Essays on the age of enterprise: 1870-1900

Edited by

David Brody
University of California at Davis

The Dryden Press
Hinsdale, Illinois

Preface

The collection makes available to the student a rich sampling of the scholarly literature—much of it scattered in historical journals—that deals with American history in the late nineteenth century. Three criteria have governed the selection of essays. A volume of this kind ought, first of all, to cover the full range of American life in the new industrial age—the worlds of business, of agriculture and labor, of the cities, of family and society, of southerners and blacks, of politics, and of Gilded Age culture. Second, I sought essays that advanced historical understanding rather than mere factual knowledge. In a few instances, where a topic has been under major debate among historians, the selected essay elucidates the historiographical issues. Mostly, however, I have preferred essays that made interpretive contributions of their own. While current work is heavily represented here, a number of older essays are included because of their pioneering quality and undiminished freshness. Finally, I sought out essays that were of methodological interest. We are in a time when new frontiers are being opened in historical research, especially through the use of social-science techniques. This vein happens to be unusually rich in the recent literature on late nineteenth-century America, and I have tried to include a full sample of the new methods in operation. The introductions to each selection have likewise been shaped by the criteria that governed my selection of the essays. They establish the historical context of the subject, and they comment on the interpretive and/or methodological issues raised by each essay, always in admiration of the skill of its author but not always in agreement with him. I should also confess a selfish motive in the construction of this volume. As one who teaches courses in late nineteenth-century American history, I have long felt the need for a meaty collection that would open up for the upper-division student the range of issues and problems of compelling interest to the historian of this period. It has always seemed to me that the best way to teach history is to show the student why the subject excited the teacher. That, at bottom, is the principle on which this collection rests.

David Brody
Kensington, California

Contents

Part I
Entrepreneurs 1

Thomas C. Cochran The Legend of the Robber Barons 3
David Brody The Psychology and Method of Steelmaking 14
Alfred D. Chandler The Beginnings of "Big Business" in American Industry 32

Part II
Workers and Farmers 57

Gerald N. Grob The Knights of Labor and the Trade Unions, 1878-1886 59
Arthur F. Bentley The Condition of the Western Farmer 74
Oscar Handlin Reconsidering the Populists 91

Part III
City Dwellers 103

Edward C. Kirkland Building American Cities 105
Roy Lubove The Tenement Comes of Age 122
Sam B. Warner Streetcar Suburbs 138

Part IV
Men and Women 151

Stephan Thernstrom Urbanization, Migration and Social Mobility 153
Richard Sennett Middle-Class Families and Urban Violence 166
James R. McGovern Anna Howard Shaw: New Approaches to Feminism 185

Part V
Southerners and Black Men 203

C. Vann Woodward Bourbonism in Georgia **205**
Lawrence C. Goodwyn Populist Dreams and Negro Rights: East Texas as a Case Study **216**
Louis R. Harlan Booker T. Washington in Biographical Perspective **237**

Part VI
Citizens and Politicians 255

Gerald W. McFarland The New York Mugwumps of 1884: A Profile **257**
Paul Kleppner The Political Revolution of the 1890s: A Behavioral Interpretation **272**
Walter LaFeber The New Empire **288**

Part VII
Culture Bearers 297

Richard Hofstadter William Graham Sumner, Social Darwinist **299**
Sidney E. Mead American Protestantism: From Denominationalism to Americanism **314**
Carl W. Condit Sullivan's Skyscrapers as the Expression of Nineteenth-Century Technology **333**

Essays on the age of enterprise: 1870-1900

Part 1
Entrepreneurs

The legend of the robber barons

Thomas C. Cochran

The late nineteenth century witnessed a fantastic expansion of America's industrial economy. This explosive growth took place within a system of essentially untrammeled free enterprise, in which innumerable private decisions, prompted by the hope of profit, led to the recruitment of capital, the exploitation of natural resources, the building of a national railroad network, and the creation of great new industries. In the process, there emerged a numerous class of American millionaires, a group of men who, sitting astride the nation's economic expansion, extracted from it huge personal fortunes. This phenomenon has posed for American historians an enduring problem of interpretation; namely, how to assess the role of the entrepreneur in the age of enterprise.

For many years, the prevailing view centered on the concept of the robber baron—the medieval figure who stationed his armed band at strategic traffic points and forced all who would pass to pay tribute to him. The image summed up the assessment of the Gilded Age businessman as one who, by force and cunning, extracted enormous profit from the economic process while making no positive contribution to it. The robber-baron notion first appeared among contemporary critics of the nineteenth century business world, was taken up enthusiastically by Progressive historians such as Charles A. Beard and Vernon L. Parrington, and given classic expression in Matthew Josephson's *The Robber Barons* (1934). If it suited the antibusiness spirit of the Progressive and New Deal eras, if it seemed to fit the notorious careers of such types as Jim Fisk and Jay Gould, the robber-baron thesis depended heavily on a convenient metaphor, did little to establish the representativeness of the few figures on which it fixed, and failed to probe the actual work of the business leader during the period of economic development. That last problem gave rise to an alternative way of assessing the American businessman. The school of entrepreneurial history, much influenced by the economist Joseph Schumpeter, took a rigorously functional approach to the study of businessmen and particularly stressed the creative aspects of entrepreneurship. The conclusions were far different from the harsh judgments of the robber-baron school. The picture that emerged was of men of exceptional energy and genius who made the crucial, innovative contributions that transformed the American economy and gave to it industrial primacy.

Thomas C. Cochran, "The Legend of the Robber Barons," *The Pennsylvania Magazine of History and Biography*, 74 (July 1950), pp. 307-321. Reprinted by permission of the publisher.

The following essay by Thomas C. Cochran, one of the deans of the entrepreneurial school, is especially noteworthy for its attention to cultural factors. Everything else being equal, why do some nations spontaneously generate industrialism, and not others? The culture provides the key, Cochran argues. The entrepreneur is the catalyst. Incorporating the larger culture and acting on it with exceptional genius and energy, he is the crucial agent for bringing a nation's cultural possibilities to bear on the factors of production. Cochran's essay reveals other strong points of the entreprenuerial approach: in his treatment of Henry Villard, an insistence on probing beneath the surface to understand business decisions and to assess the actual results; in the account of the Chicago, Burlington and Quincy's venture along the Mississippi, an acute sensitivity to the cultural variables within a single society and to the complexities of business activity.

Given its aura of scholarly objectivity, the sophistication of its research, and its openness to social-science methodology, the entrepreneurial approach has won hands down in the competition for adherents. Yet there may still be life in the robber-baron concept. Its assumptions may not hold for the businessman in relation to the economic process, but they may well provide a framework for explaining the indifference of American enterprise to the social and ecological costs of economic progress.

For further reading: Mathew Josephson, *The Robber Barons: the Great American Capitalists, 1865-1901* (1934);* William Miller, ed., *Men in Business* (1952);* Edward C. Kirkland, *Dream and Thought in the Business Community, 1860-1900* (1956);* Thomas C. Cochran, *Railroad Leaders, 1845-1890: The Business Mind in Action* (1953); Hal Bridges, "The Robber Baron Concept in American History," *Business History Review*, XXXII (1958), 1-13; Chester M. Destler, "Entrepreneurial Leadership Among the 'Robber Barons': A Trial Balance," *The Tasks of Economic History*, Supplement VI, IV (1946), 28-49; Robert H. Walker, "The Poet and the Robber Baron," *American Quarterly*, 13 (1961), 448-465; David Hamilton, "The Entrepreneur as Cultural Hero," *The Southwestern Social Science Quarterly*, 38 (1957), 248-256.

Between business history, which has concentrated attention upon the administration of the firm, and general social or economic history, which has frequently omitted business processes altogether, there is a broad, vacant area. In this twilight zone lie the relations of business leaders with similar men in other firms, the interactions of businessmen with society as a whole, and the economic effects of business decisions. Scholars viewing this area have seen such a host of related problems that a group composed of representatives from some of the East Coast universities has given the study a special name: entrepreneurial history.[1] In defining this field, the term entrepreneur has not been restricted to the conventional American textbook meaning of one who risks capital in enterprise. Rather, the older French definitions of Cantillon and Say have been re-expressed in broader language to make entrepreneur roughly equivalent to business executive. In the research of the group, the function of entrepreneurship, or business leadership, is conceived as operating in a broad socio-economic setting.

The systematic pursuit of a new interest of this kind requires a series of assumptions as to what should be examined, some tentative hypotheses about relationships and dynamics, and then historical facts against which to test and expand the original concepts.[2] The major assumption of entrepreneurial history is that it requires the exploration of the economic and social roles played by the entrepreneur: how he did his job, and what doing his particular job meant from the standpoint of his personality, his interests, and his other social roles. To gain adequate perspective, these explorations should take place in various historical settings.

What is such study likely to mean for history of the social sciences? For one thing, it will correct the elimination of man from most current economic theorizing. The necessity for including the human factor in economic equations is very obvious when we take a look at the history of a country like Venezuela. Venezuela has all of the factors usually assumed to be necessary for rapid industrial development. It has oil and iron ore, both readily available to water transportation; it has been populated for many years by people who have known of European technology; and one finds it hard in studying its history to discover any conventional economic reason for the failure of these people to develop their resources. Yet Venezuela remained a backward farming country until American oil companies began to develop it following the concessions granted in 1921, and its iron resources remained unexploited until the United States Steel Company entered the picture at a somewhat later date. The answer obviously is that the general culture of Venezuela was not such as to encourage entrepreneurship; or to carry this a step further, economic growth does not depend simply upon a population and a given body of resources and transportation facilities; it depends upon the whole cultural complex that may or may not lead to enterprise, savings, reinvestment of capital, and further development. *Time Period?*

The economists, of course, have recognized the importance of entrepreneurship abstractly; but they have failed to make any satisfactory use of this factor in setting up their equations or developing their theories. The inclusion of this factor in economic history, for example, will unquestionably reorient it in the direction of anthropological and sociological knowledge. It will not necessarily make the businessman a hero, but it will affirm the necessity of seeing economic growth in cultural terms.

For the general historian, it will mean a re-evaluation of the roles and importance of business leaders, particularly in countries such as the United States. Our present history generally has seen business leaders as parasites on a deterministic process. Historians who are in no other way determinists nevertheless seem to assume that our economic development would have gone along in good and productive paths if left to itself, whereas grasping and unscrupulous business leaders deflected this natural progress into antisocial lines for their own advantage. The corrective needed is not a eulogy of business, but real understanding of the social processes which have channeled the economic life of the nation.

An analysis of the period in which many American historians have discussed the businessman, the age of the "robber barons," will illustrate the reinterpretation that may come from entrepreneurial history. The "robber barons" are usually selected from among the railroad, industrial, and financial leaders of the period from about 1865 to 1900, and more often than not are the only businessmen who appear in college textbooks covering this period. According to the present historical mythology, they are seen as "bad" or unusually grasping and unscrupulous types in our culture against the background of a "good" public. The interest in discussing them is to illustrate business malpractices, and, presumably, to convey moralistic warnings against such activities, rather than to understand the business process in society.

In distinction to this pathological approach, the entrepreneurial historian is interested in the culture patterns and social structures which have produced these assumed types, and in whether or not the types have been correctly delineated. In pursuing such a study, the first thing is to decide what some of the major cultural themes were that guided or sanctioned the roles of these men. I think we can pick out three about which there will be little controversy: the concept of the autonomous economy that was self-adjusting; the idea that progress came through competition and the survival of the fittest; and the belief that profit or material gain was the only reliable incentive for action. These themes operated throughout the society as a whole. The truckman delivering dirt for railroad construction was as much motivated by profit and as firm a believer in these themes as was the "robber baron" who was building the road. The dissident element in the society, those who denied the value of these major themes, seem during these years to have been a relatively small, or at least uninfluential, portion of the population. Therefore, if value judgments are to be formed, they should be applied to this type of society or culture. It is rather futile to assert that the culture would have been all right if it were not for the kind of people and activities that resulted directly from its major themes.

If one accepts the additional and continuing American theme that material growth is a reliable index of progress, and its usual corollary that rapid progress is desirable, one question that may be asked of the culture as a whole is whether such progress could have taken place faster if other beliefs had prevailed. Since it is impossible to conceive deductively what the United States would have been like if built up on some other system, such a decision requires the establishment of a comparative standard. But if recourse is had to the history of another nation in order to observe the application of different cultural patterns to economic development, none seems like the United States to offer satisfying parallels. It is interesting, however, to note that in one of the somewhat similar economic situations, that of Australia, where railroads and frontier development went on through more state enterprise, about the same things were complained of that commentators here in the United States blamed upon private enterprise. In other words, a number of the difficulties seem to have been inherent in the rapid development of a pioneer area rather than in the particular means by which the development went on.

Avoiding, therefore, such unanswerable questions, and concentrating on a better understanding of the operation of American culture, let us examine the historical legend of the "robber baron" by analyzing the "case history" of Henry Villard. Villard is an interesting "robber baron" because he was brought up outside the American culture in a German bureaucratic or official family. His father was a German lawyer and judge, who ultimately became a member of the Supreme Court of the Kingdom of Bavaria. Villard, after attendance at three European universities, decided to come to the United States to try his fortune. Supported to some extent by family money, he entered journalism and built himself a successful career as a correspondent for European and American newspapers. The Civil War, particularly, gave prestige to young Villard. He was able to interview Lincoln and to offer many interesting and penetrating views of contemporary events. In the early seventies he went back to Germany, and through his family connections came to know the chief financial men of Frankfort and Munich. These contacts led to his being sent over as a representative of German bondholders in the Oregon railroad and steamship enterprises that had fallen into difficulties during the depression following the panic of 1873.

It is interesting that when Villard was placed in the position of having to make judgments regarding what should be done on the unfinished Oregon and California Railroad and in regard to the river navigation projects, he readily assumed the entrepreneurial role in just about the same form as men who had been brought up in business. In other words, the entrepreneurial role seems to have been so much a part of the cultural pattern of America, and possibly of middle class Germany, at this time, that there was no great gulf between the attitude of the professional intellectual or journalist and that of the businessman. Villard identified himself quickly with the development of the Oregon area, and, instead of advising liquidation and withdrawal for his German clients, he counseled rather the investment of still more capital in order to complete the enterprises. In this way his essential role was that of attracting foreign capital to a frontier development. It is not clear that he was ever deeply interested in problems of technology and management—that is, in just how the capital was applied for productive purposes; rather, he became a public relations man for the area, and an over-all or general entrepreneurial supervisor of where the capital should be allocated.

One factor of great importance in the Villard story is that he started new activities at just about the bottom of the deep depression that lasted from 1873 to 1879, and his ventures from then on, or at least from 1877 on, were first on a gradually rising market, and finally, from 1879 to 1882, on a market that boomed.

Villard saw quickly that the Northern Pacific Railroad, which was being built across the country from Duluth and St. Paul, would have to make, or at least should make, an agreement to connect with whatever road occupied the Columbia River valley. With this long-range plan in mind, he secured foreign and domestic help for the building of the Oregon Railroad and Navigation Company up the Columbia, at a time when Northern Pacific construction was moving very slowly into eastern Montana.

It is from this point on that the most interesting differences occur between the dramatic "robber baron" explanation of Villard's activities and the more sober and socially complex explanation offered by entrepreneurial history. The "robber baron" story is, that as Villard found the Northern Pacific management nearing the Columbia valley but unwilling to agree to make use of his facilities—that is, threatening to build either a parallel line or to cross the Cascade Mountains to Tacoma and Seattle—he decided that he must get control of the Northern Pacific. So great was his prestige for successful operation by this time that he had the boldness to ask a group of his friends in Wall Street to put up $8,000,000 for some project that he would not reveal to them. And, as the story, went, he had no difficulty in more than raising the first payment requested for this "blind pool," money which he used secretly to buy control of the Northern Pacific Railroad. The "robber baron" analogy is, of course, obvious and exciting. The "robber baron," Villard, seizes control of a strategic pass and then exacts tribute from the railroad that represents a great, nationally subsidized enterprise.[3] Villard's blind pool has all of the trappings of high drama and shady financial dealings. The "robber baron" story then goes on to assert that Villard robbed the Northern Pacific and his other properties in the course of construction in such a way so that by 1883 they were bankrupt, while he himself had become very rich.

As usual, the actual story is not so dramatic. What appears to have happened is, that when the Northern Pacific secured Drexel Morgan financing in the latter part of the year 1880, and the Drexel Morgan-Winslow Lanier syndicate learned that Frederick Billings, the president of Northern Pacific, was planning to build duplicate facilities to the coast without regard to the already existing Oregon Railroad and Navigation Company, they became worried over the economic loss involved in constructing nearly parallel lines. The bankers, not sharing in the loyalties to individual companies that presidents and other officers almost inevitably develop, could see no reason why Northern Pacific and O.R.&N. could not get together in one co-operating line. But some of the officers of Northern Pacific, particularly Billings, regarded the railroad as their greatest life work; they felt that to compromise and make the final road a joint venture between the "upstart" Villard and the great Northern Pacific enterprise was a personal defeat. Whereupon Morgan, at least, decided that the only way of bringing about a compromise and preventing unnecessary construction was to establish a common control for the two companies. Since Villard, who had, from the financial standpoint, acquitted himself well as receiver for Kansas Pacific, was now anxious to get this joint control, and assured Morgan that he independently had the resources to do so, the syndicate gave him their blessings, and even offered him their help. The "blind pool" was, therefore, chiefly a product of Villard's love of drama, of doing things in a spectacular fashion. Had he been willing to forgo these dramatic frills, control could quietly have been bought through the syndicate over about the same period. Of course, it cannot be overlooked that successfully doing the job himself gave Villard great personal prestige in Wall Street.

The difficulties from 1881 on to the completion of the road in 1883 seem to have been to some extent inevitable, and to some extent to have resulted from the usual overoptimism of American promoters. Villard formed a holding company, called the Oregon and Transcontinental Company, which was to own stocks in his various enterprises, make the construction contracts, and generally conduct the building which would weld Northern Pacific and O.R.&N. into one system. Undoubtedly, the Oregon and Transcontinental Company stock was a source of large profit for Villard; in fact, it seems probable that all the money Villard made in connection with these enterprises came from floating, buying, and selling the securities in Wall Street. It may be that Villard profited from the construction contracts, but there is no clear evidence of this, and it is quite possible, by analogy to similar situations, that the profits of construction went largely to local contractors in the West. At all events, the major difficulty was a lack of sufficient traffic to warrant the high construction cost of building railroads through the Rockies and the Oregon coastal regions. The completion of the through-line in August of 1883 was almost simultaneous with the beginning of a steady recession in general business that ended in a crisis the following March. As a result, the difficulties that the system would have experienced in paying returns under any circumstances were accentuated. When the companies were not able to pay dividends and their securities declined, Villard, temporarily losing the confidence of the banking syndicate, was forced to retire from the control of the various enterprises.

One way, therefore, of looking at this whole story is that Villard, a relatively inexperienced entrepreneur, took hold of a series of frontier developments at the bottom of the business cycle, completed them just at the peak of the boom and was then unable to steer them through the ensuing depression. Viewed from this angle, the whole development was a normal and repetitive one in both big and small business. The general history of even a small retail store or factory enterprise was often just about the same; if the enterprise started at a favorable time in the business cycle, it could last until a major depression. Then, unless it has had farsighted and unusually able management, or had been lucky in making more profit than was possible for most young enterprises, it lapsed into bankruptcy and had to be reorganized with the injection of new capital. The roles that Villard played extremely well were those of a mobilizer of capital resources for pioneer investments, and effective public relations for the development of an area. The roles that he played poorly were those of an expert railroad builder and conservative business forecaster.

What do entrepreneurial historians expect to gain from such a study? In the first place, the study of outstanding examples such as that of Villard may be instructive for the study of the normal practices and operations of business. A detailed study of the Villard enterprises will show more exactly the nature of such practices as the strategic type of entrepreneurship that went into railroad building. The seizing of the transportation route down the Columbia River is merely a dramatic example of the general type of planning done by all western railroad builders. The strategic occupation of territory was like a great game of chess. Each leading entrepreneur had to guess where his rivals were likely to build next, how he could forestall their entrance into an area by throwing a line of track through some valley or across some river, often planning these moves a decade or more ahead. Little is known of the local economic and social results of this process beyond the fact that it extended railroad transportation at an extremely rapid rate.

Trying to assess the larger economic and social effects of Villard's activities, we might note that he mobilized about $60,000,000 in capital, and applied it to western development at a social cost of perhaps one or two million dollars. That is, he may have made more money than that, but the one or two million dollars represent an estimate of what he actually spent on living and personal durable goods during these years. His other money came and went in stockmarket operations, and presumably represented a transfer of capital from one set of holders to another. The question remains: granting that this was not a high rate of commission to pay for the mobilization of so much money, was the long-run effect of the development for which the money was spent economically and socially desirable? Undoubtedly, this particular development of transportation was premature, and it was carried on at the cost of some other types of goods or services that could have been produced with the same expenditure. But this in turn raises another question from a purely nationalistic standpoint: could the foreign capital have been attracted for more prosaic and routine operations? To the extent that foreign money was invested unprofitably in western development, it was an economic loss to Germany and the other investing nations, but a net gain to the United States. As to the loss of domestic resources in these developments, it can be noted that, at least, this is what the men of the culture apparently wanted to do with their economic energy. Villard noted in his promotion activities that the word "Oregon" had a kind of popular magic to it in the seventies and early eighties. Then it was the promised land of the American West, and it stimulated the imagination of Americans along entrepreneurial lines. The historian should try to assess the extent to which the dramatic development of natural resources may actually raise the rate of saving in the community, and may increase output of energy in the population as a whole. These are, of course, very difficult and intangible problems, but yet they are just as much a part of the picture of economic development as the old stand-by of assessing the value of natural resources and the cost of getting them to market. There is a cultural paradox involved in all of this that makes it difficult for the unwary investigator. At the same time that Americans were saving at a high rate for development purposes and investing in railroad securities, they had a distrust of the railroad operator and were inclined to make the railroads a scapegoat for many of their ills. In other words, there was a kind of national Manicheaen heresy, whereby people were willing to sell themselves to the devil, to worship evil, as it were, but at the same time were not ready to forget the fact that it was really the devil and not good that they were supporting. This whole problem of ambiguity of attitude toward business leaders, and the reactions it led to on the part of the executives themselves, is one of the most fruitful fields of American cultural history.

This leads directly to the problem of social sanctions: what codes of conduct, ethics, mores, and folkways were recognized by the railroad entrepreneur? The "robber-baron" approach has implied that there were few sanctions recognized, that these men operated on the basis of nearly complete expediency. To anyone familiar with the study of cultures, this is obviously a very questionable assertion. Actually, there were many but varying sanctions operative upon the business leaders of the period. They varied with types of activity—horse-trading, for instance, having one set of ethics, banking quite another; with the conditioning of the entrepreneur, whereby a man brought up in the strict and staid business community of Philadelphia would have different ethics from one brought up in a less rigidly structured society; and with the geographical region—the frontier, in general, being an area of greater opportunity and larger adherence to the "end-justifies-the-means" philosophy than more settled areas—the mining town of Virginia City and Boston, perhaps, illustrating extreme poles.

Let us take a particular type of social sanction and see how it operated on the basis of these differing situations. One of the most important ones was the feeling of a fiduciary obligation toward stockholders and bondholders—the recognition of the fact that managers were trustees for the real owners of the property. From this standpoint, the distinction between men and regions may be brought out by analyzing the promotion of an extension up the Mississippi River by the directors of the Chicago, Burlington & Quincy Railroad.

But before proceeding to the details of these operations, it is necessary to understand some of the culture patterns of pioneer development and railroad building. The ultimate growth and welfare of the community was a rationalization that to the Westerner justified almost any means that he might employ—particularly in the handling of Easterners' capital. Added to this was the fact that railroad companies were not fitted to do their own construction work and had to let local contractors do the building. That the construction work was not done by contract simply to rob the stockholders is abundantly illustrated by the facts that the most mature and best-managed companies continued to build through contractors, even though they might readily have undertaken the work themselves, and that railroad contractors sometimes bankrupted themselves by bidding too low. The difficulties were that building was a specialized enterprise for which the railroad had no regular staff, that it was occasional rather than continuous and, therefore, did not justify the maintenance of a specialized staff, and that often the work was remote from the railroad offices and could not readily be supervised by the chief executives. In order to facilitate such large-scale work by local interests, it would often be necessary for the road itself, or the directors or large stockholders of the road, to put up cash to assist the local contractor. This would be done by buying stock in a construction company of which the operating executive would usually be a local builder. The construction company took its pay in railroad stocks or bonds, which might in the case of an old road be almost as good as cash, but in the case of many young roads might be of very speculative and dubious value. The par value of securities taken for construction work, therefore, is not a safe guide to the amount of profit actually realized by construction companies. But there is a little question that a great deal of eastern stockholders' money went west into construction companies and stayed there as profit to local entrepreneurs, including sub-contractors all the way down the line, and even to the owners of local sandbanks and hardware stores. Sometimes the eastern directors and stockholders who had advanced money for construction company stock made handsome profits; at other times, as in the case to be discussed, they lost what they had put in; but in any case, the local people were likely to make a profit. As John Murray Forbes, Boston railroad promoter and conservative financier, put it, "My feeling is . . . that the Landowners and R. Road con-tractors are the ones who too often get the whole benefit of the money that Capitalists put into the West."[4] Charles E. Perkins, long-time president of the C.B.&Q., went even further: "Iowa people make more money in farms and other industries including con-tracting and building than in railroads . . . and it is only the eastern capitalist who cannot use his money to advantage at home who is willing to risk it in western railroads and take the low average return which he gets, a return very much lower than the average of other investments in this state [of Iowa] ."[5]

This background is necessary to an understanding of the contracts for the so-called River Roads that were to go up the Mississippi from Clinton, Iowa, ultimately to Minnea-polis and St. Paul. The central western city involved in this development was Dubuque, Iowa, and the local entrepreneur who undertook to do the construction was J. K. Graves. He was a small-scale, general entrepreneur interested in banking, building, and all the wide range of local enterprises usual to the small-city capitalist. In order to undertake construc-tion on these roads, he persuaded a group of the C. B. & Q. directors, headed by ex-president James F. Joy, to put up about half a million dollars cash in return for securities of the construction company. They then entered into a contract with the two railroad companies that were to own and operate the lines after they had been built, whereby the construction company took pay partly in stocks and bonds. The rest of the bonds of these companies were to be marketed to the holders of C. B. & Q. bonds and stock, who would buy them readily because of the endorsement of their own directors; this would in turn provide additional capital that could be used to pay for the construc-tion.

Some of the members of the C. B. & Q. board, particularly John Murray Forbes and J. N. A. Griswold, were not told at the time they endorsed the sale of the bonds that their fellow directors were actually interested in the stock of the construction company. It seems probable that this knowledge was withheld because Joy and the directors who did buy such stock recognized that Forbes would not approve of their being involved in this kind of relationship. In other words, there appears to have been a difference in the business morality or sanctions recognized by James F. Joy, a western businessman, and those recognized by old, conservative, upper-class Easterners like Forbes and Griswold.

The working out of the pattern has much in common with the Villard story; Graves may or may not have been a good railroad builder. Examination of hundreds of letters to and from Graves, and letters discussing the situation among C. B. & Q. directors, has failed to provide conclusive information on this point. At least, he held the confidence of Joy and the other interested directors right up to the final failure of the enterprise. The contracts were let in the boom of 1871, and, when the depression hit after the panic of 1873, the roads had not been completed. With revenues of all kinds falling off, Graves started borrowing from the funds of the unfinished River Roads to support his other local enterprises. The result was a slowing down of construction, a default on the bonds of the River Roads, and a financial situation that would not bear close scrutiny by accountants.

In all this it is very hard to pass moral judgments. Graves had undoubtedly thought that he was doing the best thing possible for Dubuque and the surrounding country by trying to build up many enterprises at once. He had made no plans for a break in the boom and the coming of depression. As a result, he found himself hopelessly involved in ventures that could not all be kept going; yet the abandonment of any one of them then meant a postponing of all or most of the benefit that was expected to accrue from it. In this situation he tried to borrow from Peter to pay Paul, hoping that Peter would raise additional funds. The same kind of situation has turned pillars of society into scoundrels time and time again in American business history.

In the case of the River Roads, when the default occurred, Forbes and Griswold became interested in investigating the situation and soon found out the identity of the construction company's stockholders and the nature of the contracts. Forbes denounced Joy, and when the latter refused to assume personal responsibility to the C. B. & Q. investors for the interest in the River Road bonds—a procedure which would have been highly unusual—Forbes decided that Joy and certain other directors involved must be put off the C. B. & Q. board. Forbes succeeded in doing this in a proxy battle at the next stockholders' meeting and the River Roads passed ultimately into the hands of the Chicago, Milwaukee and St. Paul. This, in the long run, turned out to be a great mistake, as a decade later C. B. & Q. had to build a parallel line under less advantageous circumstances.

The quarrel was due to a conflict in sanctions based upon differences in situation. As one of Joy's followers in the matter, J. W. Brooks, a C. B. & Q. director who had had much experience in the West, put it, "Loosely as these things were done [branch-line contracts and construction in general] they as a whole have proved the salvation of the C. B. & Q. . . . we do not claim to be immaculate beyond expediency, but are content with right intentions and the good results obtained on the whole. . . ."[6]

Perhaps the above examples have demonstrated the difficulty in regarding any particular group of business leaders as "robber barons" without careful analysis of the situation involved, the popular and local codes of ethics, and the general pressure for "justification by profit" that ran all through American culture.

These illustrations have shown only limited aspects of entrepreneurial history. They have touched on, but not elaborated, the political science of the business corporation and the analysis of power within the corporation, showing only in the latter case that it is not easy to put one's finger on the exact location of control in any given instance. Real control over a situation may rest with some contractor or underling in the West, despite the façade of power in the eastern executive officers. Many other relations have not been brought out at all in these two accounts—for example, the relation of business roles to other social roles, which carries with it the discussion of the role of the business elite in relation to cultural leadership. Many railroad men, for example, were active leaders in national or state politics; others were patrons of the arts, or supporters of education. To what extent were these attitudes outgrowths of general social mores, to what extent did business sanctions indicate that these supplementary roles should be played, and to what extent were they peculiarities of the individuals?

Comparative studies need to be made of the place of entrepreneurship in varying cultures. There seems little doubt that such studies will go further toward explaining the economic progress of different regions than will any assessment of potential natural resources. It is these cultural elements, to a very large extent, that determine who will become entrepreneurs (the quantity and quality of the supply of entrepreneurship), and also the likelihood of entrepreneurial success in various types of endeavor. A culture with feudal standards of lavish living or the support of elaborate ceremonial organizations of church and state will obviously not have the capital to invest in economic development that will be available in a culture where frugal living, saving, and work are the custom.

The resources in theory and scope of interest of all the social sciences may be applied more readily to historical problems in the study of special roles and functions, such as entrepreneurship, than in the general study of the enormous conventional fields of economic, social, political or intellectual history. To learn more about how human beings behave and have behaved in history, it is wise to start with a manageable and definable group of human beings performing certain functions, rather than with the activities of the society as a whole.

Notes

1. A Research Center for Entrepreneurial History at Harvard, organized by Arthur H. Cole, is one result of the deliberations of the East Coast group.

2. It is worth noting that although data may vary in age from six months to five hundred years, any that can be collected are necessarily historical.

3. The Northern Pacific had the largest land grant of any of the western railroads.

4. John Murray Forbes to Charles S. Tuckerman, Apr. 14, 1880. President's Letters, Chicago, Burlington & Quincy Archives, Newberry Library, Chicago, Illinois.

5. Charles E. Perkins to James W. McDill, Jan. 26, 1885. President's Letters, Chicago, Burlington & Quincy Archives, Newberry Library.

6. John W. Brooks to James F. Joy, Mar. 11, 1875. Joy Collection, Michigan Historical Collections, Ann Arbor, Michigan.

The psychology and method of steelmaking

David Brody

Industrialization was an enormously complex phenomenon, involving the discovery and exploitation of natural resources, the accumulation of capital, the recruitment of labor, the building of a transportation system, and the emergence·of mass-markets. But at the heart of the industrializing process was technological change—the invention of machines, the advancement of manufacturing procedures, the introduction of new products. Innovation gave the cutting edge to the vast economic changes transforming the United States in the late nineteenth century. To observers at the time, and to succeeding generations of historians, this achievement has posed an absorbing puzzle: why and how did American industry adopt so swiftly and sweepingly the modern system of production?

These are the questions that the following essay attempts to answer in the case of the iron and steel industry—the preeminent instance of modernization. The analysis focuses on the economizing spirit of the steelmakers. This derived most directly from the market instability and intense competitiveness that placed a high premium on success at cutting the costs of production. This was, in turn, related to the technical character of steelmaking, which, unlike wrought iron, proved to be very open to technological innovation. The immediate consequence of these two conditions was to foster a spirit of rational, objective calculation and a managerial group remarkable for its energy and high motivation. The interaction of all these factors—the economizing impulse, the technological opportunity, the scientific approach, the managerial excellence—created an industry that, at the end of the nineteenth century, was the very acme of modern industrialization.

But the analysis deals only with the *proximate* causes, those acting most directly on the industry's transformation. The broader economic forces—the high cost of labor, for example—are taken essentially as given. Nor, in contrast to Cochran's entrepreneurial interpretation in the previous essay, is any specific attention paid to the larger social factors that encouraged the single-mindedness and ruthlessness of an Andrew Carnegie. The qualities that British steel men found so striking (and unsettling) in their American

Reprinted by permission of the publishers from David Brody, *Steelworkers in America: the Nonunion Era*, pp. 1-26. Cambridge, Mass: Harvard University Press, copyright, 1960, by the President and Fellows of Harvard College.

counterparts doubtless expressed in part the maturity of British industry. (This would, indeed, be the fate of the American steel industry in later years when it lost its youthful élan and let technological leadership pass to Japan and Germany.) But the differences also, clearly, had something to do with the character of English and American societies. The lack of institutional restraints by which Stanley Elkins explains the extreme form that American slavery took, for example, may provide a clue to the brilliant operation of the Carnegie Steel Company.

Why did the following essay fail to explore these broader forces behind the transformation of the steel industry? The answer relates to the uses to which the author intended to put his analysis. The essay formed the opening chapter of his *Steelworkers in America* (1960), and was intended to elucidate those industrial factors that would shape the industry's labor system. The operative ones were those directly related to the psychology and the method of steelmaking. There is, so to speak, a functional relationship between the historian's purposes and the analysis that results. To understand and evaluate the latter, the student would do well to discover the former.

For further reading: Louis M. Hacker, *The World of Andrew Carnegie, 1865-1901* (1968); H. J. Habakkuk, *American and British Technology in the Nineteenth Century* (1962);* W. P. Strassmann, *Risk and Technological Innovation: American Manufacturing Methods During the Nineteenth Century* (1959); Peter Temin, *Iron and Steel in Nineteenth Century America: an Economic Inquiry* (1964); Victor S. Clark, *History of Manufactures in the United States* (1929), vol. 2; Carroll W. Pursell, "Tariff and Technology: The Foundation and Development of the American Tin-Plate Industry, 1872-1900," *Technology and Culture*, III (1962), 267-281.

British steelmasters, visiting the United States in 1901, marveled at the progress of the iron and steel industry. Thirty years earlier, the American steel trade had been of minor consequence. Annual pig iron production had not reached one-sixth of the English output. The mills had been backward and inefficient. Now the inspecting Britons were unsettled by the mechanical perfection of American operations. From the unloading of ore to the final pass in the finishing rolls, the massive mills functioned with the efficiency of single geared machines. Twice as much pig iron was produced yearly as in Great Britain. American firms exported over a million tons of steel in 1900, recently taking orders in England itself—an unprecedented event.

The touring manufacturers pondered the success of their competitors. What accounted for the swift rise of the American industry? The Englishmen surveyed the abundant natural resources, the expanding home market, and the extensive transport system. But repeatedly their minds returned to the special character of their hosts. J. Stephen Jeans summed up the impression. "The American manufacturer is not so conservative in his methods and ideas." His decisions, regardless of "trouble, cost or interference with preconceived ideas and vested interests," rested on one chief consideration: whether they would "make for increased economy."[1] The preoccupation with economy seemed, indeed, at the root of the steelmaking achievement.

Andrew Carnegie was the preëminent example of the American type. "Carnegie never wanted to know the profits," a partner once remarked. "He always wanted to know the cost." Carnegie had very early seen the possibilities of economy. "What do you really figure we put rails at cost," he asked the superintendent of his newly constructed Edgar Thomson Works. "Cant [sic] we shade 50 dollars. If so where is there such a business." Every effort went into the reduction of production costs. By December 1878, the total charges amounted to only $36.52 a ton of steel at the Thomson Works. Twenty years later, the company was making rails for $12.00 a ton.[2]

That impulse for economy shaped American steel manufacture. It inspired the inventiveness that mechanized the productive operations. It formed the calculating and objective mentality of the industry. It selected and hardened the managerial ranks. Its technological and psychological consequences, finally, defined the treatment of the steelworkers. Long hours, low wages, bleak conditions, anti-unionism, flowed alike from the economizing drive that made the American steel industry the wonder of the manufacturing world.

The visit of British steel men in 1901 was opportunely timed. By then the Carnegie spirit ruled, and its consequences were largely completed.

The industry's economizing temper was bred in the unrestrained competition preceding the merger movement. Steelmaking then "was a merciless game . . . in the hands of strong men," the veteran Joseph G. Butler recalled. "The profits were for those who pursued business relentlessly." Before 1890 the demand for steel, chiefly railroad construction, was notoriously unstable. The industry was either "panic-stricken" or "strained to utmost capacity." The recurring imbalance between supply and demand embittered competition. Overextended companies slashed prices in the fight for existing orders in depressed years. From the boom of 1880 to the collapsed market of 1885 the price of steel rails fell from $85.00 to $27.00 a ton.[3] Only efficient producers could then survive.

Sharpened competition forced economy on the steelmakers. John W. Gates, for example, informed the superintendent of his Rankin wire works of a price collapse in 1890. "As a consequence it behooves us to be very careful in the matter of cost and I desire to impress upon your mind the importance of reducing your cost to the lowest possible figure."[4] This was the normal response to the precipitous market.

The lesson, however, was only reluctantly absorbed. For one thing, most early steel producers had also manufactured wrought iron, which, for technological reasons, was not susceptible to cheapening improvements. There was no economizing tradition in the iron trade. More important, economy was not in itself attractive. It demanded the continued reinvestment of earnings and unremitting concentration on operations. Without the competitive spur, the ordinary manufacturer would have contented himself with his established methods. The Colorado Fuel and Iron Company, for instance, seemed in a secure situation. Its plant at Pueblo supplied the Western rail market. Favored by nearby resources and strategic location, the company foresaw steady, substantial earnings. Its surplus went into an additional blast furnace instead of economizing work. Then in 1888 a railroad war broke out, freight rates fell, and Eastern railmakers were able to invade the territory. The Colorado firm could not meet Eastern prices and barely avoided bankruptcy.[5] Most concerns did not have its opportunity for complacency.

After 1887, however, the competitive situation in basic steel began to relent. Rails steadied and, more significant, the demand was becoming "general." Nine-tenths of the steel output went into rails in 1882, less than half in 1890. Surely, reasoned the *Iron Age*, "the whole country cannot at once drop into a state of collapse." Thus reassured, the industry eased its efforts for cost reduction. Profits were diverted into dividends and extensions. Prosperity was dissolving bitter rivalry and rendering unnecessary the burdensome drive for economy.

Had all steel manufacturers relaxed, the economizing spirit would have passed. Even hard times would not threaten the inefficient producers if price competition was avoided and the shrunken market fairly divided. That was, indeed, the objective of numerous efforts to establish pools and agreements.[6] A few firms, however, remained imbued with the competitive temper. Jones and Laughlins, Cambria, and Carnegie willingly joined the pools, but they were not softened by fat profits. Many prospering mills "have thought it unnecessary to economize," observed a Carnegie partner. "That has never been our history. When we have gone out of a pool, we have always been in good shape to follow the business."[7] So they were in 1893.

The ensuing business collapse put an end to the complacency of the steel manufacturers. A period of unmatched rivalry was inaugurated. When prosperity returned at the end of the decade, the rule of economy would be permanently impressed on the American steel industry.

Carnegie saw in 1893 the opening that led to domination of the market. He directed the Board to leave the rail pool. "I do not think any one can stand in our way. . . . I get no sweet dividend out of second fiddle business, and I do know that the way to make even money *is to lead*." Surveying his cost sheets, Carnegie concluded, "we needn't hesitate, take orders and run full, there's a margin."[8] The company went out to fill its order books. In New York, for instance, it contracted to furnish the Elevated Railroad with 50,000 tons of structural steel "at the lowest figure ever made." Competitors found themselves consistently undersold.

The future rested with the Carnegie Company. Other low-cost producers had economized at the expense of growth. Carnegie managed to accomplish both, mainly by the shrewd purchase of plants in difficulty. The Homestead and Duquesne mills were thus acquired in 1882 and 1890. Quickly made profitable, the earnings of the new properties soon liquidated the bond issues. Between 1888 and 1894 Carnegie's steel capacity climbed from 332,111 to 1,115,466 tons, one-fourth of the national output. He could monopolize a depressed market.

The year 1893 was disastrous in the iron and steel trade. Most plants shut down, and many firms failed. Illinois steel lost $350,000; Pennsylvania Steel went into receivership. None of Carnegie's rivals was in a position to make up the lost ground. That was part of his plan. "Now, in my opinion," Carnegie told his managers, "is the time to cause them to delay spending money to compete with us."[9]

Meanwhile, he embarked on a program to perfect economical steel manufacture. Despite the grumbling of partners that they never saw the profits (three millions in 1893, four millions in 1894), the works were rebuilt and transport facilities acquired. In 1896 Carnegie leased the vast Rockefeller holdings in the Mesabi ore fields for the exceedingly low royalty of twenty-five cents a ton. Years before, he had established a cheap coke supply by buying into the H. C. Frick Company. He was in the envious position of getting his coke at cost while the Frick firm, in whose profits he shared, was selling to his competitors at high prices. By 1897, the economizing work was completed. "This company," one journal commented,

. . . is so situated as to be absolutely in control of the market, and make the prices of steel what it will. . . . The situation is not altogether a comfortable one, and many are looking anxiously for the result. [10]

Their worst fears were soon realized.

A respite had come in 1895. Then late in 1896 the rehabilitated pools, after holding for a time, crumbled before the declining market. The ensuing contest was the bitterest in the industry's history; it tested—and proved—the validity of the economizing view. Notified of the collapse of the rail pool, Carnegie chairman Henry Frick announced: "We will at once name a lower price and take all the business we can." The Carnegie Company drove rails from $28.00 to an average of $18.00 a ton, selling large amounts at $16.00, and going to the phenomenal figure of $14.00 to capture some orders. To the astonishment of competitors, those prices were profitable for the company. It cleared $7,000,000 in 1897. Elated, Carnegie congratulated his managers: "It is a splendid year's business . . . and proves once more that there is nothing like meeting the market, taking the business, and running full."[11]

Other producers found the results less pleasing. Despite the increased demand brought out by the low prices (from five to nine million tons in two years), few companies were operating profitably. As Elbert H. Gary of Illinois Steel observed, Carnegie's low costs could not be matched. The price war, however, had stimulated tonnage far beyond his capacity. Carnegie therefore concluded an agreement with the Illinois, Colorado, and Cambria companies. He would limit himself to his natural Eastern market. "No effective competition is possible," he informed the Board. "The East is a clear field for us at $15.00 or $16.00 per ton for Rails." Bethlehem quit the steel trade, selling its rolling mills largely to Carnegie. [12] But rising prices in 1899 saved the other Eastern producers. Carnegie's campaign thus fell short of its mark.

His example, however, was stamped on the minds of the steelmasters. No longer was it possible, President John W. Gates told the stockholders of Illinois Steel, "to do business on the basis of large profits for comparatively small tonnage. . . . We must meet competition and reduce the cost of production to the minimum." Economizing efforts were quickly evident at the company's plants. Charles Schwab observed that "the South Works never showed such activity as now." Economy became the rule at Illinois Steel.[13]

Carnegie's fourteen-dollar rails—priced below their manufacturing cost—had a similar effect on the managers of the Lackawanna Company of Scranton. "That was an object lesson, that rail fight," recalled President Walter Scranton, "that made us look around to get a new location." A giant Lackawanna plant was soon rising near Buffalo, strategically situated both for resources and markets.[14]

In less striking ways, all steel producers revealed the new concern for economy. Within a few years every American steel mill achieved a rough equivalence of efficiency, and every company acquired adequate supplies of ore and coking coal. The cruel market had taught its lesson.

Competition provided the stimulus. But economizing efforts succeeded only because of the openness of steel manufacture to technological improvement. At every point in the steelmaking process, engineers were able to mechanize operations.

Wrought iron offers an instructive comparison. Before the introduction of the Bessemer converter, the iron industry had become firmly established; its output in 1866 was a million tons. Steel immediately proved superior for rails, then armor plate and structural material. But wrought iron was admittedly better suited for plate, sheet, and bar. Yet increasingly steel displaced iron. Even in the making of pipe, for which wrought iron's malleability and non-corrosiveness were ideal, steel gradually became dominant.

The 1890's saw the widespread dismantling of iron mills. The largest producer, Jones and Laughlins, had operated 110 puddling furnaces. In 1884 the firm built a five-ton converter, then two more in 1890, and began reducing its iron production. It closed down thirty-three furnaces in February 1892 because iron was being "crowded out." Its employees were advised to seek work elsewhere. Soon after, the Carnegie Company began shutting its eighty-four furnaces. The basic steel companies, all iron manufacturers in 1890, employed hardly a puddler among them in 1900.[15]

The fatal weakness of wrought iron manufacture was its resistance to mechanization. The procedures were entirely manual. The puddler agitated small batches of molten pig iron and cinder until the purified metal crystallized into balls—"coming to nature," it was called. The succeeding squeezing and rolling operations were likewise manual. Until puddling could be mechanized, no other important changes were possible.

Ironmasters had the same stimulus from the market for economy as the steel men. The two groups were, indeed, largely identical. Competition from steel lent further urgency. And experimental efforts were not lacking. The Phoenix Iron Company, for instance, in 1882 had partly perfected a mechanical puddler. The Otis Steel Company developed a revolving device. Numerous other inventions sustained the hopes of iron companies. In the end, the experimentation failed, and, after the shift to steel became general, subsided.[16] Steel production surpassed that of iron in 1892. By 1913, 23,000,000 tons of steel were rolled, while iron output was only 1,676,257 tons, half of the 1890 level.

Compared to puddling, steel manufacture offered unlimited opportunities for improvement. The basic methods of smelting, refining, and rolling had come from Europe. But Americans mechanized the processes beyond the expectation of the inventors. A remarkable inventiveness developed, pressing forward steel technology at an exceeding rapid pace. By 1900, engineers had solved the major problems of mechanization: the handling of materials, integration of production stages, and continuous rolling of steel.

Numerous devices were perfected to move the materials at the blast furnaces. A superintendent in 1910 described the changes in his department from the laborious manual methods of 1895. A huge car-dumper gripped the freight cars and turned them over, discharging the ore and limestone. At Jones and Laughlin Steel Company (the name was changed from Jones and Laughlins in 1902) the car bottom dropped, an equally effective unloading method. Electric trolleys rolled the weighed ingredients to a skip hoist that carried them to the furnace top and dumped them inside automatically. The pig casting machine and Jones mixer did away with the hot work around the sand beds. Ladle cars, an improvement that had appeared as early as 1882 at the Isabella Furnace Company, caught and carried away the molten slag. Blast furnace operation in 1910 was almost completely mechanized.[17]

Similar progress occurred in the refining processes. Electric traveling cranes simply solved the problems in feeding the Bessemer converter. But the open-hearth furnace, whose mouth was on the side, required a more complex arrangement. Boxes of pig iron were rolled on rail cars to the furnace platform. Here the arm of the Wellman charger lifted the boxes, thrust them into the furnaces, overturned and then replaced them on the car. When the Carnegie Company adopted the Wellman machine in 1897, the president reported that the cost "was notably better in Open Hearth No. I . . . a reduction of 27 cents."[18] An English visitor in 1904 could not recall an American open-hearth plant without a charger among the thirty or more he inspected.[19]

Mechanical handling permitted the enlargement of operating equipment. Blast furnaces in 1890 rarely topped 80 feet in height. Nine furnaces being built in 1901 averaged 100 feet, and Lackawanna planned one of 110 feet. Periodically, new construction was announced larger than anything in existence. Lackawanna erected a slab mill at its Buffalo works unsurpassed in capacity, an object of awe for practical steel men. The Gary mill, when completed in 1914, was even more massive. Thus was the size of optimum efficiency approached.

The second direction of improvement was to integrate production stages. Steel manufacturers early recognized the savings in connecting smelting and Bessemer operation. Started at Bethlehem and North Chicago, the practice of conveying liquid iron in ladles directly to the converters soon became general. The Jones mixer, capable of holding large quantities of molten pig iron, perfected the procedure by largely eliminating the need to cast and later remelt excess iron. To gain the advantages of integration, Carnegie, on acquiring the Carrie Furnaces, built a bridge across the Monongahela River to deliver molten iron to the Homestead plant. Republic did likewise when it erected furnaces across the Mahoning River for its Youngstown mill.[20]

Integration with rolling mills developed more slowly. Although Bessemer converters were usually located in the same plant, the ingots were not conveyed directly to the rolling department. Integration would save heat and handling, but the main stimulus came from improvements in converters and rolling mills. The capacity of both was rising rapidly. The lag in between of "facilities for getting the ingots out of the road," said Captain William Jones in 1991, "is the sticking point just now." Casting ingots on cars completely eliminated the bottleneck. When Carnegie bought the Duquesne Works, where the practice had been inaugurated in 1889, he introduced the casting cars at his other plants, and others during the competitive period hastily followed.[21] Overhead electric cranes and a mechanical plunger to strip the ingot from the mold perfected the rapid handling of steel from converter to rolling mill. Production was integrated from blast furnaces to rolling mills.

The rolling mills were the third area of advance. Here the objective was continuous, mechanical operation. In 1857 John Fritz invented the three-high roller—the first, basic step—by which metal could be given a second pass while returning to the front of the rolls. The demand for steel rails intensified experimentation. R. W. Hunt finally overcame the main obstacle in 1884 when he perfected an automatic rising and falling table for the three-high roll. Captain Jones then set out to incorporate in a mill for the Carnegie Company all the recent developments. "Instructions were given him," related Hunt, "to build the best rail mill he knew how, regardless of cost."[22] Finished in 1888, the Edgar Thomson mill became the prototype for the industry.

From the heating furnace a small electric car ran forward and tilted, depositing the ingot upon live-rolls leading to the three-high blooming mill. Provided with tables and side racks, the rolls pressed the ingot down to nine by seven inches in five passes. Automatically sheared and reheated, the lengths traveled on driven rolls to two roughing mills for ten passes and on to the finishing rail mill. The rails were then stamped, cut, cooled, and run down into waiting cars. English visitors were greatly impressed.

To stand on the floor of such a mill and to witness the conversion, in the space of half an hour, of a red-hot steel ingot weighing several tons into finished, stamped steel rails 90 feet long . . . is to gain new ideas of the possibilities of mechanism of subservience of matter to mind. [23]

The smaller products offered more formidable problems, but when finally mastered, the rolling operations would be more truly continuous. Wire rods led the way. In 1881 Charles H. Morgan attached the Bedson back-and-forth roughing mill to the Belgian looping mill, creating the first continuous rod rolling system. Another Morgan mill quickly superseded the back-and-forth method. Morgan lined in tandem a series of rolls carefully geared to take up the elongation after each pass. The metal, led by guides, emerged in finished form without interruption. Refinements quickly followed. A mill designed by William Garrett used standard billets, eliminating the need to roll smaller rod billets first. This advance capped the effort to perfect rod manufacture.

"Continuity of operation has been the touchstone throughout," said Morgan. "Operations which heretofore hindered and delayed have now disappeared . . . until it is a familiar sight to see a billet, one end still in the furnace—its length in all the reducing passes of the mill, and the other end coiled on the reel, a finished wire rod." "The development has been so rapid," concluded the inventor F. H. Daniels, "as to astonish even the most sanguine of our rod rollers." [24]

Of all the light forms, only sheet and tin plate resisted improvement. Before 1890 Wales had supplied tin plate to the United States. The McKinley tariff opened the field to Americans, and by 1900 they were producing 425,000 tons. Importing Welsh workers and methods, manufacturers immediately saw the need for "changes which will cheapen the production." They introduced heavier equipment, traveling cranes, and electric power. Machines were devised to mechanize the annealing, pickling, and polishing processes. "As soon as the manufacturing of tin plate was commenced," boasted an expert in 1899, "American enterprise and inventiveness took up the matter of introducing improvements" and carried the mills "far ahead of those in England or Wales." [25] Nevertheless, the central problem of manual, disconnected rolling methods remained unsolved.

The challenge itself sharpened the inventive effort. The first ambitious attempts to produce plate directly from molten metal ended in failure. Progress clearly would have to come along lines already established. At Monessen, Pennsylvania, stands of rolls were connected in tandem so that a sheet going through the first was fed automatically into the others. When the American Tin Plate Company acquired the plant in 1899, it applied the system elsewhere. At the Monongahela Works the output increased from 5,750 to 6,500 pounds a turn. This modest success, however, was very far from the final result envisaged by American steel men.

The Tin Plate Company determined, at whatever cost, to perfect sheet and tin plate manufacture. Charles W. Bray, the chief engineer, developed a number of ingenious devices. In its final form, the Bray arrangement mechanically heated the sheet bar, fed it through six stands of roughing rolls, and carried it to the intermediate set of three stands in tandem. The company estimated that the eight Bray mills at the Monongahela Works in

1903 produced the equal of fourteen ordinary mills. But the system was not continuous. At no point was the metal in two or more stands at the same time, and the sheets had to be finished in standard manual mills.[26]

Here progress halted. Gradually, expectation turned to pessimism. The *Iron Age* reflected the general view of 1912 that "a striking innovation in these methods has become very unlikely."[27] The Bray process, incomplete and costly, did not spread. Along with crucible steel and wrought iron, sheet and tin plate manufacture remained technologically backward. The failures here only heightened the inventive achievements elsewhere in 'he industry.

The mechanical advances would have been largely wasted without comparable improvements in the qualities of steel. Playing for high stakes, American steel men spared no effort to make a good "soft" steel. The early successes came about through the experiments of D. C. Dudley and H. M. Howe to reduce the carbon content of pig iron during the Bessemer process. It was, however, impossible to exercise adequate control in the Bessemer converters. The use of open-hearth furnaces overcame this difficulty. The culmination came in 1906 when the American Rolling Mill Company successfully made a "pure" iron—one, that is, with all the qualities of wrought iron. The way was open for the thorough displacement of the expensive puddling system.[28]

Innovations, once made, were eagerly adopted throughout the industry. American manufacturers had no commitment to standard methods and proved equipment. The steelmakers, it seemed to conservative foreign observers, were seized by a destructive passion. A Bessemer manager told the Englishman Enoch James in 1901 that his plant, supervised by the same engineer, had been rebuilt from its foundations four times. The Scranton Steel Company, for instance, started its two four-ton Bessemer converters in May 1883. By December 1885 alterations had nearly tripled the ingot output. Six months later the company replaced the straining converters.[29] Equipment, often barely worn was scrapped as soon as improved models appeared.

Companies occasionally attempted to monopolize important inventions. Carnegie, for instance, brought suit against the Cambria Company for copying his metal mixer. The United States Circuit Court validated the Carnegie patent in 1898; but infringements continued. Popplewell observed a mixer in nearly every large works he visited in 1904. The Carnegie Company attempted to control the Uehling pig casting machine, but met with a similar lack of success.[30] These disputes were not typical. Ordinarily, improvements flowed into general use easily and rapidly.

Specialization speeded the process. Once a man had demonstrated his inventive talent, he was rarely satisfied to remain a company employee. Julian Kennedy, for example, worked at Carnegie's Braddock plant until his experiments in blast furnace operation made his reputation. In 1891 he became a consulting engineer in Pittsburgh. Machine and foundry companies, led by men like Kennedy, developed into the innovating center for steel manufacture. Applying their experience and patents indiscriminately, Mackintosh, Hamphill and Company, Mesta Machine Company, and other firms built equipment for the entire industry. The one clear effort by the American Tin Plate and Sheet Steel companies in 1900 to monopolize the makers of their machinery was thwarted.[31] Any manufacturer with the means had equal access to the latest advances.

The merger movement also served to generalize technological progress. Almost the entire plant capacity for pipe, wire, hoops, sheet, and tin plate entered combinations at the turn of the century. These then were organized into the United States Steel Corporation, along with the Carnegie, National, and Federal Steel companies. Led by Carnegie men, the Steel Corporation immediately launched a modernization program. The value of its manufacturing properties, excluding the Gary Works, increased by $133,000,000—60 per cent—in one decade. The American Tin Plate Company, for instance, abandoned twenty-one mills between 1899 and 1907, and enlarged and improved many others. The half of the industry incorporated into the steel trust thus rapidly achieved a uniformly efficient level. The independent basic producers, stimulated by Carnegie's competition, did likewise. Finally, the many small finishing firms which entered the field after 1901, ordinarily without the resources to keep up with improvements, simply built the latest equipment into their new mills as part of the initial investment.

Technological requirements largely shaped the structure of the industry. The integration of every process from the blast furnace to the loading platform was necessary so that "everything worked with perfect regularity." The optimum size and arrangement for the basic mill appeared settled. "Two thousand or 2,500 tons a day would be about the point where the minimum cost in manufacturing could be reached," estimated Willis King of Jones and Laughlin. The thirty or so steel plants owned by the ten independents and the Steel Corporation were of at least that capacity and fully integrated. The finishing mills, on the other hand, generally remained small, since each machine operated independently. "A man can start in with six hot mills [in a tin plate plant] and make his product as cheaply as if he had sixty, proportionately," observed Julian Kennedy. While a steelmaking plant required a minimum investment of $20,000,000, a competitive finishing plant could be built for under $500,000. A host of companies of small capital and tonnage were soon turning out sheet, tin plate, wire, hoop, and pipe.[32]

On the margins of the industry many obsolete blast furnaces, puddling and rolling mills continued to exist precariously. But to a remarkable extent the industry made its technological advance as a unit. The accomplishment was shortly undeniable. "The results aimed at," acknowledged the German expert Dr. J. Puppe, "have been fully achieved and must command the admiration of all practical iron manufacturers."[33] American steelmaking practice was unsurpassed.

The impulse for economy, responding to unrestrained competition, fostered the inventive efforts. Technological success in turn invigorated the economizing drive. Mutually stimulating, these parallel forces profoundly influenced the psychology of the steelmasters. Concerned always with costs and improvements, they could not permit "preconceived ideas and vested interests" to obstruct their exertions. In short, they became men of calculation and inquiry. The mind of the industry was eminently rational.

When Sir Lowthian Bell visited the United States in 1890, he was appalled at the "recklessly rapid rate of driving" blast furnaces that reduced the "interiors to a wreck about every three years." The Pittsburgh furnaces, Sir Lowthian admitted, were smelting six times as much iron as those at the Clarence Works in England. But his furnaces consequently were "performing their duty as well as they did . . . 17½ years ago." This argument amused Americans. "What do we care about the lining?" asked Superintendent Charles S. Price of Cambria. "We think that a lining is good for so much iron and the sooner it makes it the better."[34] Low costs, not machines, were what Americans worshiped; and calculation showed that it was cheaper to drive a furnace than to prolong its life. Similar reckoning, devoid of sentiment or preconception, dictated the scrapping of still usable equipment, the high level of investment and, indeed, every decision.

The prerequisite for rational operation was exact information. Detailed records were not usually kept where costs were constant and methods settled, for instance, in wrought iron manufacture. Nor were such data widely used in the early years of the steel industry. Even in 1885 the Iron and Steel Association failed to gather information for a federal tariff study partly because many manufacturers "do not keep their records with sufficient minuteness. . . . Others do not care to take the trouble to compile the details."[35]

When he entered the steel trade in 1875, Carnegie adopted cost accounting methods. The general manager of the company, William B. Shinn, had been a railroad auditor. He introduced a voucher system used by railroads and Standard Oil. The detailed costs and production figures were recorded daily and each month the compiled data were presented to the Board of Managers for consideration. The report for August 1897 was characteristic.

Duquesne Steel Works. These Works produced during the month 36,355 tons of Ingots; 20,816 tons of Billets and 9,274 tons of Rails. Cost of manufacture from Pig Iron to Billets was the lowest ever obtained, being $3.55 from Pig to Billets, or 23 cents per ton less than the lowest cost ever obtained at these Works. It is now believed by the Superintendent at these Works that with his new Blowing arrangements completed and some other changes of minor character, which he is now making, that he can ultimately reduce this cost to about $3.25. . . . The practice at the Duquesne Works for the past month was the best we have ever had.[36]

The cost sheets, broken down and analyzed, were searched assiduously for slackness and points for improvement.

Charles Schwab described the procedure: "We made a careful . . . statement of each manufacture, with the cost as compared with each department, and the reasons . . . ; had the manager of that department make such explanations as were necessary. . . . Greater economies are effected by strict supervision over all departments than in any other direction." Julian Kennedy recalled his years as a Carnegie manager: "A careful record was kept of the costs. You are expected always to get it 10 cents cheaper the next year or the next month." From New York or Europe Carnegie would spot an increase in coke consumption. "This is, at least, five per cent more than it should be, and perhaps more. It should be investigated, beginning at the beginning. . . . We should do better than that."[37] The demand for excellence never slackened.

The Steel Corporation adapted the Carnegie system to its more complex organization. First, the statistics of the subsidiaries were standardized. By July 1901 a uniform system was in effect for blast furnace and open-hearth departments. The Executive Committee next established a bureau of comparative costs to determine "why costs are good and bad." Every Corporation plant sent monthly detailed forms to the New York office. The bureau compiled from these reports two sets of comparative cost sheets, a technical one for plant managers and another for higher officials. The technical sheets included practice statistics and detailed costs. Over 8,000 items were recorded in the blast furnace forms. A committee of furnace superintendents met each month, studied the figures, and recommended changes. According to President Schwab, such analysis saved over $4,000,000 in blast furnace operation alone during the first year.[38]

Decision based on exact data became habitual. When Carnegie was debating withdrawal from a beam pool, for instance, Schwab calculated the greater profitability of running full at a tenth of a cent less per pound than at three-quarters speed at the regular price. The Steel Corporation in 1908 began systematically to gather information on its competitors as a basis for its competitive policies.[39] That form of rational action was evident at every turn.

The economizing calculation, for example, was one determinant in the formation of the United States Steel Corporation. Technological advance seemed to be reaching its limits. "We cannot get Costs down any more," Frick had reported in 1898. Further economies, Schwab argued, were attainable only through organization and distribution. His eloquence strengthened J. P. Morgan's decision to undertake the unification of half the industry into one company.[40]

Appointed president of U.S. Steel, Schwab set to work putting his preachings into practice. He eliminated wasteful duplication. Ore and coal mining, coke manufacture, and lake transportation were systematized under a single management. No longer would ore pile up on one dock, while boats at the next waited weeks for a full load or departed half empty. "Now, owning all the fleet, . . . it doesn't make any difference what ore is ready." Plant specialization promised further economies. The Youngstown and South works both made rails. "One of the first things we did was to run one of these two works entirely on rails and the other on commodities best suited, thereby saving in freights, shipments and deliveries." The expectations for economy "have been fully realized," Schwab reported after the first year, and much was yet to be accomplished.[41]

Careful cost analysis also determined commercial policies. The head of a firm, said T. J. Bray of Republic, "should have constantly before him complete cost data" when making sales decisions. Here, as elsewhere, Carnegie is the best example. "The surest way to continued leadership," he lectured his managers, was "to adopt policy of selling a few finished articles which require large tonnage." Bridges were "not so good because every order different." In addition, Carnegie sought quantity orders. His company agreed to a five-year contract for steel slabs at a very low figure because of "the advantage of cheaper production on the rest of the material from that train [of rolls] ."[42] Large standard forms and capacity operation, according to the cost sheets, maximized economical production.

U.S. Steel, extending Carnegie's sales aim, became the country's quantity producer of standard lines of steel. A subsidiary sales manager reported in 1905:

Our "back-log" tonnage, and the ability to turn out enormous production, have been better than to get top prices by taking more undesirable work. . . . Even in bad times we should be able to run our works fairly full.

A car company contract was favorable because "they would order in large lengths and do their own cutting, and would take such quantities as to make desirable rollings." Long-term contracts also permitted better scheduling in transportation and production. The Steel Corporation insisted on making deliveries at its convenience from plants of its designation.[43] Premium sales, rush orders, and special products it left to the independents. Finally, U.S. Steel determined to be self-contained through the finished product. By 1907 this last step was achieved to provide the economies of standardization, scheduling, and full operation.

The cost calculation thus shaped decisions at every point in the steelmaking enterprise.

The spur of economy made the mental cast of the industry surpassingly objective and rational.

Ultimately, success or failure rested on the men who managed the furnaces and mills. They had to be a special breed. An executive, observed a prominent steelmaster, "must constantly endeavor to do a little better, accomplish a little more, save a trifle here, improve a detail there." The superintendent who repairs "on the same lines as last time, without seeing his way to improve, to strengthen, and to make more effective his furnace; we have no use for that class of men." [44] Kennedy remarked, "The pressure is always on you to make all the economies you can." Carnegie's president, J. A. Leishman, urged the recording of reasons for votes at board meetings in order to "form a correct judgment of the ability of our managers." [45] For they were the critical element in the quest for economy.

The youthfulness of American superintendents was frequently noted by English visitors. One took the Pressed Steel Car Company, employing ten thousand men, as an example: the president was thirty-eight; his assistant, thirty-six; the secretary, thirty-six; and the chief engineer was thirty-two years old. W. E. Corey and A. C. Dinkey were general superintendents of the Carnegie Company in their twenties, and Schwab became president when he was barely thirty. College men increasingly filled the managerial ranks as steel manufacture grew complex and technical, but the accent on youth remained. Of twenty-one blast furnace plants visited by Axel Sahlin in 1901, eighteen were managed by young university men. "When a college graduate, who shows that he has the right stuff in him, reaches the age of 25 or 30 years, he is ready for a position of trust," one manufacturer told Sahlin. Older, experienced men made excellent specialists, "but for managers and executives we select young men with brains and education." Lacking "time to wear themselves into a groove," they were unfettered in their efforts for improvement.[46]

They had, moreover, the vigor and enthusiasm required for peak operations. As a youthful superintendent of the Minnequa rail mill in Colorado, Tom Girdler worked practically all his waking hours. British steel men, visiting the Duquesne Works at night, found the managers still on duty, and this appeared to be the usual practice at other plants. The energy of Americans, conjectured the Englishmen, was partly the secret of their success.

But youth alone would not guarantee top performance. Steelmasters shrewdly devised incentives for their managerial forces. Charles Schwab, for instance, would not select one manager over all departments. "I put one good man at each of them and then rivalled one against the other, and in that way got better results." Rivalry was widespread. Trade journals immediately published production records, setting the mark for others to beat. The competition between the Edgar Thomson and South works became famous. In November 1891 the Thomson mill set out to beat the best twenty-four-hour mark of the South Works—1,700 tons. By the day's end 2,074 tons was the new record, soon itself to be surpassed. A huge steel broom at the Thomson Works hung above the blast furnace that had swept away the pig iron record. When the Steel Corporation was formed, President Schwab intended to "put one works as a rival against another works, as to practices, wastes, supplies, everything that goes into costs." The comparative cost sheets ranked units by cost per ton; the ambition of every manager was to reach the top.[47]

Handsome reward was the chief spur to special achievement. Carnegie dangled partnerships before his managers. They invested nothing. Shares were set aside, paid for out of accruing profit, and then awarded. The first four were chosen in 1884, and in time every responsible official became a partner. The system worked exceedingly well. It kept the managers at their peak, and guaranteed that the best men would come forward.

Carnegie had an uncanny ability for picking likely men out of the ranks; thirty of thirty-three superintendents rose from laboring jobs, some to become the leaders of the industry. He wrote Frick in 1896:

> *There is one man I should like to see given one-sixth [of one per cent] —Mr. Corey. He is worth it. . . . Perhaps there are one or two others who deserve sixths. Every year should be marked by the promotion of one or more of our young men. . . . We can not have too many of the right sort interested in the profits.*[48]

Then emerging from obscurity, W. E. Corey went on to become president of U.S. Steel. Carnegie often laid his success to the partnership policy and his "Young Geniuses." His company was renowned for its superb management.

The Carnegie incentive system seemed impractical for the corporate structure of U.S. Steel. Instead, Schwab proposed bonuses to reward performance. (The Carnegie Company had given its lesser officials bonuses.) A uniform policy, however, was not adopted until dissatisfaction arose among the executives. Under the U.S. Steel profit-sharing plan, an increasing percentage of earnings over $75,000,000 was set aside for distribution according to merit. Also, at the suggestion of the insurance magnate G. W. Perkins, a portion was held back for five years, and then shared by the executives still in the service of the Steel Corporation. Although the plan incorporated Carnegie's aim, the effect was considerably diluted.

The efficacy of bonuses was demonstrated by Schwab when he acquired Bethlehem Steel. His monetary incentives infused life into the moribund company. Schwab did not dismiss the staff, believing, as Carnegie had said, that "unsuspecting powers lie latent in willing men around us," needing only "appreciation and development to produce surprising results." They did produce surprising results; by 1915 Bethlehem was second only to the Steel Corporation. The bonus plan set a "cash premium on personal efficiency and endeavor." Bonuses were paid monthly, the men reaping their rewards directly and precisely. As Bethlehem prospered, bonuses mounted very high. Schwab's plan, like his mentor's, created a magnificent managerial organization. He became as famous for his "Boys" as Carnegie had been for his "Young Geniuses." Bonus systems, in many guises, spread through industry. [49] Excellence was generously repaid.

Security, however, was not one of the rewards. The British habit of retaining aging employees, observed an English visitor in 1901, was far distant from the American practice "of getting rid of any man, however exalted his position, when there is the least evidence that his efficiency and his power of endurance are waning." Carnegie's limited association contained an "iron clad" clause that a partner could be ejected from the firm by a three-fourths vote and his share repurchased at book value. The clause was frequently invoked. When a partner was "sent to Europe," Pittsburghers joked, it meant he was being forced out. [50] Long contracts were few, and managerial changes frequent. There was little evidence that successful men dragged "relatives up with them irrespective of actual merit and proved capacity, as in Great Britain." Sentiment had no place in the steel business.

The managerial policy worked with marvelous effectiveness. In the hands of the untiring men who superintended the steel mills the industry became the wonder of the manufacturing world.

By the opening of the twentieth century the modern character of American steel manufacture had been formed. Mechanization was nearly completed. Rational calculation prevailed. And the managerial force assured peak performance. At every point, the impulse for economy had been paramount. So it was in fixing the place of labor in the steelmaking system.

Notes

1. J. Stephen Jeans, ed., *American Industrial Conditions and Competition,* Reports of Commissioners appointed by the British Iron Trade Association (London, 1902), p. 255, and *passim* for comments.

2. Charles M. Schwab, quoted in *They Told Barron,* eds. Arthur Pound and Samuel T. Moore (New York, 1930), p. 85; Carnegie quoted in J. H. Bridge, *The Inside History of the Carnegie Steel Company* (New York, 1903), pp. 95-96.

3. Joseph G. Butler, *Recollections of Men and Events* (New York, 1927), p. 151; *Iron Age,* November 30, 1882, p. 14, February 10, 1887, p. 17, cited hereafter as *IA.*

4. John W. Gates to William Govier, April 23, 1890, Braddock Wire Company, American Steel and Wire Company Collection, Baker Library, Harvard University.

5. *Commercial and Financial Chronicle,* April 29, 1882, p. 489, March 24, 1888, p. 386, March 19, 1891, p. 427.

6. For effective pools at this period, see U.S. Commissioner of Corporations, *Report on the Steel Industry* (3 vols., Washington, 1911-1913), I, 69-71.

7. Charles Schwab, Carnegie Steel Company, Executive Board Minutes, October 22, 1900, *United States v. United States Steel Corporation,* 223 F. 55 (1912), *Government Exhibits,* VI, 1898.

8. Carnegie to H. C. Frick, February 13, 1894, Carnegie Papers, Library of Congress.

9. Carnegie Minutes, October 6, 1893, *U.S. v. U.S.S., Government Exhibits,* III, 978.

10. *Engineering and Mining Journal,* quoted in *Steel Report,* I, 78.

11. Carnegie Minutes, February 9, 1897, December 21, 1897, and Report of H. P. Bope, Assistant General Sales Agent, January 3, 1899, *U.S. v. U.S.S., Government Exhibits,* III, 1071, 1096, 1176-1179.

12. Gary, in *U.S. v. U.S.S., Testimony,* XIV, 5300; Carnegie Company Minutes, April 5, 1898, November 22, 1898, January 10, 1899, February 7, 1899, October 16, 1899, *Government Exhibits,* III, 1112, 1163, 1181, 1195, 1285.

13. Illinois Steel Company, *Annual Report* (1898); Carnegie Minutes, December 20, 1898, *U.S. v. U.S.S., Government Exhibits,* III, 1168; *Engineering and Mining Journal,* August 27, 1898, p. 242, cited hereafter as *EMJ.*

14. *U.S. v. U.S.S., Testimony,* VIII, 3200.

15. American Iron and Steel Association, *Statistical Report* (1890), pp. 44, 50; John Fritz, "The

Progress of the Manufacture of Iron and Steel," American Society of Mechanical Engineers, *Transactions*, XVIII (1897), 39-69; *EMJ*, March 5, 1892, p. 282; *Iron Trade Review*, October 15, 1914, p. 699, cited hereafter as *ITR*. The course of the Republic Iron and Steel Company, a merger of twenty-seven iron mills with a capacity of over a million tons, indicated the extent to which puddling seemed incompatible with prosperity. The company, shortly after being formed in 1899, began abandoning the iron mills, erecting in their stead a large steel plant at Youngstown. At a cost of $25,000,000 Republic became by 1914 almost exclusively a steel producer.

16. *IA*, August 19, 1882, p. 24; *EMJ*, June 9, 1892, p. 89, April 18, 1903, p. 604; Institute of Mining Engineers, *Transactions*, XXXVI (1905), 205-207, 806. On the sustained efforts of James P. Roe in later years, see *IA*, August 2, 1906, pp. 289-290, May 1, 1913, p. 1069; Mining Engineers, *Transactions*, XXXIII (1902), 551-561, and *Transactions*, XXXVI (1905), 204-215, 807-815.

17. For Carnegie's early interest in mechanical buckets ("which reduce the cost to about 6 cents") on ore boats and other economies in bringing Mesabi ore to his plants, see Carnegie to John Shaw, December 9, 1895, and James Andrews to Carnegie, December 23, 1895, Carnegie Papers.

18. Carnegie Minutes, May 11, 1897, *U.S. v. U.S.S., Government Exhibits,* III, 1083.

19. Frank Popplewell, *Some Modern Conditions and Recent Developments in Iron and Steel Production in America* (Manchester, 1906), p. 95.

20. *IA*, December 21, 1882, p. 26, August 11, 1882, p. 26, April 6, 1905, p. 1154; *EMJ*, August 13, 1898, pp. 187-189. Robert N. Grosse, "The Determinants of the Size of Iron and Steel Firms in the United States, 1820-80," unpublished Ph.D. thesis, Harvard, 1948, pp. 178-179, 190, 197, gives early history of steel and iron firms acquiring blast furnaces.

21. Jones quoted in Bridge, p. 109, also pp. 175-176.

22. R. W. Hunt, "The Evolution of American Rolling Mills," American Society of Mechanical Engineers, *Transactions*, XIII (1892), 45-69; John Fritz, *Autobiography* (New York, 1912), ch. 15.

23. Popplewell, pp. 103-105.

24. C. H. Morgan, "Some Landmarks in the History of the Rolling Mill," American Society of Mechanical Engineers, *Transactions*, XXII (1901), 31-64; F. H. Daniels, "Wire Rod Rolling Mills and Their Development," American Society of Mechanical Engineers, *Transactions*, XIV (1893), 583-618. See also, Cost Data, August 14, 1891, Washburn and Moen Mfg. Company, American Steel and Wire Collection.

25. W. C. Cronemeyer, U.S. Bureau of Census, *Twelfth Census* (1900), X, 119. On early tin plate history, see *ibid.*, pp. 111-119.

26. Hunt, Mechanical Engineers, *Transactions*, XIII, 67-68; *Iron and Steel Trade Journal*, March 24, 1900, p. 274; *IA*, September 22, 1904, p. 29, January 5, 1905, p. 1214; *EMJ*, January 17, 1903, p. 125.

27. *IA*, August 8, 1912, p. 311.

28. *EMJ*, September 2, 1893, p. 234, January 3, 1903, p. 40; *ITR*, May 14, 1914, p. 871; American Rolling Mill Company, *The First Twenty Years* (Middletown, Ohio, 1922), ch. 9.

29. *IA*, March 10, 1887, p. 19; Jeans, p. 518. Charles Schwab, *Andrew Carnegie, His Method With His Men* (Pittsburgh, November 25, 1919), pp. 9-11, tells the perhaps apocryphal story of having just remodeled a mill, only to see ways for further improvement. Carnegie told him to tear it down and do it again.

30. Carnegie to J. A. Leishman, November 12, 1895, Carnegie Papers; Bridge, pp. 79-80. In 1914, 69 metal mixers were in operation, and 112 pig casters. U.S. Bureau of Census, *Census of Manufactures* (1914), II, 216, 237.

31. *U.S. v. U.S.S., Testimony,* V, 1928-1957, 1794-1803; U.S. Industrial Commission, *Reports* (Washington, 1899-1901), I, 852, 875, 888-890, cited hereafter as *Industrial Commission.* Kennedy patended numerous appliances, which were then available, at a price, to the entire industry. See, for example, *EMJ,* February 28, 1903, p. 340, March 7, 1903, p. 379.

32. King, *Industrial Commission,* XIII, 505; Kennedy, U.S. House, Committee on the Investigation of the United States Steel Corporation, *Hearings,* 62 Cong., 2nd Sess. (1911-12), VII, 5128, cited hereafter as *Stanley Hearings.*

33. Dr. J. Puppe, "American Rolling Mill Practice," *IA*, May 15, 1913, pp. 1172-1179.

34. Bell, in British Iron and Steel Institute, *The Iron and Steel Institute in America in 1890* (London, n.d.), pp. 170, 172, 183; Price quoted in Herbert N. Casson, *The Romance of Steel* (New York, 1907), p. 362.

35. U.S. Commissioner of Labor, *Cost of Production: Iron, Steel, Coal* (Washington, 1891), p. 6.

36. September 14, 1897, *U.S. v. U.S.S., Government Exhibits,* III, 1090, and 1083-1097, for a number of such reports of 1897. On Shinn and Carnegie's early interest in cost accounting, see Bridge, pp. 85-86; Andrew Carnegie, *Autobiography* (Boston, 1924), p. 202; *EMJ,* May 7, 1892, p. 495.

37. Carnegie to J. A. Leishman, January 15, 1896, Carnegie Papers; Schwab, in *Industrial Commission,* XIII, 452; Kennedy, in *Stanley Hearings,* VII, 5115.

38. *U.S. v. U.S.S., Testimony,* XIII, 4975, XIV, 5546-5550; *Statement of the Case,* pp. 187-188; *Defendants' Exhibits,* VIII, 619, prints the first simple comparative cost sheet for the blast furnaces, July 2, 1901; U.S. Steel Executive Committee Minutes, September 9, 1902, *Stanley Hearings,* VI, 3804.

39. Carnegie Minutes, February 4, 1896, *Government Exhibits,* III, 1006; U.S. Steel, General Sales Managers' Minutes, November 20, December 16, 1908, *Stanley Hearings,* VI, 3966.

40. Frick, in Carnegie Company Minutes, September 20, 1898, *U.S. v. U.S.S., Government Exhibits,* III, 1138; *Testimony,* XIV, 5489; B. J. Hendrick, *The Life of Andrew Carnegie* (2 vols., New York, 1932), II, 129-131.

41. *Industrial Commission,* XIII, 451; U.S. Steel Executive Committee Minutes, April 12, 1901, *U.S. v. U.S.S., Testimony,* XIII, 4975; U.S. Steel, *Report to the Stockholders* (1902).

42. Bray, in *ITR,* May 28, 1914, p. 597; Carnegie Company Minutes, January 31, 1899, February 21, 1899, October 11, 1900, *Government Exhibits,* III, 1193, 1215, VI, 1896; Carnegie to J. A. Leishman, September 18, 1895, and to F. T. F. Lovejoy, December 9, 1895, Carnegie Papers.

43. Carnegie Company Directors' Minutes, March 16, 1903, October 30, 1905, *Government Exhibits,* II, 487, 502, 506. See interchange of letters between C. W. Bryan of the American Bridge Company and the Union Pacific Railroad, in which insistence on control of manufacture schedule and desire for large orders is clearly illustrated. *Government Exhibits,* XIII, Nos. 428-432.

44. Jeans, p. 500.

45. J. A. Leishman to Carnegie, December 23, 1895, Carnegie Papers.

46. Jeans, pp. 500-501.

47. Schwab, in *Industrial Commission,* XIII, 456; Bridge, pp. 107-110; *EMJ,* January 2, 1892, p. 33; *U.S. v. U.S.S., Testimony,* XIII, 4976, XIV, 5550.

48. Quoted in Hendrick, II, 42. See also Andrew Carnegie, "The Human Side of Business," *Miscellaneous Writings* (2 vols., New York, 1933), I, 9-10. Carnegie once said a fitting epitaph for him would be: "Here lies a man who knew how to get other men to work for him."

49. Arundel Cotter, *The Story of Bethlehem Steel* (New York, 1916), pp. 13-14, 20-22; New York *Times,* February 17, 1916. On other bonus systems, see, for example, *IA,* March 22, 1911, pp. 716-718, March 4, 1915, p. 518.

50. Carnegie owned over half, usually about 58 per cent of the stock. Men who left their position in the firm were required to sell their shares back at book value. This did not always work out well. When Carnegie forced Frick out, Frick sued, claiming the actual value of the company was much greater than the book value, as it was, and Carnegie had to give in. See *Government Exhibits,* III, 1334-1340; Hendrick, II, chs. 3 and 4; George Harvey, *Henry Clay Frick* (New York, 1928), chs. 16-18.

The beginnings of "big business" in American industry

Alfred D. Chandler

good into :

In the post-Civil War era, the characteristic business enterprise was small in scale, confined to a single stage of the industrial process, and limited to a local market or dependent on commission agents for access to more distant customers. By the opening of the twentieth century, the characteristic American firm was a giant in scale, corporate in form, and integrated in one direction down to the raw materials and/or in the other to include marketing and distribution. The centralized, departmentalized internal structure that resulted profoundly altered the career of the American businessman. Earlier essentially entrepreneurial, now he found himself enmeshed in a bureaucratic system of management. The giant scale of operations spelled, too, an end to genuine competition and the beginning of the modern oligopolistic market. Beyond these specifically economic consequences, the concentration of economic power would have profound and continuing implications for American politics, labor relations, and, indeed, every aspect of American life. Clearly, no economic change of the late nineteenth century matched in importance the emergence of big business. Why that happened, therefore, becomes a question of the first magnitude for American historians.

Summary of Chandler

In the following pioneering, essay, Alfred D. Chandler attempts a systematic analysis of this problem. He locates the primary cause in the rise of a huge urban market and, as a preceding factor, in the spreading railroad network that stimulated urban growth and made it accessible to American industry. Big business was a response both to expanding markets and to the new kinds of demands generated by city building. Chandler discerns a significant pattern in the ways large-scale enterprise developed. There were, to begin with, two distinct phases. The first, beginning in 1880s and lasting into the middle of 1890s, involved the industries producing consumer goods, primarily agricultural in origin, for the expanding urban markets. Among the consumer-goods industries, there were two distinct paths to large-scale organization. When essentially new products were being developed, such as dressed meat, cigarettes, and sewing machines, the need seemed to be for the creation of systems of distribution and marketing, and such firms as Swift and Company and the Singer Sewing Machine Company grew large through a process of vertical integration. For industries turning out conventional, established products, such as biscuits, sugar, and whiskey, the road to big business was mainly through horizontal integration. Intensive competition, the result of improved transportation, led to a combination movement. Once a combine was formed, it characteristically instituted internal changes to consolidate and rationalize its operations. But the initial motives were to forestall competition and only subsequently to improve industrial operations.

The second phase, which reached its peak in the half dozen years after 1897, involved the producer-goods industries, which had, Chandler argues, entered the urban market somewhat later than consumer-goods industries. Chandler suggests, too, that organizational growth now became a more complicated process because of the new role played by the financial interests, who had their own motives for encouraging mergers. Still, Chandler is able to perceive an underlying economic logic in the development of large-scale enterprise in the basic industries. Those companies turning out semifinished products, such as steel and copper, grew primarily through integration—not, however, in the direction of distribution (since this was a simple part of the enterprise) but, rather, backward toward control of raw materials, sometimes for defensive purposes, sometimes for reasons of efficiency. In finished producer-goods industries, business tended to result, as in the conventional consumer-goods fields, from an effort to control the market through the combination of competing firms, followed by further growth through moves to encompass the production of parts and to develop a "full line" of products.

Chandler correctly stresses the tentative character of his analysis. In this essay, he inaugurated (and has since carried further) a new approach to business history that focuses not on the individual firm but, rather, on institutional change cutting across firms. This is a welcome advance in what has been a rather sterile area of historical studies, but it is also one that raises serious problems, not only of research, but also of analysis. Since there is no integral connection among firms, the approach must be essentially comparative in nature, and the analysis must depend heavily on classification, as Chandler's essay does. Any attempt at sweeping conclusions will likely be vulnerable to attack. In this instance, one questions the completeness of an analysis based so heavily on market changes. Chandler may have underestimated the importance of technological factors. In the dressed meat industry, for example, the key development was the perfection of the refrigerator car in the 1870s. The expanding urban markets were actually being served quite satisfactorily by the railroad shipment of live-stock to city slaughter houses. What concentration of processing in midwestern centers offered was greater efficiency in plant operations and in the use of by-products. Likewise, technological change stimulated the competition that led to combinations and often made possible the integration that contributed to business growth. In any case, Chandler's complex essay bears close reading, both for what it has to say about the emergence of big business in America and for the possible modifications that his analysis will require.

For further reading: Edward C. Kirkland, *Industry Comes of Age: Business, Labor and Public Policy, 1860-1897* (1961);* Allan Nevins, *Study in Power: John D. Rockefeller, Industrialist and Philanthropist* (1953); Joseph Frazier Wall, *Andrew Carnegie* (1970); Eliot Jones, *The Trust Problem in the United States* (1924); Thomas R. Navin and Marion V. Sears, "The Rise of the Market for Industrial Securities, 1887-1902," *Business History Review,* 19 (1955), 105-138; Alfred D. Chandler, *Strategy and Structure: Chapters in the*

History of the Industrial Enterprise (1962);* Thomas C. Cochran, "Economic History, Old and New," *American Historical Review*, LXXIV (1969), 1561-1572.

Criteria for Selection and Analysis

The historian, by the very nature of his task, must be concerned with change. What made for change? Why did it come when it did, and in the way it did? These are characteristically historians' questions. For the student of American business history, these basic questions can be put a little more precisely. What in the American past has given businessmen the opportunity or created the need for them to change what they were doing or the way they were doing it? In other words, what stimulated them to develop new products, new markets, new sources of raw materials, new ways of procuring, processing, or marketing the goods they handled? What encouraged them to find new methods of financing, new ways of managing or organizing their businesses? What turned them to altering their relations with their working force, their customers and competitors, and with the larger American public?

The question of what constitutes the dynamic factors in American business history, dynamic in the sense of stimulating change and innovation, can be more clearly defined if the country's land, natural resources and cultural patterns are taken as given. Land and resources were the raw materials with which the businessmen had to work, and the cultural attitudes and values helped set the legal and ethical rules of the game they had to play. Within this cultural and geographic environment a number of historical developments appear to have stimulated change. These provide a framework around which historical data can be compiled and analyzed.

The following major dynamic forces are visible in the American business economy since 1815: the western expansion of population; the construction and initial operation of the national railroad network; the development of a national and increasingly urban market; the application of two new sources of power: the internal combustion engine and electricity, to industry and transportation; and the systematic application of the natural and physical sciences, particularly chemistry and physics, to industry through the institutionalizing of research and development activities.

The first, the westward expansion, appears to have provided the primary impetus, except possibly in New England, to business innovation in the years from 1815 to about 1850; the building of the railroads appears to have been the major factor from the 1850's to the late 1870's; the growth of the national and urban market from the 1880's until a little after 1900; the coming of electricity and the internal combustion engine from the early 1900's to the 1920's; and, finally, the growth of systematic and institutionalized research and development since the 1920's.

These five factors are essentially aspects of fundamental population changes and technological advances. There were, of course, other factors that encouraged business innovation and change. The coming of the new machines and mechanical devices may have been a more important stimulant to innovation in New England than the growth of her markets and sources of supply in the expanding South and West. Wars usually precipitated change. The business cycle, flow of capital, government policy and legislation all played a significant part in business innovation. But such political and financial developments appear to have intensified or delayed the more basic changes encouraged initially by fundamental population shifts and technological achievements.

The purpose of making such a list is, however, not to argue that one development was more dynamic than the other. Nor are these five factors to be considered as "causes" for change; nor are they "theses" to be argued as representing reality, nor "theories" to provide an over-all explanation of change or possibly of predicting change. They are, rather, a framework on which historical information can be tied and inter-related. They provide a consistent basis upon which meaningful questions can be asked of the data.

This framework and these questions are, it should be emphasized, concerned only with fundamental changes and innovation in the business economy. They do not deal with the day-to-day activities to which businessmen must devote nearly all of their time. They are not concerned with the continuous adaptation to the constant variations of the market, sources of supply, availability of capital, and technological developments. Nor do they consider why some businesses and businessmen responded quickly and creatively to the basic population and technological changes and others did not. But an understanding of the continuous response and adjustment would seem to require first an awareness of the meaning of the more fundamental or "discontinuous" changes.

Since historical compilation and analysis must be selective, it is impossible to undertake any historical study without some criteria either implicit or explicit for selection. Further study and analysis, by indicating the defects of this approach and framework, will suggest more satisfactory ones. In the process, an analysis and interpretation of change in the American business past should come a little nearer to reality.

The purpose of this article then is, by using the framework of basic, dynamic forces, to look a little more closely at the years that witnessed the beginnings of big business in American industry. What types of changes came during these years in the ways of marketing, purchasing, processing, and in the forms of business organization? Why did these changes come when they did in the way they did? Was the growth of the national market a major prerequisite for such innovation and change? If not, what then was? How did these innovations relate to the growth of the railroad network or the coming of electricity and the internal combustion engine?

In addition to secondary works on this period, the data used in seeking answers to these questions have been annual and other corporation reports, government documents, articles in periodicals, histories, and biographies concerning the 50 largest industrial companies in the country in 1909. Nearly all these companies, listed in Table I, had their beginning in the last years of the nineteenth century.

Major Changes in American Industry At the End Of the Nineteenth Century

Between the depression of the 1870's and the beginning of the twentieth century, American industry underwent a significant transformation. In the 1870's, the major industries serviced an agrarian economy. Except for a few companies equipping the rapidly expanding railroad network, the leading industrial firms processed agricultural products and provided farmers with food and clothing. These firms tended to be small, and bought their raw materials and sold their finished goods locally. Where they manufactured for a market more than a few miles away from the factory, they bought and sold through commissioned agents who handled the business of several other similar firms.

By the beginning of the twentieth century, many more companies were making producers' goods, to be used in industry rather than on the farm or by the ultimate consumer. Most of the major industries had become dominated by a few large enterprises. These great industrial corporations no longer purchased and sold through agents, but had their own nation-wide buying and marketing organizations. Many, primarily those in the extractive industries, had come to control their own raw materials. In other words, the business economy had become industrial. Major industries were dominated by a few firms that had become great, vertically integrated, centralized enterprises.

In the terms of the economist and sociologist a significant sector of American industry had become bureaucratic, in the sense that business decisions were made within large hierarchical structures. Externally, oligopoly was prevalent, the decision-makers being as much concerned with the actions of the few other large firms in the industry as with over-all changes in markets, sources of supplies, and technological improvements.

These basic changes came only after the railroads had created a national market. The railroad network, in turn, had grown swiftly primarily because of the near desperate requirements for efficient transportation created by the movement of population westward after 1815.[1] Except for the Atlantic seaboard between Boston and Washington, the construction of the American railroads was stimulated almost wholly by the demand for better transportation to move crops, to bring farmers supplies, and to open up new territories to commercial agriculture.

By greatly expanding the scope of the agrarian economy, the railroads quickened the growth of the older commercial centers, such as New York, Philadelphia, Cincinnati, Cleveland, and St. Louis, and helped create new cities like Chicago, Indianapolis, Atlanta, Kansas City, Dallas, and the Twin Cities. This rapid urban expansion intensified the demand for the products of the older consumer goods industries—particularly those which processed the crops of the farmer and planter into food, stimulants, and clothing.

At the same time, railroad construction developed the first large market in this country for producers' goods. Except for the making of relatively few textile machines, steamboat engines, and ordnance, the iron and nonferrous manufacturers had before 1850 concentrated on providing metals and simple tools for merchants and farmers. Even textile machinery was usually made by the cloth manufacturers themselves. However, by 1860, only a decade after beginning America's first major railroad construction boom, railroad companies had already replaced the blacksmiths as a primary market for iron products, and had become far and away the most important market for the heavy engineering industries. By then, too, the locomotive was competing with the Connecticut brass industry as a major consumer of copper. More than this, the railroads, with their huge capital outlay, their fixed operating costs, the large size of their labor and management force, and the technical complexity of their operations, pioneered in the new ways of oligopolistic competition and large-scale, professionalized, bureaucratized management.

The new nation-wide market created by the construction of the railroad network became an increasingly urban one. From 1850 on, if not before, urban areas were growing more rapidly than rural ones. In the four decades from 1840 to 1880 the proportion of urban population rose from 11 per cent to 28 per cent of the total population, or about 4 per cent a decade. In the two decades from 1880 to 1900 it grew from 28 per cent to 40 per cent or an increase of 6 per cent a decade. Was this new urban and national market, then, the primary stimulant for business innovation and change, and for the coming of big business to American industry?

Changes in the Consumers' Goods Industries

The industries first to become dominated by great business enterprises were those making consumer goods, the majority of which were processed from products grown on the farm and sold in the urban markets. Consolidation and centralization in the consumers' goods industries were well under way by 1893. The unit that appeared was one which integrated within a single business organization the major economic processes: production or purchasing of raw materials, manufacturing, distribution, and finance.

Such vertically integrated organizations came in two quite different ways. Where the product tended to be somewhat new in kind and especially fitted for the urban market, its makers created their businesses by first building large marketing and then purchasing organizations. This technique appears to have been true of the manufacturers or distributors of fresh meat, cigarettes, high-grade flour, bananas, harvesters, sewing machines, and typewriters. Where the products were established staple items, horizontal combination tended to precede vertical integration. In the sugar, salt, leather, whiskey, glucose, starch, biscuit, kerosene, fertilizer, and rubber industries a large number of small manufacturers first combined into large business units and then created their marketing and buying organizations. For a number of reasons the makers of the new types of products found the older outlets less satisfactory and felt more of a need for direct marketing than did the manufacturers of the long-established goods.

Integration via the Creation of Marketing Organization

The story of the changes and the possible reasons behind them can be more clearly understood by examining briefly the experience of a few innovating firms. First, consider the experience of companies that grew large through the creation of nation-wide marketing and distributing organization. Here the story of Gustavus F. Swift and his brother Edwin is a significant one. Gustavus F. Swift, an Easterner, came relatively late to the Chicago meat-packing business. Possibly because he was from Massachusetts, he appreciated the potential market for fresh western meat in the eastern cities.[2] For after the Civil War, Boston, New York, Philadelphia, and other cities were rapidly outrunning their local meat supply. At the same time, great herds of cattle were gathering on the western plains. Swift saw the possibilities of connecting the new market with the new source of supply by the use of the refrigerated railroad car. In 1878, shortly after his first experimental shipment of refrigerated meat, he formed a partnership with his younger brother, Edwin, to market fresh western meat in the eastern cities.

For the next decade, Swift struggled hard to carry out his plans, the essence of which was the creation, during the 1880's, of the nation-wide distributing and marketing organization built around a network of branch houses. Each "house" had its storage plant and its own marketing organization. The latter included outlets in major towns and cities, often managed by Swift's own salaried representatives. In marketing the product, Swift had to break down, through advertising and other means, the prejudices against eating meat killed more than a thousand miles away and many weeks earlier. At the same time he had to combat boycotts of local butchers and the concerted efforts of the National Butchers' Protective Association to prevent the sale of his meat in the urban markets.

To make effective use of the branch house network, the company soon began to market products other than beef. The "full line" soon came to include lamb, mutton, pork, and, some time later, poultry, eggs, and dairy products. The growing distributing organization soon demanded an increase in supply. So between 1888 and 1892, the Swifts set up meat-packing establishments in Kansas City, Omaha, and St. Louis, and, after the depression of the 1890's, three more in St. Joseph, St. Paul, and Ft. Worth. At the same time, the company systematized the buying of its cattle and other products at the stockyards. In the 1890's, too, Swift began a concerted effort to make more profitable use of by-products.

Before the end of the 1890's, then, Swift had effectively fashioned a great, vertically integrated organization. The major departments—marketing, processing, purchasing, and accounting—were all tightly controlled from the central office in Chicago. A report of the Commissioner of Corporations published in 1905 makes clear the reason for such control:[3]

Differences in quality of animals and of their products are so great that the closest supervision of the Central Office is necessary to enforce the exercise of skill and sound judgement on the part of the agents who buy the stock, and the agents who sell the meat. With this object, the branches of the Selling and Accounting Department of those packing companies which have charge of the purchasing, killing, and dressing and selling of fresh meat, are organized in the most extensive and thorough manner. The Central Office is in constant telegraphic correspondence with the distributing houses, with a view to adjusting the supply of meat and the price as nearly as possible to the demand.

As this statement suggests, the other meat packers followed Swift's example. To compete effectively, Armour, Morris, Cudahy, and Schwarzschild & Sulzberger had to build up similar integrated organizations. Those that did not follow the Swift model were destined to remain small local companies. Thus by the middle of the 1890's, the meat-packing industry, with the rapid growth of these great vertically integrated firms had become oligopolistic (the "Big Five" had the major share of the market) and bureaucratic; each of the five had its many departments and several levels of management.

This story has parallels in other industries processing agricultural products. In tobacco, James B. Duke was the first to appreciate the growing market for the cigarette, a new product which was sold almost wholly in the cities.[4] However, after he had applied machinery to the manufacture of cigarettes, production soon outran supply. Duke then concentrated on expanding the market through extensive advertising and the creation of a national and then world-wide selling organization. In 1884, he left Durham, North Carolina, for New York City, where he set up factories, sales, and administrative offices. New York was closer to his major urban markets, and was the more logical place to manage an international advertising campaign than Durham. While he was building his marketing department, Duke was also creating the network of warehouses and buyers in the tobacco-growing areas of the country.

In 1890, he merged his company with five smaller competitors in the cigarette business to form the American Tobacco Company. By 1895 the activities of these firms had been consolidated into the manufacturing, marketing, purchasing, and finance departments of the single operating structure Duke had earlier fashioned. Duke next undertook development of a full line by handling all types of smoking and chewing tobacco. By the end of the century, his company completely dominated the tobacco business. Only two other firms, R. J. Reynolds & Company and P. Lorillard & Company had been able to build up comparable vertically integrated organizations. When they merged with American

Tobacco they continued to retain their separate operating organizations. When the 1911 antitrust decree split these and other units off from the American company, the tobacco industry had become, like the meat-packing business, oligopolistic, and its dominant firms bureaucratic.

What Duke and Swift did for their industries, James S. Bell of the Washburn-Crosby Company did during these same years in the making and selling of high-grade flour to the urban bakeries and housewives, and Andrew J. Preston achieved in growing, transporting, and selling another new product for the urban market, the banana.[5] Like Swift and Duke, both these men made their major innovations in marketing, and then went on to create large-scale, departmentalized, vertically integrated structures.

The innovators in new consumer durables followed much the same pattern. Both Cyrus McCormick, pioneer harvester manufacturer, and William Clark, the business brains of the Singer Sewing Machine Company, first sold through commissioned agents. Clark soon discovered that salaried men, working out of branch offices, could more effectively and at less cost display, demonstrate, and service sewing machines than could the agents.[6] Just as important, the branch offices were able to provide the customer with essential credit. McCormick, while retaining the dealer to handle the final sales, came to appreciate the need for a strong selling and distributing organization, with warehouses, servicing facilities, and a large salaried force, to stand behind the dealer.[7] So in the years following the Civil War, both McCormick and Singer Sewing Machine Company concentrated on building up national and then world-wide marketing departments. As they purchased their raw materials from a few industrial companies rather than from a mass of farmers, their purchasing departments were smaller, and required less attention than those in the firms processing farmers' products. But the net result was the creation of a very similar type of organization.

In those industries making more standard goods, the creation of marketing organizations usually followed large-scale combinations of a number of small manufacturing firms. For these small firms, the coming of the railroad had in many cases enlarged their markets but simultaneously brought them for the first time into competition with many other companies. Most of these firms appear to have expanded production in order to take advantage of the new markets. As a result, their industries became plagued with over-production and excess capacity; that is, continued production at full capacity threatened to drop prices below the cost of production. So in the 1880's and early 1890's, many small manufacturers in the leather, sugar, salt, distilling and other corn products, linseed and cotton oil, biscuit, petroleum, fertilizer and rubber boot and glove industries, joined in large horizontal combinations.

In most of these industries, combination was followed by consolidation and vertical integration, and the pattern was comparatively consistent. First, the new combinations concentrated their manufacturing activities in locations more advantageously situated to meet the new growing urban demands. Next they systematized and standardized their manufacturing processes. Then, except in the case of sugar and corn products (glucose and starch), the combinations began to build large distributing and smaller purchasing departments. In so doing, many dropped their initial efforts to buy out competitors or to drive them out of business by price-cutting. Instead they concentrated on the creation of a more efficient flow from the producers of their raw materials to the ultimate consumer, and of the development and maintenance of markets through brand names and advertising. Since the large majority of these combinations began as regional groupings, most industries came to have more than one great firm. Only oil, sugar, and corn products remained long dominated by a single company. By World War I, partly because of the dissolutions under the Sherman Act, these industries had also become oligopolistic, and their leading firms vertically integrated.

Specific illustrations help to make these generalizations more precise. The best-known is the story of the oil industry, but equally illustrative is the experience of the leading distilling, baking, and rubber companies.

The first permanent combination in the whiskey industry came in 1887 when a large number of Midwestern distillers, operating more than 80 small plants, formed the Distillers' and Cattle Feeders' Trust.[8] Like other trusts, it adopted the more satisfactory legal form of a holding company shortly after New Jersey in 1889 passed the general incorporation law for holding companies. The major efforts of the Distillers Company were, first, to concentrate production in a relatively few plants. By 1895 only 21 were operating. The managers maintained that the large volume per plant permitted by such concentration would mean lower costs, and also that the location of few plants more advantageously in relation to supply and marketing would still reduce expenses further. However, the company kept the price of whiskey up, and since the cost of setting up a distillery was small, it soon had competition from small local plants. The company's answer was to purchase the new competitors and to cut prices. This strategy proved so expensive that the enterprise was unable to survive the depression of the 1890's.

Shortly before going into receivership in 1896, the Distillers Company had begun to think more about marketing. In 1895, it had planned to spend a million dollars to build up a distributing and selling organization in the urban East—the company's largest market. In 1898, through the purchase of the Standard Distilling & Distributing Company and the Spirits Distributing Company, it did acquire a marketing organization based in New York City. In 1903, the marketing and manufacturing units were combined into a single operating organization under the direction of the Distillers Securities Company. At the same time, the company's president announced plans to concentrate on the development of brand names and specialties, particularly through advertising and packaging.[9] By the early years of the twentieth century, then, the Distillers Company had become a vertically integrated, departmentalized, centralized operating organization, competing in the modern manner, more through advertising and product differentiation than price.

The experience of the biscuit industry is even more explicit. The National Biscuit Company came into being in 1898 as a merger of three regional combinations: the New York Biscuit Company formed in 1890, the American Biscuit and Manufacturing Company, and the United States Biscuit Company founded a little later.[10] Its initial objective was to control price and production, but as in the case of the Distillers Company, this strategy proved too expensive. The Annual Report for 1901 suggests why National Biscuit shifted its basic policies:[11]

This Company is four years old and it may be of interest to shortly review its history. . . . When the Company started, it was an aggregation of plants. It is now an organized business. When we look back over the four years, we find that a radical change has been wrought in our methods of business. In the past, the managers of large merchandising corporations have found it necessary, for success, to control or limit competition. So when this company started, it was thought that we must control competition, and that to do this we must either fight competition or buy it. The first meant a ruinous war of prices, and a great loss of profit; the second, a constantly increasing capitalization. Experience soon proved to us that, instead of bringing success, either of those courses, if persevered in, must bring disaster. This led us to reflect whether it was necessary to control competition. . . .we soon satisfied ourselves that within the Company itself we must look for success.

We turned our attention and bent our energies to improving the internal management of our business, to getting full benefit from purchasing our raw materials in large quantities, to economizing the expenses of manufacture, to systematizing the rendering more effective our selling department; and above all things and before all things to improve the quality of our goods and the condition in which they should reach the customer.

It became the settled policy of this Company to buy out no competition. . . .

In concentrating on distribution, the company first changed its policy from selling in bulk to wholesalers to marketing small packages to retailers. It developed the various "Uneeda Biscuit" brands, which immediately became popular. "The next point," the same Annual Report continued, "was to reach the customer. Thinking we had something that the customer wanted, we had to advise the customer of its existence. We did this by extensive advertising." This new packaging and advertising not only quickly created a profitable business, but also required the building of a sizable marketing organization. Since flour could be quickly and easily purchased in quantity from large milling firms, the purchasing requirements were less complex, and so the company needed a smaller purchasing organization. On the other hand, it spent much energy after 1901 in improving plant layout and manufacturing processes in order to cut production costs and to improve and standardize quality. Throughout the first decade of its history, National Biscuit continued the policy of "centralizing" manufacturing operations, particularly in its great New York and Chicago plants.

In the rubber boot, shoe, and glove industries, the story is much the same. Expansion of manufacturing facilities and increasing competition as early as 1874, led to the formation, by several leading firms, of the Associated Rubber Shoe Companies—an organization for setting price and production schedules through its board of directors. [12] This company continued until 1886. Its successor, the Rubber Boot and Shoe Company, which lasted only a year, attempted, besides controlling prices and production, to handle marketing, which had always been done by commissioned agents. After five years of uncontrolled competition, four of the five firms that had organized the selling company again combined, this time with the assistance of a large rubber importer, Charles A. Flint. The resulting United States Rubber Company came, by 1898, to control 75 per cent of the nation's rubber boot, shoe, and glove output.

At first the new company remained a decentralized holding company. Each constituent company retained its corporate identity with much freedom of action, including the purchasing of raw materials and the selling of finished products, which was done, as before, through jobbers. The central office's concern was primarily with controlling price and production schedules. Very soon, however, the company began, in the words of the 1896 Annual Report, a policy of "perfecting consolidation of purchasing, selling, and manufacturing." [13] This was to be accomplished in four ways. First, as the 1895 Annual

Report had pointed out, the managers agreed "so far as practicable, to consolidate the purchasing of all supplies of raw materials for the various manufactures into one single buying agency, believing that the purchase of large quantities of goods can be made at more advantageous figures than the buying of small isolated lots." [14] The second new "general policy" was "to undertake to reduce the number of brands of goods manufactured, and to consolidate the manufacturing of the remaining brands in those factories which have demonstrated superior facilities for production or advantageous labor conditions. This course was for the purpose of utilizing the most efficient instruments of production and closing those that were inefficient and unprofitable." The third policy was to consolidate sales through the formation of a "Selling Department," which was to handle all goods made by the constituent companies in order to achieve "economy in the distribution expense." Selling was now to be handled by a central office in New York City headquarters, with branch offices throughout the United States and Europe. Of the three great new departments, actually manufacturing was the slowest to be fully consolidated and centralized. Finally, the treasurer's office at headquarters began to obtain accurate data on profit and loss through the institution of uniform, centralized cost accounting.

Thus United States Rubber, National Biscuit, and the Distillers Securities Company soon came to have organizational structures parallelling those of Swift and American Tobacco. By the first decade of the twentieth century, the leading firms in many consumers' goods industries had become departmentalized and centralized. This was the organizational concomitant to vertical integration. Each major function, manufacturing, sales, purchasing, and finance, became managed by a single and separate department head, usually a vice president, who, assisted by a director or a manager, had full authority and responsibility for the activities of his unit. These departmental chiefs, with the president, coordinated and evaluated the work of the different functional units, and made policy for the company as a whole. In coordinating, appraising, and policy-making, the president and the vice presidents in charge of departments came to rely more and more on the accounting and statistical information, usually provided by the finance department, on costs, output, purchases, and sales.

Changes in the Producers' Goods Industries

Bureaucracy and oligopoly came to the producers' goods industries somewhat later than to those making products for the mass market. Until the depression of the 1890's, most of the combinations and consolidations had been in the consumers' good industries. After that, the major changes came in those industries selling to other businesses and industrialists. The reason for the time difference seems to be that the city took a little longer to become a major market for producers' goods. Throughout the 1880's, railroad construction and operation continued to take the larger share of the output of steel, copper, power machinery, explosives, and other heavy industries. Then in the 1890's, as railroad construction declined the rapidly growing American cities became the primary market. The insatiable demand for urban lighting, communication, heat, power, transportation, water sewerage, and other services directly and indirectly took ever growing quantities of electric lighting apparatus, telephones, copper wire, newsprint, streetcars, coal, and iron, steel, copper, and lead piping, structures and fixtures; while the constantly expanding urban construction created new calls on the power machinery and explosives as well as the metals industries. Carnegie's decision in 1887 to shift the Homestead Works, the nation's largest and most modern steel plant, from rails to structures, symbolized the coming change in the market.[15]

Also the new combinations and consolidations in the consumers' goods industries increased the demand for producers' products in the urban areas. Standard Oil, American Tobacco, Swift and other meat packers, McCormick's Harvesting Machinery and other farm implement firms, American Sugar, Singer Sewing Machine, and many other great consumer goods companies concentrated their production in or near major cities, particularly New York and Chicago.

The changes after 1897 differed from the earlier ones not only in types of industries in which they occurred but also in the way they were promoted and financed. Combinations and vertical integration in the consumer goods industries before 1897 had been almost all engineered and financed by the manufacturers themselves, so the stock control remained in the hands of the industrialists. After 1897, however, outside funds and often outside promoters, who were usually Wall Street financiers, played an increasingly significant role in industrial combination and consolidation. The change reflected a new attitude of investor and financier who controlled capital toward the value of industrial securities. [16] Before the depression of the 1890's investment and speculation had been overwhelmingly in railroad stocks and bonds. The institutionalizing of the American security market in Wall Street had come, in fact, as a response to the needs for financing the first great railroad boom in the 1850's.

The railroads, however, had made a poor showing financially in the middle years of the 1890's when one-third of the nation's trackage went through receivership and financial reorganization. The dividend records of some of the new large industrial corporations, on the other hand, proved unexpectedly satisfactory. Moreover, railroad construction was slowing, and the major financial and administrative reorganizations of the 1890's had pretty well stabilized the industry. So there was less demand for investment bankers and brokers to market new issues of railroad securities.

Industrials were obviously the coming field, and by 1898 there was a rush in Wall Street to get in on this new business. The sudden availability of funds stimulated, and undoubtedly overstimulated, industrial combination. Many of the mergers in the years after 1897 came more from the desire of financiers for promotional profits, and because combination had become the thing to do, and less from the special needs and opportunities in the several industries. Moreover, as the financiers and promoters began to provide funds for mergers and expansion, they began to acquire, for the first time, the same type of control over industrial corporations that they had enjoyed in railroads since the 1850's.

The changes in the producers' goods industries were essentially like those in the consumer goods firms before the depression. Only after 1897 the changes came more rapidly, partly because of Wall Street pressures; and the differences that did develop between the two types of industries reflected the basic differences in the nature of their businesses. Like the companies making consumer goods, those manufacturing items for producers set up nation-wide and often world-wide marketing and distributing organizations, consolidated production into a relatively few large plants and fashioned purchasing departments. Because they had fewer customers, their sales departments tended to be smaller than those in firms selling to the mass market. On the other hand, they were more concerned with obtaining control over the sources of their supply than were most of the consumer goods companies.

Here a distinction can be made between the manufacturers who made semi-finished products from raw materials taken from the ground, and those who made finished goods from semi-finished products. The former, producing a uniform product for a few large industrial customers, developed only small sales departments and concentrated on obtaining control of raw materials, and often of the means of transporting such materials from mine to market. The latter, selling a larger variety of products and ones that often required servicing and financing, had much larger marketing and distributing organizations. These makers of finished goods, except for a brief period around 1900, rarely attempted to control their raw materials or their semi-finished steel and other metal supplies. They did, however, in the years after 1900, begin to buy or set up plants making parts and components that went into the construction of their finished products.

Except in steel, integration usually followed combination in the producers' good industries. And for both makers of semi-finished and finished goods, integration became more of a defensive strategy than it was in the consumers' goods industries processing agricultural products. In the latter the manufacturers had an assured supply of raw materials from the output of the nation's millions of farms. In the former, on the other hand, they had to consider the threatening possibility of an outsider obtaining complete control of raw materials or supplies.

Integration and Combination in the Extractive Industries

By the early twentieth century nearly all the companies making semi-finished product goods controlled the mining of their own raw materials. The industries in which they operated can, therefore, be considered as extractive. This was also true of two consumers' goods industries: oil and fertilizer. The experience of these two provides a good introduction to the motives for integration and the role it played in the coming of "big business" in steel, copper, paper, explosives and other businesses producing semi-finished goods.

In both the oil and fertilizer industries, control over raw materials came well after combination and consolidation of groups of small manufacturing firms. The Standard Oil Trust, after its formation in 1882, consolidated its manufacturing activities and then created a domestic marketing organization. Only in the late 1880's, when the new Indiana field began to be developed and the older Pennsylvania ones began to decline, did the Trust consider going into the production of crude oil. Both Allan Nevins in his biography of John D. Rockefeller and the Hidys in their history of Standard Oil agree that the need to be assured of a steady supply of crude oil was the major reason for the move into production. [17] Other reasons, the Hidys indicate, were a fear that the producers might combine and so control supplies, and the desire of the pipeline subsidiaries to keep their facilities operating at full capacity. Although neither Nevins nor the Hidys suggest that the desire to obtain a more efficient flow of oil from the well to the distributor was a motive for this integration, both describe the communities and staff units that were formed at the central office at 26 Broadway to assure more effective coordination between production, refining, and marketing.

What little evidence there is suggests somewhat the same story in the fertilizer industry. Shortly after its organization in the mid-1890's, the Virginia-Carolina Chemical

Company, a merger of many small southern fertilizer firms, began, apparently for the same defensive reasons, to purchase phosphate mines. Quickly its major competitor, the American Agricultural Chemical Company, a similar combination of small northeastern companies formed in 1893, responded by making its own purchases of mines. As the latter company explained in a later annual report: "The growth of the business, as well as the fact that available phosphate properties were being fast taken up, indicated that it was the part of wisdom to make additional provision for the future, and accordingly. . . available phosphate properties were purchased, and the necessary plants were erected and equipped, so the company now has in hand a supply of phosphate rock which will satisfy its growing demand for 60 years and upwards." [18] However, neither of these companies appeared to have set up organizational devices to guide the flow of materials from mine to plant to market; nor did the managers of a third large integrated fertilizer company, the International Agricultural Corporation, formed in 1909.

Defensive motives were certainly significant in the changes in the steel industry. Here the story can be most briefly described by focusing on the history of the industry's leader, the Carnegie Steel Company. [19] That company's chairman, Henry C. Frick, had in the early 1890's consolidated and rationalized the several Carnegie manufacturing properties in and about Pittsburgh into an integrated whole. At the same time, he systematized and departmentalized its purchasing, engineering, and marketing activities. The fashioning of a sales department became more necessary since the shift from rails to structures had enlarged the number of the company's customers.

Then in 1896 the Carnegie company made a massive purchase of ore lands when it joined with Henry W. Oliver to buy out the Rockefeller holdings in the Mesabi Range. As Allan Nevins points out, the depression of the 1890's had worked a rapid transformation in the recently discovered Mesabi region. [20] By 1896, the ore fields had become dominated by three great interests: the Oliver Mining Company, the Minnesota Mining Company, and Rockefeller's Consolidated Iron Mines. A fourth, James J. Hill's Great Northern Railroad, was just entering the field. Frick's purchases, therefore, gave the Carnegie company an assured supply of cheap ore, as well as providing it with a fleet of ore ships. Next, Frick and Carnegie bought and rebuilt a railroad from Lake Erie to Pittsburgh to carry the new supplies to the mills.

Yet the steel company's managers did little to coordinate systematically the mining, shipping, and manufacturing units in their industrial empire. These activities did not become departments controlled from one central office but remained completely separate companies under independent managements, whose contact with one another was through negotiated contracts. This was the same sort of relation that existed between the Frick Coke Company and Carnegie Steel from the time Frick had joined Carnegie in 1889. If the Carnegie company's strategy had been to provide a more effective flow of materials as well as to assure itself of not being caught without a supply of ore and the means to transport it, then Frick and Carnegie would have created some sort of central coordinating office.

The steel industry responded quickly to the Carnegie purchases. [21] In 1898, Chicago's Illinois Steel Company, with capital supplied by J. P. Morgan & Company, joined the Lorain Steel Company (with plants on Lake Erie and in Johnstown, Pennsylvania) to purchase the Minnesota Mining Company, a fleet of ore boats, and railroads in the Mesabi and Chicago areas. Again, little attempt was made to coordinate mining and shipping with manufacturing and marketing. In the same year, many iron and steel firms in Ohio and

Pennsylvania merged to form the Republic and National Steel Companies. Shortly thereafter, a similar combination in the Sault Sainte Marie area became the Consolidated Lake Superior Company. These three new mergers began at once to set up their marketing organizations and to obtain control by lease and purchase of raw materials and transportation facilities. In 1900, several small firms making high-grade steel did much the same thing by the formation of the Crucible Steel Company of America. In these same years, the larger, established steel companies, like Lackawanna, Cambria, and Jones & Laughlin obtained control of more supplies of ore, coke, and limestone and simultaneously reorganized their manufacturing and marketing organizations. Like Carnegie and Federal, they at first made little effort to bring their mining and coke operations under the direct control of the central office.

In copper, defensive motives for integration appear to have been somewhat less significant. In the 1890's, mining, smelting and refining were combined on a large scale. During the 'eighties the railroad had opened up many western mining areas, particularly in Montana and Arizona; a little later the new electrical and telephone businesses greatly increased the demand for copper. Mining firms like Anaconda, Calumet & Hecla, and Phelps Dodge moved into smelting and refining, while the Guggenheims' Philadelphia Smelting & Refining Company began to buy mining properties. [22] In the copper industry, the high cost of ore shipment meant that smelting and—after the introduction of the electrolytic process in the early 1890's—even refining could be done more cheaply close to the mines. Of the large copper firms, only Calumet & Hecla and the Guggenheims set up refineries in the East before 1898, and both made use of direct water transportation.

After 1898, several large mergers occurred in the nonferrous metals industries. Nearly all were initially promoted by eastern financiers. Of these, the most important were Amalgamated Copper, engineered by H. H. Rogers of Standard Oil and Marcus Daly of Anaconda, the American Smelting and Refining Company which the Guggenheims came to control, and United Copper promoted by F. Augustus Heinze. United Copper remained little more than a holding company. Amalgamated set up a subsidiary to operate a large refinery at Perth Amboy and another, the United Metals Settling Company, with headquarters in New York City, to market the products of its mining and processing subsidiaries. The holding company's central offices in New York remained small and apparently did comparatively little to coordinate the activities of its several operating companies. The Guggenheims formed a much tighter organization with direct headquarters control of the company's mining, shipping, smelting and marketing departments. On the whole, there appears to have been somewhat closer coordination between mining and processing in the large copper than in the major steel companies.

Lowering of costs through more effective coordination appears to have been a major motive for consolidation and combination in three other businesses whose raw materials came from the ground: explosives, paper, and coal. [23] The mergers that created the Pittsburgh Coal Company in 1899 and greatly enlarged the Consolidation Coal Company in 1903 were followed by a reorganization and consolidation of mining properties and then by the creation of large marketing departments which operated throughout most of the country. The merger of close to 30 paper companies, forming the International Paper Company in 1899, was followed first by consolidation and reorganization of the manufacturing plants, next by the formation of a national marketing organization with headquarters in New York City, and then by the purchase of large tracts of timber in Maine and Canada. These three activities were departmentalized under vice presidents and controlled from the New York office. In all these cases, the central office was responsible for the flow of materials from mine or forest to the customer or retailer.

The explosive industries underwent a comparable sweeping change in 1902 and 1903. Since the 1870's, price and production schedules had been decided by the industry's Gunpowder Trade Association, and almost from its beginning, that Association had been controlled by one firm, the E. I. DuPont de Nemours & Company. However, the member concerns had retained their own corporate identities and managements. In 1902, the DuPonts bought out a large number of these independent companies through exchanges of stock, and then consolidated them into a single centralized organization. In the process, plants were shut down, others enlarged, and new ones built. A nation-wide selling organization was created, and centralized accounting, purchasing, engineering and traffic departments formed. Once the new organization was completed, then the company's executives obtained control of their raw materials through the purchase of nitrate mines and deposits in Chile.

Except possibly in paper, the control of price and production does not appear to have been a major motive for the initial combinations in the extractive industries making producers' goods. In steel before 1901, and in nonferrous metals and coal, there were several combinations, but none acquired as much as 20 per cent of the market. Nor is there any evidence that the creators of the different mergers, while they were forming their organizations, were arranging with one another to set over-all price and production schedules. In explosives, control of competition could not have been a significant reason for the 1902 changes since the DuPont company had enjoyed such control since the 1870's. In coal and explosives, and possibly in copper, the major motive for combination, consolidation, and the integration of supply with the manufacturing and marketing processes seems to have been an expectation of lowered costs through the creation of a national distributing organization, the consolidation of manufacturing activities, and the effective coordination of the different industrial processes by one central office. In steel and possibly copper, the desire for an assured supply of raw materials appears to have been more significant in encouraging combination and integration.

Changes and Integration in the Finished Producers' Goods Industries

Control of price and production was, on the other hand, much more of an obvious motive for combination and resulting consolidation in the industries manufacturing finished products or machinery from the semi-finished materials produced by the extractive firms. Concern over supply, however, was also a cause for change, for after 1898 the users of steel, copper, coal, and other semi-finished materials felt threatened by the growing number of combinations among their suppliers. In any case, between 1898 and 1900 there was a wave of mergers in these industries, largely Wall Street financed, which led to the formation of American Tin Plate, American Wire & Steel, American Steel Hoop, National Tube, American Bridge, American Sheet Metal, Shelby Steel Tube, American Can, National Enameling & Stamping Company and a number of other combinations among steel-fabricating firms. [24] At the same time, there were many amalgamations in the power machinery and implement businesses, such as American Car & Foundry, American Locomotive, Allis-Chalmers, International Steam Pump, and International Harvester. The largest combination among the copper users, the American Brass Company, came a little later, in 1903, after the Guggenheims, Rogers and Heinze had completed the major copper mergers.

Nearly all these combinations quickly consolidated their constituent companies into a single operating organization. Manufacturing facilities were unified and systematized, over-all accounting procedures instituted, and national and often world-wide distributing organizations formed. Many set up central traffic and purchasing departments; some even began to assure themselves control over supply by building up their own rolling mills and blast furnaces. As American Wire & Steel and National Tube began to make their own steel, they cancelled contracts with Carnegie and other semi-finished steel producers. This development, in turn, led Carnegie to develop plans for fabricating his own finished products.[25]

The resulting threat of overcapacity and price-cutting led to the formation of the United States Steel Corporation.[26] This giant merger, which included Carnegie, Federal and National Steel, and the first six of the fabricating companies listed above, continued on as a combination. Although the activities of the various subsidiaries were re-formed and redefined, there was no consolidation. United States Steel remained a holding company only, and the central office at 72 Broadway did comparatively little to coordinate the operations of its many subsidiary companies.

After 1901, the fabricators and the machinery manufacturers made little attempt to produce their own steel or copper. Nor did the makers of semi-finished products try, for some years to come, to do their own fabricating. Possibly the metal users realized that even with the formation of United States Steel they were fairly certain of alternative sources of supply. Also they may have found that once they had combined they had enough bargaining power to assure themselves of a supply of steel and other materials more cheaply than they could make it themselves.

While such firms no longer sought to control their basic materials, many, particularly the machinery makers like General Electric, Westinghouse, American Car & Foundry, International Harvester and, a little later, General Motors, began to purchase or set up subsidiaries or departments to make parts and components.[27] Here again the motive was essentially defensive. Since much of their manufacturing had now become mainly assembling, they wanted to be sure to have a supply of parts available at all times. The lack of a vital part could temporarily shut down a plant. However, they expected to take only a portion of the output; a major share was sold to outsiders. One outstanding exception to this pattern was Henry Ford. He came to control his raw materials as well as his parts and components, and rarely sold such parts to outside companies. But Ford's insistence on having a completely integrated organization from mine to market, concentrated largely in one huge plant, proved to be one of the most costly mistakes in American business history.

Control of parts and accessory units led to a diversification of the types of products these manufacturing companies made and sold. Such diversification brought, over time, important changes in business organization. Even more significant for stimulating product diversification was the new "full line" strategy adopted by a number of these recently consolidated concerns. Such a policy, initiated largely to help assure the maximum use of the new departments, encouraged technological as well as organizational change.

Pioneers in developing "full lines" in the producer's goods industries were the two great electrical companies: General Electric and Westinghouse. Unlike most any other of the leading American industrial companies in 1900, these two had begun as research and development rather than manufacturing organizations. Because of their origins, they had the skilled personnel and the necessary equipment to move, in the mid-1890's, from making lighting equipment alone to manufacturing many lines of electric traction and power machinery products. [28] Allis-Chalmers, International Steam Pump, and American Locomotive began, shortly after their formation and subsequent consolidations, to develop new lines using electric and gasoline engines. [29] International Harvester, building up a number of farm implement lines, also started to experiment with the use of the gasoline engine for machinery on the farm. In this same first decade of the twentieth century, rubber, explosive, and chemical companies began to turn to industrial chemistry in their search to develop broader lines of products.

Continuing diversification came, however, largely in industries where science, particularly chemistry and physics, could be most easily applied. And it was in these industries, and in those which were directly affected by the coming of two new sources of power, electricity and the internal combustion engine, that the major innovations in American industry came after 1900. The chemical, automotive, power machinery, rubber, and petroleum industries led the way to the development of new processes and products, new ways of internal organization and new techniques of external competition as the new century unfolded. The metals industries and those processing agricultural goods have, on the other hand, changed relatively little since the beginning of the century. In these industries, the same firms make much the same products, use much the same processes, and compete in much the same manner in the 1950's as they did in 1900's. For them the greatest period of change came in the last decade of the nineteenth century.

Conclusion: The Basic Innovations

The middle of the first decade of the new century might be said to mark the end of an era. By 1903, the great merger movement was almost over, and by then the metals industries and those processing agricultural products had developed patterns of internal organization and external competition which were to remain. In those years, too, leading chemical, electrical, rubber, power machinery and implement companies had initiated their "full line" policy, and had instituted the earliest formal research and development departments created in this country. In this decade also, electricity was becoming for the first time a significant source of industrial power, and the automobile was just beginning to revolutionize American transportation. From 1903 on, the new generators of power and the new technologies appear to have become the dominant stimuli to innovation in American industry, and such innovations were primarily those which created new products and processes. Changes in organizational methods and marketing techniques were largely responses to technological advances.

This seems much less true of the changes during the 20 to 25 years before 1903. In that period, the basic innovations were more in the creation of new forms of organization and new ways of marketing. The great modern corporation, carrying on the major industrial processes, namely, purchasing, and often production of materials and parts, manufacturing, marketing, and finance—all within the same organizational structure—had its beginnings in that period. Such organizations hardly existed, outside of the railroads, before the 1880's. By 1900 they had become the basic business unit in American industry.

Each of these major processes became managed by a corporate department, and all were coordinated and supervised from a central office. Of the departments, marketing was the most significant. The creation of nation-wide distributing and selling organizations was the initial step in the growth of many large consumer goods companies. Mergers in both the consumer and producer goods industries were almost always followed by the formation of a centralized sales department.

The consolidation of plants under a single manufacturing department usually accompanied or followed the formation of a national marketing organization. The creation of such a manufacturing department normally meant the concentration of production in fewer and larger plants, and such consolidation probably lowered unit costs and increased output per worker. The creation of such a department in turn led to the setting up of central traffic, purchasing, and often engineering organizations. Large-scale buying, more rational routing of raw materials and finished products, more systematic plant lay-out, and plant location in relation to materials and markets probably lowered costs still further. Certainly the creators of these organizations believed that it did. In the extractive and machinery industries integration went one step further. Here the motives for controlling raw materials or parts and components were defensive as well as designed to cut costs through providing a more efficient flow of materials from mine to market.

These great national industrial organizations required a large market to provide the volume necessary to support the increased overhead costs. Also, to be profitable, they needed careful coordination between the different functional departments. This coordination required a steady flow of accurate data on costs, sales, and on all purchasing, manufacturing, and marketing activities. As a result, the comptroller's office became an increasingly important department. In fact, one of the first moves after a combination by merger or purchase was to institute more effective and detailed accounting procedures. Also, the leading entrepreneurs of the period, men like Rockefeller, Carnegie, Swift, Duke, Preston, Clark, and the DuPonts, had to become, as had the railroad executives of an earlier generation, experts in reading and interpreting business statistics.

Consolidation and departmentalization meant that the leading industrial corporations became operating rather than holding companies, in the sense that the officers and managers of the companies were directly concerned with operating activities. In fact, of the 50 companies with the largest assets in 1909, only United States Steel, Amalgamated Copper, and one or two other copper companies remained purely holding companies. In most others, the central office included the heads of the major functional departments, usually the president, vice presidents, and sometimes a chairman of the board and one or two representatives of financial interests. These men made major policy and administrative decisions and evaluated the performance of the departments and the corporation as a whole. In the extractive industries a few companies, like Standard Oil (N.J.) and some of the metal companies, were partly holding and partly operating companies. At Standard Oil nearly all important decisions were made in the central headquarters, at 26 Broadway, which housed not only the presidents of the subsidiaries but the powerful policy formulating and coordinating committees. [30] But in some of the metals companies, the subsidiaries producing and transporting raw materials retained a large degree of autonomy.

The coming of the large vertically integrated, centralized, functionally departmentalized industrial organization altered the internal and external situations in which and about which business decisions were made. Information about markets, supplies, and operating performance as well as suggestions for action often had to come up through the several levels of the departmental hierarchies, while decisions and suggestions based on this data had to be transmitted down the same ladder for implementation. Executives on each level became increasingly specialists in one function—in sales, production, purchasing, or finance—and most remained in one department and so handled one function only for the major part of their business careers. Only he who climbed to the very top of the departmental ladder had a chance to see his own company as a single operating unit. Where a company's markets, sources of raw materials, and manufacturing processes remained relatively stable, as was true in the metals industries and in those processing agricultural goods, the nature of the business executive's work became increasingly routine and administrative.

When the internal situation had become bureaucratic, the external one tended to be oligopolistic. Vertical integration by one manufacturer forced others to follow. Thus, in a very short time, many American industries became dominated by a few large firms, with the smaller ones handling local and more specialized aspects of the business. Occasionally industries like oil, tobacco, and sugar, came to be controlled by one company, but in most cases legal action by the federal government in the years after 1900 turned monopolistic industries into oligopolistic ones.

Costs, rather than interfirm competition, began to determine prices. With better information on costs, supplies, and market conditions, the companies were able to determine price quite accurately on the basis of the desired return on investment. The managers of the different major companies had little to gain by cutting prices below an acceptable profit margin. On the other hand, if one firm set its prices excessively high, the other firms could increase their share of the market by selling at a lower price and still maintain a profit. They would, however, rarely cut to the point where this margin was eliminated. As a result, after 1900, price leadership, price umbrellas, and other evidences of oligopolistic competition became common in many American industries. To increase their share of the market and to improve their profit position, the large corporations therefore concerned themselves less with price and concentrated more on obtaining new customers by advertising, brand names, and product differentiations; on cutting costs through further improvement and integration of the manufacturing, marketing, and buying processes; and on developing more diversified lines of products.

The coming of the large vertically integrated corporation changed more than just the practices of American industrialists and their industries. The effect on the merchant, particularly the wholesaler, and on the financier, especially the investment banker, has been suggested here. The relation between the growth of these great industrial units and the rise of labor unions has often been pointed out. Certainly the regulation of the large corporation became one of the major political issues of these years, and the devices created to carry out such a regulation were significant innovations in American constitutional, legal, and political institutions. But an examination of such effects is beyond the scope of this paper.

Reasons for the Basic Innovations

One question remains to be reviewed. Why did the vertically integrated corporation come when it did, and in the way it did? The creation by nearly all the large firms of nationwide selling and distributing organizations indicates the importance of the national market. It was necessary that the market be an increasingly urban one. The city took the largest share of the goods manufactured by the processors of agricultural products. The city, too, with its demands for construction materials, lighting, heating and many other facilities, provided the major market for the metals and other producers' goods industries after railroad construction slowed. Without the rapidly growing urban market there would have been little need and little opportunity for the coming of big business in American industry. And such a market could hardly have existed before the completion of a nation-wide railroad network.

What other reasons might there have been for the swift growth of the great industrial

Table I
The Fifty Largest Industrials
(Numbers indicate relative size according to 1909 assets)

Consumers' Goods Companies

Agricultural Processing	*Extractive*	*Manufacturing*
3. Am. Tobacco	2. Standard Oil	4. Int'l. Harvester
8. Armour & Co.	26. Va.-Carolina Chem.	10. U.S. Rubber
9. American Sugar	35. American Agri. Chem.	12. Singer Mfg. Co.
13. Swift & Co.		
30. Nat'l. Biscuit		
33. Distillers' Securities		
50. United Fruit		

Producers' Goods Companies

Agricultural	*Extractive*	*Manufacturing*
6. Central Leather	1. U.S. Steel	7. Pullman
18. Corn Products Co.	5. Amalgamated	15. Gen. Elec.
21. Am. Woolens	(Anaconda) Copper	16. Am. Car & Foundry
	11. Am. Smelting &	19. Am. Can
	Refining	22. Westinghouse
	14. Pittsburgh Coal	24. DuPont
	17. Colo. Fuel & Iron	29. Am. Locomotive
	20. Lackawanna	36. Allis-Chalmers
	23. Consolidation Coal	44. Int. Steam Pump
	25. Republic Steel	46. Western Electric
	27. Int'l. Paper	
	28. Bethlehem Steel	
	31. Cambria Steel	
	33. Associated Oil	
	34. Calumet & Hecla	
	37. Crucible Steel	
	38. Lake Superior Corp.	
	39. U.S. Smelting & Ref.	
	40. United Copper	
	41. National Lead	
	42. Phelps Dodge	
	43. Lehigh Coal	
	45. Jones & Laughlin	
	48. Am. Writing Paper	
	49. Copper Range	

corporation? What about foreign markets? In some industries, particularly oil, the overseas trade may have been an important factor. However, in most businesses the domestic customers took the lion's share of the output, and in nearly all of them the move abroad appears to have come after the creation of the large corporation, and after such corporations had fashioned their domestic marketing organization.

What about the investor looking for profitable investments, and the promoter seeking new promotions? Financiers and promoters certainly had an impact on the changes after 1897, but again they seem primarily to have taken advantage of what had already proved successful. The industrialists themselves, rather than the financiers, initiated most of the major changes in business organization. Availability of capital and cooperation with the financier figured much less prominently in these industrial combinations and consolidations than had been the case with the earlier construction of the railroads and with the financing of the Civil War.

What about technological changes? Actually, except for electricity, the major innovations in the metals industries seem to have come before or after the years under study here. Most of the technological improvements in the agricultural processing industries appear to have been made to meet the demands of the new urban market. The great technological innovations that accompanied the development of electricity, the internal combustion engine, and industrial chemistry did have their beginning in these years, and were, indeed, to have a fundamental impact on the American business economy. Yet this impact was not to be really felt until after 1900.

What about entrepreneurial talent? Certainly the best-known entrepreneurs of this period were those who helped to create the large industrial corporation. If, as Joseph A. Schumpeter suggests, "The defining characteristic [of the entrepreneur and his function] is simply the doing of new things, and doing things that are already done, in a new way (innovation)," Rockefeller, Carnegie, Frick, Swift, Duke, McCormick, the DuPonts, the Guggenheims, Coffin of General Electric, Preston of United Fruit, and Clark of Singer Sewing Machine were all major innovators of their time. [31] And their innovations were not in technology, but rather in organization and in marketing. "Doing a new thing," is, to Schumpeter a "creative response" to a new situation, and the situation to which these innovators responded appears to have been the rise of the national urban market.

There must be an emphasis here on the words, "seem" and "appear." The framework used is a preliminary one and the data itself, based on readily available printed material rather than on business records are hardly as detailed or accurate as could be desired. More data, more precise and explicit questions, and other types and ranges of questions will modify the generalizations suggested here. For the moment, however, I would like to suggest, if only to encourage the raising of questions and the further compilation and analysis of data, that *the* major innovation in the American economy between the 1880's and the turn of the century was the creation of the great corporations in American industry. This innovation, as I have tried to show, was a response to the growth of a national and increasingly urban market that was created by the building of a national railroad network—the dynamic force in the economy in the quarter century before 1880. After 1900 the newly modified methods of interfirm and intrafirm administration remained relatively unchanged (as did the location of major markets and sources of raw materials) except in those industries directly affected by new sources of power and the systematic application of science to industry. In the twentieth century electricity, the internal combustion engine, and systematic, institutionalized research and development took the place of the national urban market as the dynamic factor in the American industrial economy.

Notes

1. The factors stimulating the growth of the American railroad network and the impact of the earlier construction and operation of this network on the American business economy and business institutions is suggested in Chandler, *Henry Varnum Poor—Business Editor, Analyst, and Reformer* (Cambridge, 1956), especially chaps. 4, 6-9.

2. Swift's story as outlined in Louis F. Swift in collaboration with Arthur Van Vlissingen, *The Yankee of the Yards—the Biography of Gustavus Franklin Swift* (New York, 1928). The United States Bureau of Corporations, *Report of the Commissioner of Corporations on the Beef Industry, March 3, 1905* (Washington, 1905), is excellent on the internal operations and external activities of the large meat-packing firms. There is additional information in the later three-volume *Report of the Federal Trade Commission on the Meat Packing Industry* (Washington, 1918-1919). R. A. Clemen, *The American Livestock and Meat Industry* (New York, 1923) has some useful background data.

3. *Report of Commissioner of Corporations on the Beef Industry,* p. 21.

4. Some information on James B. Duke and the American Tobacco Company can be found in John W. Jenkins, *James B. Duke, Master Builder* (New York, 1927), chaps. 5-7, 10. More useful was the United States Bureau of Corporations, *Report of the Commissioner of Corporations on the Tobacco Industry* (Washington, 1909).

5. The story of Bell is outlined in James Gray, *Business Without Boundary, the Story of General Mills* (Minneapolis, 1954), and of Preston in Charles M. Wilson, *Empire in Green and Gold* (New York, 1947).

6. The early Singer Sewing Machine experience is well analyzed in Andrew B. Jack, "The Channels of Distribution for an Innovation: the Sewing Machine Industry in America, 1860-1865," *Explorations in Entrepreneurial History,* Vol. IX (Feb., 1957), pp. 113-141.

7. William T. Hutchinson, *Cyrus Hall McCormick* (New York, 1935), Vol. II, pp. 704-712.

8. The major sources of information on combination and consolidation in the distilling industry are Jeremiah W. Jenks, "The Development of the Whiskey Trust," *Political Science Quarterly,* Vol. IV (June, 1889), pp. 296-319; J. W. Jenks and W. E. Clark, *The Trust Problem* (rev. ed.; New York, 1917), pp. 141-149. The annual reports of the Distilling and Cattle Feeding Company and its various successors provide some useful additional data, as does the Industrial Commission, *Preliminary Report on Trusts and Industrial Combinations* (Washington, 1900), Vol. I, pp. 74-89, 167-259, 813-848, and Victor S. Clark, *History of Manufactures in the United States* (New York, 1929), Vol. II, pp. 505-506. Changes in taxes on liquors also affected the company's policies in the early 1890's.

9. *Annual Report of the President of the Distillers Securities Company* for 1903.

10. The information on National Biscuit comes largely from its annual reports.

11. *Annual Report of the National Biscuit Company for the Year Ending December, 1901,* January 3, 1902. References to centralizing of manufacturing facilities appear in several early annual reports. As this was written before Theodore Roosevelt had started to make the Sherman Act an effective antitrust instrument and Ida Tarbell and other journalists had begun to make "muck raking" of big business popular and profitable, the Biscuit Company's shift in policy could hardly have been the result of the pressure of public opinion or the threat of government action.

12. The background for the creation of the United States Rubber Company can be found in Nancy P. Norton, "Industrial Pioneer: the Goodyear Metallic Rubber Shoe Company" (Ph.D. thesis, Radcliffe College, 1950), Constance McL. Green, *History of Naugatuck, Connecticut* (New Haven, 1948), pp. 126-131, 193-194, and Clark, *History of Manufactures,* Vol. II, pp. 479-481, Vol. III, pp. 236-237. The company's annual reports provide most of the information on its activities.

13. *The Fifth Annual Report of the United States Rubber Company, March 31, 1897,* pp. 6-7.

14. This and the following quotations are from the *Fourth Annual Report of the United States Rubber Company, May 25, 1896,* pp. 4-5, 7-8.

15. Clark, *History of Manufactures,* Vol. II, Chap. 19.

16. The story of the shift from rails to industrials as acceptable investments is told in Thomas R. Navin and Marian V. Sears, "The Rise of the Market for Industrial Securities, 1887-1902," *Business History Review,* Vol. XIX (June, 1955), pp. 105-138. Government securities were, of course, important in the years before 1850 and during and after the Civil War, but in the late 1870's and 1880's as in the 1850's, railroads dominated the American security exchanges. As Navin and Sears point out, some coal and mining firms were traded on the New York Exchange, but the only manufacturing securities, outside of those of the Pullman Company, were some textile stocks traded on the local Boston Exchange. The connections between the railroad expansion and the beginnings of modern Wall Street are described in detail in Chandler, *Poor,* chap. 4.

17. Ralph W. Hidy and Muriel E. Hidy, *Pioneering in Big Business, 1882-1911* (New York, 1955), pp. 176-188, Allan Nevins, *Study in Power, John D. Rockefeller, Industrialist and Philanthropist* (New York, 1953), Vol. II, pp. 1-3. Nevins adds that another reason for the move into production was "partly to limit the number of active wells and reduce the overproduction of crude oil," Vol. II, p. 2, but he gives no documentation for this statement.

18. *Annual Report of the American Agricultural Chemical Company*, August 14, 1907, also the same company's *Annual Report* dated August 25, 1902. In addition to the annual reports of the two companies, Clark, *History of Manufactures,* Vol. III, pp. 289-291, provides information. There is a brief summary of the story of the International Agricultural Corporation in Williams Haynes, *American Chemical Industry—A History* (New York, 1945), Vol. III, p. 173.

19. The information on the Carnegie Steel Company is taken from Burton J. Hendrick, *The Life of Andrew Carnegie,* 2 vols. (New York, 1932), George Harvey, *Henry Clay Frick, the Man* (New York, 1928), James H. Bridge, *The Inside Story of the Carnegie Steel Company* (New York, 1903.)

20. Nevins, *Rockefeller,* Vol. II, p. 252.

21. The experience of the other steel firms comes primarily from their annual reports and from prospectuses and other reports in the Corporation Records Division of Baker Library. A company publication, *J & L—The Growth of an American Business* (Pittsburgh, 1953) has some additional information on that company. Also, books listed in footnote 26 on the United States Steel Corporation have something on these companies. Two other steel companies listed in Table I made major changes somewhat before and after the period immediately following 1898. One, the Colorado Fuel & Iron Co., established in 1892, quickly became an integrated steel company in the Colorado area. The Bethlehem Steel Corporation was formed in 1904 when Charles F. Schwab, formerly of the Carnegie company and the United States Steel Corporation, reorganized the finances, corporate structure, and administrative organization of the bankrupt United States Shipbuilding Company.

22. Information on the mining companies came from their annual reports and from Isaac P. Murcosson's two books, *Magic Metal—the Story of the American Smelting and Refining Company* (New York, 1949), and *Anaconda* (New York, 1957), also Clark, *History of Manufactures,* Vol. II, pp. 368-369.

23. The story of the leading explosives, paper, salt and coal companies comes from annual reports and also from Charles E. Beachley, *History of the Consolidation Coal Company 1864-1934* (New York, 1934), George H. Love, *An Exciting Century in Coal* (New York, 1955), the company-written, *The International Paper Company, 1898-1948* (n.p., 1948), William S. Dutton, *DuPont—One Hundred and Forty Years* (New York, 1940), and *U.S. v. E. I. DuPont de Nemours & Company et al. in Circuit Court of the United States for the District of Delaware, #280 in Equity (1909), Defendants' Record Testimony,* Vol. I, and for the paper industry, Clark, *History of Manufactures,* Vol. III, pp. 245-252. The American Writing Paper Company, though less successful, had many parallels to International Paper.

24. The best brief summary of these mergers and the formation of the United States Steel Corporation is in Eliot Jones, *The Trust Problem in the United States* (New York, 1924), pp. 189-200. The companies' annual reports and prospectuses provide additional material.

25. Hendrick, *Carnegie,* Vol. II, pp. 116-119.

26. The beginnings and the operation of the United States Steel Corporation are outlined in Abraham Berglund, *The United States Steel Corporation: A Study of Growth and Combination in the Iron and Steel Industry* (New York, 1907), Arundel Cotter, *The Authentic History of the United States Steel Corporation* (New York, 1916), Ida M. Tarbell, *The Life of Elbert H. Gary, the Story of Steel* (New York, 1925).

27. This generalization is based on the annual reports of the several companies.

28. As is well described in Harold C. Passer, *The Electrical Manufacturers* (Cambridge, 1953).

29. The development of new lines by Allis-Chalmers, International Steam Pump, and American Locomotive is mentioned in their annual reports in the first decade of the twentieth century. International Harvester's similar "full line" policies are described in Cyrus McCormick, *The Century of the Reaper* (New York, 1931), chaps. 6-9, and United States Bureau of Corporations, *The International Harvester Co., March 3, 1913* (Washington, 1913), especially pp. 156-158.

30. Hidys, *Pioneering in Big Business,* chap. 3 and pp. 323-388.

31. Joseph A. Schumpeter, "The Creative Response in Economic History," *Journal of Economic History,* Vol. VII (May, 1947), p. 151, and also his *Theory of Economic Development,* trans. Redvers Opie (Cambridge, 1934), pp. 74-94.

Part II
Workers and farmers

The knights of labor and the trade unions, 1878-1886

Gerald N. Grob

good intro

Industrialization profoundly altered the situation of American labor in the second half of the nineteenth century. Increasingly drawn into a factory system that subjected him to a tightening discipline, his valued skills made obsolete by the new technology, his aspirations for advancement either crushed or at least divorced from the idea of personal independence, more and more sharply designated as a member of the laboring class, the workingman of this era struggled to find the solutions to his difficulties. Two principle responses emerged. One directed itself against the entire economic order that was pressing the workingman down. The other accepted the new system, and aimed at gaining for the workingman the best possible treatment. These two impulses—comprehensive social reform and trade unionism—went back to the early days, without, in fact, any distinct line separating them. Men and organizations shifted back and forth, with trade unionism normally dominant during prosperous years, and reform activity during hard times when unions lost effectiveness. But as labor institutions stabilized and the economic system matured, the inherent incompatibility between the two forms of labor action became increasingly acute. In the 1880s American workers made a choice. A climactic battle developed between the Knights of Labor and the trade unions (which in 1886 joined together in the American Federation of Labor). Trade unionism won, and thereby established itself as the primary form of labor organization in American society.

This fateful struggle forms the theme of Gerald Grob's essay. He defines the issue essentially in institutional terms. Aiming at reform of the economic order, the Knights of Labor adopted a form of organization that would best advance the educational and cooperative work that Terence V. Powderly and other leaders hoped would lead to the cooperative commonwealth. This meant a high degree of centralization and a organizational structure that was geographical in character—district assemblies and, beneath them, local assemblies (which could be either mixed, i.e., open to all kinds of people, or trades, i.e., open to those of a single occupation or industry). Trade unionism, on the other hand, developed a decentralized system in which each national union was autonomous (even after these formed the AFL) and in which organizational divisions

Gerald N. Grob, "The Knights of Labor and the Trade Unions, 1878-1886," *The Journal of Economic History*, XVIII (June 1958), pp. 176-192. Reprinted by permission of the publisher.

Sees Knights as Reactionary Utopians looking to past

were strictly along occupational lines. There was, in theory, no reason why these two kinds of organizations could not have coexisted, so long, that is, as each adhered to its own institutional form and objectives. But they could not do so. The Knights of Labor, as Grob points out, made room for trade-union bodies, even national unions in a few instances. And, especially during the Knights' upsurge in the mid-1880s, there was a good deal of movement from the trade unions into the Knights. This institutional overlapping, Grob argues, forced the trade unions to declare the war on the Knights that would end in the permanent defeat of reform unionism in America.

Why should this overlapping have occurred? Grob does not say, but the answer is implicit in his line of argument and in his evidence. During the 1880s, there seems to have been a massive, unarticulated acceptance among American workingmen of the trade-union mode of thinking. This was happening even within the Knights of Labor. Its ambivalence goes a long way toward explaining its curious twists and turns, its forays into collective bargaining, its strike activity, and also its fluctuating efforts at incorporating a trade-union structure within its fold. The unions proposed in 1886 that each organization consistently stick to its preferred strategy. This actually made good sense, but only if the Knights of Labor intended to adhere to its reform purposes. The Knights could not accept the offer precisely because of its ambivalence on this fundamental question. The institutional analysis that Grob offers here rests on a change going on within the American working class: as men abandoned hope for a return to the past and accepted the inevitability of the new industrial order, economic unionism became the primary institutional mode for American labor. This explained the Knights' unwillingness (or inability) to embrace fully labor reformism. The conflict with the trade unions therefore became inescapable, and, since it failed to abandon reform and resolve its internal ambivalence, probably also spelled the ultimate defeat of the Knights of Labor.

For further reading: Gerald N. Grob, *Workers and Utopia* (1961);* Norman J. Ware, *The Labor Movement in the United States: 1860-1895* (1929);* Philip Taft, *The AFL in the Time of Gompers* (1957); John R. Commons, *et al., A History of Labour in the United States* (1918-1935), vol. 2; Lloyd Ulman, *The Rise of the National Trade Union* (1955); Robert A. Christie, *Empire in Wood: a History of the Carpenters' Union* (1956); Terence V. Powderly, *The Path I Trod* (1940); Samuel Gompers, *Seventy Years of Life and Labor* (1925), 2 vols.

The year 1886 was destined to be a crucial one in the history of the American labor movement. The eight-hour crusade, the numerous strikes, the Haymarket bomb, the entrance of workingmen into the political arena at the state and national levels, and the mushroom growth of labor organizations all contributed to the agitation and excitement of the year. Yet the importance of these events was overshadowed by a development that was to have such far-reaching implications that it would determine the future of the labor movement for the succeeding half century. That development was the declaration of war by the trade unions against the reform unionism of the Knights of Labor.

The struggle between the Knights and the other unions represented a clash of two fundamentally opposing ideologies. The Knights of Labor, on the one hand, grew out of the reform and humanitarian movements of ante-bellum America, and was the direct descendant, through the National Labor Union, of the labor reform tradition of the Jacksonian era. Banking on the leveling influence of technological change, its leaders sought to organize the entire producing class into a single irresistible coalition that would work toward the abolition of the wage system and the establishment of a new society. "We do not believe," a high official of the Knights remarked, "that the emancipation of labor will come with increased wages and a reduction in the hours of labor; we must go deeper than that, and this matter will not be settled until the wage system is abolished."[1] The leaders of the Knights therefore emphasized education and co-operation, and they bitterly opposed their constituents' participation in such affairs as the Southwest and stockyards strikes of 1886, as well as the very popular eight-hour movement of that same year.

The reform ideology of the Knights, in turn, had an important impact upon the development of its structure, which followed a heterogeneous rather than a homogeneous pattern. Minimizing the utility of organization along trade lines, the Order emphasized instead the grouping of all workers, regardless of craft, into a single body.[2] Highest priority therefore was given to the mixed local assembly, which included all workers irrespective of their trade or degree of skill. Neither a trade, plant, nor industrial union, the mixed assembly could never be more than a study or debating group. Including many diverse elements (even employers), it could not adapt itself to meet the problems of a specific industry or trade. The mixed assembly might agitate for reform or participate in politics, but it could never become the collective bargaining representative of its members.

Given the predominance of the mixed over the trade local, the structure of the Knights inevitably developed along geographical rather than jurisdictional lines, and the district assembly, which included mixed as well as trade locals, became the most characteristic form of organization. The highest governmental body of the Knights—the General Assembly—was not intended as a medium for collective bargaining. Indeed, its very inclusiveness precluded such a possibility.

The trade unions, on the other hand, rejected the broad reform goals of the Knights, emphasizing instead higher wages, shorter hours, and job control. Such objectives were clearly incompatible with an organizational structure such as that developed by the Knights. Eschewing the multitrade local that had been so prevalent during the 1860's and was being perpetuated by the Order, the trade unions began to stress the craft-industrial form of organization both at the local and national levels. A relative scarcity of labor, together with a rapidly expanding economy, had created a favorable environment for the trade unions. Gambling on the hope that the rise of a national market made organization along trade rather than geographical lines more effective, union leaders chose to concentrate upon the task of organizing the workers along trade lines into unions designed for collective bargaining rather than social reform.[3]

Therefore, given the inherent differences in ideology and structure, the conflict between the Knights and the trade unions was, if not inevitable, certainly not an unexpected or surprising development.[4] Undoubtedly the antagonistic personalities of partisans on both sides hastened an open rift.[5] Yet the hostilities between the Knights and the trade unions cannot be explained solely in terms of personalities, for the conflict was not simply a struggle for power between two rivals. It was a clash between two fundamentally different ideologies—with the future of the labor movement at stake.

I

The contest between trade unionists and reformers for control of the labor movement developed on two planes. Commencing first as an internal struggle within the Knights, it eventually expanded and soon involved the national unions. Within the Knights the struggle revolved around the unresolved question as to which form of organization best met working-class necessities. On the surface the issue of mixed versus trade locals was simply a structural problem. In reality, however, the differences between the two forms indicated the existence of a fundamental cleavage in ultimate objectives, for the mixed assembly could be utilized only for reform or political purposes, while the trade assembly was generally a collective bargaining organization.

Although the national leadership of the Knights regarded the mixed assembly as the ideal type of unit, a large proportion of its local assemblies were trade rather than mixed. The first local, composed of garment cutters, were strictly craft, and remained so to the end. Most of the other locals that followed were also trade assemblies.[6] On January 1, 1882, according to the *Journal of United Labor,* there were 27 working districts and over 400 local assemblies. Of the latter, 318 were trade and only 116 were mixed. Thirteen additional districts, not functioning, had 53 trade and 87 mixed locals, attesting to the relative instability of the mixed form of organization. Of the 135 locals attached directly to the General Assembly, 67 were trade and 68 were mixed.[7]

Despite the wide latitude given them to organize trade local assemblies, the trade element within the Knights nevertheless found it difficult to function efficiently. Local trade assemblies, no matter how inclusive in their particular area, were often ineffective when operating in a market that was regional or national rather than local in character. So long as employers could find a ready supply of nonunion labor elsewhere, efforts at collective bargaining by locals would be ineffective. The only solution lay in national organization, and the trade exponents within the Knights pressed for national and regional trade districts that would transcend the limited geographical area normally encompassed by the local or district assembly.

The General Assembly, therefore, meeting in January 1879, authorized the establishment of autonomous national trade districts within the framework of the Knights. But only nine months later the Assembly completely reversed itself by declaring that trade locals were "contrary to the spirit and genius of the Order," and it returned exclusive jurisdiction over all locals to the district assembly of their area.[8]

In December 1881, however, the Federation of Organized Trades and Labor Unions, predecessor of the American Federation of Labor (A.F. of L.), held its first convention. Of the 107 delegates persent, no less than 50 came from the Knights.[9]

The following September the General Assembly heard the secretary of the Knights warn that trade sentiment was growing rapidly. "Many Trades Unions have also written me," he remarked, "stating that they were seriously meditating the propriety of coming over to us in a body, freely expressing the opinion that their proper place was in our Order."[10] To prevent any mass exodus from the Order to the rival Federation, and also to recruit members from the trade unions, the General Assembly enacted legislation authorizing and encouraging the formation of national and regional trade districts. This move was reaffirmed and even extended at the meetings of the General Assembly in 1884 and 1886.[11]

While permissible, at least in theory, the establishment of trade districts was not a simple matter. The basic philosophy of the Knights militated against organization along craft lines, and the establishment of autonomous trade units within the framework of the Order aroused strong opposition. "I do not favor the establishment of any more National Trade Districts," Terence V. Powderly, head of the Knights from 1879 to 1893, told the General Assembly in 1885, "they are a step backward." [12] Other reform unionists, echoing Powderly's sentiments, charged that trade districts violated the fundamental principles of the Knights. [13] Holding tenaciously to their reform concepts, the leaders of the Knights were insistent in their demands that organization should not proceed along trade lines.

Applicants for trade districts therefore could not always be certain that charters would be granted them, even though they had met all the formal requirements. In some cases charters were granted without any questions. Window Glass Workers' Local Assembly (L.A.) 300 was chartered as a national trade district at a time when such districts were contrary to the laws of the Knights, and the telegraphers were organized nationally in 1882 as District Assembly (D.A.) 45. For a while these two were the only national districts, although before 1886 there were two district assemblies composed of miners, five of shoemakers, three of railroad employees, and one each of printers, plumbers, leather workers, government employees, and streetcar employees. Between 1883 and 1885 the General Assembly went on record as favoring the establishment of trade districts of shoemakers, plate-glass workers, and plumbers. [14] On the other hand, after sanctioning the formation of builders' districts in 1882, it refused the following year to permit these districts to be represented on the General Executive Board. [15] Even while passing legislation authorizing trade districts, the General Assembly refused to allow woodworkers, cigarmakers, and carpenters to organize trade districts. Furthermore, it passed a resolution stating that no charter for a trade district would be granted unless the applicants could demonstrate to the satisfaction of the General Executive Board that the craft would not be effectively organized under the system of mixed or territorial districts. [16] The attitude of the board, however, was often conditioned by the antitrade unionism of its officers. In 1886, for example, it refused to sanction the request of five building trade locals that they be permitted to withdraw from D.A. 66 and organize their own district. At the same time it empowered a New Hampshire local to change from a trade to a mixed assembly. [17]

Trade units, generally speaking, were authorized usually in efforts to attract workers to join the Knights. Thus the International Trunkmakers Union came into the Order as a trade district. [18] Once inside, however, workers found it considerably more difficult to secure trade charters. After affiliating in 1882, to cite one case, the plumbers later left the Knights when they encountered difficulty in obtaining a charter for a national trade district, and they established the International Association of Journeymen Plumbers, Steam Fitters, and Gas Fitters. [19]

The hostility of the national leadership of the Knights was not the sole obstacle to the formation of trade units. Mixed and territorial districts, which were first in the field and were already established as functioning organizations, were also antagonistic toward trade districts. If the latter were formed, not only would a mixed district suffer a loss of membership to a trade district, but it would also surrender its absolute jurisdiction over a given territorial area, since the autonomous trade district would exercise control over the entire craft in that area.

The General Assembly and the General Executive Board often supported the mixed and territorial districts in disputes with trade districts. Frequently the district's consent was a prerequisite to secession and the establishment of a trade district. This consent was not easily obtained. In 1886 D.A. 30 of Massachusetts turned down an application by four of its locals for permission to withdraw and form a national trade assembly of rubber workers.[20] While the General Assembly supported a district court decision that members of trade locals could not be compelled to join mixed locals, the General Executive Board refused to force trade members of mixed locals to transfer to trade assemblies.[21]

Even after obtaining a charter, trade districts encountered difficulties with the mixed district in their areas. Dual jurisdiction often led to friction, though in theory the system of mixed and trade districts appeared perfectly harmonious and compatible. For example, D.A. 64 of New York City, composed of workers in the printing and publishing business, became embroiled in a rivalry with D.A. 49 (mixed). In 1883 D.A. 64 failed to get exclusive jurisdiction over all workers in the trade. Soon afterward D.A. 49 charged that the printers were accepting locals not of their trade, and that these locals had also withdrawn from D.A. 49 without permission. An investigation by the secretary of the General Executive Board disclosed the D.A. 64 had been initiating lithographers, type-founders, pressmen, and feeders in order to strengthen itself as a bargaining unit, and that it had not engaged in raiding forays against D.A. 49. Although the Board upheld D.A. 64, the decision did not resolve the rivalry, and the two districts continued their feud.[22]

With the single exception of L.A. 300, trade districts did not enjoy any appreciable measure of success between 1878 and 1885.[23] The far-reaching reform goals of the Knights and its structural inclusiveness left the advocates of trade organization in the position of a perpetual minority. The expansion of the Knights into the more sparsely populated regions of the South and West, moreover, further diminished trade influence, since the mixed assembly was dominant in rural areas. Lacking a majority, the trade members were unable to establish a central strike fund or concentrate on collective bargaining, and they found that their immediate goals were being subordinated to and sacrificed for more utopian objectives.

II

The struggle between trade unionists and reformers within the Knights, however, was completely overshadowed by the rupture of relations in 1886 between the Knights and the national unions. The latter, stronger and more cohesive than the trade districts of the Order, were better able to take the lead in the conflict between reform and trade union-ism. Disillusioned with labor reformism, the trade unions acted upon the premise that the traditional programs of the past were no longer suitable to the changing environment, and they led the assault against the Knights of Labor in 1886.

During the early 1880's, however, it was by no means evident that the Knights and the national unions were predestined to clash. The Federation of Organized Trades and Labor Unions permitted district assemblies of the Knights to be represented at its annual con-ventions,[24] and many trade union leaders also belonged to the Order.[25] Local unions and assemblies often cooperated in joint boycotts, and expressions of friendliness by the national unions toward Powdely and other officials of the Knights were not uncom-mon.[26] The International Typographical Union expressed appreciation in 1882 for the aid given it by the Knights in a number of cities, and then went on to adopt resolutions recommending cooperation with other labor organizations and permitting its members to join any body that would further the interests of the craft in their particular locality. [27] In other words, the national unions regarded the Knights as a valuable economic ally.

In turn, the Knights vehemently denied having any hostile designs upon the trade unions, and in a number of prominent cases before 1885 it acted accordingly. [28] Nevertheless, with its structural inclusiveness and reform ideology, it was perhaps inevitable that the Order, in its efforts to bring all workingmen into a single organization, would undercut trade union organizational efforts. Thus the General Assembly authorized a committee in 1883 to confer with union representatives in the hope of incorporating all the trade unions within the Knights. [29]

In the absence of any national or international union, the absorption of local unions by the Knights in the form of trade assemblies created no friction. Indeed, isolated local unions were eager to affiliate with such a powerful national organization. [30] By 1886, therefore, the Knights claimed nearly eleven hundred local assemblies, many of which undoubtedly represented local trade unions having no parent national union.

When, however, the Knights began to organize workingmen in trades already having national organizations, friction was quick to arise. The trouble that followed the Order's expansion into the realm of the trade unions was not simply a jurisdictional rivalry between similar organizations. As discussed above, the Order and the national unions had opposing conceptions of the legitimate functions of the labor movement, which in turn had led to different structural forms. The expansion of the Order's mixed units thus served to undermine the economic functions of the trade unions, since the heterogeneous character of the former prevented them from exercising any appreciable degree of economic power. Furthermore, the structural diversity of the Knights caused trouble when its trade assemblies sought to perform tasks that logically fell within the purview of the trade unions. [31] The national unions, moreover, took the position that geographical trade assemblies were inadequate to meet the challenge of a nationalized economy, and in fact were little better than mixed district assemblies. In defense, union officials generally refused to consent to a mutual recognition of working cards, [32] and they demanded that the Knights cease interfering in trade affairs. [33]

The Knights, however, did not heed the warnings of the national unions, and its organizers continued their sporadic work in trades having national unions. "Every week," John Swinton reported in 1885, "Trades Unions are turned into Local Assemblies, or Assemblies are organized out of Trade Unions." [34] As early as 1881 a district leader attempted to capture a typographical union local, and by 1884 there were over forty local assemblies of printers in the Knights. [35] The overzealous activities of the Order's organizers also led to trouble with the Bricklayers and Masons International Union. [36]

The trade unions continuously charged that the Order had accepted scabs and unfair workers. [37] It is probable that the unions greatly exaggerated this grievance, but there is little doubt that the existence of two labor organizations, each purporting to accomplish different ends, created a disciplinary problem. Intraunion disagreements frequently concluded with one party seceding and joining the Order as a local assembly. Thus the trade unions found that the Knights were attracting dissidents who normally might have remained in the union. [38]

Despite the proselytizing activities of the Knights, there was no general conflict with the other unions before July 1885. At this time the membership of the Order was slightly over 100,000, and examples of clashes with the trade unions were generally the exception rather than the rule. When differences did arise, the trade unions often made conciliatory efforts at peaceful adjustment. Thus the convention of the International Typographical Union agreed in 1884 to its president's suggestion that he confer with Powderly in order to iron out existing grievances, although it refused to sanction a proposed amalgamation with the Order.[39]

In only one major case—that involving the Cigar Makers International Union—did the differences between a national union and the Knights erupt in open hostilities before 1886. Historians, placing much emphasis upon this particular conflict, have credited Adolph Strasser and Samuel Gompers, the leaders of the Cigar Makers, with the dual responsibility of helping to precipitate the internecine war between the national unions and the Knights, and then founding the A.F. of L. as a rival national federation.[40]

While the national unions generally supported the Cigar Makers in its struggle with the Knights,[41] it is improbable that sympathy for the Cigar Makers would have led to a fight with the Order. Undoubtedly Strasser and Gompers exerted great efforts to induce the unions to lend them support. The fact is also incontrovertible that both were determined, forceful, and sometimes ruthless men. Nevertheless, their efforts would have been useless unless a solid basis of discontent had already existed. In other words, for the unions to break with the Knights, there must have been more compelling reasons than simply the activities of two individuals.

III

To understand the conflict that split the labor movement, the rapid growth of the Knights after 1885 must be examined. In the twelve months between July 1885 and June 1886 the Order's membership increased from 100,000 to over 700,000. This growth, at least in part, came about at the expense of the other unions. In many cases workers abandoned their trade unions to join the Knights. The Journeymen Tailors National Union found that many of its locals had transferred to the Knights, resulting in a considerable loss of membership. A vice-president of the Amalgamated Association of Iron and Steel Workers complained in 1886 that some sublodges in his area had been disbanded because of inroads by the Order.[42] Further difficulty was caused by overzealous organizers who made determined efforts to transform trade unions into local assemblies. In February 1886 the secretary of the Journeymen Bakers National Union protested against such activities. "We never knew," responded the secretary-treasurer of the Knights, "that the K. of L. was proscribed from bringing into its fold all branches of honorable toil."[43]

The Knights, in other words, had adopted an organizational policy diametrically different from that of the trade unions. The traditional concept of organization held by the A.F. of L. (the representative of the trade unions) required that federal labor unions (local units including workers of all trades having no separate unions of their own) be splintered into separate homogeneous craft units as soon as there were enough workers in that locality to form such bodies. The aim of such a policy was to develop the collective bargaining potentialities of the various trades. The Knights, on the other hand, sought to reverse this strategy and proceed in the opposite direction, and it encouraged the combining of trade units into mixed assemblies, which at most were reform or political units.

Beneath the structural and organizational differences of the two groups, therefore, lay opposing goals.

To what extent did the Knights encroach upon the domain of the trade unions? Peter J. McGuire of the Carpenters claimed that between 150 and 160 trade unions, including the Molders, Boiler-Makers, Bakers, Miners, Typographical, and Granite Cutters, had grievances against the Order.[44] Only in the case of the Bricklayers and Masons International Union, however, is the evidence fairly complete. In response to a survey conducted in the summer of 1886, the union's secretary received eighty-seven replies. Eight locals reported the existence of bricklayers and masons assemblies within their jurisdiction, four claimed the Knights were working for subunion wages, and three asserted the Knights were working longer hours. "But there are a large number of such men scattered throughout the country who belong to mixed assemblies," the secretary reported—and herein lay the union's major grievance.[45] The complaints of the Bricklayers and Masons were echoed by most of the other major national unions.[46]

In general, the national unions were fearful of the Knights for two closely related reasons. The mixed assembly, in the first place, was incompatible with trade union goals. In theory both structural forms could exist side by side, each pursuing its own ends. Thus the mixed assembly could concentrate on reform and politics, while the trade unions could develop their collective bargaining functions. This *modus vivendi*, however, presupposed that workers could belong simultaneously to both trade unions and mixed assemblies. At a time when the labor movement's primary problem was to organize and stay organized, such an assumption was unwarranted, and trade union leaders recognized the mutual hostility of the mixed assembly and trade union.

In the second place, trade union officials opposed the chartering of trade assemblies within the Knights for the reason that these units had proved incapable of developing collective bargaining and other union institutions. Furthermore, the geographical and regional organization of the Knights meant that there was little hope for the mature evolution of the national trade assembly. Since local trade assemblies were often ineffective when operating in an environment marked by a nationalized economy and the geographical mobility of labor, trade union leaders argued that these units were attempting to perform functions that logically belonged to the national unions, and in the long run tended to undermine the standards of membership and employment that the unions had struggled so fiercely to establish.[47]

By the spring of 1886 relations between the trade unions and the Knights had so deteriorated that a collision appeared imminent.[48] Five prominent unionists therefore called for a meeting of union leaders to arrange a settlement of differences, while at the same time Powderly summoned the General Assembly in a special session to consider, among other things, the troubles with the trade unions. The conference of trade union officials then appointed a committee of five to draw up a plan of settlement. Under the moderating influence of McGuire, who played the leading role, the committee drew up a "treaty," which it submitted to the General Executive Board of the Knights on May 25, 1886.[49]

By the terms of this treaty the Knights would refrain from organizing any trade having a national organization, and also would revoke the charter of any existing trade assembly having a parent union. In the second place, any workers guilty of ignoring trade union wage scales, scabbing, or any other offense against a union, would be ineligible for membership in the Order. Third, any organizer who tampered with or interfered in the internal affairs of trade unions would have his commission revoked. Finally, local and district assemblies were not to interfere while trade unions engaged in strikes or lockouts, and the Knights would not be permitted to issue any label or trade-mark where a national union had already done so.[50]

On the surface it appears surprising that the trade unions, which claimed to represent about 350,000 workers (although their actual membership was about 160,000), would present such a document to an organization having 700,000 members. Yet the treaty was neither a bargaining offer nor a declaration of war.[51] It was rather the logical outcome of the duality that had pervaded the labor movement since the Civil War. Under its terms the labor movement would be divided into two separate and distinct compartments. The Knights of Labor, on the one hand, would continue its efforts to abolish the wage system, reform society, and educate the working class. The national unions, on the other hand, would be left paramount in the economic field, and the Order would no longer be permitted to exercise any control over wages, hours, working conditions, or the process of collective bargaining. In other words, trade unionism and reform unionism had come to a parting of the ways.

In one sense the treaty was an expression of the fear of the skilled workers that they were being subordinated to the interests of the unskilled.[52] Yet the polarization implied in such an interpretation should not be exaggerated, for it cannot be said that the Knights themselves represented the unskilled workers. The Order was not an industrial union, nor did it emphasize collective bargaining. It was rather a heterogeneous mass that subordinated the economic functions of labor organizations to its primary goal of reforming society. The mixed assembly, while including workers of all trades and callings, was in no sense an industrial union, since it was not organized either by industry or factory. Moreover, the trade unions had never excluded the unskilled from the labor movement; they simply maintained that organization along craft lines was historically correct. "In truth," remarked Gompers, "the trade union is nothing more or less than the organization of wage earners engaged in a given employment, whether skilled or unskilled, for the purpose of attaining the best possible reward, [and] the best attainable conditions for the workers in that trade or calling."[53]

The General Assembly of the Knights, in turn, submitted its own proposals to the union committee. Its terms included protection against unfair workers, a mutual exchange of working cards, and the holding of a joint conference before either organization presented wages and hours demands to employers.[54] Clearly the Assembly's position was in fundamental disagreement with that of the trade unions. The latter had demanded unitary control over the economic field, while the Knights had demanded equal jurisdiction over membership and working standards. Thus neither side evinced willingness to compromise over basic issues.

Although failing to conclude a settlement with the trade unions, the special session of the General Assembly did not close the door to further negotiations. For the time being, therefore, the conflict remained in abeyance. While matters were pending, however, the Knights made a determined effort to end friction by intensifying its campaign to bring the national unions under its control. The national unions, however, recognized that the structure of the Knights was incompatible with trade union objectives, and the policy of the Order was only partially successful. Some of the smaller unions, including the Seamen's Benevolent Union, the Eastern Glass Bottle Blowers' League, and the Western Green Bottle Blowers' Association, joined the Knights. [55] The American Flint Glass Workers Union, on the other hand, refused to go along with the other glassworkers because of an earlier dispute with the Order. [56] In New York City the Knights made a determined but unsuccessful attempt to capture the German shoemakers and the Associated Jewelers. [57] Most of the larger and more important unions emphatically rejected the Order's overtures. The members of the Amalgamated Association of Iron and Steel Workers overwhelmingly defeated a referendum on the subject, while a similar poll conducted by the secretary of the Bricklayers and the Masons resulted in the same conclusion. The Iron Molders' convention turned down the merger proposal by the vote of 114 to 27. [58] Furthermore, the Typographical Union, the Carpenters, the Plumbers and Gas Fitters, the coal miners, and the Stationary Engineers all rejected the invitation to join the Knights.[59]

At the regular meeting of the General Assembly in October 1886 further negotiations between the trade unions and the Knights again ended in failure. The action by the Assembly in ordering all workers holding cards in both the Knights and the Cigar Makers International Union to leave the latter under pain of expulsion, [60] was interpreted by both sides as constituting a final break and an open declaration of war. [61] The trade union committee therefore issued a call on November 10, 1886, for all unions to send representatives to a convention in Columbus, Ohio, on December 8, to form an "American Federation or Alliance of all National and International Trade Unions." Out of this meeting came the A.F. of L. Completely dominated by the national unions, the December convention excluded assemblies of the Knights from membership, and then proceeded to establish the new organization on a firm foundation. [62]

Thus by the end of 1886 the die had been cast, and the Knights and national unions prepared for war. Why had all negotiations failed? Undoubtedly the intractability of leaders on both sides contributed to the difficulties, but there were also those who had made sincere efforts to head off the impending conflict. The trade unions, furthermore, had encountered jurisdictional rivalries with the Knights, but this has been an endemic problem of the labor movement, and one which has not always had an unhappy ending.

The conflict between the Knights and the trade unions, then, had a much broader significance than the negotiations between them indicated, and represented the culmination of decades of historical development. The Knights, growing out of the humanitarian and reform crusades of ante-bellum America, emphasized the abolition of the wage system and the reorganization of society. To achieve this purpose it insisted on the prime importance of the mixed assembly, which would serve as the nucleus of an organization dedicated to reform. The trade unions, on the other hand, accepted their environment, and sought to take advantage of the relative scarcity of labor and the rising scale of production. Hence they emphasized the collective bargaining functions of labor organizations, thus tacitly accepting the workers' wage status.

Perhaps grounds for compromise did exist, but neither side was prone to make any concessions. The national unions, by insisting upon strict trade autonomy as a *sine qua non* of settlement, were in effect demanding that the Knights should virtually abandon any pretense at being a bona fide labor organization. It is true that the unions could have organized as national autonomous trade districts if the Knights had been ready to grant permission. The leaders of the Knights, however, were unwilling to permit their organization to be transformed into what the A.F. of L. ultimately became. Indeed, after 1886 many national trade districts left the Order because of their inability to function within the framework of that body. [63] The national unions, moreover, were not encouraged by the experiences of trade districts within the Knights before 1886. Finally, there was the simple element of power, and both the trade unions and the Knights, as established organizations, were adamant in their refusal to surrender any part of it.

Between reform and trade unionism, therefore, existed a gulf that the leaders of the 1880's were unable to bridge. By 1886 this chasm had widened to such a degree that co-operation between the two seemed virtually impossible and war seemed to be the only solution. Reform and trade unionism had at last come to a parting of the ways, and upon the outcome of the ensuing struggle hinged the destiny of the American labor movement.

Notes

1. *The Laster*, IV (Nov. 15, 1891), 3.

2. For the antitrade unionism of the national leadership of the Knights see the *Journal of United Labor*, I (June 15, 1880), 21 (hereinafter cited as JUL); Knights of Labor, *Proceedings of the General Assembly*, 1880, p. 169; 1884, pp. 716-17; 1897, p. 37 (hereinafter cited as K. of L., *GA Proc.*); Terrence V. Powderly, *Thirty Years of Labor: 1859 to 1889* (Columbus: Excelsior Publishing House, 1889), pp. 155-56; Powderly Letter Books, Catholic University of America, Washington, D.C., Powderly to James Rogers, Dec. 19, 1892; Gerald N. Grob, "Terrence V. Powderly and the Knights of Labor," *Mid-America*, XXXIX (January 1957), 41-42.

3. See Lloyd Ulman, *The Rise of the National Trade Union* (Cambridge: Harvard University Press, 1955), pp. 348-77.

4. See Carroll D. Wright, "An Historical Sketch of the Knights of Labor," *Quarterly Journal of Economics*, I (Jan. 1887), 155; *Cigar Makers' Official Journal*, XI (June 1886), 6; *The Carpenter*, VI (Feb. 1886), 4, (Apr. 1886), 4.

5. Norman J. Ware emphasized the importance of conflicting personalities. Ware, *The Labor Movement in the United States 1860-1895* (New York: D. Appleton and Company, 1929), pp. 162-63, *et passim*.

6. See Wright, "An Historical Sketch Knights of Labor," p. 146.

7. Ware, *Labor Movement*, p. 158. The statistics on trade locals in the Knights are unsatisfactory and misleading, since many of them admitted workers belonging to different trades.

8. K. of L., *GA Proc.*, Jan. 1879, pp. 69-70, 72; Sept. 1879, pp. 98, 129.

9. Federation of Organized Trades, *Proceedings*, 1881, pp. 7-9 (1905 reprinting).

10. K. of L., *GA Proc.*, 1882, pp. 296-98. See also the statement of the General Executive Board in *ibid.*, p. 334.

11. *Ibid.*, pp. 364, 368; 1884, pp. 705-7, 776; 1886, pp. 265-66.

12. *Ibid.*, 1885, p. 25.

13. See the *JUL*, VII (June 25, 1886), 2100; *John Swinton's Paper*, Sept. 6, 1885; K. of L., *GA Proc.*, 1884, pp. 716-17.

14. K. of L. *GA Proc.*, 1883, pp. 438, 443, 502; 1884, p. 787; 1885, pp. 127, 133; *Jul*, V (Dec. 10, 1884), 856.

15. K. of L., *GA Proc.*, 1882, pp. 325, 347; 1883, pp. 445, 498.

16. *Ibid.*, 1882, pp. 311, 351; 1883, pp. 349-40, 498, 502.

17. *Ibid.*, 1886, pp. 126-27.

18. *Ibid.*, 1883, p. 506; 1884, p. 619. This was also the case in the affiliation of the harness workers. *JUL*, IV (June 1883), 511; (July 1883), 520-21. The Knights also aided the barbers, horse railway men, miners, railway men, and ax makers in attempts to get them to join.

19. New York Bureau of Labor Statistics, *Annual Report*, V (1887), 202-3.

20. *Quarterly Report of District Assembly No. 30 . . . July . . . 1886* (Boston, 1886), p. 69. For a somewhat similar case see New York Bureau of Labor Statistics, *Annual Report*, V (1887), 202-4.

21. K. of L., *GA Proc.*, 1885, pp. 102-3, 140; 1886, p. 130.

22. *Ibid.*, 1883, pp. 467, 508; 1884, p. 617; 1885, pp. 125, 135; 1887, pp. 1714, 1757.

23. Even the successful career of L.A. 300 cannot be attributed to the Knights. It was due primarily to the skilled nature of the trade which permitted the window glass workers to organize thoroughly, restrict output, and regulate apprenticeship requirements. See Pearce Davis, *The Development of the American Glass Industry* (Cambridge: Harvard University Press, 1949), pp. 126-30.

24. Federation of Organized Trades, *Proceedings*, 1882, pp. 5, 16, 20, 23.

25. For a partial list of trade union leaders belonging to the Knights see *The Painter*, II (Feb. 1888), 3.

26. See *Iron Molders' Journal*, XIX (June 30, 1883), 9; XX (June 30, 1884), 10; XXI (Nov. 30, 1885), 14; Amalgamated Association of Iron and Steel Workers, *Proceedings*, 1882, p. 955; *The Craftsman*, II (Jan. 17, 1885), 2 (Aug. 15, 1885), 2.

27. International Typographical Union, *Proceedings*, 1882, pp. 43, 58, 62, 78, 83, 87.

28. See K. of L., *GA Proc.*, 1882, p. 270; 1884, pp. 707, 787; 1885, pp. 73, 138.

29. *Ibid.*, 1883, pp. 460, 467, 505-6. See also Powderly Letter Books, Powderly to J. P. McDonnell, Sept. 24, 1882.

30. Ohio Bureau of Labor Statistics, *Annual Report*, IX (1885), 28; Grace H. Stimson, *Rise of the Labor Movement in Los Angeles* (Berkeley: University of California Press, 1955), p. 45.

31. Differences over wages, hours, and working conditions frequently ensued between trade assemblies and local and national unions, especially since no formal co-ordinating bodies existed. For an example of such a disagreement see K. of L., *GA Proc.*, 1884, pp. 703, 764, 768.

32. Iron Molders International Union, *Proceeding*, 1882, pp. 15, 54-55.

33. See the *National Labor Tribune*, July 7, 1883, cited in John R. Commons, ed., *History of Labour in the United States* (4 vols: New York: Macmillan Company, 1918-1935), II, 353. "With other trade unionists," Gompers recalled, "I joined the Knights of Labor for the purpose of confining that

organization to theoretical educational work and to see that the Trade Unions were protected from being undermined or disrupted." Gompers Letter Books, A.F. of L.–C.I.O. Building, Washington, D.C., Gompers to N.E. Mathewson, Oct. 10, 1890.

34. *John Swinton's Paper*, Apr. 12, 1885.

35. *JUL*, II (Sept.-Oct. 1881), 158, *John Swinton's Paper,* March 2, 1884.

36. Bricklayers and Masons International Union, *Proceedings*, 1884, p. 9; Powderly Papers, Henry O. Cole to Powderly, Mar. 9, Apr. 28, 1883.

37. *The Carpenter*, III (Feb. 1883), 3; International Typographical Union, *Proceedings*, 1884, p. 12.

38. For typical examples see *The Carpenter*, III (Oct. 1883), 2; VI (Mar. 1886) 4; VIII (Feb. 15, 1888), 1; Robert A. Christie, *Empire in Wood: A History of the Carpenters' Union* (Ithaca: Cornell University Press, 1956), pp. 50-51; *John Swinton's Paper*, Feb. 1, 8, 1885; K. of L., *GA Proc.*, 1885, pp. 106, 109, 140.

39. International Typographical Union, *Proceedings*, 1884, pp. 12, 65-66, 70, 72, 102.

40. See especially Ware, *Labor Movement*, pp. 258-79, 285, *et passim*, and Commons, *History of Labour*, II, 401-2.

41. *Iron Molders' Journal*, XXII (Mar. 31, 1886), 14; *The Craftsman*, III (Aug. 7, 1886), 2.

42. John B. Lennon, "Journeymen Tailors," *American Federationist*, IX (Sept. 1902), 599; Amalgamated Association of Iron and Steel Workers, *Proceedings*, 1886, p. 1793.

43. New Haven *Workmen's Advocate,* Dec. 10, 1887.

44. K. of L., *GA Proc.*, 1886 special session, pp. 50-51.

45. Bricklayers and Masons International Union, *Proceedings*, 1887, pp. 70-75.

46. *Iron Molders' Journal*, XXII (Feb. 28, 1886), 10, 14, (Apr. 30, 1886), 8, (Aug. 31, 1886), 6; XXIII (Dec. 31, 1886), 7; *The Craftsman*, III (May 15, 1886), 3; *Granite Cutters' Journal*, X (Apr. 1886), 3; *The Carpenter*, VI (May 1886), 2; *Cigar Makers' Official Journal*, XI (Apr. 1886), 6; *Printers' Circular*, XXI (June 1886), 66; International Typographical Union, *Proceedings*, 1886, pp. 90, 93-94; Iron Molders International Union, *Proceedings*, 1886, pp. 16, 25, 31.

47. See *The Craftsman*, III (Feb. 6, 1886), 2, (Mar. 20, 1886), 1; *The Carpenter*, XXIV (Dec. 1904), 5.

48. *John Swinton's Paper*, Mar. 21, 1886; Illinois Bureau of Labor Statistics, *Biennial Report*, IV (1886), 160-61.

49. Bricklayers and Masons International Union, *Proceedings*, 1887, pp. 63-66; *The Carpenter*, VI (May 1886), 2, (June 1886), 3; *Cigar Makers' Official Journal*, XI (June 1886), 7; K. of L., *GA Proc.*, 1886 special session, pp. 1-2; Powderly Letter Books, Powderly to P. J. McGuire and Adolph Strasser, May 11, 1886.

50. A.F. of L., *Proceedings*, 1886, p. 16 (1905-06 reprinting).

51. Cf. Ware, *Labor Movement*, p. 284.

52. Perlman has interpreted the conflict between the Knights and unions largely as one between

skilled and unskilled workers. Commons, *History of Labour,* II, 396-97. Undoubtedly the skilled workers feared the Knights. The Knights, however, was not necessarily an organization of unskilled workers, as the large number of trade assemblies would indicate. While the unions jealously guarded their autonomy and independence, the conflict that developed in 1886 was more than simply a struggle between the skilled and unskilled, although this aspect was an important element.

53. Gompers Letter Books, Gompers to George H. Daggett, Jan. 4, 1896. See also Gompers to Albert C. Stevens Nov. 1, 1889; Gompers to Frank D. Hamlin, May 6, 1890; Gompers to Charles W. Nelson, Apr. 29, 1892.

54. K. of L., *GA Proc.,* 1886 special session, pp. 53, 55, 67.

55. *JUL,* VIII (Aug. 20, 1887), 1476; K. of L., *GA Proc.,* 1887, p. 1334; *John Swinton's Paper,* July 25, 1886; David A. McCabe, *The Standard Rate in American Trade Unions* (Baltimore: The Johns Hopkins Press, 1912), pp. 155-56. The glassworkers probably joined the Order in the hope of emulating the success of L.A. 300.

56. *Iron Molders' Journal,* XXII (Feb. 28, 1886), 10; *Cigar Makers' Official Journal,* XI (Aug. 1886), 6; Secretary of Internal Affairs of the Commonwealth of Pennsylvania, *Annual Report,* XVI (1888), Pt. III, Section F, pp. 18-19.

57. *The Carpenter,* VI (Oct. 1886), 1.

58. Amalgamated Association of Iron and Steel Workers, *Proceedings,* 1886, pp. 1807-08, 1818-19, 1846; 1887, pp. 1959-62; Bricklayers and Masons International Union, *Proceedings,* 1887, pp. 71, 76; Iron Molders International Union, *Proceedings,* 1886, pp. 17-20.

59. *John Swinton's Paper,* June 20, 1886; *The Carpenter,* VI (Oct. 1886), I. See also *Locomotive Firemen's Magazine,* X (Mar. 1886), 141.

60. K. of L., *GA Proc.,* 1886, pp. 200, 282.

61. See Joseph R. Buchanan, *The Story of a Labor Agitator* (New York: The Outlook Company, 1903), p. 314.

62. Bricklayers and Masons International Union, *Proceedings,* 1887, pp. 79-80; A.F. of L., *Proceedings,* 1886, pp. 13-15. A committee from the Knights was also present at the trade union convention in December 1886 but no agreement was reached. See A.F. of L., *Proceedings,* 1886, pp. 17-18; K. of L., *GA Proc.,* 1887, pp. 1445-47.

63. The shoemakers, miners, machinists, garmentworkers, carriage and wagonworkers, and potters all seceded from the Knights after 1886 because of their inability to function efficiently within the existing framework of the Order. For evidence on this point see the following: *The Laster,* I (Mar. 15, 1889), 1; *Shoe Workers' Journal,* XI (July 1910), 11; United Mine Workers of America, *Proceedings,* 1911, I, 581; *JUL,* VIII (May 19, 1888), 1; *Journal of the International Association of Machinists,* VII (July 1895), 238; *Garment Worker,* III (Sept. 1896), 4; *Carriage and Wagon Workers Journal,* II (Jan. 1, 1901), 113; United States Industrial Commission, *Report of the Industrial Commission* (19 vols: Washington, D.C., 1900-02), XVII, 59, 209; Theodore W. Glocker, *The Government of American Trade Unions* (Baltimore: The Johns Hopkins Press, 1913), p. 54.

The condition of the western farmer

Arthur F. Bentley

For American farmers engaged in staple-crop agriculture, the late nineteenth century was a time of deepening economic distress. Why was the farmer's lot so hard in this period? The large factor was declining commodity prices, the result primarily of world trade conditions. What seems less clear is why an adverse price movement should have had so disastrous an effect on American farmers. The Populists did not lack answers: the railroads charged excessive and unfair freight rates; eastern loan companies burdened farmers with exhorbitant interest rates; manufacturers, middle men, and processors sold dear to farmers and bought cheap from them; and, above all, the deflationary effect of the gold standard compounded all the farmer's price and credit problems. Where was the truth in this welter of charges?

In recent years, a number of historians have turned their hand to aspects of this question. But surprisingly, one of the best, if overlooked, studies dates back to 1893 when Arthur F. Bentley, who would go on to a major career in political science, published a short monograph on farm conditions in the Nebraska township of Harrison, a major portion of which is reprinted below. A local study cannot, as Bentley stresses, explain the large factors, but it can show in a precise way their impact on American farmers, and, equally important, can uncover sources of distress attributable to the farmers themselves. Bentley's study is particularly revealing on the latter score. Farming was less profitable in the late 1880s than earlier for all farmers in Harrison township, but some would continue to make a living, while others were surely going under. The crucial factor, Bentley shows, was farm indebtedness, which, in turn, was related to the timing of arrival in the township. Those farmers who came at the time of initial settlement in the early 1870s took up farms as homesteaders or at little cost through preemption or by purchase from the railroad. As a group, they were not heavily mortgaged in the 1880s, as were those who came later and purchased from original settlers. The latecomers were precisely the ones who were failing. Why should indebtedness have been so burdensome? Not because of high interest rates, Bentley demonstrates. These had fallen steadily, and

Arthur F. Bentley, *The Condition of the Western Farmer as Illustrated by the Economic History of a Nebraska Township*. Baltimore: Johns Hopkins University Press, 1893, pp. 7-10, 25-28, 43-46, 48-52, 67-70, 76-86.

stood at only 7 percent at the end of the 1880s. The crucial problem was the high valuation of land in relationship to the income it would produce. Of the two variables, farm prices are taken as essentially a given factor, since price movements are not the result of local conditions. But land values are local in character; they are what farmers say they are. And it was, Bentley argues, the unrealistically high valuation that Harrison farmers placed on their land—a reflection of the speculative and optimistic instincts of American farmers—that spelled probable ruin for any man who purchased a Harrison farm with the expectation of carrying the mortgage through the income the farm would produce.

Besides its significant findings, Bentley's essay is important for its empirical methodology. Bentley drew his conclusions on the basis of quantitative data developed from local sources. In a time when modern historians are increasingly stressing research into statistical and other "hard" evidence, it is refreshing to discover a model study of that kind dating back to very distant predecessors.

For further reading: Fred A. Shannon, *The Farmers' Last Frontier: Agriculture, 1860-1897* (1945);* Allen G. Bogue, *From Prairie to Corn Belt: Farming on the Illinois and Iowa Prairies in the Nineteenth Century* (1963);* Allen G. Bogue, *Money at Interest: the Farm Mortgage on the Middle Border* (1953);* Merle Curti, *The Making of an American Community: A Case Study of Democracy in a Frontier County* (1959);* P. H. Johnstone, "Old Ideals versus New Ideas in Farm Life," in Department of Agriculture, *Farmers in a Changing World* (1940); Theodore Saloutos, "The Agriculture Problem and Nineteenth-Century Industrialism," *Agricultural History*, XXII (1948), 156-174.

The study on which this paper is based was suggested by the desire of the writer to obtain some actual knowledge of the true economic condition of the farmers in the western states. The farmers' movement, culminating in its attempt to change the policy of the government in many important particulars, had for its *raison d'être* the depressed financial condition of the agricultural classes. Against this position, the other political parties urged that the financial depression affected all classes alike, and that in no way did farmers have greater difficulty in attaining prosperity than persons in other lines of activity. Realizing the worthlessness of the isolated examples cited for proof, as well by one side as by the other, the author undertook the present investigation.

Two ways lie open to one desiring to find an answer to such a question as that set before us. Either many and varied statistics for the whole region under consideration may be collected and examined, or a study in miniature may be made of some little district which can fairly lay claim to being typical of the whole region. . . .

In comparison with a statistical investigation on a large scale, this form of study has advantage in that we get from it a better knowledge of the real life of the farmer. Where the figures are on a very large scale, all sense of the actual economic life of the individual is lost, and that sense, it may well seem, is the true object of inquiry and the one from which the most benefit can be derived. Again, the detailed study gives us the best opportunity to investigate the local causes of changes in financial condition. The causes which would tend to produce depression among agriculturalists fall in general into two classes: those due to the general economic condition of society, and those more directly connected with the local conditions of agriculture. The first class of causes is entirely without the scope of our inquiries, but in seeking the facts of the present status of the farmers, we obtain naturally, and in the same process, knowledge of the local conditions and of their effects during the years which the study covers.

The boundaries of Harrison Township (or Precinct, as it was called before the county adopted township organization) coincide exactly with those of the congressional township known as township eleven, range eleven, west of the sixth principal meridian, and thus it contains very nearly thirty-six square miles. Its southeast corner is, as nearly as may be, the geographical center of Hall county. The main channel of the Platte river lies, at its nearest point, about five miles distant, while the northwestern corner of the township is some thirteen or fourteen miles distant from the river. The lands are what we have designated in this paper as "second bottom" lands. The surface is very slightly undulating, so slightly indeed that one who was not a close observer might call it an almost perfect level. Through the northwestern quarter of the town runs a small stream, Prairie Creek, and there is one other streamlet which contains running water only at certain times of the year. The fertility of the land is, on the whole, of a very high grade; this matter, however, will receive more careful attention hereafter.

The first settlement in Hall county, on that part of the "second bottom" lands which is drained by Prairie Creek, had been made in the year 1871, but it was not until 1872 that a claim of any sort was taken within the limits of Harrison township. By the end of that year, however, entries of some kind had been made on all of the government land therein. The first entry was in the latter part of March, when two pre-emptions were filed on quarter sections in the southeastern part of the township. In April nine entries were made, most of them homesteads, near the two claims taken in March; two, however, were pre-emptions, placed in the western part of the town by ranchers who hoped, while controlling under their own claims but a few hundred acres, to be able to have the use of many thousands of acres of unclaimed land around them for grazing their cattle. Needless to say, the rapidity of settlement surprised these men so greatly that they gave up their claims in disgust and moved farther away. In May there were six entries; in June, eleven; in July, six; in August, twelve; in September, nineteen; in October, three; and in November two. This includes, it must be remembered, only the first entry on each tract of ground, the total number of such entries being seventy; and as the government land originally available for entry consisted of sixty-four quarter-sections, the average number of acres taken on each entry was 146.3.

Of these original entries, fourteen were pre-emptions, forty-seven were homesteads, and nine were soldiers' homestead declaratory statements, intended to mature in due time into homesteads proper,—all but four, in fact, doing so. It is proper, then, to say that there were fourteen pre-emptions as against fifty-six homesteads; that is, four-fifths of all entries were homesteads. This shows, at least, the relative estimation in which the two ways of taking land were held. It might at first sight seem that the taking of a homestead indicated that the settler came with the intention of residing permanently, but did not have sufficient means to purchase the land he desired, even at the very low prices demanded by the government; thus it would follow that four-fifths of the entries were made by settlers who were lacking the means necessary for pre-emption. But such a conclusion must be looked at with caution, for in considering the individual cases we find that here and there a well-to-do "speculator"[1] took a homestead, while on the contrary a pre-emption was occasionally taken by one whose possessions were as nearly nil as they well could be, and whose hopes for paying up on a pre-emption must have been based entirely on some wild notion of fabulous crops in the first years. Of the fourteen pre-emptions mentioned above, only one was paid up, that one being one of the two taken by the ranchmen whom we have spoken of before. Three men relinquished, their pre-emptions to take homesteads on the same land, and four relinquished in order to take timber-claims on the same land; the remaining four gave up their holdings in the township altogether and moved away. This relinquishment of pre-emptions occurred almost entirely in the fall of '74, when the time given by law for "proving up" had expired, and the holders found themselves unable to pay the amounts required to complete their title under the pre-emption laws. It must be remembered that this land being within the Union Pacific ten-mile limit, pre-emptors were obliged to pay the government the double minimum price, $2.50 per acre. . . .

The last entry made on government land in the township was in February, 1884. In all 159 entries had been made, of which ninety-seven were homesteads, fourteen soldiers' homestead declaratory statements, twenty-five pre-emptions, and twenty-three timber claims.

We have noticed above the number of entries made on land in the various months. By referring to these figures it will be evident that the number of entries in August and September, 1872, formed nearly half of the total number in that year. Now, many of those who made entries at this time did not actually enter into possession of the land until the following spring, and, evidently, those who took possession in the fall could do little more than get some kind of habitation in readiness, and a very little, if any, breaking done, before winter set in and put a stop to work. So their first year saw, practically, no farming undertaken.

Those not familiar with the subject sometimes think of the conditions of colonization under our present land laws as having been of such a character that the empty-handed settler could, through the mediation of the government, soon become the possessor of a well-equipped farm. But a very little reflection shows us that the gift of the soil is by no means all that is needed as the foundation for a farm. To convert the raw prairie into a habitable and income-producing farm is not an easy task, and quite a little capital is needed to do it satisfactorily. Prof. Rodney Welch makes the following estimate of the necessary expenses.[2]

Registering, etc.	$50.00
Horses and implements	500.00
Furniture, small stock, etc.	200.00
House (sod), stables and seed	150.00
Breaking forty acres sod	100.00 $1000.00

To this must be added the cost of sustenance for self and family during the year, or perhaps two years, which intervened before regular crops could be raised. The country being new, little work could be found by which the income could be helped out. It would be perfectly safe to say that the ordinary immigrant had very much less means than the amount mentioned, and was much hindered in his work by his lack of sufficient capital. Those who came out to their claims with practically no capital were usually forced to leave before much time had passed, though here and there a prosperous farmer is to be found who started out with not even a team with which to plow his land. . . .

Farming in this township seems to have been at its best in the middle part of the period that has elapsed since colonization began. After the drawbacks attending the first settlement were past, the prosperity of the settlers was at its highest point, and in the later years, while the older settlers have in the main increased their wealth, but at a much slower rate than before, yet those who have come in as purchasers from the older settlers have, almost without exception, fallen behind rather than gained in their net wealth.

When Harrison township was first settled, land in limited quantities could be purchased from the government by actual settlers for $2.50 an acre. At the same time the Union Pacific Railroad was asking $4 an acre for its lands. As the government land was all so quickly taken, and as sales were made by the railroad company at its own prices, we can consider the actual value of the lands from 1872 to 1874 to have been about $4 an acre. During the two or three years following 1874 there was absolutely no sale for farming land, but after immigration began again in 1878, the railroad price may be considered as indicative of the actual marketable value of the lands. In '78 and '79, $5 and $6 per acre were the current prices. From 1880 to 1884 land of the average quality brought from $6 to $8 per acre. These were the prices, of course, for unimproved land sold on long time and easy terms. A settler who wished to sell for cash would get very much less, unless the improvements represented a substantial sum. With the exception of two or three years prior to 1891 or '92, land has, since 1880, steadily increased in value, though usually it has been of rather slow sale, because owners have habitually asked prices for it above what purchasers were willing to pay. At the present time, land with good average improvements will sell with comparative readiness for about $25 an acre, though owners often claim that they would refuse any offer of less than $30 to $35 an acre. . . .

There are in general four ways in which the farmers have made use of the capital of others. These are, first, by obtaining credit with retail dealers with whom they trade; second, by borrowing with real estate security; third, by borrowing with chattel security (and this includes most of the debt on agricultural implements, for the part of the price of such implements which is not paid in cash is usually secured by mortgage on the machinery itself); and fourth, by borrowing with unsecured promissory note or with personal security. The first method is relatively unimportant, as the total amount of credit so obtained has necessarily been quite small. Let us then pass to the consideration of the three other forms.

When the township was settled, money could only be borrowed on chattel security, and was very difficult to obtain even at the high rates then offered and demanded; for capitalists were few, and the condition of the borrower was such as to warrant only the smallest line of credit. Moreover, the insecurity of the loan made the interest required very high. But in time real estate became of importance as security. The agent of the first company that loaned money upon real estate in this part of Nebraska appeared about 1875, and twelve per cent was the rate of interest demanded, with a bonus of from ten per cent to twenty-five per cent for commission. The rates have gradually lowered; in 1880 they were eight per cent interest and two per cent commission; then seven and two; later, seven and one; and now the current rate is six and one, while a certain large life insurance company will make all good loans of over $2000 that are desired at six per cent without commission. But for a long time the chattel mortgage held its own and was the form of security regularly in use for borrowing money; even the most well-to-do did not hesitate to allow such mortgages to appear on record against them. This has changed to a certain extent, however, and real estate or personal security is coming to be given in preference by the more prosperous farmers. Chattel mortgages are still frequently given by cattle-feeders as security for their extra purchases of stock for winter feeding, but even in this line of business they are less common than formerly. The amount of money now borrowed on personal security, or simply on individual note, is not large, for only the more prosperous can so borrow and they are just those who want to and who do borrow the least. I was allowed to examine the books of a bank that does perhaps the greater part of the business of this township, and found only an insignificant amount of this last variety of paper.

Those few settlers who were able to borrow of a father or of other relatives in the eastern states had a very great advantage, especially in the first years of residence, as in trying times they could count on aid without having to pay the exorbitant interest charged by local lenders. Many were the occasions for borrowing in the early days; but most of the debt was incurred either to provide sustenance during a year of lost crops, or to make improvements, or to settle an unpaid balance of purchase money.

It will be necessary later to discuss in detail the use of credit in its relation to agricultural prosperity; but two general incentives to mortgaging may be here mentioned, the influence of which has been felt throughout a great part of the history of the township, but especially during the earlier days. The first incentive grew out of the appreciation in the price of land, the farmer being led into realizing this in advance by means of mortgaging; as fast as he could increase his loan he would do so, and use the sum obtained sometimes to make good deficiencies and losses, or for current expenditure, and sometimes for investment, whether legitimate or speculative, upon his farm. The second incentive lay in the fact of the relatively large returns of crop in proportion to the cost of the land. In the early days the farmer's profits were very high in proportion to the amount of capital employed, whenever his crops were at all good; and this often led him to purchase and cultivate more land than he was able to manage; then if bad crops, which he had not counted on, came, he would become hopelessly involved in debt. It is true the farmer may often have suffered from excessive interest and grasping creditors; but it was less frequently the avarice of the lender that got him into trouble than the fact that he was too sanguine and too prone to believe that he could safely go in debt, on the assumption that crops and prices in the future would equal those in the present.

During the years 1872 and '73 all the agricultural produce of Hall county could be readily sold to the new settlers, at prices so high as to make shipments to outside markets unprofitable. During the three following years it was necessary to bring grain into the country rather than ship it out, on account of successive crop failures caused by grass-hoppers and drouth; but with '77 a period of fairly good crops began, and during most of the time from then until '84 the markets in the western part of Nebraska, and in the Black Hills and other near regions in which settlement was just beginning, gave better prices for corn and oats than could be realized by shipping them to eastern grain centers. Between '85 and '87 the activity in railroad building in states to the west gave rise to good markets for corn, and quite high prices prevailed. From 1877 to 1883, Chicago was by far the best market for wheat, but since 1883 the local mills have competed with it and absorbed a good share of the crop. Since 1887 it has been necessary to ship most of the grain to eastern markets, or sometimes to the South, and this is especially the case when crops are heavy. While therefore during a great part of the period we are considering the prices obtained for grain have been somewhat better than could be obtained by shipments to the eastern markets, yet since 1877 the price of wheat has been to a great extent affected by the net price to be obtained by shipping to Chicago, and since 1887 the Chicago prices have had a by no means inconsiderable effect on the selling price of all grains. It is unfortunately impossible to obtain records showing the prices which grains have brought in the local markets, but Table V. gives the average prices for corn and wheat and oats in Chicago for each year since 1872.

Table V
Average Chicago Prices of Corn, Wheat, and Oats[3]

	Corn "No. 2" cts. per bushel	Wheat "No. 2" Spring cts. per bushel	Oats "No. 2" cts. per bushel
72	34.3	111.5	26.1
73	32.3	102.9	25.6
74	59.3	97.6	41.7
75	54.8	88.9	41.
76	40.	92.6	28.3
77	42.7	121.5	29.5
78	36.9	95.2	22.3
79	35.6	99.6	26.8
80	37.7	105.7	29.8
81	50.	114.8	37.8
82	67.5	116.6	43.6
83	53.8	101.7	34.5
84	51.6	83.	29.1
85	43.	83.9	29.
86	37.	76.6	27.6
87	39.5	75.6	26.
88	46.8	90.	28.6
89	34.	85.5	22.2
90	39.3	89.2	30.9
91	58.4	96.6	39.1

In attempting to estimate, on the basis of the preceding table of prices, the profits which the farmer has been able to make on his grain, we should next have to take into account the cost of raising the grain and the cost of transporting it to market; and though we shall be unable to discuss this matter in detail here, a few facts bearing on the subject may not be out of place.

The cost of raising corn in Nebraska has been investigated by the Nebraska Bureau of

Labor and Industrial Statistics, and in its report for 1891-92 the estimates of some six or seven hundred farmers are given, which make the average cost of the production of corn per acre to be $6.40, and therefore, figuring forty bushels of corn to the acre, the cost per bushel would be 16 cents. The method of this estimate is, however, faulty, in that the cost of husking and cribbing is estimated by the acre and not by the bushel, as it should be, and thus the size of the crop is entangled from the start with the cost per acre. Leaving out these items of husking and cribbing, the average cost per acre shown by the report is $4.90. From this latter figure, the cost per bushel should be estimated according to the size of the crop, and then an addition made to cover cost of husking and cribbing. Moreover, the figures given in the report do not include cost of hauling to market, which is for the farmers of Harrison township from one to two cents a bushel. The cost to the farmers we are considering of corn delivered by them at the marketplace cannot be estimated under from eighteen to twenty cents per bushel for a fairly good year, that is when the crop averages from thirty-five to forty bushels to the acre.

The report of the Bureau indicates that the cost of raising corn in the eastern counties is greater than in the western counties of the state. The reasons suggested for this are that the item of interest on the investment in the land in the newer counties is less than in the older ones, as is also the amount of cultivating which it is found necessary to give the land. Analogy with this conclusion would suggest that the cost of raising corn in Harrison was less in earlier days than now, and therefore, though the freight rates were much higher then than at present, yet the price which the farmer had to realize for his corn in order to make a profit from it was less than now.

Table VI
Freight Rates (in Cts. per Cwt.)

Grand Island to Omaha (150 miles)				Grand Island to Chicago (650 miles)			
Date effective	Corn	Wheat	Oats	Date effective	Corn	Wheat	Oats
January 1, 1883	18	19½	18	January 7, 1880	32	45	32
April 16, 1883	15	16½	15	September 15, 1882	38	43	38
January 10, 1884	18	19½	18	April 5, 1887	34	39	34
March 1, 1884	17	19½	17	November 1, 1887	25	30	25
August 25, 1884	20	20	20	March 21, 1890	22½	30	25
April 5, 1887	10	16	10	October 22, 1890	22	26	22
November 1, 1887	10	12	10	January 15, 1891	23	28	25
March 7, 1888	9½	11¾	9½				
December 15, 1888	10	12	10				

As to freight rates on grain, Table VI. will show all the changes since 1880-83 in the rates between Grand Island and Omaha, and between Grand Island and Chicago. A comparison made between the figures in the table itself will show how large the local rates have been as compared with through rates.[4] A comparison[5] of the rates here given with the Chicago prices of grain as seen in Table V. will show how much of the value of the product is absorbed in finding a market for it. If further deduction is made from the Chicago price for the commissions of two middlemen, we will begin to appreciate the position and feelings of the farmer who said that when he bought his farm he thought he was really going to own the land, but that he soon discovered that he only held it on an uncertain tenure from the railroad companies. It will be noticed that the proportion of the market price which is paid for freight is much higher for corn and oats than for wheat, and in the former grains often runs over one-third of the total price.

Table XVIII
Real Estate Mortgages Owed by Residents, with
Reference to the Mode of Acquisition of the Lands[6]

A. Settled on Government Land	No.	Acres	Amount of debt	Average size of farm, acres	Average debt per man	Average debt per acre
a. Original home unmortgaged:						
1. No mortgage on any land	9	1,680		186.66		
2. Additional lands only mortgaged[7]	5	1,280	$3,950.00	256.00	$790.00	$3.09
b. original home mortgaged	4	640	3,300.00	160.00	825.00	5.16
B. Settled on Railroad Land						
a. Lands unmortgaged	3	720		240.00		
b. Lands mortgaged	16	3,000	23,400.00	187.50	1,462.50	7.80
C. Purchasers of Land from Individuals						
a. Lands unmortgaged	4	440		110.00		
b. Lands mortgaged	33	5,200	48,769.61	157.57	1,477.87	9.38

These figures are very striking from almost every point of view. First, we observe that half of all the settlers on government land have their lands entirely free from mortgage, while only four have mortgages upon their original homes; in the case of those who have mortgages upon their additional lands, the average debt per acre is very low, being only $3.09. Of those who have their original homes mortgaged, two came in among the last of those who took government land; two have very small mortgages; moreover, the average debt per acre on the property of these is itself quite low, being $516. Then again we notice that the size of the farms among these settlers averages larger than among either of the other classes; the homes of those, especially, who have additional lands which they have mortgaged are much larger than those of any of the others. Not one of these settlers on government land who has a mortgage to take care of can be said to be at all seriously embarrassed by it, and some of them are, despite their mortgages, as well off as any men in the township.

Take up next the settlers on railroad land and what a difference! There are only three of them without mortgage, as against sixteen holding mortgaged farms, and the average debt per acre on those lands which are mortgaged is $7.80, or half again as much as the average debt borne by those settlers on government land who have their original homes mortgaged. Following the analogy of class "A," we would expect to find the mortgaged farms larger than those which are clear, and we shall find this to be the case in class "C"; but in class "B," the unmortgaged farms are considerably larger on the average than the mortgaged; this points to something exceptional in these particular cases and in investigating the cases in detail we find this indication borne out in fact. Of the three purchasers of railroad land who have their lands unmortgaged, two are brothers who had been farmers in Germany, and who, coming to America with considerable property, were able not only to buy and pay for comparatively large farms, but to put considerable money in bank— certainly a very exceptional state of affairs with the ordinary settler on a Nebraska farm. The third case is that of a man who bought railroad land at an early date and farmed it for a number of years, but on the death of his wife drifted away into other employments. Having made the final payments on his land, and having inherited more land in the immediate neighborhood, he has now come back with a new wife, once more to try his luck at farming.

When we come to purchasers, we find only four unmortgaged farms, as against thirty-three mortgaged ones. The average size of the farms is very much smaller, being only one hundred and ten acres for the unmortgaged and about one hundred and fifty-seven acres for the mortgaged. The average debt per acre is higher than in either of the other classes; in fact, so much higher that, despite the comparative smallness of the farms, the average debt per farm is higher than elsewhere.

It has already been remarked that none of the settlers on government land are in poor circumstances, while among their ranks the great majority of the most prosperous farmers are to be found. Of the settlers on railroad land, nearly all would be included if they were as a class described as quite heavily mortgaged, but with debts not so great as to make it seem probable that any of them will be unable to extricate themselves with time. The only case here to be ranked among those whose future prospects are doubtful is that of a man whose agricultural experience has been very limited, and as he seems to have almost no capital, and labors under still other disadvantages, it is doubtful how long he will be able to hold out. But now, when we turn from the purchasers of land from the railroad company to class "C," the purchasers from other owners, we find as marked a change in conditions as we noticed in passing from class "A" to class "B." The mortgages are heavier, the well-to-do are comparatively rare, and there are many persons in very poor circumstances. In fact, there are quite a number with whom it seems to be only a question of time, and a short time at that, when they will have to give up their holdings. One is almost tempted to draw the moral that the would-be purchaser, at least the one whose means are not sufficient to pay entirely for his farm and then tide him over all subsequent periods of hard times, had almost better throw his money away than invest it in farming operations in Nebraska, at the current prices of land and under the present agricultural conditions; unless, indeed, he be possessed of unusual energy and ability. . . .

Conclusion

It remains now to summarize briefly the facts shown respecting the condition of the farmers in Harrison township since its settlement, with a view to learning something of the various economic influences that during that time have been operative upon western agriculture, as far as they may be exemplified in this township. As will be seen, our data permit us to examine only such influences as can be seen plainly at work in individual cases. Matters like the burden of indirect taxes, or the effect of changes in the value of the circulating medium, which can be observed only on the wide scale, are here excluded.

We have had before us a class of farmers owning lands of steadily increasing value. Of those who are still residents, about half got their lands either as gifts from the government, or on very easy terms from the Union Pacific Railway Company; the remainder purchased their farms from other owners than the railway company, at prices ranging from seven or eight dollars an acre in earlier times to twenty-five or thirty dollars in late years; in most cases these paid a good part of the purchase money in cash. The farmers of this township have on the average a little over a quarter section of land each, and usually from 125 to 135 acres in a quarter section is plow-land. A large proportion of the farms are mortgaged, and the debt on such as are mortgaged is on the average something over one-third the actual value of the farms. When a tract of land is once encumbered, the tendency is often for the mortgage on it to increase in size as the rise in the value of the security makes a larger loan possible. The mortgages on lands obtained from the government or the railway company are in general lighter than those on lands purchased from individual owners, and the condition of the farmers owning such lands is correspondingly more prosperous. This we find natural to a certain extent, inasmuch as purchasers are very rarely able to pay in full at the time of purchase, and so usually start out encumbered by a mortgage debt; but the frequent increase in the size of mortgages thus incurred, and the corresponding unprosperous condition of those who are to pay them, is indicative of the fact that in very many instances the real burden of a mortgage has been much greater than one would infer from the mere knowledge of its amount.

We must note, however, that there is among the residents of the township, as nearly as can be judged, a comparative freedom from floating debt. The chattel mortgage debt, of which the sum-total is comparatively small, is confined mainly to those most heavily burdened with debt on real estate, and can be interpreted in general as emphatic evidence of the poor financial condition of the least prosperous farmers.[8] The appreciation in the value of lands furnishes us the clue to the lack of floating debt among the more prosperous farmers; for whenever any amount of such debt has accumulated, the farmer, unless his land is already mortgaged to the maximum, is usually able to augment his loan on the basis of the increased value of the land, and, with the funds thus obtained, to pay off his smaller debts. This expedient is usually resorted to; for the rate of interest on the real estate loan is considerably less than that on smaller loans with other security, and there is in addition an advantage in being free from the annoyance of having continually to provide for the satisfaction of small debts coming due at frequently recurring intervals. As to improvements on land, our tables have indicated that these are much better on the farms of settlers on government land than on the farms of other classes, and that it is mainly on the farms of the later purchasers that the debt is not represented by improvements. We note that the number of resident owners has greatly decreased in late years, and also that the number of farmers failing in comparatively late years from what seemed unavoidable causes directly connected with their farming operations, has been larger than at any other period in the history of the township. The drought of 1890 had undoubtedly very much to do with this fact, but a cause is also to be found in the temporary cessation of increase in land value in the years just prior to 1890 or '91, and the consequent inability of the debtors to increase their loans so as to make good past deficiencies with the proceeds.

With the knowledge now arrived at of the condition of the farming classes, let us pass in review the various economic influences which have affected them so far as those influences are exhibited by the material collected in this monograph. What is said about these forces must be understood to apply to the farmers of normal ability, who have at their service an average amount of capital. Unusual shiftelessness or misfortunes may have accelerated the failure of some, and unusual ability may have given positive prosperity to other, but such elements we may for the time leave to a certain extent out of consideration. It seems sufficiently evident from Part II. of this paper that over and above those who have failed owing to personal causes, there are men whose ruin or financial embarrassment has had behind it causes which cannot be so localized; and their lack of success has been described as due to prevalent agricultural conditions, a phrase which we are now to analyze.

However, of the conditions possibly unfavorable to the farmer, we evidently have no data here from which to examine those which may be connected with the whole econony of our industrial society, such as indirect taxes, changes in the value of money, the modern distributive process, and perhaps also the influence on prices of the greatly increased production from the recently opened prairie states. Other matters, however, of a less wide-reaching character we are in a position fairly to examine.

From our account of the farmers' condition, it is clear that the central fact is the rise in the value of land. For it is this rise that has given the opportunity for the continued increase of mortgage debt; and even a temporary cessation in it has been followed by an increased number of failures among the farmers. We may almost infer that in many cases the greater part of the wealth that the farmer of average ability now has must be attributed to this rise in value; for very often the value of the improvements and personal property is covered by the mortgage debt, and this means that the amount of profits which have been realized and invested upon the farm has been very small. Indeed, in many cases the present farmer's equity in his land would be little or nothing were it not for this rise in value, while he would have been unable without it to obtain the means to reach even as advanced a system of cultivation as is in vogue at present. It must be admitted, however, that this conclusion will hold good only for the farmer of average ability. A man of poor personal habits, or one who is shiftless in his management, will dissipate the increment in the value of his land as fast as he can make use of it as security for new loans. On the other hand, a skilful, energetic, economical farmer, who knows how to avail himself of every advantage, will probably be able, with average good luck, to pay off in time even a heavy debt incurred in the purchase of his farm. But even with these qualifications, should fortune not favor him he may fail miserably; for he is dependent on credit, and credit, though it furnishes wings to the man fit to use them, so long as the wind of fortune is fair, becomes a dead weight to drag down the less able, or even the competent when fortune fails. If there were space to consider the individual cases of the farmers in Harrison township, we should find a few young men whose ability has been such as to enable them thus to overcome the hindrance of heavy debt at the start and become in the end prosperous farmers.

Probably the only other persons besides these exceptionally able ones who have succeeded in making considerable profits and saving any part of them are those farmers who received their land in early times from the government. These, having a clear start, were enabled in most cases to avoid the burden of heavy debt, and consequently, in a year of good crops, they could at once invest their profits permanently on their farms.

It may well seem that these statements in regard to the frequent unprofitableness of farming operations are not in harmony with such facts as that the market price of land is at present increasing rapidly, and that there is now a more eager demand for good agricultural land than has obtained for a number of years; and again that land is now being eagerly sought by renters who are willing to pay a larger proportion of the produce for rent than ever before, and who will in some cases even pay a quite high cash rent. It might be said that in order to occasion such a demand for lands to purchase and to rent, farming must be very profitable, or at least that the chances of high profits in it must be very good, and this would not agree with our preceding inferences. Attention should, however, be directed to one or two influences of importance which, apart from the profitableness of the investment, might create a high demand for land.

In the first place, although the available free government land has been practically exhausted, yet the tradition of cheap farms easily obtainable still lingers in the minds of the people, and so the home-seeker still turns his thoughts toward the West, where prices of land are really low in comparison with those current further east. But the conditions make it necessary for him to resort to new methods of acquiring the desired land. If he has some little capital he will probably try to purchase as large a farm as possible with what means he has at his disposal for the first cash payment; then, giving a mortgage for the balance of the purchase money, he will trust to Providence for the ability to meet the debt when it comes due. If the newcomer has not money enough to purchase land in any way, he will seek for a farm to rent with the hope that he may before long become an owner himself. In these facts we see a prominent reason why the demand for land may have increased without regard to the income produced by it, until its selling price, and as well its rental, have become much higher than the income really warrants. The possibility of such influences having their effect upon the demand for land is made greater by one of the characteristics of investment in farming operations, which may be specially mentioned; this is the slowness with which the true rate of agricultural profits can be estimated, owing to the great variations from year to year in the size of the crops and in the prices at which farm products will sell.

A special case of this migration of home-seekers to the newer western states is exemplified on a considerable scale by the large parties of farmers who at the present time (March, 1893) are leaving Illinois for Nebraska, the Dacotas, and neighboring states. As the value of land in such states as Illinois increases, the younger generation finds it constantly growing harder to acquire farm homes of their own. Consequently it often happens that the owner of a small farm sells it, perhaps to a non-resident landowner, and moves with his sons further west, where the proceeds from the old farm will purchase enough land for both father and sons.

But again, a cause for the increased demand for farming lands may be sought in the deeper relations underlying all industrial society. Farming may be an uncertain means of getting a living, and yet it, or the ideas of it current in the eastern states, may seem to many a laborer so much better than his existing lot, or may actually be such an improvement upon it, that he is only too glad to seek to better himself by means of it; and thus he helps to swell the already overcrowded ranks of agriculturalists, and so raises the price of their primary necessity—the land.

Though the special peculiarities in the character of the income derived from farming operations should by no means be left out of account in considering the status of the farmers, yet a brief mention of these peculiarities must suffice here. In the first place, the irregularity in the amount of the income from year to year has very important effects. Though even the tenant farmer may almost always feel confident that a sufficient supply of food is assured him, no matter how poor the crop, still every farmer is liable to have his year's profits totally wiped out, or even to suffer quite a heavy loss if the season should be very bad; for the margin between the normal net income and the sum of the living expenses and the interest on the investment is often very narrow. Thus while a well-to-do farmer may be able to recuperate in succeeding years from a heavy loss of crops, yet such a blow may be too great for one who is poorer or deeply indebted, and may effect his ruin before he has time to attempt to repair his losses. The effects of bad management in wiping out this margin of profit are very similar to those of bad seasons, and when poor management and poor crops are found in conjunction, there is little hope for the farmer.

It should be remarked, however, that while the crop failure of 1890 ruined many farmers who were already heavily encumbered with debt, still in some cases indirect results of a very different kind can be traced. For many of those farmers whose affairs were in moderately good condition and who had sufficient energy to cause them at once to set to work to recover their lost ground, have really profited by their experience. They have become much more conservative, and are less inclined to enter upon speculative transactions, especially where they would have to make use of credit. Consequently they will soon be in better position to resist heavy losses, should such again befall them.

Next, in regard to direct taxes, it has been seen that these are by no means so high as seriously to affect the farmer's prosperity, being probably in no case above four or five mills on the dollar of true valuation.

Freight rates have played a more important role, especially since of late years it has become necessary to ship large amounts of surplus products to distant markets; and they often absorb a large part of the gross price for which the product sells. Whether the responsibility for this deduction from the farmer's receipts lies with railroad companies which charge excessive rates, or with the conditions which make necessary the shipment of grain for such great distances, must be decided from other evidence than that which we have gathered.

The influence of the use, and more especially of the abuse, of credit will require a more extended treatment, for it is by no means a simple matter and needs to be looked at from several points of view. In the first place, the mere borrowing of money cannot be said to be in itself a harmful thing. Credit has a tendency to multiply as well the opportunities for gain of the man who makes use of it, as to make greater his dangers of loss; but it is only rarely that it can be called the direct cause of either gain or loss. Merely to say that the farmer pays too high interest for his money is in no way an explanation of his financial difficulties; for the rate of interest is adjusted by a competition acting with comparative freedom, and we must go back of it to consider the earning power of the material things in which the borrowed money is invested.

The economic significance of a mortgage debt depends partly on the previous financial condition of the debtor, but perhaps to a still greater extent on what is the corresponding item on the opposite side of his balance-sheet. As to this latter, we must consider whether there stands back of the debt an asset, the liquidation of a loss in the past, or a present personal expenditure. If the money is borrowed for either of the last two purposes, then the debt will be a dead weight, to be provided for from other sources. If the item offsetting it in the accounts is an asset, then one must consider further whether it has the actual present value of the debt; for in so far as it has not, the debt will be a drag, just as in the cases above. If the asset does actually have a value equal to the debt, then we must examine first whether it is likely to appreciate or depreciate, and second whether it is income-producing or not. If income-producing, then such income must be investigated as to its amount, as to the regularity with which it accrues, and the probability of its permanence.

Applying these principles, we shall be able to see why a mortgage bearing seven per cent interest, that represents in part a payment for high-priced land, in part a new house, and in part losses or expenses in excess of income, may perhaps be more burdensome to the farmer of to-day than a small loan at three per cent a month given by an early settler who had practically no means to obtain the funds to begin cultivation or even to make the first payment on cheap land. For the early settler could reasonably expect to make and save both principal and interest out of a single crop, while the variable income of the farmer to-day may often fall so low as to fail to yield sufficient surplus to pay the interest on that part of the debt which is represented by income-producing assets, much less on the remainder of it.

In the region which we are considering, capitalization of all agricultural property is too high (it has been previously maintained that the basis of capitalization is not so much income as a demand arising from other causes), and from this two results follow: first, that the rate of income from land is low compared to that from other investments, and second, that the marginal amount of money that can be borrowed on the land is high in just the proportion that the capitalization is high. Now under these circumstances let a farmer pay the rate of interest which is current in the money markets, and if the debt is large or long-continued, the tendency is for him steadily to lose. It must of course be remembered that agriculture is a highly uncertain occupation, so that a succession of good crops may entirely overcome this normal loss, or a succession of poor ones may greatly increase it.

What we have thus far said of the use of credit has been of such general application as to apply to all borrowers alike, but it will now be necessary to show how borrowing becomes a much greater evil to certain classes of farmers than to others. It is a fact often commented upon that the small *entrepreneur* who is out of debt takes pride in his condition and usually avoids investments or speculations which would make the use of credit necessary to him, while one who had once become heavily encumbered becomes callous to the inconveniences caused by his indebtedness, and often does not hesitate to plunge deeper if possible; moreover, the latter will become reckless in his speculations, because if he is successful the gain is his, and if he loses, much of the loss falls on his creditors. Now, as has before been pointed out, an exceptionally energetic man can sometimes attain prosperity even though he starts out with a heavy debt incurred for purchase money, and if he meets with good fortune he can gradually free himself from his burden. But under the prevailing conditions, the man of just ordinary ability, who is owing a heavy debt, will be more likely than not to allow it to grow continually larger; and not only will the effect of the debt be seen in making more grievous the ill effects of losses or misfortunes, but when a man's credit is exhausted or badly strained he will often be unable to avail himself of opportunities which he would otherwise have had to make profits, as for instance when he is forced to sell his grain at a low price when, had he been able to wait on the market, he could have realized a much larger sum.

Perhaps the effect of his debt on a heavily mortgaged man may be summed up by saying that in order to use the money profitably, the borrower must be a man of normal ability; if his qualities are exceptionally good he may profit greatly by his loan; but if they are under the average, or if fortune should go against him, his debt will almost surely operate to increase his troubles. Any man who undertakes farming in Nebraska at the present day requires, in order to be assured of success, at least three things,—first, that he have some little capital, second, that he possess good business qualificatons, and third, that he escape any extraordinary misfortunes. If he lack any one of these, or is seriously deficient in it, his success will be much retarded, if not rendered entirely impossible. And though the same statement would probably be true of almost any business enterprise, yet it seems clear from the facts that it applies with especial emphasis to the western agriculturalists of the present time.

Thus far what has been said in discussing the various economic influences at work has been said mainly from the point of view of the unsuccessful farmers. The term unsuccessful must not only be taken to include those who have failed completely owing to causes of a general nature or of nature not clearly personal (for these latter causes have been excluded from our consideration), but it also includes the many who are still struggling for success, though badly embarrassed by debt. In brief, it comprises all those who have to a greater or less extent fallen short of the measure of success which their efforts seemed to deserve. Nor should it be forgotten that to the men classed as successful the same conditions have applied as to the unsuccessful, though not with equal results; for the successful ones are those whose energy or business ability or external advantages have been so great as to enable them to overcome in some degree, at least, all the unfavorable influences.

And now let us see what this measure of success is which the more successful in the township have attained. The largest landowner among them has 480 acres of land, while only four or five, all told, own over 240 acres apiece. Of those who have more than one quarter section of land, the great majority have had some exceptional advantage, such as a capital greater than the average, when they first came to the country, or external help of some kind, as land or money received by inheritance, or they have been men of exceptional thrift. In no case can the improvements be called more than comfortable, and it is rare to find an exceptionally good house without noticing that the outbuildings have to some extent been sacrificed to it, or *vice versa*. In few cases will the income from his farm support the owner after he has retired from active life. To the writer it seems that the condition of the successful farmers more strongly indicates the disadvantages under which they have labored than the condition of the more or less unsuccessful ones. For here we see good business men who have carefully labored for many years, and who come now toward the close of their active careers, feeling fortunate if their farms are unencumbered and their property sufficient to support them in their old age, while they live with their descendants who have taken their places in the active operations of agriculture. It is true these men have had little inherited wealth behind them, but they are among the men who have helped to build up a new country, and who, it would seem, should have as much share in the prosperity of the new territory they have helped to open, as those who cast their lot with the towns and cities.

The farmer who has once become fairly well equipped, and who is not burdened with a heavy debt, has, it is true, certain advantages which make his lot in some ways quite desirable. If not in debt, he feels sure of a comfortable living even in poor years, and a small deficit is easily tided over. Moreover, he is in a position to make advantageous use from time to time of a small line of credit for temporary purposes; and, being able to get money at very low rates, may sometimes be able to make very profitable investments.

As compared with the pioneer farmer of twenty years ago, the farmer of to-day requires a much larger capital, and in consequence the cost of production of the grain that he raises is higher. Not only is it found necessary to give the land slightly more cultivating, but also there must be figured into the cost the interest on the investment in the land, which was very small in the early days, but is of considerable importance now. Then the standard of living, by which each family gauges its expenditure, is much higher than formerly, and the enforced economies of the pioneer period cannot be practiced, and indeed ought not to be demanded or expected. The markets are no better to-day than before. In short, if the farmer of to-day expects to achieve the same success as the pioneer achieved, he must, except where good fortune and the possession of unusual personal qualities are combined, have capital in sufficient amount to offset the free land and low cost of living of the pioneer period.

Notes

1. The term "speculator," as used here and at other places in this paper, always refers to residents. It includes both those who took government land and resided thereon just long enough to "prove up," and those who, coming later and purchasing land from the railroad company or from other settlers, had a speculation as their prime motive, but who really made their living out of the farms for one or more years, while waiting for an opportunity to sell at a profit.

2. *The Forum*, Vol. VIII., No. 5.

3. For fuller tables see "Statistical Information Pertaining to Chicago Markets," Howard, Bartels & Co., Chicago.

4. It must, however, be remembered that the through rates are not strictly to be found by adding the local Nebraska rates to the Omaha-Chicago rates, there being usually some deduction for through traffic.

5. In making comparisons with the preceding table, figure wheat at 60 lbs. per bushel, oats at 32 lbs., and corn (shelled) at 56 lbs.

6. In this table the percentage of partial payments has not been deducted, as the figures are used only for comparison, and by omitting this deduction the matter is much simplified.

7. The mortgages against these five men cover 480 acres of their lands, and, the total amount of their debt being $3950, the average amount they owe on each mortgaged acre is $8.23.

8. However, in a more recently settled township, or in a township where the farmers were in the habit of buying cattle on a large scale to feed, on credit, this rule would not hold.

Reconsidering the Populists

Oscar Handlin

The economic distress suffered by the farmers of Harrison township (and the comparable hardships in the cotton district of the South) gave rise to the Populist movement, which, during the 1890s, threatened a major upheaval of the nation's political and economic life. The movement had a short life: partial absorption by the Democrats, the election of 1896, and then the rise of farm prices killed Populism before it reached full stride. But the problems of historical explanation have not died. Populism has proved to be one of the most intractable issues of late nineteenth century historiography; indeed, of all American history. Part of the difficulty arises from the multilayered nature of Populism. It aimed at easing the economic problems of the farmers. But it also stood for major political reform and, beyond that, for radical change of the entire economic order. Populism also generated a rhetorical and crusading zeal that seemed to hold implications alien to the American reform tradition. What meaning and significance are to be assigned to these elements, not to say how are they to be united into a coherent whole? To compound the problems of interpretation, Populism evoked powerful responses pro and con in its own time, and became afterward one of those historical events whose meaning seemed deeply relevant to contemporary life. So historians have tended to approach Populism not with cool detachment, but on the contrary with the battle cries of their own time ringing in their ears. All of this has combined to give a remarkable turbulence to Populist historiography, especially in recent years.

The first generation of historians, writing from a perspective of hard-money conservatism, treated Populism as an agrarian aberration, a cranky and unreasoning attack on monetary responsibility, and one fully meriting national repudiation. Historians of the Progressive era, especially under the influence of Charles A. Beard and Frederick Jackson Turner, treated Populism as a central event in American liberal reform, and stressed especially the contribution it made to subsequent political and economic change. The classic exposition of this view is John D. Hicks' *The Populist Revolt* (1931). The fireworks really began after World War II, with the publication of Richard Hofstadter's *Age of Reform* (1955). Hofstadter was writing under the shadow of McCarthyism, and his

Oscar Handlin, "Reconsidering the Populists," *Agricultural History*, XXXIX (1965), pp. 68-74. Reprinted by permission of the publisher.

particular concern was to find the roots of this frightening phenomenon. His key idea was to distinguish between conventional "interest" politics—in which people act in rational response to perceived economic interests—and another mode of politics in which people act, in response to social or psychological concerns, usually without a clear perception of their motives. This second form of politics Hofstadter applied to Populism (and, in the guise of status politics, to Progressivism). Pointing to the agrarian rhetoric, the cataclysmic thinking, the belief in conspiracy, the apparent anti-semitism, Hofstadter suggested that psychological motives had activated Populism, and given it a distinctly illiberal cast. (Elsewhere, Hofstadter was more explicit in locating the roots of the modern radical right in the Populist tradition.) Others took up Hofstadter's theme, often without his careful qualifications and distinctions. In the heated debate which ensued, much effort was devoted to attacks on the accuracy of Hofstadter's dark characterization of Populism. Perhaps the best example is Walter Nugent's *The Tolerant Populists* (1963). Much of this response aimed at restoring Populism to its place in the liberal reform tradition, but in the case of Norman Pollack, the objective was to identify Populism as a genuine radical movement, which is the theme of his *Populist Response to Industrialism* (1966). The sum of all this scholarly debate, unfortunately, does not seem to have advanced our understanding of Populism very far, although it has drawn attention to the complexities of the subject, and there are hopeful signs of greater sophistication in the most recent work such as for example, in Sheldon Hackney's *Populism to Progressivism in Alabama* (1969).

Given the tangled state of current Populist historiography, Oscar Handlin's plea for restraint in the following essay has particular value. Handlin, of course, does not come to the debate an entirely disinterested observer. His 1951 article on Populist attitudes towards the Jews provided some of the groundwork for Hofstadter's thesis, and was subsequently the target for sharp criticism. Handlin in fact takes pains to show—quite rightly—the distortion to which his analysis was subjected, and to make this an instance of the kind of partisam history against which his essay is directed. Certainly Handlin is right in his conclusions that Populism will be fully understood only when historians stop treating it in terms of good and bad and start exploring the social and institutional context from which the movement arose.

For further reading, in addition to the preceding works cited: Chester M. Destler, *American Radicalism: 1865-1901* (1946);* Michael P. Rogin, *The Intellectuals and McCarthy: the Radical Specter* (1967);* Theodore Saloutos, "The Professors and the Populists," *Agricultural History*, XL (1966), 235-254; C. Vann Woodward, "The Populist Heritage and the Intellectual," *American Scholar*, XXIX* (1959-1960), 55-72; Victor C. Ferkiss, "Populist Influences on American Fascism," *Western Political Quarterly*, X (1957), 350-357; Norman Pollack, ed., *The Populist Mind* (1967);* ——, "The Myth of Populist Anti-Semitism," *American Historical Review*, XLVIII (1962), 76-80.

The treatment of American populism in the last three decades reveals the extent to which history is still far from being a cumulative science which steadily refines the understanding of the past through successive scholarly discoveries. If any figure of speech is appropriate, it is that of the treadmill, with regressions and standstills as frequent as advances. A good deal has been written on the subject; progress, alas, has been slight.

Most of the difficulty arises from a pervasive Manichaeanism which interprets history as the battlefield between the forces of light and those of darkness—the good guys against the bad guys. In this drama, which can be pushed indefinitely back into the past, the honest, the altruistic and the patriotic constantly battle the greedy and the corrupt in defense of national virtue. This formulation has the virtue of simplicity and of clear identification of heroes and villains; its drawback lies in its slight correspondence with actuality.

The heated emotions the populist movement aroused among contemporaries have extended into the historical literature. Although the political issues of the 1890's have faded, the heat they engendered persists.

Well before the New Deal, the populists had captured the sympathy of the American historian.[1] Their agrarianism, their advocacy of the cause of the oppressed poor, their situation as game independents facing up to the entrenched and powerful, and their spontaneous grassroots origins gave them a heroic cast in the accounts of writers influenced by progressive ideas. Charles A. Beard summarized the prevailing attitude in *The Rise of American Civilization*: The populists were the culmination of the long history of agrarian protest and an integral element in the struggle for American democracy. A more definitive academic statement of this position came from John Hicks in 1931. "Thanks to this triumph of Populist principles, one may almost say that, in so far as political devices can insure it, the people now rule . . . the acts of government have come to reflect fairly clearly the will of the people."[2]

Such firm commitments have impeded every effort to interpret the character of the movement. Each bit of fresh evidence must meet the test of whether it casts the populists in the role of heroes or villains.[3] The result is a sterile round of argument that has added little to the understanding of the subject.

The extended—and pointless—discussion of whether the populists were anti-Semitic is a glaring illustration. In 1951, when I attempted to assess the attitude of Americans towards Jews at the end of the nineteenth century, I found that by 1900, "the favorable prevailing temper of tolerance had produced a great willingness to accept the Jew as a desirable and equal participant in the emerging culture of the nation." But, I added, widely held stereotypes, which in the 1890's were not derogatory in intent, provided the materials which anti-Semites would use after 1910. The attitudes of the populists were no different from those of any other group except insofar as their insistence upon a bankers' conspiracy deepened the popular image of the mysterious international Jew. Nothing in the subsequent literature has in the least challenged those conclusions.[4]

Instead, it was necessary to ascribe to me views I did not express, so that they could be refuted. If Professor Nugent concluded that I wrote that the populists "swum with the racist current of the period" and "were personally guilty of some degree of overt anti-Semitism," it was not from anything he read in my text, but from the exigencies of his own argument.[5]

The need to cast the populists as either heroes or villains turned the discussion about the false question of whether they were proto-Nazis or tolerant. Richard Hofstadter, using essentially the same evidence as I, added the pejorative designation "anti-Semitism," although he qualified his characterization more carefully than his critics think. The choice of that term was unfortunate for it stirred up a hornet's nest. Vann Woodward, Norman Pollack, John Higham and Walter T. K. Nugent in their zeal to defend the populists have thoroughly befogged the issue.[6]

The tortuous apologetics of the defenders are wider of the mark than Hofstadter's blanket indictment. John Higham, for instance, clamps the whole subject into a dubious cyclical device. To relieve the agrarians of blame, he argues that the patrician intellectuals and the underprivileged masses of the cities of the east "were more deeply engaged in ethnic conflict" and therefore more venomous and fierce in their anti-Semitism than the rural radicals or rustic pamphleteers of the west. But in any case, he argues, anti-Semitism could not have been activated by decisive internal forces because it "ebbed and flowed on an international level," rising everywhere in the 1880's and 1890's and declining between 1900 and 1918.[7]

It takes utter disregard of the evidence to contrive this apologia. There was no advance in anti-Semitism in the last two decades of the nineteenth century; and the period in which Higham asserts that "anti-Semitism made no significant advances" was uncomfortably marked by the East Side riots, the Leo Frank case and the first overt discrimination in employment. Actually, anti-Semitism slowly took form in the first decade of the twentieth century, gained strength in the second, and reached the peak of its intensity in the 1920's and 1930's. No cycles—however useful Higham may find them in obscuring the "American traditions, circumstances, or habits of mind" by which populists and others prepared the ground for anti-Semitism in the United States![8]

The supererogatory task of refuting the charge of populist anti-Semitism also leads to other extraordinary perversions. To demonstrate the benign intentions of *Caesar's Column*, Walter Nugent explains that, "The idea that the Jewish nation was reborn out of the revolution's chaos . . . showed Donnelly's admiration for the ancient chosen people." Reference to the passage in question reveals the quality of that admiration. Donnelly has the revolutionary Jew abscond with "one hundred million dollars that had been left in his charge. . . . He took several of his trusted followers, of his own nation, with him" and proposed to "revive the ancient splendors of the Jewish race, in the midst of the ruins of the world." Those who seek—needlessly—to rehabilitate the populists can even believe that an author "used the word 'Shylock' about a dozen and a half times but never made it specifically Jewish."[9] What a mass of error would be cleared up by the recognition that the populists were neither exceptionally tolerant nor exceptionally prejudiced! They shared the attitudes of most other Americans before 1900. On this issue, there was a "consensus."

The same defensive attitude has confused his critics with reference to a much more important element in Hofstadter's account—the incisive analysis of the irrational element in populist thought. The idea that politicians were subject to other than rationally calculated drives is not after all in itself startling; populists, like Democrats and Republicans, were human beings. Yet the suggestion that their agrarianism or their belief in an Anglo-Wall Street conspiracy did not rest on pure reason alone has evoked an instinctive response which justifies them as farsighted men whose analysis of the problems of their time was essentially correct. Professor Pollack, for instance, feels compelled to demonstrate that they were progressive (or radical or socialist) in order to prove that they were not a "source for later proto-fascist groups, McCarthyism, anti-Semitism, xenophobia, and anti-intellectualism."[10]

The techniques of defense are significant. The standards of judgment applied to the populists differ from those used for their opponents. There is an assumption that the reforms proposed were self-evidently valid. And indefensible ideas are written off as irrelevant eccentricities.

Protestations of concern for the interests of the people and for the general welfare were part of the common rhetoric of politicians and businessmen in the last quarter of the nineteenth century. John D. Rockefeller was not a hypocrite when he described himself as steward of God's gold, nor was James G. Blaine when he proclaimed his intention "to elevate and dignify labor—not to degrade it." [11] Nevertheless, however sincere were these statements, the historian will not overlook personal ambition or class and sectional motives in accounting for the actions of the men who made them. By the same token, he ought not explain the behavior of the farmers, editors and lawyers who became populists by their expressions of belief in "the brotherhood of man." No party was free of politicians who sought passes from the railroads or were willing to take flyers in mineral lands or who proved corrupt and inept or who were able to "work both sides of the street" or who balanced tickets and sought the votes of Negro and immigrant groups while opposing the entry of non-existent contract laborers and condoning segregation. [12] To take professions of virtue and of disinterestedness in the case of any of them—whether Wall Street bankers or populists—is hazardous.

Too often also the defenders have uncritically assumed that the populists were correct in their assessment of the problems they faced and the reforms they advocated. Certainly in the periods of falling prices and depression of the 1880's and 1890's, American farmers, like American laborers, had genuine grievances; but it does not follow that they understood their own situation or that their "folk-wisdom" provided them with simple solutions to complex philosophical questions. [13]

"What really irked them," writes Professor Nugent, "was not commerce, but the abuse of commerce, not loans and interest but usury, not banking but special privilege, not enterprise but speculation"—as if those differentiations were clear and precise. [14] It is easy enough to paraphrase the populist literature in denunciations of "monopoly" and in demands for the "equitable distribution of wealth"; it is not so easy to determine just what those concepts meant.

When it comes to specifics, the failure of analysis is glaring. "More and more wealth of all kinds was concentrating in fewer and fewer hands." "Who does not know that no man can be nominated for president by either party who is not approved by the money power of New York and Boston? Who does not know that the railroad barons, democrats and republicans though they be, are ONE in the halls of Congress?" [15] The Senate was a corrupt rich men's club; political machines perverted democracy; not overproduction but plutocratic monopoly, deflation and excessive distribution costs caused the farmers' difficulties. These judgments are accepted as statements of fact with scarcely any effort to go beyond the data presented by their advocates. Nor is there any more careful scrutiny of the remedies proposed. The direct election of senators and the primary would reform politics; monetary inflation, cooperatives and government ownership would raise farm incomes and lower consumer prices. [16]

Can we assume that the advocates of those changes were wiser, more enlightened, more concerned with the public welfare than the opponents? In the perspective of the experience of the past half-century, these propositons are by no means self-evident. Direct election has not altered the character of the Senate and the primary has not weakened the political machine. Agricultural surpluses have not disappeared, cooperatives have had a negligible effect on distribution costs, and government ownership, to the extent that it was adopted, caused no cures. The discrepancy between results and expectations is not decisive—conditions have changed since the 1890's—but it is a warning against the passive assumption that the populists understood what ailed them or knew what was good for them. It certainly leaves open the possibility that the populists may have clung to their nostrums for reasons that were as non-rational as those which attached the goldbug or Bourbon to his own.

Finally, the defensive accounts obscure, or write off as harmless eccentricities, the inexplicable peculiarities of some of the populists. Thus Mary Ellen Lease's racist visions of world conquest and Ignatius Donnelly's belief in the lost continent of Atlantis or in the Baconian authorship of Shakespeare's plays seem altogether irrelevant. Walter Nugent shrugs when the populist legislature of Kansas, elected in 1896, failed to enact a railroad regulation bill and launched into a debate on a measure "to give statutory force to the ten commandments." Vann Woodward argues that the two parts of Tom Watson's life are unconnected and he finds no meaning in his subject's worship of Napoleon. [17] These aberrations become negligible in the eyes of those who feel the need to justify the populists.

Apologia has obscured the genuine problems that the scholars now concerned with populism ought to address. Once we cease to worry about whether the populists were more farsighted and more virtuous than their contemporaries, we shall be able to confront the characteristics really distinctive of the movement.

Populism drew together many discontented elements in American society—farmers, laborers, social reformers and intellectuals. The very diversity of these groups renders futile the quest for a single ideology among them. Socialists and currency men, Bellamy Nationalists and Knights of Labor could unite in complaints against the contemporary capitalism and in resentment of the moral deficiences of the new wealth but not in their vision of the future; significantly, Norman Pollack's book which seeks to define such an ideology deals with criticism of existing conditions, not with proposals for the future. [18]

The process of voicing these grievances produced not a common set of ideas but a common style. Populist literature and oratory were laden with a rhetoric that appealed to the emotions. The audience was again and again summoned to "put on the bright armour of chivalry, ride forth to the rescue and smite the dungeon-door with the battle-axe of Lionheart." It therefore responded with "impulsiveness and emotionalism" to "anything from an economic doctrine to a political platform." What was true of Kansas was often true elsewhere; the election of 1890 could "hardly be diagnosed as a political campaign. It was a religious revival, a crusade, a pentecost of politics in which a tongue of flame sat upon every man, and each spake as the spirit gave him utterance." Senator Peffer once explained that "the Alliance is in a great measure taking the place of the churches"; he was correct in more ways than he knew. The style had recognizable antecedents as far back as the Great Awakening. And it was particularly compelling for those in the audience reared in the evangelical denominations. [19]

Sensational revelations of conspiracies which threatened the safety of the republic spiced the treatises on money or on the trusts. The authors and speakers were, of course, sincere; they believed absolutely in the gospel for which they sought converts. But the villainies they exposed did not become known through research or investigation; although some of the authors worked industriously to compile their data, in the end the consipiracy of the gold gamblers could only be inferred. But it had to be true because only thus could the discrepancy between events and faith be reconciled.[20]

The populist faith rested consistently upon one article: the competence of the common man—in whom a divine spark dwelt—to deal adequately with all the problems of life. Control by the mass of the people could solve every difficulty; the direct election of Senators, the primary, cooperatives and government owenrship were ultimately means of establishing that control. The voice of the people was the voice of God, even when it would, later, be sounded by a lynching mob.[21]

Most populists in the 1890's, however, learned to accept a distinction between the people as they were and as they should be, if for no other reason than because the majority voted incorrectly. "The very fool workingmen who are deprived of the means of subsistence will continue to vote for the perpetuation of the system which is constantly adding to the number of unemployed just as often as they get a chance," wrote the Topeka *Advocate*.[22]

The populist could only explain away the failure of the people to elect those who would best serve them by references to the corrupting power of conspiracy. And he had no doubt about who were the unregenerate and who the redeemed. "The government is the *people* and *we* are the people," announced Jerry Simpson. "Old man Peepul is on top. Aunt Sarah Jane is on top. We country folks are on top, and everybody is going to be happy." Virtue was safe on the farm, in danger in the urban setting. An agrarian promised land was the true home of the people; the apocalyptic visions of *Caesar's Column* exposed the alternative. Hence the hostility to the city, the resentment of its power to draw men from the farms and the mistrust of the strange populace that clustered there.[23]

The awareness that the people as they were were not the same as the people as they should have been also turned many populists against the institutions which deceived and misled as well as oppressed the common man. The business corporations, entrenched in Wall Street, were an obvious target: but the mistrust and hostility also spilled over to the hireling subsidized press, to the universities and occasionally to the churches which were all tools of the capitalists and unresponsibe to the popular will.

One can neither accept these categorizations at face value as valid nor dismiss them offhand as aberrations. Properly viewed, the relationship of the populists to the social institutions of their complex society can shed light on both the movement and the objects of its attack.

The bitterness of the attack is comprehensible in terms of the lack of understanding on the part of the opponents of the populists. The scorn and sometimes the practical penalties visited upon the dissidents were enough to account for their resentment. But, in addition, significant changes in the institutional life of the nation made the position of those who did not fit uncomfortable. The elaboration of a formal network of organization and of communication the articulation of particular elements into a highly structured system, professionalism, and the appearance of centralized controls were novel and tended to separate institutions from the life of the people. But these developments were not the products of any conscious plot, nor did they result in the dominance of the plutocrats. The populists sensed, but neither understood nor knew how to deal with, the growing distance between institutions and people."[24]

Their sweeping mistrust of the social and cultural authority being established in these years led to a total reliance upon common sense, unfettered by external discipline. The professors who were wrong on the question of silver were also in error on the authorship of *Hamlet*. The same kind of reasoning led Donnelly to his conclusions in both cases. The eccentricities referred to earlier were the direct product of the rejection of the standards sustained by the dominant institutions of the nation. More important, the populists could not perceive that within the respectable churches and universities and even within some of the great business corporations important forces were at work to give these institutions a new sense of social purpose.

The political party was the institution with which the populists were most involved—first in the effort to capture control from within, then in the formation of a separate organization, and finally in the fusion of 1896. Yet while the course of specific campaigns has been exhaustively studied, we still lack an adequate analysis of the political party as a functioning institution in this period. It is significant that Professor Hicks' judgment has been allowed to stand: "Populist propaganda in favor of independent voting did much to undermine the intense party loyalties that had followed in the wake of the Civil War." Indeed, Professor Pollack seems to assume that there was "a need for the formation of a third party" in the 1890's, although he also argues that there was not a need for a third party in 1896.[25]

Yet in these years the Democratic and Republican organizations took their modern form and the two-party system became firmly entrenched in American politics. The pressures that operated on the dominant parties also affected the populists and—in ways that have not yet been explored—markedly influenced both tactics and objectives. For instance, an examination of the situation in the national and state legislatures of the populists as politicians and not as reformers would throw light on the fluctuations in their support in 1894 and on the maneuvers that led to fusion two years later. Professor Hollingsworth has called attention to the failures of leadership in this period; we need also to know why so much more was demanded of it.[26]

Above all, we need to know far more than we do about the audience that responded to populist appeals. Their statements of grievances are eloquent evidence of the economic hardships these people suffered. But this is partial evidence only and must be filled out from other sources. Complaints of debt are frequent, for instance; but we have only fragmentary information on the process by which indebtedness snowballed. Ben Tillman traced his personal downfall back to 1881 when "the devil tempted me to buy a steam engine and other machinery, amounting to two thousand dollars, all on credit." The devil, in the guise of a city slicker, has remained a convenient scapegoat; one scholar has concluded that an "avalanche of credit" from the east tempted the western farmers "to extravagance, over-investment and speculation."[27]

Such explanations tell only half the story. Why did some agriculturalists and not others yield to temptation? Why was the incidence of debt high not in the poorest sections but in those in which land values rose rapidly? Studies like those of Allan Bogue reveal that interest rates were falling and that it was by no means a simple matter to attract eastern or European funds into the west. And the farmers were by no means reluctant victims. Tillman himself recalled that, "My motto was, 'It takes money to make money, and nothing risk nothing have'." Denunciations of the competitive system were readily heard in hard times, but a speculative, acquisitive atmosphere seemed characteristic of many regions just before they turned populist and just after they left the faith. It would help to know to what extent the farmers—and editors, lawyers, doctors and small-town businessmen—who became populists remained spiritually boomers and sooners.[28]

We catch only fragmentary glimpses, beneath the definable economic grievances, of more pervasive causes of discontent. However idyllic the images of the happy husbandman, the audience knew well enough the isolation of the Great Plains, the dreariness of life in the rural South, the debilitating effects of illness, the devastation of climatic disasters. No change in railroad rate or cotton prices could transform these harsh conditions. The alliances, like the granges earlier, were social before they were political organizations; and perhaps the intensity of the emotions of their members owed something to the repressed consciousness that some among their problems were utterly beyond their control.[29]

In sum, what is called for is an effort to understand rather than to defend or attack the populists. They were neither saints nor sinners, but men responding to the changes that were remaking America in their time. They have to be comprehended in that light.

Notes

1. Van Woodward is in error in the chronology of the shifts in attitude toward the populists ("The Populist Heritage and the Intellectual," *American Scholar*, XXIX [1959-60], 55 ff.).

2. Charles A. and Mary R. Beard, *Rise of American Civilization* (New York, 1927), II, 278 ff., 556 ff.; John D. Hicks, *Populist Revolt* (Minneapolis, 1931), 422; John D. Hicks, "The Persistence of Populism," *Minnesota History*, XII (1931), 3 ff.; John D. Hicks, "The Legacy of Populism in the Western Middle West," *Agricultural History*, XXIII (1949), 225 ff.

3. See the candid account in Walter T. K. Nugent, *The Tolerant Populists; Kansas Populism and Nativism* (Chicago, 1963), 3 ff.

4. Oscar Handlin, "American Views of the Jew at the Opening of the Twentieth Century," *Publications of the American Jewish Historical Society*, XL (1951), 323 ff. To keep the chronology accurate, it is well to point out that this essay was written before the onset of the McCarthyite hysteria. See also Oscar Handlin, "How U.S. Anti-Semitism Really Began," *Commentary*, XI (1951), 541 ff.; and *Adventure in Freedom* (New York, 1954), 174 ff.

5. Nugent, *Tolerant Populists*, 15, 16.

6. Richard Hofstadter, *Age of Reform* (New York, 1955), 61 ff., 76 ff.; C. Vann Woodward, "Populist Heritage and the Intellectual," *American Scholar*, XXIX, 55 ff.; Norman Pollack, "Hofstadter on Populism," *Journal of Southern History*, XXVI (1960), 478 ff.; and "Myth of Populist Anti-Semitism," *American Historical Review*, LXVIII (1962), 76 ff.; John Higham, "Anti-Semitism in the Gilded Age." *Mississippi Valley Historical Review*, XLIII (1957), 559 ff.; and "Social Discrimination against Jews in America," *Publication of the American Jewish Historical Society*, XLVII (1957), 1 ff.

7. Higham, "Anti-Semitism," *M.V.H.R.*, XLIII, 571, 572 ff.; Woodward, "Populist Heritage and the Intellectual," *American Scholar*, XXIX, 64.

8. Higham, "Anti-Semitism," *M.V.H.R.*, XLIII, 571; Higham, "Social Discrimination," *Jewish Historical Society*, XLVII, 13 ff.

9. Nugent, *Tolerant Populists*, 113; Ignatius Donnelly, *Caesar's Column* (W. B. Rideout, ed., Cambridge, 1960), 283. Pollack similarly misstates the case when he asserts, "Donnelly never attacked radical Jews" ("Myth of Populist Anti-Semitism," *Am. Hist. Rev.*, LXVIII, 78).

10. Norman Pollack, *Populist Response to Industrial America* (Cambridge, 1962), 6.

11. James G. Blaine, *Words on the Issues of the Day* (Boston, 1884), 285.

12. Pollack, *Populist Response*, 14; Nugent, *Tolerant Populists*, 78, 131, 150, 203 ff.; Hicks, *Populist Revolt*, 71; Roscoe C. Martin, *People's Party in Texas* (Austin, 1933), 94 ff., 111 ff., 226 ff.; Jack Abramowitz. "The Negro in the Agrarian Revolt," *Agricultural History*, XXIV (1950), 95, n. 47; Francis B. Simkins, *The Tillman Movement in South Carolina* (Durham, 1926), 140 ff.; Martin Ridge, *Ignatius Donnelly* (Chicago, 1962), 305. On the contract laborers, see Charlotte Erickson, *American Industry and the European Immigrant* (Cambridge, 1957).

13. Pollack, *Populist Response*, 7, 9.

14. Nugent, *Tolerant Populists*, 95 ff.

15. Nugent, *Tolerant Populists*, 103; Pollack, *Populist Response*, 79.

16. James C. Malin, "Mobility and History," *Agricultural History*, XVII (1943), 178; Pollack, "Hofstadter on Populism," *Journ. So. Hist.*, XXVI, 490. For studies which cast doubt upon these propositions, see Chester M. Destler, "Agricultural Readjustment and Agrarian Unrest in Illinois," *Agricultural History*, XXI (1947), 107 ff.; Theodore Saloutos, "The Agricultural Problems and Nineteenth-Century Industrialism," *Agricultural History*, XXII (1948), 162 ff., 166 ff.; Ralph A. Smith, " 'Macuneism' or the Farmers of Texas in Business," *Journal of Southern History*, XIII (1947), 243, 244. On money, see Milton Friedman and Anna J. Schwartz, *Monetary History of the United States 1867-1960* (Princeton, 1963), 91 ff., 113 ff., 119 ff.; Charles Hoffman, "The Depression of the Nineties," *Journal of Economic History*, XVI (1956), 164. The best summary of national data is still Fred A. Shannon, *The Farmer's Last Frontier* (New York, 1945), 291 ff. which, however, takes for granted such assumptions as that ton-mile rates should have been the same throughout the country.

17. Nugent, *Tolerant Populists*, 204; Woodward, "Populist Heritage and the Intellectual," *American Scholar*, XXIX, 67.

18. Pollack, *Populist Response, passim*; Destler, "Agricultural Readjustment," *Agricultural History*, XXI, 115; Chester M. Destler, *American Radicalism 1865-1901* (New London, 1946), 15 ff.

19. C. Vann Woodward, *Tom Watson, Agrarian Rebel* (New York, 1938), 41, 138, 139; Hicks, *Populist Revolt*, 159.

20. Norman Pollack is himself the victim of the same faulty logic, "Hofstadter on Populism," *Journ. So. Hist.*, XXVI, 493; Paul W. Glad, *Trumpet Soundeth; William Jennings Bryan and His Democracy, 1896-1912* (Lincoln, 1960), 49 ff.

21. Woodward, *Watson*, 445; R. C. Miller, "Background of Populism in Kansas," *Mississippi Valley Historical Review*, XI (1925), 469 ff.; Glad, *Trumpet Soundeth*. 34.

22. Pollack, *Populist Response*, 62.

23. Nugent, *Tolerant Populists*, 77; Woodward, *Watson*, 428.

24. See, e.g., Simkins, *Tillman Movement*, 142 ff.; Ridge, *Donnelly*, 209, 264, 266, 370.

25. Hicks, *Populist Revolt*, 409; Pollack, "Hofstadter on Populism," *Journ. So. Hist.*, XXVI, 487, 498.

26. J. Rogers Hollingsworth, *The Whirligig of Politics* (Chicago, 1963), 235 ff.; Woodward, *Watson*, 278 ff.; George H. Mayer, *The Republican Party* (New York, 1964), 243 ff.; Stanley L. Jones, *Presidential Election of 1896* (Madison, 1964), 77 ff., 246 ff.; Martin, *People's Party in Texas*, 141 ff.

27. Simkins, *Tillman Movement*, 51; Hicks, *Populist Revolt*, 23.

28. Allan G. Bogue, *Money at Interest* (Ithaca, 1955), 83 ff., 263 ff., 269 ff.; Allan G. Bogue, *From Prairie to Corn Belt; Farming on the Illinois and Iowa Prairies in the Nineteenth Century* (Chicago, 1963), 177; Malin, "Mobility and History," *Agricultural History*, XVII, 181 ff.; Simkins, *Tillman Movement*, 51 ff.: Pollack, *Populist Response*, 18, 27; Nugent, *Tolerant Populists*, 54 ff.; Hofstadter, *Age of Reform*, 42, 58; Martin Ridge, *Ignatius Donnelly*, 17 ff.; Glad, *Trumpet Soundeth*, 46; Woodward, "Populist Heritage and the Intellectual," *American Scholar*, XXIX, 62.

29. Hicks, *Populist Revolt*, 128 ff.; William D. Sheldon, *Populism in the Old Dominion* (Princeton, 1935), 40 ff.; Theodore Saloutos, *Farmer Movements in the South 1865-1933* (Berkeley, 1960), 69 ff.

Part III
City dwellers

Building American cities

Edward C. Kirkland

The United States experienced an enormous urban growth in the late nineteenth century: city population multiplied fivefold between 1860 and 1900. It is a truism, of course, to connect urbanization with the industrial development proceeding so rapidly in this era. But of what, precisely, did this connection consist? Historians have stressed the ways industrialism tended to concentrate population. This actually had not been so before the Civil War, when manufacturing tended to be dispersed so as to be close to raw materials (as in the iron industry) or at waterpower sites (as in the case of textiles). Improved transportation and new power sources, first steam and then electricity, permitted the concentration of industrial activity, and the growing scale of production further increased the factory populations in industrial centers. But, if industrialization thus stimulated urban growth, there were other aspects to the relationship.

In the following essay, one of the most valuable chapters in his *Industry Comes of Age*, Edward C. Kirkland shifts the focus to the building of American cities and, by so doing, opens up for consideration some overlooked connections between urbanism and industrialism. The late nineteenth century saw a great upsurge of city construction: the value of building permits in 1890 was greater than for any year prior to 1925; the massive water and sanitation systems now were constructed; and there was a huge investment in electrification and rapid transit. This urban building, Kirkland points out, was decisive in sustaining the nation's industrial expansion in the 1880s and after, at a time when railroad construction, the primary economic stimulus of the post-Civil War decade, was on the wane. So the cities were as much the cause as they were the result of industrial growth. There was also a striking parallel between urban and industrial expansion. The latter depended heavily, as we have seen, on technological innovation, but so, in fact, did the former. Before the city could expand beyond the limitations of size that operated in the first half of the nineteenth century, a wide range of technological problems had to be overcome relating to sanitation, mass transportation, communications, and high-rise construction. The Gilded Age city was as much an arena for technological innovation,

From *Industry Comes of Age: Business, Labor, and Public Policy, 1860-1897*, by Edward C. Kirkland. Copyright ©1961 by Holt, Rinehart and Winston, Inc., pp. 237-261. Reprinted by permission of Holt, Rinehart and Winston, Inc. Footnotes omitted.

Kirkland suggests, as was the factory, and was no less dependent on inventive genius for its growth in the late nineteenth century than was American industry. Finally, there were the questions of public policy in city building, which were the significant counterparts to those involving private industry. What form and/or what degree of control should government assert over economic activity and how should it exercise control? The question was not, at bottom, so very different either for city or factory, although the possibility of public ownership was real in the former case, never so in the late nineteenth century in the latter case. What is striking about Kirkland's findings on city-related enterprise is the absence of ideological controversy. Questions of municipal vs. private ownership and, in the event of the latter, the degree of public regulation seemed to have been decided essentially on practical grounds and on the basis of previous experience. One may then ask whether the issues of public regulation of the railroad and of competition then agitating the country were not actually conceived more in comparable practical terms than historians have assumed?

All the foregoing ideas emerge from Kirkland's effort at breaking down the barrier between urban and economic history. By this basic strategy, he is able to discover a much wider network of relationships between the city and industrialization than can be perceived when these two subjects are compartmentalized, and, more specifically, to see the city both as a stimulus to and a participant in industrialization and not merely as a consequence of it.

For further reading: Blake McKelvey, *The Urbanization of America* (1963);—— *Rochester, The Flower City, 1855-1890* (1948); Sam B. Warner, *The Private City* (1968);* Constance M. Green, *American Cities in the Growth of the Nation* (1957); Bessie L. Pierce, *A History of Chicago* (1937-1957); Bayrd Still, *Milwaukee: The History of a City* (1948); Harold Passer, *The Electrical Manufacturers, 1875-1900* (1953); Seymour Mandelbaum, *Boss Tweed's New York* (1965).*

Urban Growth and the Welfare of the Economy

To those who believed that the welfare of the American economy depended upon the production of capital goods, the decade of the eighties brought forebodings. The most obvious support for this theory had been the construction of the railroad network. Its constantly extending mileage had given employment and business directly to thousands; it had also stimulated auxiliary activities such as the iron and steel industry and the engineering trades. Now railroad expansion was slowing down. What was to take its place? What power was now to pull the economy forward?

Though the answer was by no means obvious, the new generative factor was the growth of American cities. There had been cities, of course, in the colonial era, and in the first half of the nineteenth century population had gone cityward as well as westward. But after the Civil War the railroads and the industrialization of the economy compelled urbanization at rapid speed. In 1860 the number of places in the United States with a population of 8,000 or over was 141; in 1900, it was 545. At the same time there was a progressive increase in the absolute totals of urban dwellers. Whereas in 1860 just over

5,000,000 people lived in cities, in 1900 the urban population was just under 25,000,000. The eighties was the decade *par excellence* of urban growth; for those ten years the Federal Census reported "A very large increase in urban population."

The startling accessions of population to cities came from two migrations: one from the country to the city and the other from abroad. On the whole the former, at least in quantitative terms, was probably the more important. Since the country-city migration was merely a population displacement within the national boundaries, it is hard to estimate its net effects. In 1891 the *Commercial and Financial Chronicle*, brooding over the decline of New Hampshire and Massachusetts small towns, expressed distress at this "decay" and "the melancholy story of the farming towns" but added that so long as Massachusetts "as a whole, is showing such vigor, there is no room for lamentations over the drift of population away from the barren hillsides." On the other hand, immigrants from abroad represented an addition to the economy. These were producers and consumers the United States had not had before. And they came fast and numerously in the late nineteenth century. In 1882 their number, 788,991, set a record up to that time and one not to be surpassed until 1903.

Though not all immigrants went to cities, and the enlarging population, wherever located, was a stimulus to the economy, there were differences between cities and rural regions which were of profound importance. The compacting and concentration of population stimulated economic activities, for example urban transportation and the provision of electricity from a central station, which a dispersed population in those days could neither have called into being nor supported. Where people were gathered in communities, standards of taste, convenience, and economic necessity compelled other improvements. For instance, officials of Augusta, Maine, complained in 1880: "The method of keeping . . . the main street in condition, is to haul on gravel in the summer and grade up in places where needed. In the fall and spring this makes a road-bed of 6 or 8 inches of mud. . . . Then in the spring our streets are scraped and the gravel that was hauled in is again carted out." This was a road condition to which country dweller had become, perforce, reconciled. It was humiliating to an aspiring city if "not a single paved street exists."

Furthermore, in the country the building of houses and barns was apt to be assimilated to the partially self-sufficing regime of the farm; in the urban communities it was set apart and organized into commercial construction, the building industry. In 1900, 63 per cent of the establishments in the building trade were located in the country's 209 cities and construction expenditures on farms constituted less than 10 per cent of the nation's total. Finally, in the city considerations of the relation between sanitation and health, to mention no other factors, raised problems that had to be met by community rather than individual or familial action. The provision of pure water and the disposal of waste meant that in the city reliance upon public policy in social and economic matters came earlier and went deeper than elsewhere in the United States.

The problems and challenges inherent in these figures and circumstances induced in some a state of ecstasy. As F. C. Howe of Cleveland was to write: "The possibility of a free, orderly, and beautiful city became to me an absorbing passion. . . . I had an architectonic vision of what a city might be. I saw it as a picture. It was not economy, efficiency, and business methods that interested me so much as a city planned, built, and conducted as a community enterprise. . . . The city was the enthusiasm of my life. And I saw cities as social agencies that would make life easier for people, full of pleasure, beauty, and opportunity." Whatever Howe might dream, the city wore a very material aspect. It had to be built. To some extent the increase in municipal debt mirrored this necessity. Though such debts might occasionally represent operational costs they were primarily capital expenditures. In 1860 net municipal indebtedness in the country was estimated at $200,000,000; in 1880 it was $725,000,000, and in 1902 $1,433,000,000. Whereas early in the period these sums were fed into the economy via city subscriptions to railroad securities, or other forms of railroad subsidy, the revulsion against the railroad-aid policy in the hard times after 1873 meant that municipal expenditures for other purposes became more important.

Unhappily for purposes of historically measuring and tracing such expenditures, statistical data cannot be pushed very far back into the nineteenth century. But the investment in municipal water works in 1905 was estimated at "considerably more than a billion dollars"; in gas works, plants and distributing systems, the sum in 1900 was $567,000,506, about twenty times what it had been in 1860. In 1860 neither central electric power stations nor electric railways existed. In 1902 the issued capitalization and funded debt of electric stations selling power in the commercial market was $627,515,875. At the same date for street railways the capitalization and funded debt was $2,308,282,099.

The Choice of Public or Private Enterprise

Cities could turn over the provision of municipal services to private enterprise or furnish them at first hand through municipal ownership and operation. Though state legislatures restricted the capacity of cities to go into debt and otherwise limited their functions, cities remained public corporations chartered for public purposes. In favorable circumstances the legal hindrances to activity were not excessive. In 1897 the appellate division of the New York Supreme Court, validating New York City's issue of bonds for the construction and ownership of a subway, asserted that it was a principle of our nation's policy "to foster and protect private enterprise." Nonetheless the municipal ownership of a subway system was neither "socialism nor paternalism." There were other purposes cities could fulfill by their energy and expenditure. It was futile to formulate "a complete definition of 'a city purpose' . . . in view of the fact that reasons may arise which we are unable to foresee or now consider." In the same decade the justices of the Massachusetts Supreme Court unanimously approved a wide area for the municipal provision of public services.

If the city chose to fulfill its functions through the agency of a private corporation, the transfer of responsibility was usually effected by the grant of a franchise, either from the state or city government depending upon the date and jurisdiction. Such contractual documents permitted a private corporation to acquire property through eminent domain and to use the streets to lay pipes, install conduits, put down rails, or string wires. "The political science of the street is of fundamental importance in most municipal problems," commented one expert. Since the streets were generally not wide enough to accomodate competition, a franchise was usually equivalent to a monopoly grant. The franchise grant might or might not contain time limitations, rate and service regulations, provisions for recapture, or provide for payments by the grantee. In other words, it roughly resembled the earliest railroad charters.

The Improvement of Streets

Even the most confirmed advocate of private enterprise admitted that streets were a legitimate responsiblity of government. Expenditures for this purpose were, of course, not large so long as the making of streets did not depart widely from that of country roads. Cities graveled their streets or, as in Philadelphia, used an abudant supply of local materials for cobblestones. Though these methods had the advantage of cheapness, such streets were dirty, rough, noisy, uneven, damaging to traffic and uncomfortable for riders. The rationale for innovation was not long in coming. "Smooth and clean highways are a wise investment from every point of view, and that so long as the work is done in a thorough and scientific manner, the result is worth having, regardless of cost. No city should think itself rich enough to prosper without them, and no city is so poor that it can not afford them if it has any reason whatever for continued existence. Good roadways are cheap at any cost, and bad ones are so disastrously expensive that only a very rich country, like the United States, can afford them."

Apparently about the time of the Civil War, eastern cities became aware of the possibilities and advantages of paving their streets with small granite blocks. Soon quarries in Massachusetts and Maine, along the coast or accessible to it, became interested in the paving-stone industry. A specialized craft of stone cutters recruited from Yankees and immigrants from the British Isles began hammering out the "New York block" eight to twelve inches long, seven to eight inches deep, and three-and-one-half to four-and-one-half inches wide. Coastal sailing vessels distributed the product to cities up and down the Atlantic and there were even some shipments to the interior. On the whole cities without easy access to quarries relied upon other materials. After the mid-seventies pioneer communities in the Midwest were laying down brick pavements, a material far superior to wooden blocks, which in spite of their tendency to decay and heave, were also a contemporary fashion. Chicago was noted for its "floating pavements" of cedar block, "which are said to rise with the floods of water filling the roadways after heavy rainfalls." Finally, taking a cue from the experiences of Paris and London, American cities about 1870 began the use of asphalt. At first the raw material came from the great Pitch Lake deposit in Trinidad; by the end of the century the refining of American crude oils was producing a domestic supply.

Though cities owned the streets and could improve them through their own officials and employees, the task could also, without a franchise, be turned over to private contractors. Like all jobs, these contracts were much sought after and there frequently grew up a political alliance between the city government and favored contractors. The latter provided a labor force, frequently Irish or Italian, and the labor force provided voters at election time.

Water and Sewerage

Cities had also to face the problem of providing abundant supplies of water for their own use, for fire fighting, for industrial purposes, and for their own populations. After research during the closing decades of the nineteenth century had validated the germ theory of disease, the water had to be pure. Building dams and aqueducts, installing pumping apparatus to raise the water to standpipes or high basins, laying out an elaborate distribution system of water mains was an expensive business. Generally speaking, whether the municipality should build and own the works or turn the job over to a private corporation depended upon the empirical consideration of what was the less painful way of raising the money. On the one hand municipal officials and citizens were loath to increase city debt; on the other, private capitalists, though they were sometimes granted subsidies and a monopoly of providing water service, hesitated to invest in enterprises in the determination of whose rates social and sanitary considerations were more important than the law of supply and demand. Though ancient Rome had undertaken the task of water supply and classical precedents meant a great deal to Americans, more influential in the United States was the example of its two leading cities. In Philadelphia the Fairmount works opened in 1799-1801, and in New York, where the original Croton system was opened in 1842, water works were municipal undertakings. Since New York had earlier experimented with private enterprise, its eventual choice of public ownership and operation was all the more influential.

Interlocked with the water problem was the provision of improved sewage facilities. In some instances, as in Chicago and Milwaukee, the sewers emptied into the lakes from which the cities drew their water supplies; everywhere the wider employment of water closets raised problems of disposal. Slowly and quarrelsomely, most municipalities brought themselves to provide facilities through the sale of bonds and the levy of assessments upon abutting property owners. In Chicago the heroic measure of reversing the flow of the Chicago River, into which most waste was dumped, away from Lake Michigan and into the Mississippi was completed in 1871 at the cost of $3,000,000.

Lighting

The provision of modern lighting facilities had, of course, to wait upon the course of invention. In 1816, Baltimore, the first American city to do so, introduced illuminating gas made from coal. In the seventies a dual transformation affected the gas industry. The Standard Oil group became definitely interested in piping and selling natural gas, used primarily for industrial and heating purposes, and also in the production of gas, oil, a derivative from petroleum, which was used to produce water gas, a product with superior illuminating qualities. These changes, of course, soon confronted the competition of electric lighting. Frank Brush's invention of an improved arc light devised a source of illumination peculiarly fitted for the outdoors. The Edison incandescent light early in the eighties was designed for interior use, and it was not until a later date that it competed with the arc light for street illumination. In any case, the advent of electrical lighting slowed the expansion of gas as an illuminant. In many ways the problems connected with lighting were like those of providing water. There was a dual market for the product—a private one, homes and businesses, and a public one, street lighting. Both gas and electricity had to use the streets, the one for mains, the other for wires or conduits.

Urban Transportation

As cities grew in population and enlarged in area, a new problem emerged—urban transportation. Before the Civil War the omnibus and the horse-car furnished public conveyances. Horse-car lines were often adjuncts to speculation in suburban real estate. But these methods were hazardous, uncomfortable, and inefficient. They so heightened street congestion, already intense enough, that a person could proceed on foot more quickly to his destination. More rapid means of locomotion had been introduced into the city incidental to the search by steam railroads for convenient urban terminals. Though railroads secured franchises permitting them to lay rails along the streets, such documents were usually foresighted enough to prohibit locomotives from traveling along city thoroughfares and to insist that there steam should give way to mule or horse-power.

One obvious solution for the dilemma was to construct roadways at different levels and to permit locomotives and cars to travel the elevated one. Still there were real business uncertainties in such undertakings. In view of the proclivity of steam trains to jump the track or to run off bridges, elevated railroads threatened dangers. There was also considerable doubt whether people would take the trouble to walk upstairs for improved transport. Whatever the attitude of passengers, abutting property owners were quickly aware that an iron elevated structure along the street and the frequent passage of noisy trains was likely to diminish rather than enhance the value of their property. Nevertheless the need was so great that a Rapid Transit Commission appointed by the Mayor of New York recommended in the early seventies for two of the north and south avenues in the city an elevated system capable of carrying 15,000 passengers a day. By the next decade elevated roads had demonstrated their success. Eastern cities imitated New York, and in the early nineties Chicago, destined to become the city of "El's," already had its lines.

Eventually the elevateds were electrified. So were the surface lines. Cities, unless in special circumstances like San Francisco's, discarded the use of an endless cable beneath the pavement to tow cars and relied, particularly after Sprague's demonstration in Richmond, upon an overhead electric wire or an underground one with which a shoe from the car made contact. By the nineties there "was an active 'boom' in electric railway building" and speculation. "It is stimulated by the apparent cheapness of electricity as compared with horse power, by the expectation of large profits, and in some cases probably by the hope of successful deals in the securities of the company."

Private capitalists solicited and secured the franchises for these networks of urban transportation and operated the completed enterprises. Whereas local capital had once undertaken this task, capitalists without local ties moved into the enterprise. A hope of steady dividends prosaically earned from operations was hardly their aim. Instead they applied to urban transportation the most dubious devices of speculation and personal enrichment developed in the railroad world: the construction company, the lease, consolidation, stock-watering and Wall Street speculation. In some cases those practicing these arts in the new area were railroad men; for instance, in the eighties Jay Gould applied his unquestioned talents to the New York elevated system. He transferred its complicated affairs to the arena of Wall Street, journalistic rumors, and the courts. Eventually the growing returns from the consolidations he put together placed the stock on a dividend basis and made it one of the "blue chips" in the Gould estate.

In street railways a national "syndicate" appeared, originating in Philadelphia. Its leaders, Peter A. B. Widener and William L. Elkins, started their business careers, as had John D. Rockefeller, in the provision trades. Clearly this occupation as a training ground and reservoir of capital possessed a magic of its own. Dabbling in politics, Widener, Elkins, and others had by 1884 gathered within their Philadelphia Traction Company at least half the street car lines of the city. Elkins, who had invested in oil and had sold out to the Standard, once remarked, "Give me the Broadway franchise and the coal-oil trade of Philadelphia and I will retire." Actually this was a rather limited objective. In 1886 the Philadelphia group, with the alliance of broker Charles T. Yerkes, invaded Chicago. In the resulting process of consolidation and leasing, the capitalization of the various enterprises roughly doubled and cable cars superseded the horse-drawn ones.

In New York City William Collins Whitney, a graduate of Yale and a reform anti-Tweed Democrat who had married a Standard Oil fortune, formed an alliance with T. F. Ryan, a Virginia farm boy now a broker. Whitney once remarked of his associate, "If Ryan lives long enough, he'll have all the money in the world." Whitney and Ryan called to their assistance the Philadelphians Widener and Elkins and were also fortunate enough to retain as counsel Elihu Root to plot a path through the intricacies of New York law and politics, though in the latter area Whitney himself was adroit enough. These capitalists went ahead to consolidate all the surface lines of New York City. The first instrument was the Metropolitan Traction Company, a holding company incorporated in New Jersey. Like holding companies elsewhere, it exchanged its stock for the concerns it acquired; it also leased enterprises. In 1893 their corporate means of expansion became the Metropolitan Street Railway Company of New York. Whatever the legal form, the battle for consolidation was waged in the city and state governments and with frequent recourse to the courts. A trail of injunctions and receiverships marked this continual litigation. Nor were the vacillations of securities on Wall Street forgotten.

Though Whitney's brother became the urban transportation magnate of Boston through his own efforts, the Widener-Elkins-Whiteney-Ryan syndicate at the end of the century were reputed to have built up the street railway systems in New York, Chicago, Philadelphia, and Pittsburgh and in at least one hundred cities and towns from Maine to Pennsylvania. In addition they had become influential in gas and electric-lighting companies as far west as Omaha and as far south as St. Augustine. The united capitalization of their street railways was a billion dollars and of their lighting companies $300,000,000.

The Movement for Municipal Ownership

By the end of the nineteenth century there was a considerable movement for government ownership of certain industries. In its national phase this movement, which sometimes touched the railroads, focussed on the telephone and telegraph. But the objective eliciting the most expenditure of words and effort was the municipal ownership of public utilities. In one sense this is surprising, for earlier circumstances had certainly cast a dark shadow over the wisdom of enlarging both the sphere of municipal activity and the size of municipal debts. The experience of communities in financing railroad expansion had not turned out well; debt repudiations and scaling wrote an epitaph to the policy. What is more, events in New York City immediately after the Civil War unveiled a most discouraging example of municipal enterprise.

There the municipality had fallen into the merciless hands of a group of unsavory officials, whose leader was William Marcy Tweed, boss of Tammany Hall. With great persistence and courage, reform elements opposed to Tweed in 1871 finally rid the city of his tyranny and documented a noisome record of graft and corruption. The methods of the Tweed Ring in looting the city and enriching itself had diversity and also a certain simple charm. A favorite device was to suggest to contractors who worked for the city that they increase their bills and kick back the surplus to the conspirators. Thus a County Court House which really cost about $3,000,000 was made to stand on the books at $11,000,000. Toward the end of their rule, Tweed and his associates were taking as their own about 85 per cent of the city's expenditures. "If to the amount stolen outright is added the amount extravagantly and wastefully expended in sinecure offices, the performance of unnecessary work, fraudulent contracts, it is safe . . . to say that one-half the city debt of $130,000,000 represents absolute plunder," concluded Lalor's *Cyclopedia of Political Science*. An investigating committee estimated that if a private corporation had run the city, it would have done so for about one-tenth the stated costs. Incidentally most of Tweed's expenditures were for unquestioned "public" purposes.

The Tweed experience bit deep. Methods of improvement, advocating city home rule and centralized and responsible city government, seemed inadequate to stem the "evils arising out of our attempts to rule the large populations of our cities, made up of foreign and floating elements, through a government in form republican." The real cure, some felt, was the abandonment of democracy in the city and the restriction of the ballot to those owning property. Americans were not allowed to forget the bearing of this episode upon municipal and state ownership. In 1891 Godkin, editor of the *Nation* and a fanatic for laissez faire, answered the question, What is the State? with an answer complete for New York City, "the little Tammany junta."

If one were likely to forget this equation, events in Philadelphia reminded him of it. Acting on the assumption that gas lighting was a public function and should not be delegated to a private corporation, the city in 1841 took over the gas plant and entrusted its management to twelve trustees appointed by the Councils of the city government. Most paradoxically this arrangement was known as the "gas trust." It became a political machine. It employed 15 per cent more workers than necessary. Since it never established a depreciation fund, the original plant decayed and the mains leaked so badly that it was impossible to maintain pressure. Few extensions of service were made, and the coal used for the gas was purchased at extravagant prices. Finally, in 1880 a committee of investigation concluded: "One could not conceive a large business plant, run upon business principles, in such a condition without reflecting unfavorably upon its owners." After a decade of struggling with direct municipal operation, the Councils leased the city gas properties in 1897 to the United Gas Improvement Company for $10,000,000. This concern, a trust of quite a different character, owned plants in other cities. For a time the improvements in service and modernization which it introduced gained wide popular approval for it. Be that as it may, the Philadelphia story of public ownership was characterized by one crusader for public ownership as "the most disastrous failure of its kind in the country. It was a huge inescapable argument against the advocates of public ownership. . . ."

Despite such discouragements the advocates of municipal ownership had made considerable headway. The group was composed of college professors, mostly economists, who led a far from routine academic existence: John R. Commons and Richard T. Ely of the University of Wisconsin, E. J. James of the University of Pennsylvania, Edward W. Bemis, from the University of Chicago and eventually a consultant to cities desiring to install municipally owned gas works, and Frank Parsons, a lecturer in the law school of Boston University and a freelance teacher elsewhere. Of the reformers, Parsons was the most important. His *The City for the People*, published in 1899, crammed together in encyclopedic style arguments in behalf of municipal ownership. Though its obliviousness to differing contexts or circumstances and its insistent note diminish its persuasiveness, the book reveals one intellectual prop of the group as a whole, reliance upon foreign precedents: Germany's railroads, Berlin's telephone, Glasgow's tramways and gas and electric works. A later volume by Parsons discovered the usefulness of New Zealand precedents. Along with professors, American portraitists of Utopias played their part. In 1888 Edward Bellamy published *Looking Backward, 2000-1887.* An advocate of nationalized industries, Bellamy proposed as one preliminary step the public ownership of local public utilities. Bellamy inspired an organized movement, whose Nationalist clubs and their agitation were one explanation for the passage in Massachusetts in 1891 of a statute permitting cities and towns to own their gas systems.

A contemporary of Bellamy was Henry George. The classic statement of his position, *Progress and Poverty,* appearing in 1879, had focussed upon the evils arising from monopoly in land and proposed to abolish them by a single tax upon its unearned increment. Among the many converted by George's philosophy was Tom L. Johnson, a Cleveland millionaire with a fortune derived from among other sources, street railways. Johnson saw monopoly in public utilities as one explanation for poverty. As a successful candidate for mayor of Cleveland, he devoted his immense knowledge and convictions to an attack upon urban monopoly as "Privilege." Since Cleveland was forbidden by law to own street railways, Johnson proposed as a solution the lease of the existing private lines to an operating company of five trustees appointed by the mayor of the city. The lines were to be limited to an agreed return upon their stock, and the rates they charged were placed upon a sliding scale, with a minimum of three cents, depending upon the level of earnings. To bludgeon the old companies into this agreement, Johnson threatened to build competitive lines on parallel streets and charge a three-cent fare. There were mayoralty campaigns elsewhere—Chicago, for instance—which were won on the issue of municipal ownership.

In his ten-years war, Tom Johnson had the support of the Cleveland *Plain Dealer.* This was symptomatic, for the campaign for municipal ownership had considerable journalistic backing. For several years, before he established his Municipal Ownership League and ran for mayor of New York in 1905, William Randolph Hearst had been heating up the issue. In his early career in San Francisco he had been the advocate of municipal ownership of the city's water works; when he invaded New York with the New York *Journal* in the nineties he attacked the Gas Trust and proposed a municipal gas works. Certainly the conjunction of the professional reformers and the notorious editor of sensationalism was puzzling. Still it was not the first time in history that the dragon and St. George were on the same side.

Leaders to be effective had to have followers, and journalists had to have readers who could be persuaded. Generally the crusaders for municipal ownership pictured themselves as relying upon the "people" and it would be folly to deny that Hearst's sensational journalism had more positive influence in the crowded sections of New York than in the homes of tycoons. But businessmen also had a stake in efficient municipal services and in low prices for them. They might use water, gas, and electricity in large quantities in business and industrial establishments. Also, since they paid wages, they were interested in lowering the cost of living for wage receivers. If street transportation were not available and cheap, they might have to erect company housing near places of work. So even the apostles to laissez faire were willing to grant to municipalities a range of activities vouchsafed to few other forms of government.

Thus Charles E. Perkins, president of the Burlington Road, thought that "the inhabitants of a small, compact community, like a city, in the exercise of local self-government . . . may wisely and economically combine to procure gas, water, horse-cars, and perhaps other conveniences, granting special privileges in the streets, which are limited in number and extent, and limiting prices in consideration of such privileges. . . ." An executive of the New York Edison Company, concerned as to where to draw the line between the permissible and the forbidden, concluded: "Good roads, it is conceded, must be provided by the commonwealth, as also sewerage; water supply is usually, though not always, considered a municipal function; lighting, communication and transportation are on debatable ground; there are few in this country who approve public bakeries or store-houses, although bread is a necessity of life. Somewhere within this range is the point where democracy becomes socialism. It is important to limit the function of the municipality at this point, and not be misled by the phrase that 'a city is a business corporation.' . . . The real limits of municipal activity must be found in an alert and wholesome public opinion which will prevent steps that lead by easy reaches into socialistic enterprises, pure and simple."

Vague and fatuous though this distinction was, it had as much touch with reality as the prodigies of reconciling fact and theory undertaken by the advocates of municipal ownership. The strength of their attachment to municipal ownership and of their belief in democratic government confronted them with a dilemma when they looked realistically at the level of politics and political administration in the cities of America. So American advocates of municipal enterprise were compelled to dismiss the Philadelphia gas trust as "that parody on popular government" or elaborate a doctrine of purification in which theory refined fact. Thus it was private enterprise that corrupted city governments, and the responsibility of public enterprise would act as a cleansing agent.

The main thread of their argument was not, however, circular or contradictory. Obviously a franchise was a privilege, a thing of value. Its recipients proceeded to capitalize it. Thus Whitney's consolidation in 1901 of New York street railways issued securities to a par value of $165,000,000; the net value of the physical property was $60,000,000. The differential was the capitalized value of the franchises which Whitney thought, being combined, were worth a good deal more than when they were separate. It was performances such as these that gave substance to the frequent charge against the private managers of urban utilities that their stock was heavily watered. Without doubt there were many unfairnesses and short-cuts in this matter of capitalization. Also, as elsewhere in the economy, managers and investors were capitalizing in the basis of estimated earnings rather than actual investment.

Favoritism and extortion were not the whole explanation of this over-capitalization. While certain utilities such as water and gas works had been long enough in existence to be stabilized and the results of their operation anticipated, electricity as light and electricity as power for street railways were new arrivals. Technical advances and manufacturing changes were so rapid that costs, including that for equipment, fell rapidly; experience with these new industries was so lacking that there was a blindness to proper charges for depreciation. As in the case of new industries, there was a spectacular increase in patronage and use. In short, since over-optimism was common, business misjudgments about capitalization and profits understandably resulted. The ideological case for capitalizing prospective earnings was posted, as in manufacturing, upon a certain check by competition. But of course in municipal utilities such competition was unfeasible. So advocates of municipal ownership correctly emphasized the inherent monopoly of public utilities as an explanation of their high and discriminatory charges.

Achievements of Municipal Ownership

In terms of adoption municipal ownership had considerable success. In provision of sewers it was universal; "Copies of sewer franchises, are like rare books, hard to get." In the case of waterworks, of the 3,326 installations in the United States in 1899 only 46.27 per cent were owned and operated by private owners, while 53.73 per cent were owned and operated by the communities in which they were located. At the same date, of the 965 gas works, 1.45 per cent were municipally owned; of the 3,032 electric light plants 15.17 per cent were municipal. In street railways, private enterprise swept the boards. When the National Civic Federation investigated the merits of public and private operation early in the twentieth century, it was compelled to turn to publicly owned tramways in England for a yardstick of performance. As to the reasons for these variations the concentration of municipally owned gas and electric works in the smaller places gives a hint. Individuals as opposite as Tom Johnson and Charles E. Perkins believed the close oversight of operations justified municipal enterprise in such communities. Waterworks which did not require a large labor force were less vulnerable to the spoils system and hence more acceptable to voters. Though private enterprise was historically entrenched in the gas business, electric light and power arrived later, at a time when the municipal ownership movement had acquired momentum.

In terms of comparative economic performance, it is hard to come by a dispassionate appraisal of the merits of public and private municipal enterprise during this period. The contemporary literature abounds with exceptions, assumptions, and short-run judgments. Though much ink had already been spilled on matters of rates, service and efficiency, the National Civic Federation when it undertook an investigation in 1907, headed the introduction to its resulting volume with the assertion that until the Federation took up the matter "no definite effort had been made to determine impartially and scientifically the relative merits of private and public ownership and operation of public utilities." However, in 1888 A. T. Hadley, an economist and president of Yale, had dared to appraise contemporary accomplishments. Sensitive to the larger context surrounding the movement for municipal ownership abroad and in America, he concluded: "What the advocates of state ownership really fail to show is the combination of liberal policy and wise administration in the same instance. . . . This is a damaging omission. As far as it exists, it renders the argument for state management of industry totally inconclusive. . . . Successful administration is found, but without the more liberal policy which is the main argument for government activity. Liberal policy is sometimes found, but is almost invariably accompanied by mistakes in administration."

Regulation of Municipal Enterprise

Between private and public ownership lay the compromise of public regulation of private enterprise. As we have seen, state and nation turned to this middle way in the case of railroads, but champions of municipal ownership would have none of it. Tom Johnson, for instance, believed monopoly was more than a match for a prying or regulatory government. It would always win. Moderates were more sympathetic to regulation, for state ownership "may be compared to a man who protects himself against a boy with a snowball by killing the boy. The social industrialism is no more necessary than the homicide is." At different times in different jurisdictions legislation which had once let the government give franchises free or without stipulation, exacted, for this money-making privilege, a flat fee or a percentage of receipts, or stipulated the franchise must be sold at auction to the highest bidder. Franchise grants were limited in duration and the city was authorized to recapture the property after a certain period. Rates and services were also regulated. All this resembled the old effort to regulate railroads through provisions in their charters.

As in the case of railroads, the regulatory movement gravitated into the hands of that new governmental discovery, the commission. In Massachusetts, for instance, street railways were placed under the control of the Massachusetts Railroad Commission when it was established in 1869. Through the decades the degree of regulation over both means of transportation revealed the same evolution: rate-making changed from recommendations to mandates, and the Commission could prescribe measures for public safety and comfort, and finally in the nineties place severe limitations upon the methods of capitalization. In 1885 The Commonwealth established a Board of Gas Commissioners and two years later changed its name to the Board of Gas and Electric Light Commissioners. Explicitly accepting the monopoly character of these new enterprises, the General Court authorized these Boards to investigate rates upon complaint and if they deemed proper, order a reduction in price and, in the case of gas, an improvement in quality. The anti-stock watering statutes of the Commonwealth also caught within their dragnet the gas and electric utilities.

As in the case of the railroad commission, these regulatory agencies put great emphasis upon reports, publicity, and complaints of wrong from individuals. But a panegyrist of this device confessed it was of limited utility. It would work neither in a "corporation-ridden state" like Pennsylvania, nor "in South Carolina half of whose population ten years of age and over is illiterate." The prerequisites to success were "that a large body of the people of the state shall be intelligent and educated; that they shall be devoted to reading and discussion; that associated efforts shall be habitual and frequent; that population shall be considerably dense; and that resentment against wrong and whatever limits the common welfare shall be quick and energetic." This proviso seemed to require, as in the case of most utopias, the regeneration of mankind or at the very least their elevation to the standard *homo sapiens* had attained in Massachusetts.

Urban Building

Private expenditures for residential and business purposes were the most important contribution American cities made to the economy. An index of the dollar value of building permits in terms of 1913 dollars reveals how important this stimulus was. The index reached a peak in 1890 which was not approached again until 1925. Such figures, as usual, obliterate distinctions. But so can the impressionistic, qualitative observations of travelers. In an oft-quoted sentence Lord Bryce, after excepting a few historic American cities, remarked, "American cities differ from one another only herein, that some of them are built more with brick than with wood, and others more with wood than brick." Actually, building followed a straight-line evolution from wood to brick to stone. For stone was the prestige building material, granite enjoying the highest favor. Governmental buildings—customs houses, post-offices, courthouses, and jails—were built of it, as were buildings having a public aspect—banks, hotels, churches, markets, and railroad stations. Since granite was hard to work and therefore expensive, those with lesser means turned to softer stones, and brownstone fitted the prescription perfectly. Since its chief deposits lay along the lower Connecticut River, it could be shipped cheaply by water; the large blocks, straight from the quarry, were easily worked up and fitted near the spot of construction. Brownstone fronts dominated the domestic architecture of Boston's Back Bay and flowed like a chocolate tide along the avenues and cross streets of New York. The birthplace of Theodore Roosevelt had a brownstone front; Commodore Vanderbilt gave the material a certain cachet when he built his palace on Fifth Avenue of it. To the Commodore, granite, like the law, was "too slow," and he wanted the building done before he died. Of the stone buildings in New York, over three-quarters had brownstone fronts, and its use penetrated even to Chicago. The slate quarries, which furnished fire-proof roofing, and the lime quarries, whose product was processed in kilns to make interior finish plaster, were associated industries. All in all, the number of building stone quarries in the United States increased from 1,444 in 1850 to 5,764 in 1902.

Houses with brownstone fronts usually had side and rear walls of brick. In some communities, for example Philadelphia, brick had been the traditional material for super-structures of the more pretentious early buildings. By century's end, even the slums of Philadelphia were brick single-family houses. Since the costs of transportation increased rapidly with the distance such heavy materials were carried, nearly every city was rimmed with clay pits from which its buildings had been dug. Every state in the Union, except two in the Far West, reported brickyards. Nonetheless there was a tendency for the industry to gravitate to deposits of superior clay and to utilize at these locations brick-making machinery.

In the United States even the interior structure of stone and brick edifices—flooring, beams, roofs—was generally of wood. Furthermore there were factors which made it the preferred material for the whole building. Forests were abundant. Moreover a revolutionary new technique for building houses and working wood kept prices down. In the 1830's an ingenious migrant from New England to Chicago invented the balloon frame. Previously a frame house had been composed of heavy timbers fitted together; the balloon frame used a multitude of lighter pieces and relied upon the exterior boarding to give the structure rigidity and strength. The house utilized the principle of the box. Later, multiplication and refinement of woodworking machinery released workers from making blinds, sash, doors, and mouldings by hand in a shop during the winter and transferred this task to a shop using machinery all the year round, thus doing the work more cheaply and in some instances performing prodigies hand workers could not attempt.

The census of 1880 observed that, "Having a larger and more rapidly increasing population than any other country that is noted for its consumption of iron, we are consequently the largest consumers of nails and spikes in the construction of dwellings and public buildings, stores, warehouses, offices and similar structures." So pronounced were the advantages of wooden construction that great American cities clung to it even after the Chicago fire of 1871 demonstrated its danger.

Whatever the building façade, the interior was mechanized. The American stove, "works of real art," "handsome, bright, cheerful, healthful, and clean," and one of the early triumphs of American mass production, gave way to an industry of steamfitting and heating apparatus. The same domestic mechanization created the indoor bathroom and toilet, thus benefiting the porcelain industry.

American construction now began to utilize new materials of the industrial age. In New York City Peter Cooper, the ironmaster, decided to support the floors of his Cooper

Union on horizontal rolled iron beams. By 1859 his plant was rolling beams 4 feet long and 9 inches deep. Somewhat earlier Harpers rebuilt their burned down publishing plant with one seven stories high, using iron beams supported by iron columns; instead of brick or stone, it had a cast-iron front. By the eighties architects were considering the feasibility of a building whose support was a metal frame or cage and whose walls were simply filler between the beams and columns. In 1885 the plans of a Chicago engineer, W. LeBaron Jenney, materialized in the ten stories of the Home Insurance Company building, the "first skyscraper." Of course steel had now superseded iron. Whereas the census of 1880 had mentioned neither iron nor steel for buildings, the census of 1900 noted the production of 856,983 tons of structural shapes of iron and steel. Unhappily it did not specify what proportion went into buildings.

The construction industry stimulated the economy directly. Materials had to be manufactured and put together or installed. Occupations ranging from sophisticated manufacturing such as wood working to the handicrafts of carpenter, mason, painter, plumber, and plasterer boomed. In 1900, expenditures on construction turned out an annual product valued at $1,946,000,000. In the sixties an American calculator had surmised by extrapolation from data then available that there was "a vast annual demand for 130,000 new houses" and foresaw that the better construction and luxuries of a "modern house" with "modern improvements" constantly increased the expenditure per house. For the decade as a whole he put their total cost at $1,300,000,000. This was quite unlike the course of affairs in the "old and stationary countries of Europe," where "old cities" were already built and there was consequently "no active and continued demand for labor and capital to provide new dwellings to accommodate swelling numbers."

The American ideal of owning one's home was deep-seated. Home ownership conferred prestige, showed others that the owner was getting ahead and reassured him that he was "Americanized." In farming the dream was widely realized; in urban living, much less so. In New York City in 1900, rented homes constituted 87.9 per cent of the total; in Chicago 74.9. Since urban population was notably on the wing, it relied on rented properties. Builders of all sorts relied in large part on borrowed money. The owner did not issue stock, he encumbered the property with a mortgage. Though most figures for construction in the late nineteenth century contain a good deal of surmise, it seems reasonably accurate to say that the non-farm mortgage debt rose from $3,811,000,000 in 1890 to $4,661,000,000 in 1900. While the major share of this mortgage debt was held by individuals, savings banks and insurance companies under legal restrictions were also large holders.

Such arrangements facilitated home ownership without funds; they also aided speculative tenement building. Builders who went into this operation generally bought the land from an owner, borrowing money from him for the purchase; the latter frequently lent a portion of the funds for the purchase of material. When the building was done, the builder tried to sell it as soon as possible to an investor who would put in some money of his own and purchase the mortgages accumulated along the way. Land owner and builder hoped to make their gains by marking up the value of the property in the course of these transactions.

By the mere fact of its existence, the city regulated the kind of edifices it had. Even with minimum planning, the city had to lay out the pattern of the streets. In Philadelphia the rectangular system or gridiron went back to its founder, William Penn. Between 1808 and 1811, three commissioners appointed by the New York state legislature laid out the gridiron plan of north and south avenues and cross streets for New York City and applied it from the old town of crooked streets on lower Manhattan to 155th Street. Chicago also had the gridiron. While this design had the advantage of fixing precise boundaries for property and thus facilitating its conveyance, it necessarily determined the size of the conventional lot: in New York, 25 feet frontage and 100 feet in depth, and in Chicago "The shoe-string lot," also with 25 foot frontage but often 125 feet deep. Both sizes were ill-adapted for tenement construction, a tenement being a house occupied by three or more families. When multi-family houses were built with higher standards they came to be called apartment houses and furnished abode for the well-to-do and middle classes.

Although tenements appeared in New York as early as the 1830's, it was in the seventies, as congestion deepened, that the typical brick tenement, five or six stories high, appeared, occupying most of the front part of the narrow lot. Since Chicago lots were a little deeper and the city could spread out over the prairie, tenements there became wooden houses two or three stories high. There was one on the front of the lot, one in the rear on an alley, and sometimes one between.

Families were crowded into these dwellings until the density of population per square mile became record-making. In 1893 well over half the population of New York City lived in tenements; in thirty-two acres of the eleventh ward, there were 986.4 persons per acre, a density which only parts of Bombay approached. The crowded urban regions by their filth and lack of ventilation bred more than their share of mortality and illness; to them also were ascribed prostitution, drunkenness, crime, poverty, and the break-down of family life. The more conservative feared they were seed beds of social discontent and revolution.

Charity societies, settlement houses staffed by professors, divines, and social service workers, and individual reformers such as Jacob Riis protested the growth of slums. The particularities of their indictment and proposed remedies would seem to fall within the "public purpose," the responsibility for which in other matters majority opinion had often assigned to city governments. Some European precedents, to which American reformers were usually attune, pointed in the same direction. But though there were many who asserted that private philanthropy and the self-denial of rich men would remove the slum, rare was the proposal to do so through municipally owned housing. For local authorities to spend public money "competing with private enterprise in housing the masses is bad principle and worse policy." Since housing was not a "natural monopoly," public housing lacked that justification.

The answer was regulatory legislation. In New York after years of investigation and report, the legislature passed the first tenement house law in 1867. Successive years saw amendments or new acts until the passage of a general tenement house act in 1901, "the most significant regulatory act in America's history of housing." It was widely copied elsewhere. This act "would not have been possible except for the vogue of restrictive legislation that so largely dominated American thought at the opening of the twentieth century. Whereas in 1867 it had been thought sufficient to give each sleeping room ventilation by transom to another room or hall and to prescribe one toilet or privy for each twenty occupants, by 1901 the law restricted tenement houses to 70 per cent of the lot, required for every room a window opening upon street, yard, or court, compelled the installation of running water and a private toilet in each apartment, and prescribed a certain minimum of cubic feet of space for each occupant. The evolution of these requirements had been accompanied by a tightening of administration through the Board of

Health or Building Department and had culminated in a Tenement House Department in 1901. Some provisions of the act were to govern only future construction; others were to compel the alteration of "old-law tenements."

As in other aspects of the economy, the regulatory movement headed into a dilemma. If pushed far enough to accomplish the sanitary and social objectives sought for, it might so increase expenses of construction and hence rents as to defeat its purposes. For a while housing reformers were able to console themselves with the reflection that alterations in "old-law tenements" benefited the landlord by decreasing vacanies and increasing the rents which the occupants ought to be willing to pay. But as congestion continued and new-law tenements were not constructed fast enough, and as apartments in old-law tenements continued in use into the twentieth century, regrets that regulation had not started earlier and chiding landlords for greed hardly seemed an adequate clarification of the situation. What the reformers wanted was expansion under standards which the community could approve. But one employer had noted in the eighties, "Capitalists consider tenement houses a poor investment, paying poor returns."

The tenement comes of age

The hallmark of the new age was the city, and the blight on the city was the tenement and slum. By 1890, one out of every three Americans lived in cities (defined as those over 8,000 in population); three cities—New York, Chicago, Philadelphia—had gone over the million mark. The urban world provided the setting for the new industrial order, for multiplying financial and trade activity, for the magnificent wealth and national culture visible in fine mansions, in museums and opera houses. But the city was also the site of burgeoning slums, inhabited mainly by immigrants living in squalor and misery. In 1890, New York City's Tenth Ward on the Lower East Side housed 57,000 people. The population density amounted to 334,080 per square mile, roughly ten times the city's average. What made possible this incredible crowding was the tenement, the multifamily dwellings so designed as to maximize the use of valuable city land for the urban poor. Of New York's 81,000 dwellings in 1890, 35,000 were tenements. Those containing 21 persons or more housed 1 million of the city's population of 1½ million.

In the following essay Roy Lubove analyzes the response of civic-minded Americans to the slums during the Gilded Age. Two major points emerge. First was the great concern aroused by slum problems. Never during this era were these minimized or ignored. On the contrary, for reasons that Lubove develops in his essay, reformers considered ending of the slum blight as essential to the health of the American social order. It may be argued, in fact, that the ideals of preindustrial America, still much alive in the late nineteenth century, injected a sense of urgency that would not be matched in the twentieth century when people came to accept slums as inevitable. Lubove's second finding concerns the failure to develop workable modes of reform in this era before Progressivism. Two approaches emerged: legal regulation that imposed high standards on tenement builders and owners and the model-tenement movement that aimed at encouraging voluntary housing reform. Neither held out any real hope of success. There were, for one thing, the intractable economic realities that had led to tenement building in the first place, above all, the high cost of land in close proximity to the job opportunities open to the urban

From Roy Lubove, *The Progressives and the Slums: Tenement House Reform in New York City, 1890-1927*. Pittsburgh: University of Pittsburgh Press, 1962, pp. 25-48.

poor. Of at least equal importance were the prevailing notions of individualism and property rights. The ideological factor explained why tenement-housing legislation, first enacted in New York in 1867, was so feebly drawn. The economic factor explains why even modest regulation proved unenforceable. The model-tenement movement attempted to satisfy the individualistic requirements of the era, but there proved to be no way to overcome the prevailing economic constraints. The model-tenement advocates were never able to make their plans desirable as investments—and this was the crux of their approach. When New York housing reformers attempted to meet the commercial builders entirely on the latter's terms, the awful result was the dumb-bell tenement that would be the bane of the Lower East Side for decades to come.

Lubove's analysis locates the central weakness of urban reform in the Gilded Age: not in the recognition of the problems, but in the insurmountable limits to effective action deriving both from the ideological and economic spheres.

For further reading: Jacob Riis, *How the Other Half Lives* (1890);* Moses Rischin, *The Promised City: New York's Jews, 1870-1914* (1962);* Arthur M. Schlesinger, *The Rise of the City* (1933);* Robert H. Bremner, *From the Depths: the Discovery of Poverty in America* (1956);* "The Big Flat. History of a New York Tenement House," *American Historical Review*, LXIV (1958), 54-62; Gordon Atkins, *Health, Housing and Poverty in New York City: 1865-1910* (1947); Ray Ginger, *Altgeld's America, 1890-1905* (1958).*

[1]

The jurisdiction of the newly-established Metropolitan Board of Health extended over New York, Kings, Westchester, and Richmond counties and a few towns in the present Borough of Queens. The Board consisted of nine commissioners—four appointed by the governor, three of whom had to be physicians; the health officer of the Port of New York; and four police commissioners. A sanitary superintendent, appointed by the Board, supervised the work of fifteen sanitary inspectors.[1]

The Board's authority to regulate tenement conditions was embodied in the Tenement House Law of 1867. This law was enacted upon the recommendation of a state legislative committee which had investigated the New York and Brooklyn tenements shortly after the establishment of the Metropolitan Board of Health. The committee discovered that the 15,511 tenements reported by the Council of Hygiene had increased to over 18,000. More than half were in "bad sanitary condition." The squalor of basement and cellar habitations defied imagination. In the lower streets of the city they were "subject to regular periodical flooding by tide water, to the depth of from six inches to a foot; frequently so much as to keep the children of the occupants in bed until ebb-tide."[2] The committee's findings generally confirmed the low estimate placed upon New York's sanitary condition by the Council of Hygiene.

The housing act of 1867 defined a tenement as follows:

A tenement house within the meaning of this act shall be taken to mean and include every house, building, or portion thereof which is rented, leased, let or hired out to be occupied, or is occupied as the home or residence of more than three families living independently of another, and doing their cooking upon the premises, or by more than two families on a floor, so living and cooking, but have a common right in the halls, stairways, water closets or privies, or some of them.[3]

The "more than three families" provision was a serious error. Some of the city's worst tenements were occupied by only three families.[4] Twenty years passed before this fault was corrected. Otherwise, the legal definition of a tenement remained the same into the twentieth century.

On the whole, the standards established by the Tenement House Law of 1867 were low. Many of its provisions were vague, leaving too much discretionary authority with the Board of Health. In relation to fire protection, for example, the law required all tenements to have a fire escape *or some other means of egress* approved by the inspector of public buildings in Manhattan and in Brooklyn by the assistant sanitary superintendent. An inconveniently located wooden ladder thus satisfied the legal requirements, if approved by these officials. To ventilate dark interior bedrooms, the law compelled only the construction of a window connecting with a room which did communicate with the outer air. The law set no limit to the percentage of the lot which a tenement might cover. Although ten feet had to separate the rear of any building from another, a tenement might extend to the lot line if no other building existed. The Board of Health was authorized to modify even this modest ten foot requirement.

The reports of the inspectors for the Council of Hygiene were glutted with uncomplimentary references to the poor sanitary and drainage systems in tenement districts. Privies, often unconnected to sewers and located in rear yards, overflowed. In some places, the contents seeped through rotten foundations into cellars.[5] The sanitary requirements set by the act of 1867 represented little progress. Cesspools were forbidden—except where unavoidable. Water closets and privies had to connect with sewers—where such existed. A landlord was obligated to provide only one water closet or privy for every twenty inhabitants, and it could be located in the yard. The manner and material of water closet construction was left again to the discretion of the Board of Health. Finally the tenement landlord satisfied the law if he furnished a water tap somewhere in the house or yard.

The Tenement House Law of 1867 at least had symbolic value. It represented the acceptance in principle of the community's right to limit the freedom of the tenement landlord and builder. However, the low standards of the law and its successors through 1901 involved a very shaky compromise between entrepreneurial rights and the rights of the community to protect its citizens. Housing legislation before 1901 was also characterized by inadequate provision for enforcement. An understaffed Board of Health, often subject to political pressures from landlords or builders influential with Tammany, found it difficult to ensure compliance with the law.[6] Burdened with many other duties, the Board of Health had not the time or resources to inspect periodically thousands of tenements or to prod indefinitely uncooperative landlords. It was difficult to force elusive "estates, receivers, agents and non-residents" to obey the legislation, and the "poverty of small owners, struggling to retain property heavily mortgaged" intensified the problems of enforcement.[7] Legal compulsion was at best a slow and often futile procedure. Two major problems inherited by Progressive housing reformers were an ineffective tenement code and the creaky machinery of enforcement.

[2]

Housing reformers of the post-Civil War decades experimented further with the model tenement program which had its small beginnings in the AICP's "Workmen's Home" and in the program of sanitary legislation urged by the Council of Hygiene. A key development of the period was the emergence of Alfred T. White of Brooklyn as the chief spokesman for the model tenement ideal. The example of White's three groups of model tenements, built between 1877 and 1890, greatly influenced a generation of reformers seeking a solution to the problem of the ever-expanding tenement slums

The discrepancy in standards between the model tenements erected by White and other "investment philanthropists" and the ordinary commercial tenement built under the housing laws, was very apparent; but the few built housed only a small fraction of New York's tenement population and the vast majority had to depend for their protection upon legislative restrictions over builders and landlords. Conceivably, had the housing reformer not overestimated the potentialities of the model tenement, he might have pressed harder for legislation which would make all tenements model, at least in relation to such basic necessities as light, air, ventilation, fire protection, and sanitary facilities. One consequence of the minimal legislative controls over building development was the birth and proliferation after 1879 of the notorious *dumb-bell tenement*. The dumb-bell, indeed, did not even originate in the minds of building speculators, but was the contribution of reformers willing to accept the terms imposed by the commercial builder.

The history of the dumb-bell begins in 1877 when Henry C. Meyer established a trade journal, the *Plumber and Sanitary Engineer*. Shortly after the Civil War, Meyer had founded a company which manufactured water, gas, and steam installation supplies. Anxious to boost sales, he hoped that his journal would convince architects, plumbers, and engineers of the safety of his type of equipment. Meyer chose Charles F. Wingate, a civil engineer, as his editor. A relative of the secretary of the AICP, Wingate had assisted in the preparation of the Association's annual reports and in the process had become an authority on the housing problem. Wingate interested Meyer in housing reform, and the latter decided that a competition for an improved tenement sponsored by his journal would increase circulation. Accordingly, the *Plumber and Sanitary Engineer* in December 1878, announced a prize competition for a tenement on a 25 x 100 foot lot. The design which best combined maximum safety and convenience for the tenant, and maximum profitability for the investor, would win.[8]

In the next few months approximately two hundred plans were submitted by architects. Exhibited at the Leavitt Art Gallery on Clinton Place, they aroused considerable public interest.[9] The plans were judged by a committee of five: R. G. Hatfield, a consulting architect;[10] Charles F. Chandler, president of the Board of Health; Robert Hoe, a printing press manufacturer; and two clergymen, Dr. Potter of Grace Church and Dr. John Hall, Meyer's own clergyman. The gentlemen of this committee, despite their explicit denial that the "requirements of physical and moral health"[11] could be satisfied by a tenement on a 25 x 100 foot lot, awarded first prize to the dumb-bell design of James E. Ware.

The widespread adoption of the dumb-bell by builders was assured by a provision of the Tenement House Law of 1879. Partly as a result of the interest in tenement reform stimulated by the *Plumber and Sanitary Engineer* competition, a group of clergymen and laymen held a conference early in February 1879. This conference, which included Dr.

Stephen Smith, Alfred T. White, and Charles Loring Brace of the Children's Aid Society, resolved that the clergy of the city would preach on the tenement problem on Sunday, February 23. After the ministers had spoken, two public meetings were held in the evening and various speakers explained the pressing urgency of tenement reform. The following week Mayor Cooper presided over an important public meeting at Cooper Union, which resulted in the formation of a Committee of Nine to plot a reform strategy. Upon the recommendation of this committee, an Improved Dwellings association was formed to provide housing for "persons unable to pay more than eight to ten dollars per month." The "New York Sanitary Reform Society," a voluntary private association designed to work for the improvement of tenement conditions, also originated in the Committee's recommendations. Finally, the Committee of Nine prepared and introduced into the state legislature a bill amending the Tenement House Law of 1867. After considerable delay "owing to the vigorous opposition of many landlords through the agency of their representatives at Albany," [12] the legislation passed. It required, significantly, that every tenement bedroom have a window opening directly to the street or yard unless sufficient light and ventilation could be provided "in a manner and upon a plan approved by the board of health." This provision of the law requiring a window in all tenement bedrooms, combined with the descretionary authority granted to the Board of Health, paved the way for the dumb-bell tenement.

Ware's prize tenement, with various modifications, was the characteristic type of multiple dwelling erected for the working class in New York between 1879 and 1901. The dumb-bell was essentially a front and rear tenement connected by a hall. Situated on a pinched 25 x 100 foot lot, the dumb-bell was usually five or six stories high and contained fourteen rooms to a floor, seven on either side running in a straight line. One family occupied the first four of these seven rooms, a second family the remaining three rooms to the rear. The dumb-bell thus harbored four families to a floor. The hallways and stairwell were dimly lit by windows fronting upon the air shaft. Water closets, two to a floor or one to every two families, were located opposite the stairs.

Of the fourteen rooms on each floor, ten depended for light upon the narrow air shaft. This was an indentation at the side of the building about twenty-eight inches wide and enclosed on all sides. It proved to be not only inadequate for the purpose of providing light and air, but a positive hindrance to the health and comfort of tenants. The shaft was a fire hazard, acting as a duct to convey flames from one story to the next. It became a receptacle for garbage and filth of all kinds. It was noisy with the quarrels and shouts of twenty or more families. Its stale air reeked with the cooking odors from twenty or more kitchens.

Meyer and his associates had attempted the impossible; the architect could not reconcile the tenant's welfare and the investor's profit. Two dozen families could not be housed comfortably in a six-story building compressed into a lot 25 x 100 feet in dimension. The building occupied 75 per cent to 90 per cent of the lot. The front parlor, the most spacious room, measured only 10½ x 11 feet. Bedrooms were about 7 x 8½ feet in size. Amenities such as landscaping or children's play areas were out of the question.

Meyer explained his acquiescence in the 25 x 100 foot lot on the grounds that "the problem in New York then was the single lot, and that any architect could make a design for a large block; but that it was an attempt to emphasize and solve the New York problem that the competition was instituted." [13] Far more useful, however, would have been an attempt by Meyer or the Committee of Nine to condemn the single lot as unfit

for tenement construction. The 25 x 100 foot lot mostly benefited land owners, speculators, realtors, builders, and landlords who found it a convenient parcel to buy, build
upon, and sell. This narrow subdivision may have made sense in 1800, when most dwellings were built for single-family occupancy. By 1879 it had outlived its usefulness.

The prize awards of the *Plumber and Sanitary Engineer* were criticized by contemporaries who realized that the dumb-bell was a negative contribution to the solution
of the housing problem. The New York *Times* observed that if the prize plans were the
best possible, then the housing problem was virtually insolvable. Perhaps, the *Times*
sardonically reflected, "the gentlemen who offered the prizes really desired to demonstrate this to the public before proposing any other scheme." Dr. A. N. Bell, editor of the
Sanitarian, complained that "the prizes were won by the most ingenious designs for
dungeons." If the dumb-bell is the best, then "how much is the best worth?" wondered
the *American Architect and Building News*.[14]

[3]

The housing legislation between 1879 and 1890 contained some useful provision, but did
nothing to alter the dumb-bell pattern. The 1879 law limited, for the first time, the
amount of lot space a tenement could occupy. The 65 per cent limitation, however, was
nullified by the discretionary authority granted the Board of Health. A provision requiring a window of at least twelve square feet in any room used for sleeping was also diluted
by discretionary power given the Board of Health, which could approve a substitute.
Finally, the law provided for thirty sanitary police, under the Board's supervision, to
enforce the housing code.

The widespread interest in housing conditions stimulated by the *Plumber and Sanitary
Engineer* competition subsided until 1884, when a series of lectures by Felix Adler,
founder of the Ethical Culture Society, again aroused and coalesced the energies of
reformers. Growing out of Adler's denunciation of the tenement blight in 1884 was the
first of a series of official state tenement house commissions. The investigations and
report of the tenement house commission of 1884, which included Adler and Charles F.
Wingate among its membership, resulted in further amendments to the tenement code in
1887, mostly of a superficial character. The number of sanitary police was increased from
thirty to forty-five. The law established a standing (and quite ineffectual) tenement house
commission composed of New York's mayor and several department heads. Tenement
landlords now had to provide one water closet for every fifteen instead of every twenty
inhabitants, as well as running water on every floor. For administrative purposes, the law
required owners of tenements to file their names and addresses annually with the Board
of Health. Moreover, the Board was required to make semiannual inspections of every
tenement. Neither of these latter provisions was successfully enforced.[15]

We have suggested, although it would be difficult to prove, that reformers might have
labored for higher standards of restrictive legislation had they not been so dazzled by the
potentialities of the model tenement. The intense interest in model tenements throughout
the period was always disproportionate to the actual accomplishments of "investment
philanthropy." The model tenement, in theory, had many advantages over restrictive
legislation. It circumvented the troublesome task of enacting and enforcing housing
codes, a process which often involved the compromise of standards and principles.
Second, even if restrictive legislation prevented the worst tenements from being built, it

did not guarantee a sufficient supply of good ones at moderate rentals. The model tenement, a strictly private venture accompanied by voluntary limitations upon profit, promised a safe, sane solution to the housing problem in a capitalist society.

One of the first notable model tenement projects after the Civil War emerged not in New York but in Boston, where Dr. H. P. Bowditch helped organize the Boston Cooperative Building Company in 1871. Limiting dividends to 7 per cent, the Company opened its first buildings in 1872 and ultimately constructed five tenement estates. The tenements were small, with one family to a floor, and each apartment contained running water. This latter convenience, however, was canceled out by cellar toilets. A few years after the Company began operations, Robert Treat Paine decided to offer workers the benefits of model homes rather than tenements. He financed the construction of four- to six-room single-family homes with bath, and arranged for long-term mortgage payments. Paine organized a limited-dividend Workingmen's Building Association in 1880 to expand his operations.

Despite the work of Paine and the Boston Cooperative Building Company, the undisputed evangelist of model-tenement gospel in the postwar period was Alfred T. White of Brooklyn. Born in 1846, White was educated at Rennselaer Polytechnical Institute. After the Civil War he joined his father as a partner in the importing firm of W. A. and A. M. White. A wealthy man in search of a philanthropy, White discovered in housing reform an outlet for his benevolent impulse: "It is time to recognize that if the intelligent and wealthy portion of the community do not provide homes for the working classes, the want will be continually supplied by the less intelligent class and after the old fashion." In White's estimation, the need for improved low-income housing had become imperative, for "the badly constructed, unventilated, dark and foul tenement houses of New York . . . are the nurseries of the epidemics which spread with certain destructiveness into the fairest homes; they are the hiding-places of the local banditti; they are the cradles of the insane who fill the asylums and of the paupers who throng the almshouses; in fact, they produce these noxious and unhappy elements of society as surely as the harvest follows the sowing. . . . "[16]

In 1872 White began preparing plans for a model tenement when he learned of Sir Sydney Waterlow's philanthropic work in London. Waterlow in 1863 had erected a tenement whose distinctive features were an exterior stairwell and two-room-deep apartments. White patterned his own buildings after the Langbourn Estate of Waterlow's Improved Industrial Dwellings Company, including the outside stairwell which dispensed with the "foulness of interior dark unventilated halls and stairways," and served as a sturdy, accessible fire escape.[17] Located in Brooklyn and completed in 1877, White's initial tribute to "philanthropy and 5 per cent" was an immediate, influential success. He demonstrated, presumably, that a capitalist could provide "well-ventilated, convenient, and agreeable" housing for workers.[18] According to White, his "Home Buildings" on Hicks and Baltic Streets near the Brooklyn waterfront swiftly captured the attention of the Children's Aid Society, the AICP, and the State Charities Aid Association. Among the visitors, "keen in their interest," were Theodore Roosevelt, Sr., and Louisa Lee Schuyler, both of the State Charities Aid Association, D. Willis James, at whose home the first conference leading to the formation of the Committee of Nine had been held, and Josephine Shaw Lowell, founder of the New York Charity Organization Society, who referred to the new tenements as a "realization of an Arabian Night's Dream."[19]

The "Home Buildings" accommodated forty families; and each apartment, only two rooms deep to ensure sufficient light and ventilation, included a sink and water closet. White completed a second adjoining unit the same year and then purchased a 200 x 250 foot tract on the next block. The "Tower Buildings" arose on this site (Hicks, Warren, and Baltic Streets) in 1878-79. Finally, White compressed thirty-four cottages into a narrow alley or passageway running from Warren to Baltic Street. These were attached six- to nine-room houses, arranged in two parallel rows. Altogether White was landlord to 267 families. He prohibited boarders or lodgers, set high standards of maintenance and upkeep for his tenants, and demanded prompt weekly payments of rent in advance.

Following White's lead, others promoted model tenement companies in the next decade. The Improved Dwellings Association, organized in 1879 as a consequence of the Committee of Nine's recommendations, opened its Manhattan tenements for occupancy in 1882. The Tenement House Building Company, organized in 1885, was ready for business two years later. Its property was located on squalid Cherry Street in the fourth ward. Pratt Institute inaugurated another philanthropic venture in 1887, when it opened its Astral Apartments in Greenpoint, Brooklyn, and White rounded out the decade's good works with his "Riverside Buildings" in 1890.

White's objectives were representative of most other model tenement enthusiasts of the period. He insisted, above all, that such tenements must be profitable. Otherwise, they would not inspire imitators. And if model tenements failed financially, opponents of restrictive legislation would use this as an argument "*against* efforts to secure legislative action seeking to impose healthful restrictions on existing or future buildings."[20] Furthermore, the reformer must never view housing as a charity in which the poor got something for nothing, thus weakening their character and self-reliance. It was a business venture; the purpose of the model tenement was to prove that good housing paid.

White advised prospective investors to build in districts already invaded by speculators. "You can afford to pay as much for land as they can; and high cost is no detriment, *provided* the value is made by the pressure of people seeking residence there."[21] White's insistence upon profitability and his advice to philanthropists to emulate the example of the speculative builder indicate his essentially conservative outlook. Neither White nor his contemporary housing reformers were radicals, toying with imaginative reconstructions of the social and economic order. Their aim was more modest—to provide safe, comfortable, and even pleasant housing for low-income groups within the framework of the capitalist-profit system. Apart from the genuine structural merits of the model tenement, it is not surprising that the businessmen, clergymen, and social workers who participated in the housing movement were so united in its endorsement. The model tenement represented no challenge whatever to economic orthodoxy. It was a painless and ostensibly effective solution to the housing problem.

White recommended that model tenement investors determine the prevailing rents in the neighborhood selected for construction. The buildings should then be planned to return the same average rentals and simultaneously assure tenants "as many conveniences as this average rental will allow."[22] White's last unit, the "Riverside Buildings," are a good example of his objectives in practice and they indicate, generally, the kind of accommodations which the model tenement companies hoped to provide. The Riverside Buildings were six stories high. They contained 3 one-room, 91 two-room, 161 three-room and 23 four-room apartments. Rents ranged from $1.40 a week for a single room with scullery on the ground floor to $3.60 a week for a four-room apartment. These rents, which the unskilled worker could afford to pay, were unusuaully low even by the standards of the model tenement. White, of course, built in Brooklyn, where land prices were much cheaper than in Manhattan. The Riverside Buildings provided a separate water closet for each family and such outdoor amenities as children's sandboxes, grass-lined courts and summer band concerts. Most important of all, White broke from the confines of the 25 x 100 foot lot and grouped his buildings around a large central court. They covered only half the land and since no apartment was more than two rooms deep, every room was assured plentiful light and ventilation.[23]

Model tenement zealots like White were certain that the policy of investment philanthropy would inspire widespread emulation. After all, the model tenement idea courted two of the strongest instincts in human nature—self-interest and altruism. By helping the poor at a profit, one served both humanity and one's pocket. Unfortunately, capitalists in the 1880's were no more prepared to minister to humanity in this fashion than had been their counterparts in 1850's, when the AICP had sponsored its model tenement. Why should wealthy businessmen with loose capital accept dividends of only 4 or 5 per cent in an age of great material expansion when more profitable investments beckoned elsewhere?

Housing, as a rule, did not attract the large aggregations of capital necessary to build model tenements in contrast to the cheaper dumb-bells with their smaller lot dimensions and lower structural standards. Concentrated ownership of tenement land or property, such as that of the Astor family or Trinity Church, was not typical. Low-income housing appealed mostly to the capitalist (builder or landlord) of relatively small means.[24] It required a comparatively modest equity, which was all he could afford. Yet the tenement landlord might anticipate average profits of 6 or 7 per cent on his investment. Tenement property in the 1880's sometimes paid much more—even 15 or 18 per cent.[25] In effect, those who could afford the large capital investment required to build model tenements were not particularly interested; they had better uses for their capital which did not involve the annoyance of dealing with ignorant or careless tenants. On the other hand the small entrepreneurs, sometimes immigrants themselves, who owned the lion's share of New York tenements, were not prepared to sacrifice their profits for the sake of humanity. The altruism and self-restraint upon which model-tenement enthusiasts depended were remote from the realities of the market place. Until reformers could incorporate the standards of the model tenement in restrictive legislation, housing conditions would not improve for the majority of workers.

[4]

Why was it that an affluent and comfortably situated gentleman like Alfred T. White devoted so much time, energy, and money to improving the housing of the poor? Why, in the words of the AICP, was there "no social question, except that of labor itself, of deeper interest to the community at large?"[26] We cannot wholly appreciate the attitudes and goals of housing reformers until we grasp the full social implications of the tenement problem. The tenement slum was the product of mighty social and economic upheavals in American society. For most reformers it was also a cause.

The quality of a city's housing is inextricably linked to broader social and economic trends. It is related, for example, to the generally accepted standard of living, the pace of urban and industrial expansion, the level of technology, the accepted role of government in the urban economy, and social and moral ideals. The decade or two after the Civil War has been described as the age of the robber barons, the gilded age, the age of enterprise, the great barbecue. Its dominant features—industrialization, urbanization, immigration, westward expansion—were not new phenomena in American life, but their magnitude was unprecedented. In 1860 there were only nine cities with over 100,000 population. By 1880 there were twenty. The nine cities in 1860 contained a little over 2,500,000 inhabitants. The corresponding figure for the twenty cities in 1880 was 6,000,000. In 1854, some 400,000 immigrants from Europe landed in the United States, the record number before the Civil War. After 1880, yearly immigration rarely fell below 400,000. In 1859, approximately 1,300,000 wage earners toiled in 140,000 industrial establishments. By 1889, over 4,000,000 labored in 355,000 factories. The value of manufactured products in the same thirty-year period rose from less than two billion dollars to more than nine billion.[27]

However one might characterize the two decades after the Civil War, one thing is certain. The machine and the city had shattered the Jeffersonian-Jacksonian vision of the yeoman, agrarian republic. The economic vitality of the new era centered in the factory, not the farm. The city, rather than the small town, became the undisputed symbol of America's productive energies, cultural and intellectual attainments, economic and social opportunities. New men of wealth in the great cities superseded the older planter and merchant aristocracy and, as Veblen explained, created new canons of consumption. The stone and marble palaces of the rich lined Fifth Avenue in New York. The lavish excesses of the wealthy excited the imagination of *hoi polloi*. It became the custom on New Year's day, for example, to leave window curtains partly undrawn on Fifth Avenue, permitting strollers to view "the richly furnished, brightly lighted drawing rooms, with their elegantly dressed occupants."[28] The excitement and diversity of city life, its economic possibilities most vividly manifested by the *nouveau riche*, attracted those persons dissatisfied with the stale routine of the farm or village.

But the color of the city, the avenues it opened to material success and cultural stimulation, were balanced by less glamorous features. The city reflected as well the acute social tensions and maladjustments of an expanding and fluid industrial society.

The Jeffersonian-Jacksonian ideal had been that of a roughly equalitarian society. A nation composed of small property owners, mostly farmers and artisans, would insure political democracy, widely diffused intelligence, virtue, and patriotism. Although extreme Jacksonians had certain qualms about the unsettling effects on the economy of business enterprise, most Americans could easily reconcile enterprise with stability and virtue. Men would be rewarded for their toil in proportion to their thrift, initiative, ability, and sobriety. Work and business were thus tests of character, and the entrepreneur the instrument of the community's moral and economic progress. Even the most doctrinaire Jacksonian agreed that the threat to social stability came not from business enterprise as such, but from monopoly and special privilege.

What happened to the certainties of the equalitarian society in an industrial-urban age? They lingered on in men's minds, but they obviously had less applicability in the urban metropolis, with its striking contrasts between wealth and poverty. The artisan became a wage earner in a factory. No longer the master of his economic destiny, he found that his standard of living and his range of opportunities were increasingly controlled by remote and impersonal forces—the absentee capitalists, the laws of the market place, technological innovations. A permanent laboring class had formed that owned neither its homes nor the tools of its trade. But the equalitarian dream was based upon a nation of men who owned their homes, worked for themselves, and lived close to the soil. Could the new proletariat be relied upon to exercise sound political judgment when it had no material interest in honest government? No wonder corruption and bossism pervaded urban politics. Could such a class appreciate the rights of property and not look with envy upon the acquisitions of the more prosperous and successful? No wonder the middle class reacted furiously to such assertions of working-class discontent as the railroad strikes of 1877 and the Haymarket explosion of 1886. Were these a portent of the future—a nation of cities filled with a rootless, ignorant proletariat ogling the wealth of their betters and prepared to expropriate it by violent means? "The city's beautiful homes, splendid with costly furniture; the prancing horses and sparkling carriages; the silks and seal-skins and the bright and dainty dresses of rich children," seemed to the worker "to have been filched from his own poor fireside and from his shabby little ones." What did one have in common with a man who believed that "you and your class have wronged him?"[29]

At the same time that the city exposed the breakdown of America's ideal of the classless society, it revealed a corresponding division by race and nationality. Large cities like New York, Chicago, and Boston developed foreign quarters whose life and culture seemed to diverge at every point from that of native, middle-class Americans. Here was another serious menace to America's social homogeneity and the stability of her institutions.

Could these foreigners, most of them belonging to the wage-earning proletariat and many of them Catholics, be depended upon to preserve the "pure high faith of our fathers," the faith that had "promoted at once free-thinking and right-thinking, power and purity, personal liberty and personal responsibility?" How many of these same foreigners—whose ranks after 1880 increasingly included the hot-tempered, unpredictable Italian and the querulous, clannish Jew plucked from the Pale and ghettos of eastern Europe—would "join the ranks of the misguided and incorrigible men who openly or secretly long for the coming of anarchy and chaos?" The presence of the foreigner not only intensified the "great and growing gulf . . . between the working class and those above them," but created an even worse class problem than existed in Europe. In America disparities in wealth were intensified by "still greater differences in race, language, and religion."[30]

Within the urban community, the most vivid expression of the class and ethnic tensions troubling American society was the slum. Here the working-class and immigrant population concentrated. Measured by American standards of physical health, moral deportment, language, customs, traditions, and religion, the tenement population almost seemed to belong to a different species of humanity. The housing reformer believed that if he could improve the housing of the poor, this would reduce the class and ethnic conflict splitting the urban community into enemy camps. Better housing was needed not only to protect the health of the entire community, but to Americanize the immigrant working-class population, to impose upon it the middle-class code of manners and morals.

[5]

Charles F. Wingate, former editor of the *Plumber and Sanitary Engineer*, included among the moral disadvantages of tenement life "the growth of intemperance and immorality," "the disruption of families, the turning of children into the street, the creation and fostering of crime." If such charges were true, then New York had indeed allowed a civic Frankenstein to gestate within its womb. By 1890, the city's 81,000 dwellings included 35,000 tenements. These tenements, however, contained an overwhelming percentage of the city's total population of approximately 1,500,000. Those tenements alone which housed twenty-one persons or more contained a total population in excess of 1,000,000.[31]

In the American hierarchy of values, stable and harmonious family life loomed high. Whatever else failed, the moral influence of the family unit over the individual would maintain the integrity of the community. But New York was a city of the homeless. Many of its people grew up "without the education, discipline, and moral influence of a separate family life and the interest in the community which the owning of a bit of land gives." These were the "natural tool of demogogues." A generation of tenement life had already "destroyed in a great measure the safeguards which a genuine home erects around a people." This left "vice and ignorance as the foundation stones of the municipality."[32]

As in the past, the feature of tenement life which critics singled out most frequently was the enforced overcrowding. The tenement heaped people and families together; by force of example, the impure infected the virtuous. As Wingate explained: "Every tenement-house is a community in itself, and the malign example of vice cannot fail to exert its full influence. The drunkard, the wife or child beater, the immoral woman, and the depraved child infect scores of their neighbors by their vicious acts. How is it possible to preserve purity amid such homes, or to bring up children to be moral and decent?"[33]

There in the tenements "young girls are found sleeping on the floor in rooms where are crowded men, women, youths and children. Delicacy is never known; purity is lost before its meaning is understood. . . ." [34] Boys growing up in the company of thieves and vagabonds formed into the gangs of "toughs" who roamed the city in search of thrills. These, the children of immigrants, were described by Charles Loring Brace as "the dangerous classes of New York." Ignorant and insensitive, they were "far more brutal than the peasantry from whom they descend." [35] When the parent could no longer control his child, the tenement indeed had sapped the roots of the family.

The tenement environment responsible for crime, hoodlumism, and sexual impurity also fostered alcoholism. Poor food, filthy surroundings, and "the constant inhalation of vitiated air" poisoned the organism and predisposed "these unfortunates to a continual desire for stimulation." [36] The environment was more responsible for intemperance than any inherent addiction of the tenement poor to liquor. If "Mr. Millions" had to suffer through life in a cramped tenement apartment, one sympathetic observer noted, he would very likely be inclined to send for his bottle of rum and "solace himself with the great East Side comforter."[37]

How could the immigrant and his children develop into desirable citizens, how could they be assimilated into the American community if the tenement warped their personalities? It even warped their bodies. The poor fell prey to "the slow process of decay . . . called 'tenement-house rot'." Infantile life was "nipped in the bud." Deformed youth gave way at the age of thirty to "loathsome" decrepitude. The typical immigrant was "a European peasant, whose horizon has been narrow, whose moral and religious training has been meager or false, and whose ideas of life are low." How could he possibly be rescued if, segregated in his tenement ghetto, he remained impervious to the elevating influence of

American moral and cultural doctrine? Perhaps it was necessary to restrict immigration, the source of so much turmoil. The foreigners who came here to "herd together like sheep in East Side tenement-houses" were more an incubus than a boon to the nation.[38]

Although the American middle-class community and the immigrant worker were conscious of each other's existence, there was a little personal association between them. The city became a world marked by physical proximity and social distance.[39] The American reacted with hostile contempt to the foreigner's unwillingness or inability to shed his old world customs, language, and companions. He blamed the foreigner for having caused the tenement blight. He resented the fact that "all forms of misgovernment and political corruption in the City feed on this un-Americanized mass, which has now grown so great that the native element is merely tolerated."[40] The foreigner, for his part, could either ignore or rankle under the whiplash of such criticism. Whatever his reaction, he could not suddenly shed his foreignness and merge silently into the American community. The city was divided into two worlds.

If the homogeneity of urban society had disintergrated under the strains caused by industrialism and immigration, the tenement system in the eyes of reformers thwarted any possibilities of reintegration. Since "the bad almost inevitably drag down the good; and the good have not the chance to lift up the bad,"[41] it was impossible for the foreigner to adopt the standards of personal cleanliness and behavior essential to his Americanization.

The tenement reformer had great faith in the reformatory powers of an improved housing environment. It was true, as some complained, that many "perfectly honest and virtuous" persons conscientiously abstained from soap and water, twisted out balusters for kindling wood, and unhesitatingly emptied garbage from the nearest window.[42] Reformers replied to such pessimism that the poor could not always help themselves, that they "never knew cleanliness or comfort or anything but squalor." It was their normal condition. On the other hand, such squalor not only served to "prevent the adoption of better habits," but threatened to "produce a race adapted to the surroundings." Thus John Cotton Smith, rector of Ascension Church, admitted that it was useless to carry on mission work among the poor until their physical conditions had been improved. They would only remain impervious to elevating moral influences. In words reminiscent of the AICP, the New York *Times* argued that it was futile to expect "decency, purity of life, and obedience to moral and political law" to arise out of wretched physical squalor.[43]

Conceivably, housing reformers placed excessive faith in the potency of a changed physical environment. The latter cannot necessarily transcend the limitations imposed by historical and cultural conditioning. The slum, after all, was a way of life, not simply houses. Habits and attitudes of the tenement population were affected by such fundamental influences as ethnic background, level of education, employment opportunities, and personal ambitions. The immigrant's adaptation to American life was influenced also by what he expected from this country. The immigrant who viewed his residence here as only temporary did not always care how he lived, so long as he found work, and this transient immigrant would remain especially resistant to efforts to transform his life.[44] Because the quality and tone of tenement life were moulded by factors other than overcrowding, poor sanitary facilities, a paucity of light or ventilation, and similar inconveniences, housing reform had limited applicability as an instrument of social control. As Thomas and Znaniecki have explained in their analysis of the Polish peasant, changes of material environment will not necessarily affect "mentality and character of individuals and groups." A change of material conditions might "help or hinder . . . the development of corresponding lines of behavior, but only if the tendency is already there, for the way in which they will be used depends on the people who use them."[45]

Tenement reformers, however, did not usually ponder such subtleties. They exposed the moral and physical condition of the tenement population and arraigned the tenement itself as the nursery of the squalor and degradation spreading incessantly before their eyes. They transmitted their faith in the beneficent powers of better housing conditions to most reformers of the Progressive generation.

Notes

1. In 1870 the Board was reorganized to include only the City of New York (Manhattan and the Bronx).

2. "Report of the Committee on Public Health, Medical Colleges and Societies, Relative to the Conditions of Tenement Houses in the Cities of New York and Brooklyn," *New York State Assembly Documents*, No. 156, Mar. 8, 1867, 3, 4, 6.

3. *New York State Laws*, Ninetieth Session, 1867, Chap. 908, Sec. 17.

4. This was the conclusion reached by the New York State Tenement House Commission of 1884. "Report of the Tenement House Commission," *New York State Senate Documents*, No. 36, Feb. 17, 1885, 9. Hereafter cited as Tenement House Commission of 1884, *Report*.

5. Council of Hygiene, *Report*, 151.

6. New York *Times*, Mar. 25, 1879, 40, May 25, 1879, 6.

7. See the testimony before the Tenement House Commission of 1884 of Roger S. Tracy, a sanitary inspector for the Board of Health, and William P. Prentice, attorney and counsel to the Board. Tenement House Commission of 1884, *Report*, 170, 132, 135.

8. For Meyer's account of the founding of his journal see Henry C. Meyer, *The Story of the Sanitary Engineer, Later the Engineering Record. Supplementary to Civil War Experiences* (New York, 1928). On the contest itself consult the *Plumber and Sanitary Engineer*, II (1878), 1, 32.

9. New York *Times*, Feb. 10, 1879, 8; *American Architect and Building News*, V (1879), 57; *Plumber and Sanitary Engineer* II (1879), 90.

10. Hatfield died before the awards were made. He was replaced by James Renwick.

11. *Plumber and Sanitary Engineer*, II (1879), 90.

12. For the sequence of events beginning with the conference at the home of D. Willis James to the formation of the Committee of Nine and the enactment of the Tenement House Law of 1879, consult the following: Committee of Nine, *Final Report*, May 31, 1879; James Gallatin, *Tenement House Reform in the City of New York* (Boston, 1881); Henry E. Pellew, "New York Tenement Houses," *The Sanitarian*, VII (1879), 107-11; *Plumber and Sanitary Engineer*, II (1879), 89. The members of the Committee of Nine were H. E. Pellew, W. Bayard Cutting, R. T. Auchmuty, D. Willis James, C. P. Daly, C. Vanderbilt, W. W. Astor, James Gallatin, and F. D. Tappen. Most of these served on the Board of Directors of the New York Sanitary Reform Society and were connected in some capacity with the Improved Dwellings Association. The quotation is from Gallatin, 6.

13. Meyer, *Story of the Sanitary Engineer*, 13.

14. New York, *Times*, Mar. 16, 1879, 6; *The Sanitarian*, VII (1879), 226; *American Architect and Building News*, V (1879), 81, 97.

15. The Tenement House Commission of 1884 included, besides Adler and Wingate, Joseph W. Drexel, chairman; S. O. Vanderpoel; Oswald Ottendorfer; Moreau Morris; Anthony Reichardt; Joseph J. O'Donohue; Abbot Hodgman; William P. Esterbrook.

16. Alfred T. White, *Improved Dwellings for the Laboring Classes: The Need, and the Way to Meet It on Strict Commercial Principles, in New York and other Cities* (New York, 1879), 41, 2.

17. Alfred T. White, *Thirty-Five Years' Experience as an Owner* (New York, 1912), 3.

18. New York *Times*, Nov. 5, 1877, 4; *American Architect and Building News*, IV (1878), 208; Tenement House Commission of 1884, *Report*, 75; Charles L. Brace, "Model Tenement Houses," *Plumber and Sanitary Engineer*, I (1878), 48.

19. White, *Thirty-Five Years' Experience as an Owner*, 4, 5.

20. Alfred T. White, "Better Homes for Workingmen," National Conference of Charities and Correction, *Proceedings*, 1885, 368.

21. *Ibid.*, 370-71.

22. *Ibid.*, 371.

23. For a description of the Riverside Buildings see E. R. L. Gould, *The Housing of the Working People*, Eighth Special Report of the Commissioner of Labor (Washington, D.C., 1895), 177-81.

24. Gustavus Myers, *History of the Great American Fortunes* (Modern Library: New York, 1936), 160-62. Henry C. Meyer, testifying before a Royal Housing Commission in England, claimed that New York's 21,000 tenements were divided among 18,000 owners. Meyer, *Story of the Sanitary Engineer*, 33.

25. Tenement House Commission of 1884, *Report* 83, 105, 106.

26. AICP, *Forty-fifth Annual Report*, 1888, 21.

27. The statistics were drawn from U.S. Department of Commerce: Bureau of the Census, *Historical Statistics of the United States, 1789-1945* (Washington, D.C., 1949).

28. James D. McCabe, *New York by Sunlight and Gaslight, A Work Descriptive of the Great American Metropolis* (New York, 1882), 174.

29. Samuel L. Loomis, *Modern Cities and Their Religious Problems* (New York, 1887), 61. Josiah Strong complained that "socialism not only centers in the city, but is almost confined to it; and the materials of its growth are multiplied with the growth of the city." Josiah Strong, *Our Country: Its Possible Future and Its Present Crisis* (New York, 1885), 132; New York *Tribune*, Jan. 16, 1885, 4.

30. Loomis, *Modern Cities and Their Religious Problems*, 81, 66; New York *Times*, May 2, 1887, 4.

31. Charles F. Wingate, "The Moral Side of the Tenement-House Problem," *The Catholic World* XLI (1885), 160; "Dwellings and Families in 1890," Extra Census Bulletin, No. 19, U.S. *Census*, 1890, 17, 27.

32. New York *Times*, Mar. 2, 1879, 6; Edward Crapsey, *The Nether Side of New York; or, The Vice,*

Crime, and Poverty of the Great Metropolis (New York, 1872), 116. Also New York *Tribune*, Apr. 20, 1884, 6; New York *Times*, Mar. 1, 1879, 8.

33. Wingate, "The Moral Side of the Tenement-House Problem," 160-61.

34. New York *Times*, Dec. 3, 1876, 6. Charles Loring Brace, founder of the Children's Aid Society, expressed a similar point of view: "If a female child be born and brought up in a room of one of these tenement-houses, she loses very early the modesty which is the great shield of purity. Personal delicacy becomes almost unknown to her. Living, sleeping, and doing her work in the same apartment with men and boys of various ages, it is well-nigh impossible for her to retain any feminine reserve, and she passes almost unconsciously the line of purity at a very early age." Charles Loring Brace, *The Dangerous Classes of New York, and Twenty Years' Work Among Them* (New York, 1880), 55.

35. *Ibid.*, 27. Josiah Strong complained that "the hoodlums and roughs of our cities are, most of them, American-born of foreign parentage." Strong, *Our Country: Its Possible Future and Its Present Crisis*, 41-42. See also Edward Self, "Evils Incident to Immigration," *North American Review*, CXXXVIII (1884), 85.

36. "The Sanitary and Moral Condition of New York City," *The Catholic World*, VII (1868), 556.

37. New York *Times*, Jan. 7, 1883, 9.

38. Wingate, "The Moral Side of the Tenement-House Problem," 162; Strong, *Our Country: Its Possible Future and Its Present Crisis*, 40; New York *Times*, May 15, 1880, 4.

39. For a sociological analysis of the physical proximity and social distance which characterize urban life, consult two essays in Ernest W. Burgess, ed., *The Urban Community* (Chicago, 1926). The first is E. S. Bogardus, "Social Distance in the City"; the second is Nicholas J. Spykman, "A Social Philosophy of the city." Useful also is Louis Wirth, "Urbanism as a Way of Life," *American Journal of Sociology*, XLIV (1938), 1-24.

40. New York *Times*, May 15, 1880, 4.

41. J. O. S. Huntington, "Tenement-House Morality," *Forum*, III (1887), 516.

42. *American Architect and Building News*, XV (1884), 205. For similar sentiments see the remarks of Henry Bergh quoted in the New York *Times*, Mar. 7, 1879, 3, and the remarks of Henry Bergh quoted in the New York *Times*, Mar. 7, 1879, 3, and the remarks of several speakers at a meeting at Cooper Union Institute on Mar. 11, also quoted in the *Times*, Mar. 12, 1879, 2.

43. New York *Tribune*, Feb. 6, 1884, 4; New York *Times*, July 1, 1878, 2, Feb. 24, 1879, 4.

44. David Brody has pointed out that the "one essential" for immigrant steelworkers was "not wages, working conditions, or living standards, but employment itself." *Steelworkers in America: The Nonunion Era* (Cambridge, Mass., 1960), 105.

45. William I. Thomas and Florian Znaniecki, *The Polish Peasant in Europe and America* (Dover Publications: New York, 1958), I, 13.

Streetcar suburbs

Sam B. Warner

When Jacob Riis published his famous *How the Other Half Lives* in 1890, he gave an enduring focus to American urban history. Especially for the formative period of the late nineteenth century, city life has been defined in terms of the urban poor—the recent immigrants and tenement house dwellers whose mean lives Riis described in graphic detail. But what of the half about whom Riis did not write? The rising middle-class, equally as numerous as the urban poor and just as much a product of the forces of industrialization, has only recently begun to find its historians. Among these, no one has matched the brilliant contribution made by Sam B. Warner in *Streetcar Suburbs* (1962). Warner focused on three outlying towns—Roxbury, West Roxbury, and Dorchester—that became, in the late nineteenth century, suburban communities within the greater Boston area. By what process did this development occur? To answer this fundamental question required pathbreaking historical research. First of all, Warner worked through and analyzed the one surviving record of suburban growth, the thousands of building permits for the dwellings erected in the three towns between 1870 and 1900. In addition to this laborious job, Warner employed another technique equally unusual among library-bound scholars: he walked the streets of Roxbury, West Roxbury, and Dorchester studying and photographing the physical remains of this era of suburban development, most of it still surviving. By these methods, Warner was able to reconstruct a part of urban history that,—because it did not generate the standard kinds of historical evidence, would have been thoroughly resistant to conventional historical research.

Warner's pioneering study has opened up the middle-class dimension of American urbanization. The key is indicated in the title of Warner's book. Until the second half of the nineteenth century, Boston was a walking city, its dimensions limited by the distance a man could go on foot in a reasonable time. The perfection of urban transporation, coming simultaneously with Boston's shift of emphasis from commerce to industry, led to a vast enlargement of the urban area. It was the middle class that seized the

Reprinted by permission of the publisher from Sam B. Warner, Jr., *Streetcar Suburbs: the Process of Growth in Boston, 1870-1900*. Cambridge, Mass.: Harvard University Press, Copyright, 1962, by the President and Fellows of Harvard College and the Massachusetts Institute of Technology, pp. 153-166.

opportunity thus opened to move out of the central city as the car tracks reached into the countryside. Motivated by the rural ideal that captivated men's imagination as an urban nation emerged, white-collar Bostonians abandoned their city to the uses of business and industry and to the unfortunates lacking the means to escape, Public agencies contributed greatly by the creation of municipal facilities well timed and on terms favorable for the swift suburban growth; and land developers did the job of transforming the countryside into building lots. But the actual financing and construction of houses, Warner emphasizes, was accomplished by a multitude of individuals, each building either for his own use or on speculation a house or two at a time. This was nineteenth-century enterprise at its freest. But those thousands of individuals' decisions resulted, not in chaos, but in a striking set of patterns in the architectural and social order of suburban Boston. By 1900, the building process had run its course (for Roxbury, West Roxbury, and Dorchester, at any rate). A score or more of American cities were ringed by suburbs housing the middle class in solid comfort and at arms length from the problems of the central cities.

The selection reprinted below is the last chapter in Warner's book. In it, he traces the consequences of the suburban process, which he has spelled out with immense precision and imagination. What emerges most strikingly is a sad irony, the juxtaposition of a veritable triumph of nineteenth-century America—its technology, its opportunities, and its material progress—and the resulting urban ills that confound America in 1972.

For further reading: Richard Sennett, *Families Against the City* (1970); J. W. Reps, *The Making of Urban America* (1965); Robert Fogelson *Fragmented Metropolis: Los Angeles, 1850-1930* (1967); Harold C. Syrett, *The City of Brooklyn, 1860-1898* (1944); Nelson M. Blake, *Water for the Cities* (1956); Oscar Handlin, *Boston's Immigrants, 1790-1880: a Study in Acculturation* (1959);* S. B. Warner, Jr., *The Private City* (1968).*

Two qualities mark off the Boston of 1900 from all preceding eras: its great size and its new suburban arrangement. In 1850 the metropolitan region of Boston encompassed a radius of but two or three miles, a population of two hundred thousand; in 1900 the region extended over a ten-mile radius and contained a population of more than a million. A change in structure accompanied this change in scale. Once a dense merchant city clustered about an ocean port, Boston became a sprawling industrial metropolis. In 1850 it was a fairly small and unified area, by 1900 it had split into two functional parts: an industrial, commercial, and communications center packed tight against the port, and an enormous outer suburban ring of residences and industrial and commerical subcenters. By examining in detail the method of building one part of the great outer suburban ring, this book has attempted to discover something about the society that underwent this transformation and to elicit some of the consequences of this new physical arrangement of people.

In Roxbury, West Roxbury, and Dorchester the parade of 25,000 new houses arranged by grid streets and frontage lots, the regular progress from one architectural style to the next, the constancy of basic house design, and the clustering of buildings by the income levels of their owners witness uniformity of behavior among individual decision makers.

Both positive and negative factors contributed to the uniformity of decisions of the 9,000 private builders. Positively, these middle class homeowners and amateur investors shared a sympathy for the suburban style of living which was then developing in metropolitan Boston. There existed a consensus of attitude which made each decision maker to some degree favorable to the new shingle and later colonial revival styles of architecture. This same consensus caused each man to build houses much like those of his neighbors and to seek to locate in a neighborhood or on a street which was popular with families of an income similar to his own. Finally, this same consensus encouraged each man to seek and to perpetuate the new suburban environment which emphasized the pleasures of private family life, the security of a small community setting, and the enjoyments of an increased contact with nature. The strength of this consensus grew with the passage of time. Every year more and more middle class families lived in the suburbs. Every year, too, the streetcar and utility networks brought a steady increase in land available for settlement so that successively closer approximations to the desired environment became possible.

Negatively, suburban builders were repelled by conditions in the central city. The unending immigrant invasion, the conversion of old houses and the encroachment of industry and commerce heightened the contrast between the new suburbs and the central city. Negatively, too, the limited financial position of homebuilders disciplined their choices of houses and neighborhoods and controlled their methods of land division.

The policies of the large institutions concerned with building supported and disciplined these individual choices. The role of the larger agents was essential. At the municipal scale, utilities had to be laid before most men would be willing to build. Adequate streetcar service also preceded homebuilders and their customers. At the neighborhood scale the arrival of new families attracted by a new improved transportation service, or the expansion of adjacent neighborhoods, or the departure of old families because of housing obsolescence, all encouraged one kind of building and discouraged others. At his peril a man built cheap rental units in outer suburbs, or expensive singles in old inner suburbs. The patterned spread of various kinds of new construction bears witness to the power of the informal neighborhood regulation of building. It was a power based upon the sensitivity of individual landowners to the economic standing of their neighbors.

The behavior of the large institutions concerned with suburban building also encouraged individual landowners to repeat in their building the popular suburban architecture, engineering, and economic grading of neighborhoods. Late nineteenth century Boston was a fast-growing metropolitan society made prosperous by the new industrial technology and propelled by the energy of thousands of individual capitalists. The middle class was one of the principal beneficiaries of this prosperity, and its well-being and rapid enlargement gave this large segment of Boston society the confidence to stress its equalitarianism and the willingness to exploit each new technological device. The rise of thousands of families of the most diverse ethnic backgrounds to a middle class competence, like their quick adoption of each new invention, was taken as proof of the success of the society.

The City of Boston and the later metropolitan boards enthusiastically adopted the new sanitary engineering. These institutions undertook to see that all new neighborhoods would be built to the latest standards, and at great expense attempted to service the old parts of the city. This enormous undertaking not only made the new devices available to Boston's homeowners, but also stimulated the universal acceptance of middle class criteria for home services. In the suburbs all the new regulations for plumbing, gas fitting, and building and fire safety were perhaps more important as official affirmations of middle class norms than for policing an occasional offender. With the cooperation and example of the large institutions almost all new suburban building from 1870 to 1900 included safe construction, indoor plumbing, and orderly land arrangement. From the prosperity of the middle class and its enthusiastic acceptance of the new sanitation and transportation technology came the popular achievement of the late nineteenth century suburbs: a safe environment for half the metropolitan population.

The orientation of the large institutions toward the benefit of the suburban builders also assisted the small landowners. The street railways and other utilities rapidly extended their service to outlying metropolitan villages. In so doing they encouraged private development of distant land. This policy was aimed at taking advantage of the general growth of the city, but it also reflected a belief that public agencies should assist private undertakings. Similarly, the Park Department carefully avoided land which was thought to be suited to private construction, taking instead the marshes and uplands at the edges of areas then building. In effect, the Park Department landscaped the margins of private developments. In the new neighborhoods the City of Boston built schools at a very rapid rate and its official architecture and landscape design mirrored the fashions of private builders. Public policy held installation charges for new utilities and streets to below cost, much of the expense being borne by general taxation and general rates. When the city bargained with gas and electric companies for the extension of its lighting it often bargained in behalf of residential users as well, endeavoring to see that they too would be connected to the new lines and served at reasonable rates.[1] The combined effect of all these policies was to greatly assist the individual builder to develop the vacant land outside the old city.

At the level of homeowners' decisions the class character of neighborhoods played a more supportive than immediately disciplinary role. Though the migration of various income groups ultimately determined the uses, rents, and fate of neighborhoods, at the moment of construction the power of regulation lay only in the example set by the behavior of others. The presence of houses of similar cost and style encouraged a man to build his own house in keeping with existing ones. No laws, however, prevented him from building something different.

The variety of ethnic backgrounds of families living within the surrounding houses also encouraged the builder of a new house to minimize any ethnic hostilities he might possess. If no Catholic, Methodist, or Episcopal church yet existed in his neighborhood the presence of recently built churches and schools all over the suburbs allowed a new resident to expect one soon. Just as curbs and gas lights might still be a few years in coming to his street, so, too, the arrival of his particular church, club, and school, was merely a matter of time.

To all these characteristics—the speed of building, the mass arrival of new families, the separation of families by economic class, the universality of the new high standards of light, air, land, and sanitation—must be added the effect of the omnipresent newness. Whether a man lived in a lower middle class quarter of cheap three-deckers, or on a fashionable street of expensive singles, the latest styles, the freshly painted houses, the neat streets, the well-kept lawns, and the new schools and parks gave him a sense of confidence in the success of his society and a satisfaction at his participation in it. These physical expressions gave him the willingness to abide by the rules of the society whether the rules took the form of building regulations or the less specific directions of group imitation. The very extent of newness in the suburbs, which by 1900 dwarfed the old central city, made these areas a source of pride for Boston's metropolitan society. Today suburbs are increasingly assigned all the evils of American society; but in the late nineteenth century they created a widespread sense of achievement.

The general contemporary satisfaction with suburbs came from their ability to answer some of the major needs of the day. To be sure, the costs of new construction were such as to exclude at least half the families of Boston; but the suburban half, the middle class, was the dominant class in the society. To middle class families the suburbs gave a safe, sanitary environment, new houses in styles somewhat in keeping with their conception of family life, and temporary neighborhoods of people with similar outlook. In an atmosphere of rapid change, the income-graded neighborhoods rendered two important services to their residents. Evenness of wealth meant neighbors who would reinforce an individual family's efforts to pass on its values to its children. The surrounding evenness of wealth also gave adults a sense of a community of shared experience, and thereby gave some measure of relief from the uncertainties inherent in a world of highly competitive capitalism.

In addition to benefiting their own residents, in one important way the suburbs served the half of Boston's population which could not afford them. The apparent openness of the new residential quarters, their ethnic variety, their extensive growth, and their wide range of prices from fairly inexpensive rental suites to expensive single-family houses—these visible characteristics of the new suburbs gave aspiring low-income families the certainty that should they earn enough money they too could possess the comforts and symbols of success. Even for those excluded from them, the suburbs offered a physical demonstration that the rewards of competitive capitalism might be within the reach of all.

The rendering of these important social services gave Bostonians of the late nineteenth century a confidence that at least in the suburbs they had struck a successful compromise among the conflicts then active in their society. The suburban city, however, was a compromise which had all the faults of its virtues. Many of the same devices that gave power and dynamism to its building contained within them unresolved conflicts. These conflicts, in turn, worked to destroy much of what the suburb hoped to achieve.

Homeownership was one suburban goal, but the high down payments and short-term, nonamortizing mortgages of the unregulated mortgage market restricted homeownership to one quarter of Boston's families. A pleasant landscape was another goal, but the lack of training and limited financial capabilities of subdividers condemned the new streetcar suburbs to the progressive destruction of their natural setting. Under the grid street and frontage lot system of land division natural contours were thrown away for the short-term advantages of easy marketing and cheap utility and street construction. Once all the narrow lots had been occupied, a band of tiny front lawns and a row of street trees was about all the venture a suburban development could offer.

The suburb, the home of property owners and settled family life, was thought by contemporaries to be an environment that encouraged individual participation in community life. Compared to transient conditions in older parts of the city the suburbs were more conducive to integration of the individual into some sort of community activity.[2] Their physical arrangement, however—the endless street grids and the dependence upon the downtown for work and shopping—failed to provide local centers where all the residents of a given area might, through frequent contact, come to know each other and thereby be encouraged to share in community-wide activities.

Aside from class segregation there was nothing in the process of late nineteenth century suburban construction that built communities or neighborhoods: it built streets. The grid plan of the suburbs did not concern itself with public life. It was an economically efficient geometry which divided large parcels of land as they came on the market. The arrangement of the blocks of the grid depended largely upon what farm or estate came on the market at what time. The result was not integrated communities arranged about common centers, but a historical and accidental traffic pattern.

Where a railroad station and arterial streets came together, stores, churches, and sometimes schools were built to serve some of the needs of the residents of the area. In Dorchester, for example, there were historic village clusters that grew with the increase of population around them: Meeting House Hill, Harrison Square, Codman Square, Lower Mills. Other clusters—such as Fields Corner, Grove Hall, and Columbia Square—were largely the work of the new streetcar transportation network. Most characteristic of the new suburban order was the commercial strip which followed the main transportation lines and had no center at all. Washington street, Dorchester, from Codman Square to Grove Hall lacked any historic center. It was simply a long row of little stores which served those passing by and those living in the houses behind.

This centerless tendency was intensified by the Boston School Department's building policy which placed schools on inexpensive land on the side streets. In this way the schools formed partial centers by themselves which were often isolated from the commercial and social centers. The most dramatic example was the placing of Dorchester High School in Ashmont with the consequent destruction of the town's old educational center at Meeting House Hill. Roxbury High School was similarly mislocated. In West Roxbury, however, the school building policy maintained the historic center at Eliot Square. By this municipal money-saving policy the child of the suburbs was isolated from the center of his community in the same way his mother was separated from her husband's work.

An amorphous and weak neighborhood structure was the consequence of compounding communities with a mix of side-street grids, commercial strips, and small historic centers. A family living near the corner of Tonawanda street and Geneva avenue in central Dorchester during the 1890's shopped locally on Geneva avenue, and went to Boston for major purchases. If they happened to be Congregationalists their church stood on their corner. The father went to Boston on the Old Colony Railroad or took the streetcar down Dorchester avenue. The children went to primary school, however, in a different neighborhood on the other side of Dorchester avenue. If the family was not Congregational they had to go to a third neighborhood for church, and, of course, social clubs were scattered through the town. A similar family living twelve doors up Tonawanda street had an entirely different orientation. Its business area lay along the Washington street strip.

As a result of the centerless character of most suburbs, community life fell into fragments. Groups formed about particular churches, clubs, schools, and ward club rooms; rarely did any large fraction of the population of a suburban area participate in any joint endeavor. When, through accident, the historic political boundaries of a town coincided with the building pattern of a new suburb local politics provided a framework for community activities. Nevertheless, even these conditions were unfavorable to the development of meaningful community life. The limited subject matter of town politics, and the frequently narrow income band of the residents of new bedroom suburbs, together generated an enervating parochialism which hung heavy over such community life as existed.[3]

In 1900 the new metropolis lacked local communities that could deal with the problems of contemporary society at the level of the family and its immediate surroundings, and it lacked a large-scale community that could deal with the problems of the metropolis.[4] As a result Boston community life fell into a self-defeating cycle. Each decade brought an increase in the scale and complexity of economic and social life; each decade's problems demanded more wide-scale attention, more complex solutions. Because of the physical arrangement of the new metropolis, each decade also brought an ever greater fragmentation of the community life into town and ward politics, church groups, clubs, and specialized societies of all kinds. The growing parochialism and fragmentation resulted in a steady relative weakening of social agencies. Weakness, in turn, convinced more and more individuals that local community action was hopeless or irrelevant. From this conviction came the further weakening of the public agencies. The self-defeating cycle, begun by the streetcar metropolis, has continued with increasing severity to this day. It has proved, both for the metropolis and its constituent political units, an iron cycle, a cycle which once established, is difficult to break.

The inattention of late nineteenth century Bostonians to the fragmentation of their community life was not an accidental oversight, it was a matter of principle, the principle of individualistic capitalism. Above all else the streetcar suburbs stand as a monument to a society which wished to keep the rewards of capitalist competition open to all its citizens. Despite ignorance and prejudice, during this period of mass immigration, the suburbs remained open to all who could meet the price.

By 1900 about half the families of metropolitan Boston had come to share this new environment. The wealth brought to the society by its industrial technology, and the special practices of suburban building, made this mass achievement possible. The manner in which the nineteenth century building process physically separated the metropolitan population into two sections—the middle class section of families who could afford new construction, and the lower class section of families who could not—assisted some of the open equalitarian goals of the capitalist society. In the suburbs families of similar economic standing lived next to each other, and their similarity of economic position helped them to learn to ignore their differences of religion and national background. The great extent of the new suburbs, moreover, left room for fine gradations of the middle class population. Middle class families were free to choose among hundreds of possible locations, free to find a neighborhood which suited both their ethnic feelings and their progress up the economic ladder.

The infrangible and enduring problems of the suburbs also derive from the principle of open capitalist competition. At any moment in the late nineteenth century half the metropolitan society was not successful, half the society remained apart from the achievements of the suburbs. The process of new construction, since it was tied to the abilities of individual builders erecting houses for their own immediate use or profit, took no effective responsibility for the lower income half of the society. As a result, contemporary progress in housing for lower class families was slow and uncertain, limited to slight improvements in sanitaton, structural safety, and fire prevention.

By sheer enlargement of their numbers, and by the obsolescence of middle-income structures, low-income groups could and did reach the new suburbs. Most often, however, they could occupy them only by destroying much of what the suburb had achieved. Because the late-comers possessed but small sums for rent, secondhand houses in the suburbs often had to be divided and redivided so that a single became a double or a triple, to a two-family house was added an attic apartment, and so forth. Even where slightly higher incomes made division of structures unnecessary the cost of maintaining old wooden houses often prevented the newcomers from keeping up their houses and lots to the level originally intended. Though not included in their rent bills, the progressive deterioration of their environment was one of the prices of low-income tenancy.[5]

Neither the architecture nor the land planning of the new suburbs took any account of the possible subsequent users. A satisfactory single-family house brought, when divided, two or three cramped and mean apartments, each one often well below the building's original standards for light, air, and sanitation. The reduction in floor area per person brought an immediate and obvious retreat from the norms of the first owner. The garden setting for the street often disappeared under the feet of running children; back yards and porches filled with the overflow and trash from the houses; planted playgrounds required tar to support increased use; and the large country parks grew to weeds because of lack of time and interest among their new users.

By assigning building to the activities of thousands of individual middle class land-owners the metropolitan society allowed itself to build a physical environment which would become, by its own terms, the unsatisfactory home of half its members. By this means also the society received a physical plan which was destructive to its democratic processes. The essence of the new metropolitan plan was the separation of the vast areas of new construction from the old central city.

The literature of late nineteenth century reformers tells the consequences of this division. For the middle class the inner area of low-income housing became an unknown and uncontrolled land. Here, in one ward vice and drunkenness flourished out of reach of middle class supervision; in another ward nationalist demagogues, institutionally isolated from the rest of the metropolis and responsible only to the majority of the ward, held free rein in the search for their own profit. Such troublesome manifestations of the divided society gave much concern to contemporaries. They were but symptoms of the serious consequences of the physical division of classes.

Most important, the concentration in a solid two-mile area of foreign languages, poverty, sweatshops, and slum housing gave the suburban middle class a sense of hope-lessness and fear. Much of the work of reformers in the twentieth century progressive era had to be devoted to the task of educating in the middle class to the conditions of modern industrial cities. It was a task undertaken with the middle class faith that through knowledge would come a willingness to take action.[6]

Opposing reformers' goals of knowledge and action stood the structure of the streetcar metropolis which had damaged the fabric of the society. In part the rural ideal bore responsibility for the arrangement of the metropolis, for it had encouraged middle class families to seek escape from the conditions of modern industrial life into an isolated family environment. More important, the dominant ideal of individualistic capitalism with its accompanying unwillingness to bring private profit to account had caused the economic division of the society. The slums and the suburbs were the physical expression of this division. The conditions of the central city which so dismayed the middle class were the product of its failure to control the distribution of income, its failure to regulate housing and working conditions, its failure to develop an adequate welfare program for the sick and unfortunate, and its failure to devise a community program for integrating the thousands of new citizens who every year moved to the metropolis. These things, neglected, bore a harvest of middle class fear. From fear came the late nineteenth century paradox of the growth of an economically integrated regional city of over a million inhabitants accompanied by an increase in the parochialism of its political and social units.

In 1870 many middle class suburbanites regarded Boston as their achievement, something they wished to join in order to create a political union of homes, jobs, and community. Such sentiment gave popularity to the mid-century annexation movement. From about 1850 to 1873 almost every city and town around Boston had an annexationist group, and the question of the advantages and disadvantages of union with Boston was seriously debated. In 1868 Roxbury joined Boston; in 1870 Dorchester, and in 1873 Charlestown, Brighton, and West Roxbury, voted for unification.

The year 1873 marked the end of the annexation movement. That year the residents of Brookline voted to remain separate. This political defeat, and the Depression of 1873-1878 ended public concern over the metroplitan expansion of Boston. With the return of prosperity, however, the movement never revived. Instead, the legislature created in the late 1880's and early 1890's three specialized state-managed agencies which undertook to serve metropolitan needs for water, sewer, and park building.

The sudden and permanent collapse of the annexation movement had two causes: the first concerned municipal services; the second, the idea of community. During the middle years of the nineteenth century some of the larger and more prosperous of the peripheral towns and cities had built their own waterworks and expanded their street and educational services so that they approximated some of the high standards of Boston. In 1870 Charlestown, Cambridge, and Brookline had satisfactory independent waterworks. These same towns and Dorchester and Roxbury possessed advanced educational facilities. Other towns, however, lacked the tax base and access to the rivers and lakes necessary for high-quality municipal service. The metropolitan agencies, by building a unified drainage and water supply for the whole metropolis, put all the region's towns in a position to meet modern municipal standards.

The motive of services having been withdrawn, there remained only the idea of community. Annexation debates had always concerned themselves with this question. Annexationists appealed to the idea of one great city where work and home, social and cultural activities, industry, and commerce would be joined in a single political union. Boston, they said, would share the fate of Rome if the middle class, which heretofore had provided the governance of the city and the force of its reforms, abandoned the city for the suburbs.[7]

Opponents of annexation countered with the ideal of small town life: the simple informal community, the town meeting, the maintenance of the traditions of rural New England. They held out to their audience the idea of the suburban town as a refuge from the pressures of the new industrial metropolis. Nor were the opponents of annexation slow to point out that the high level of city services maintained by Boston meant higher taxes, and further, they frankly stated that independent suburban towns could maintain native American life free from Boston's waves of incoming poor immigrants.[8]

As early as 1851 West Roxbury estate owners led a successful move to separate the rural part of the town of Roxbury from its industrial half. In 1873 middle class Boston commuters who had moved to West Roxbury reversed this decision by a close vote, and the town joined Boston. The new commuters wanted the high level of services offered by Boston, and they were confident that the middle class could govern the enlarged city to its own satisfaction.

By the 1880's, with but one exception, no suburban town ever again seriously considered annexation.[9] The segregation of the metropolitan population brought about by the interaction of the expansion of street railway transportation and the suburban building process had by the mid-1880's given a permanent set to political life. In the fact of the continually expanding size of the metropolis, by contrast to the continual waves of poor immigrants that flooded the central city and destroyed its old residential neighborhoods, the new suburbs offered ever new areas of homogeneous middle class settlement. Here, most immigrants spoke English, most were Americanized, and here the evenness of income lessened the scope of political conflict. It was already apparent in the 1880's that to join Boston was to assume all the burdens and conflicts of a modern industrial metropolis. To remain apart was to escape, at least for a time, some of these problems. In the face of this choice the metropolitan middle class abandoned their central city.

Very soon the middle class began to reap the harvest of its action. Already by 1900 Boston was something to be feared and controlled. Many of its powers of self-government had been taken from it by the state or voluntarily abandoned by tax-conscious voters to put a check on demands for public improvements.[10] Beyond Boston the special suburban form of popularly managed local government continued to flourish. In suburbs of substantial income and limited class structure, high standards of education and public service were often achieved. Each town, however, now managed its affairs as best it could surrounded by forces largely beyond its control. New transportation, new housing, new industries, new people, the great flow and vigor of the metropolis, lay beyond the knowledge and competence of these individual agencies. In the years to come World Wars and depressions would unleash antidemocratic forces that threatened the foundations of the society: its democratic institutions, its property, its ethnic harmony, the chance of each citizen to prosper through capitalist competition. Confronting these challenges stood a metropolitan society physically divided by classes, politically divided by about forty parochial institutions. So divided, the society denied itself the opportunity to end, through common action against common problems, the isolation of its citizens and the fear they held toward each other. So divided, the metropolis was helpless to solve its own problems.

During the years 1870 to 1900 industrial capitalism was, comparatively, a new thing, and a mass suburban metropolis like Boston had never existed before anywhere in the world. To rely on individual capitalists, to expect that each man building for himself would build a good environment for a democratic society was perhaps a reasonable error to have made. Today, some of the problems confronting the streetcar city have been solved or passed by. Except for the American Negro, immigration conditions are over. The automobile allows a less rigid class arrangement and less dense housing than was possible under streetcar transportation. Zoning, large-scale subdivision planning, and new financial institutions have made suburban building somewhat more orderly, and have opened homeownership to a greater proportion of the society. Most important of all, the great twentieth century national reforms of progressive taxation and labor, factory, and welfare legislation have allowed more widespread participation in the profits of industrialism.

Despite these changes the two great problems first met in the streetcar city remain unsolved. Even by popular standards one enormous segment of the population still lives in an unsatisfactory physical environment. More serious, because it is a condition which affects all others, the growing metropolitan society as a whole remains shut up in an ever larger number of specialized social and political units, its citizens isolated from one another, its society needlessly uncontrolled because of the weakness of its agents.

Notes

1. *Boston Transcript*, March 6, 1893, p. 1.

2. Josiah Quincy, *Moderate Houses for Moderate Means, A Letter to Rev. E. E. Hale* (Boston, 1874); R. A. Woods and A. J. Kennedy, eds. "The Zone of Emergence," [(c. 1912; ms. on deposit at the South End House, Boston)] chapters on Dorchester and Roxbury.

3. Even the most active municipal government in the metropolitan region, the City of Boston, under-took to deal with a rather narrow range of subject matter in its municipal affairs. Nathan Matthews, *The City Government of Boston*, (Boston, 1895) pp. 174-182; Quincy, *The Development of American Cities.*
   The limitation of municipal subject matter was reflected in the city's expenditure patterns: in the period 1868-1871 Boston spent 62.0 percent of its budget on real estate affairs (water, sewers, streets, and public grounds); in the period 1883-1886, 50.4 percent; in the period 1903-1906, 52.2 percent (included rapid transit). C. P. Huse, *The Financial History of Boston*, (Cambridge, 1916) p. 366.

4. Contemporary recognition of the problem of the scale of governmental units: Sylvester Baxter, *Greater Boston; A Study for a Federated Metropolis* (Boston, 1891); Massachusetts Metropolitan Commission, *Report to the Massachusetts Legislature* (Boston, 1896), pp. 17-19, 33-34.

5. Woods and Kennedy, "The Zone of Emergence," chapters on Roxbury and Dorchester; A. B. Wolfe, *The Lodging House Problem*, (Cambridge, 1913) pp. 1-26, 34-37.

6. One of the basic attempts of the nineteenth century settlement house movement was to discover the facts of the existence of "the other half." In Boston, the first friut of this effort was R. A. Woods, *The City Wilderness* (1898). The title meant to convey both a sense of social disintegration and the fact that to middle class Bostonians this was an unknown land. The same tone follows through all this group's work, *Americans in Process (1903)*, and "The Zone of Emergence" (c. 1912). For the general reform background: Arthur Mann, *Yankee Reformers in an Urban Age* (Cambridge, 1954), espec. 126-200.

7. Boston City Council and Roxbury City Council, *Reports in Relation to the Annexation of Rox-bury, etc.* Roxbury City Document no. 3 (Boston, 1867); John H. Clifford, *Argument on the Question of the Annexation of Roxbury to Boston before the Legislative Committee, Thursday, February 23, 1865* (Boston, 1867); Nathaniel W. Coffin, *A Few Reasons in Favor of the Annexation of a Part of the Town of Dorchester to the City of Boston* (Boston, 1867); Committee in Favor of the Union of Boston and Roxbury, *Report* (Boston, 1851).

8. Josiah Quincy, Sr., *Annexation of Roxbury and Boston. Remonstrance of Bostonians against the Measure* (Boston, 1865); *Considerations Respectfully Submitted to the Citizens of Boston and Charlestown on the Proposed Annexation of the Two Cities* (Boston, 1854); Arthur W. Austin, *Address at the Dedication of the Town-House at Jamaica Plain, West Roxbury* (Boston, 1860); Rufus Choate, *Speech on Application of Samuel D. Bradford and Others To Set Off Wards 6, 7, & 8 of the City of Roxbury as a Separate Agricultural Town* (Boston, 1851); B. W. Harris, *The Annexation Question, Closing Argument for the Remonstrants Against the Annexation of Dorchester to Boston* ... (Boston, 1869); Roxbury Committee Opposed to the Annexation to Boston, *A Word for Old*

Roxbury (Roxbury, 1851), *Another Word for Old Roxbury, In Reply to the Report of the Committee in Favor of Annexation* (Boston, 1852); Alfred D. Chandler, *Annexation of Brookline to Boston* (Brookline, 1880), pp. 15, 18.

9. Review of the whole late nineteenth and early twentieth century metropolitan government movement, a movement that was always alive but never in danger of being achieved: Joseph H. Beale, "The Metropolitan District," *Fifty Years of Boston* (Elisabeth M. Herlihy ed., Boston, 1932), pp. 116-127. Complete bibliography of the metropolitan and annexation pamphlet literature: Katherine McNamara, *The Boston Metropolitan District* (Cambridge, 1946).

10. Loss of Boston's home rule: Henry Parkman, Jr., "The City and the State, 1880-1930," *Fifty Years of Boston*, pp. 128-147.

Part IV
Men and women

Urbanization, migration and social mobility

Stephan Thernstrom

America was a society in flux in this era of swift industrial and urban growth. What was the experience of the mass of inhabitants of the new world of the Gilded Age? This is a question of utmost interest to social historians, but one exceedingly difficult to answer. What evidence remains to reconstruct the lives of urban dwellers of the late nineteenth century? What questions should one ask of the evidence? Both the research and formulation of issues have posed quite intractable problems to social historians. One of the pioneering younger leaders of this group, Stephan Thernstrom, proposes one line of inquiry in the suggestive essay reprinted below. Thernstrom focuses on mobility. This is a topic about which, as Thernstrom shows, some usable evidence exists (not least of all, from his own work). And clearly, too, mobility was a central experience of urban Americans of the Gilded Age. Thernstrom uses mobility in two senses: geographical (i.e., the movement of people from place to place) and social (i.e., the movement of people up, or down, the economic and status gradations of society).

The importance of geographic mobility in this era seems irrefutable. The cities grew through an influx from rural areas. The movement of native Americans fleeing from the farms Thernstrom considers more important than the better-known immigration of European peasantry. More arresting is Thernstrom's discovery, mainly in his own researches, of a high rate of movement, especially among the poor and unsuccessful, out of the cities, presumably to other cities. Social mobility presents more complex and puzzling problems. Thernstrom rejects the notion that Gilded Age America was a particularly fluid society. There was little correspondence between the rags-to-riches mythology of Horatio Alger and the actual recruitment into the business elite, whose background was mostly middle class in character. Nor does there seem to have been much downward mobility from the middle class. On the other hand, upward mobility was widely experienced by urban Americans, not in dramatic leaps but more slowly, by promotion one or two rungs up the occupational ladder and/or through the acquisition of property. (This modest upward mobility would apply, in fact, to movement into the

Stephen Thernstrom, "Urbanization, Migration and Social Mobility in Late Nineteenth-Century America," in *Towards a New Past: Dissenting Essays in American History*, ed. Barton J. Bernstein. New York: Pantheon Books, 1968, pp. 158-175. Reprinted by permission of the publisher.

business elite, although Thernstrom does not say so.) Finally, Thernstrom draws a significant connection between geographic and social mobility, a connection quite at odds with the conventional identification of migration with opportunity. This probably held, Thernstrom acknowledges, for the already successful. But the bulk of the urban transients came from among the unsuccessful, and for them movement signified failure and held out little or no promise of a better future.

What consequences can be drawn from this picture of American mobility? Thernstrom stresses the relative absence of social conflict, a fact quite remarkable in view of the stresses to which American society was then subject. It was important, first of all, that the newcomers to the cities were rural people, both those from Europe's peasant villages and those from America's farms. The experience of upward mobility, modest although it may have been, naturally encouraged acceptance of the social order. And those who failed to rise tended to be constantly on the move, and so incapable of developing the group or class identity essential to effective protest.

Thernstrom's essay, as he himself emphasizes, is tentative rather than conclusive in nature. Much of the essential evidence is still missing or is fragmentary, and the conclusions leave room for debate. It does not necessarily follow, for example, that transiency prevents class consciousness or organizational development. In the case of the I.W.W., just the reverse seems to be true. And, as Lloyd Ullman (see below) has shown, the institutional growth of the trade union movement was closely connected to the existence of transient craftsmen. The great value of this essay is its success in opening up a major area of historical inquiry. Not only does Thernstrom pose questions to which historians will have to address themselves. He also demonstrates the importance of a sociological perspective (which he wears lightly but utilizes most effectively) for the study of social history. And he shows, too, the uses of statistical data and methodology for answering the key questions in this area.

For further reading: Stephan Thernstrom, *Poverty and Progress: Social Mobility in a Nineteenth-Century City* (1964);* Stephan Thernstrom and Richard Sennett, eds., *Nineteenth Century Cities* (1969);* Gerd Korman, *Industrialization, Immigrants and Americanization: the View from Milwaukee* (1967); Rowland T. Berthoff, *British Immigrants in Industrial America, 1790-1950* (1953); Lloyd Ulman, *The Rise of the National Trade Union* (1955); Ray Ginger, "Managerial Employees in Anthracite, 1902: A Study of Occupational Mobility," *Journal of Economic History*, XIV (1954), 146-157; Seymour Lipset and Reinhard Bendix, *Social Mobility in Industrial Society* (1963).*

The United States, it has been said, was born in the country and has moved to the city. It was during the half-century between the Civil War and World War I that the move was made. In 1860, less than a quarter of the American population lived in a city or town; by 1890, the figure had reached a third; by 1910, nearly half. By more sophisticated measures than the mere count of heads, the center of gravity of the society had obviously tilted cityward well before the last date.

If to speak of "the rise of the city" in those years is a textbook cliché the impact of this great social transformation upon the common people of America has never been sufficiently explored. This essay is intended as a small contribution toward that task. It sketches the process by which ordinary men and women were drawn to the burgeoning cities of post-Civil War America, assesses what little we know about how they were integrated into the urban class structure, and suggests how these matters affected the viability of the political system.

I

The urbanization of late nineteenth-century America took place at a dizzying pace. Chicago, for instance, doubled its population every decade but one between 1850 and 1890, growing from 30,000 to over a million in little more than a generation. And it was not merely the conspicuous metropolitan giants but the Akrons, the Duluths, the Tacomas that were bursting at the seams; no less than 101 American communities grew by 100 percent or more in the 1880s.[1]

Why did Americans flock into these all too often unlovely places? There were some who were not pulled to the city but rather pushed out of their previous habitats and dropped there, more or less by accident. But the overriding fact is that the cities could draw on an enormous reservoir of people who were dissatisfied with their present lot and eager to seize the new opportunities offered by the metropolis.

Who were these people? It is conventional to distinguish two broad types of migrants to the American city: the immigrant from another culture, and the farm lad who moved from a rural to an urban setting within the culture. It is also conventional in historical accounts to overlook the latter type and to focus on the more exotic of the migrants, those who had to undergo the arduous process of becoming Americanized.

This is regrettable. To be sure, immigration from abroad was extremely important in the building of America's cities down to World War I. But the most important source of population for the burgeoning cities was not the fields of Ireland and Austria, but those of Vermont and Iowa. The prime cause of population growth in the nineteenth-century America, and the main source of urban growth, was simply the high fertility of natives living outside the city.

We tend to neglect internal migration from country to city, partly because the immigrants from abroad seem exotic and thus conspicuous, partly because of the unfortunate legacy left by Frederick Jackson Turner's frontier theory, one element of which was the notion that the open frontier served as a safety valve for urban discontent. When there were hard times in the city, according to Turner, the American worker didn't join a union or vote Socialist; he moved West and grabbed some of that free land. This theory has been subjected to the rather devastating criticism that by 1860 it took something like $1,000 capital to purchase sufficient transportation, seed equipment, lifestock, and food (to live on until the first crop) to make a go of it; that it took even more than $1,000 later in the century; and that it was precisely the unemployed workmen who were least likely to have that kind of money at their command. It is estimated that for every industrial worker who became a farmer, twenty farm boys became urban dwellers.[2] There was an urban safety valve for rural discontent, and an extremely important one. The dominant form of population movement was precisely the opposite of that described by Turner.

Since scholarly attention has been focused upon immigrants from abroad, upon Oscar Handlin's "Uprooted," it will be useful to review what is known about their movement to the American city and then to ask how much the same generalizations might hold for native Americans uprooted from the countryside and plunged into the city.

Immigration is as old as America, but a seismic shift in the character of European immigration to these shores occurred in the nineteenth century, as a consequence of the commercial transformation of traditional European agriculture and the consequent displacement of millions of peasants.[3] Compared to earlier newcomers, these were people who were closer to the land and more tradition-bound, and they generally had fewer resources to bring with them than their predecessors. One shouldn't overwork this; a substantial fraction of the German and Scandinavian immigrants had enough capital to get to the West to pick up land. But some of the Germans and Scandinavians, and most men of other nationalities, had just enough cash to make it to the New World and were stuck for a time at least where they landed—New York, Boston, or wherever. They swelled the population appreciably and the relief rolls dramatically, particularly in the pre-Civil War years, when they entered cities which were basically commercial and had little use for men whose only skill in many cases was that they knew how to dig. Eventually, however, the stimulus of this vast pool of cheap labor and the demands of the growing city itself opened up a good many unskilled jobs—in the construction of roads, houses, and commercial buildings, and in the manufacturing that began to spring up in the cities.

That they were driven off the land in the Old World, that they arrived without resources, immobilized by their poverty, and that they often suffered a great deal before they secured stable employment is true enough. But these harsh facts may lead us to overlook other aspects which were extremely significant.

One is that immigration was a *selective* process. However powerful the pressures to leave, in no case did everyone in a community pull up stakes. This observation may be uncomfortably reminiscent of the popular opinion on this point: that it was the best of the Old World stock that came to the New—the most intelligent, enterprising, courageous. But this should not lead us to neglect the point altogether. The traits that led some men to leave and allowed them to survive the harrowing journey to the port, the trip itself, and the perils of the New World, could be described in somewhat different terms: substitute cunning for intelligence, for example, or ruthlessness for courage. Still, whatever the emphasis, the fact remains: as weighed in the scales of the marketplace, those who came—however driven by cruel circumstance—were better adapted to American life than those who remained in the village or died on the way.

The other main point about the immigrants, and especially those who suffered the most extreme hardships—the Irish in the 1840s and 1850s, the French Canadians in the 1870s, the Italians and various East Europeans after 1880—is that they appraised their new situations with standards developed in peasant society. Lowell was terrible, with its cramped stinking tenements, and factory workers labored from dawn till dark for what seems a mere pittance. Children were forced to work at a brutally early age; the factories and dwellings were deathtraps. But Lowell was a damn sight better than County Cork, and men who knew from bitter experience what County Cork was like could not view their life in Lowell with quite the same simple revulsion as the middle-class reformers who judged Lowell by altogether different standards. It is not so much the objectively horrible character of a situation that goads men to action as it is a nagging discrepancy between what *is* and what is *expected*. And what one expects is determined by one's reference group—which can be a class, an ethnic or religious subculture, or some other entity which defines people's horizon of expectation.[4] Immigration provided an ever renewed stream of men who entered the American economy to fill its least attractive and least well rewarded positions, men who happen to have brought with them very low horizons of expectation fixed in peasant Europe.

That those Americans with greatest reason to feel outrageously exploited judged their situation against the dismally low standards of the decaying European village is an important clue to the stunted growth of the labor movement and the failure of American Socialism. Working in the same direction was what might be called the Tower of Babel factor. A firm sense of class solidarity was extremely difficult to develop in communities where people literally didn't speak each other's language. Even in cases where groups of immigrant workers had unusually high expectations and previous familiarity with advanced forms of collective action—such as the English artisans who led the Massachusetts textile strikes in the 1870s—they found it hard to keep the other troops in line; a clever Italian-speaking or Polish-speaking foreman could easily exploit national differences for his own ends, and if necessary there were always the most recent immigrants of all (and the Negroes) to serve as scabs to replace the dissenters en masse.

A somewhat similar analysis applies to the migrants who left the Kansas farms for Chicago. They were linguistically and culturally set apart from many of their fellow workers; they too had low horizons of expectation fixed in the countryside and brought to the city. The latter point is often missed because of the peculiar American reverence for an idealized agrarian way of life. As we have become a nation of city dwellers, we have come more and more to believe that it is virtuous and beautiful to slave for fourteen hours a day with manure on your boots. Recently that sturdy small farmer from Johnson City, Texas, remarked that "it does not make sense on this great continent which God has blessed to have more than 70 per cent of our people crammed into one percent of the land." A national "keep them down on the farm" campaign is therefore in the offing.[5] But it is damnably hard to keep them down on the farm after they've seen New York (or even Indianapolis), and it was just as hard a century ago, for the very good reason that the work is brutal, the profits are often miserably low, and the isolation is psychologically murderous. Virtuous this life may be, especially to people who don't have to live it, but enjoyable it is not—not, at least, to a very substantial fraction of our ever shrinking farm population.

This applies particularly to young men and women growing up on a farm. Their parents had a certain stake in staying where they were, even if it was a rut. And the eldest son, who would inherit the place eventually, was sometimes tempted by that. But the others left in droves, to tend machines, to dig and haul and hammer—or in the case of the girls, to sell underwear in Marshall Field's, to mind someone else's kitchen, or in some instances to follow in the footsteps of Sister Carrie.

There were some large differences between native-born migrants to the cities and immigrants from another land, to be sure. But the familiar argument that native workmen "stood on the shoulders" of the immigrant and were subjected to less severe exploitation is somewhat misleading. The advantages enjoyed by many America-born laborers stemmed more from their urban experience than their birth, and they did not generally accrue to freshly arrived native migrants to the city. The latter were little better off than their immigrant counterparts, but then they too were spiritually prepared to endure a great deal of privation and discomfort because even the bottom of the urban heap was a step up from the farms they had left behind. The two groups were one in this respect, and perceptive employers recognized the fact. In 1875, the Superintendent of one of Andrew Carnegie's steel mills summed up his experience this way: "We must steer clear as far as we can of Englishmen, who are great sticklers for high wages, small production and strikes. My experience has shown that Germans and Irish, Swedes and what I denominate 'Buckwheats'—young American country boys, judiciously mixed, make the most honest and tractable force you can find."[6]

II

The move to the city, therefore, was an advance of a kind for the typical migrant. Were there further opportunities for advancement there, or did he then find himself crushed by circumstance and reduced to the ranks of the permanent proletariat? Did his children, whose expectations were presumably higher, dicover correspondingly greater opportunities open to them? Remarkably little serious research has been devoted to these issues. Historians who see American history as a success story have been content to assume, without benefit of data, that the American dream of mobility was true, apparently on the principle that popular ideology is a sure guide to social reality. Dissenting scholars have been more inclined to the view that class barriers were relatively impassable, an assumption based upon generalized skepticism about American mythology rather than upon careful empirical study. Some recent work, however, provides the basis for a tentative reappraisal of the problem.

We know most about mobility into the most rarified reaches of the social order regarding such elite groups as millionaires, railroad presidents, directors of large corporations, or persons listed in the *Dictionary of American Biography*. What is most impressive about the literature on the American elite is that, in spite of many variations in the way in which the elite is defined, the results of these studies are much the same. It is clear that growing up in rags is not in the least conducive to the attainment of later riches, and that it was no more so a century ago than it is today.[7] There have been spectacular instances of mobility from low down on the social scale to the very top—Andrew Carnegie, for instance. But colorful examples cannot sustain broad generalizations about social phenomena, however often they are impressed into service toward that end. Systematic investigation reveals that even in the days of Andrew Carnegie, there was little room at the top, except for those who started very close to it.

Furthermore, this seems to have been the case throughout most of American history, despite many dramatic alterations in the character of the economy. It seems perfectly plausible to assume, as many historians have on the basis of impressionistic evidence, that the precipitous growth of heavy industry in the latter half of the nineteenth century opened the doors to men with very different talents from the educated merchants who constituted the elite of the preindustrial age, that unlettered, horny-handed types like Thomas Alva Edison and Henry Ford, crude inventors and tinkerers, then came into their own; that the connection between parental wealth and status and the son's career was loosened, so that members of the business elite typically had lower social origins and less education, and were often of immigrant stock. Plausible, yes, but true, no. It helped to go to Harvard in Thomas Jefferson's America, and it seems to have helped just about as much in William McKinley's America. There were the Edisons and Fords, who rose spectacularly from low origins, but there were always a few such. Cases like these were about as exceptional in the late nineteenth century as they were earlier. The image of the great inventor springing from common soil, unspoiled by book-larnin', is a red herring. It is doubtful, to say the least, that the less you know, the more likely you are to build a better mousetrap. And in any event it was not the great inventor who raked in the money, in most cases—Henry Ford never invented anything—but rather the organizer and manipulator, whose talents seem to have been highly valued through all periods of American history.

These conclusions are interesting, but an important caution is in order. It by no means follows that if there was very little room at the top, there was little room anywhere else. It is absurd to judge the openness or lack of openness of an entire social system solely by the extent of recruitment from below into the highest positions of all. One can imagine a society in which all members of the tiny elite are democratically recruited from below, and yet where the social structure as a whole is extremely rigid with that small exception. Conversely, one can imagine a society with a hereditary ruling group at the very top, a group completely closed to aspiring men of talent but lowly birth, and yet with an enormous amount of movement back and forth below that pinnacle. Late nineteenth-century America could have approximated this latter model, with lineage, parental wealth, and education as decisive assets in the race for the very peak, as the business elite studies suggest, and yet with great fluidity at the lower and middle levels of the class structure.

Was this in fact the case? The evidence available today is regrettably scanty, but here are the broad outlines of an answer, insofar as we can generalize from a handful of studies.[8] At the lower and middle ranges of the class structure there was impressive mobility, though often of an unexpected and rather ambiguous kind. I will distinguish three types of mobility: geographical, occupational, and property, and say a little about the extent and significance of each.

First is geographical mobility, physical movement from place to place, which is tied up in an interesting way with movement through the social scale. Americans have long been thought a restless, footloose people, and it has been assumed that the man on the move has been the man on the make; he knows that this little town doesn't provide a grand enough stage for him to display his talents, and so he goes off to the big city to win fame and fortune, or to the open frontier to do likewise. When you examine actual behavior instead of popular beliefs, however, you discover that things are more complicated than that.

It proves to be true that Americans are indeed a footloose people. In my work on Newburyport, a small industrial city, I attempted to find out what fraction of the families present in the community in the initial year of my study—1850—were still living there in the closing year, 1880, one short generation. Less than a fifth of them, it turned out—and this not in a community on the moving frontier, like Merle Curti's Trempealeau County, where you would expect a very high turnover. There the true pioneer types, who liked to clear the land, became nervous when there was another family within a half day's ride of them and sold out to the second wave of settlers (often immigrants who knew better than to try to tame the wilderness without previous experience at it). But to find roughly the same volatility in a city forty miles north of Boston suggests that the whole society was in motion.

The statistics bear out the legend that Americans are a restless people. What of the assertion that movement and success go hand in hand, that physical mobility and upward social mobility are positively correlated? Here the legend seems more questionable. It seems likely that some who pulled up stakes and went elsewhere for a new start did improve their positions; they found better land, or discovered that they possessed talents which were much more highly valued in the big city than in the place they came from. What ever would have happened to Theodore Dreiser in small-town Indiana had there been no Chicago for him to flee to?

But the point to underline, for it is less commonly understood, is that much of this remarkable population turnover was of quite a different kind. As you trace the flow of immigrants into and then out of the cities, you begin to see that a great many of those who departed did so in circumstances which make it exceedingly hard to believe that they were moving on to bigger and better things elsewhere. There is no way to be certain about this, no feasible method of tracing individuals once they disappear from the universe of the community under consideration. These questions can be explored for contemporary America by administering questionnaires to people and collecting life histories which display migration patterns, but dead men tell no tales and fill out no questionnaires, so that part of the past is irrevocably lost. But some plausible inferences can be drawn about the nature of this turnover from the fact that so many ordinary working people on the move owned no property, had no savings accounts, had acquired no special skills, and were most likely to leave when they were unemployed. They were, in short, people who had made the least successful economic adjustment to the community and who were no longer able to hang on there. At the lower reaches of the social order, getting out of town did not ordinarily mean a step up the ladder somewhere else; there is no reason to assume that in their new destinations migrant laborers found anything but more of the same. When middle-class families, who already had a niche in the world, moved on, it was often in response to greater opportunities elsewhere; for ordinary working people physical movement meant something very different.

That is a less rosy picture than the one usually painted, but I think it is more accurate. And we should notice one very important implication of this argument: namely, that the people who were least successful and who had the greatest grievances are precisely those who never stayed put very long in any one place. Students of labor economics and trade union history have long been aware of the fact that there are certain occupations which are inordinately difficult to organize simply because they have incessant job turnover. When only 5 percent or 1 percent of the men working at a particular job in a given city at the start of the year are still employed twelve months later, as is the case with some occupations in the economic underworld today (short-order cooks or menial hospital workers, for instance), how do you build a stable organization and conduct a successful strike?

An analagous consideration applies not merely to certain selected occupations but to a large fraction of the late nineteenth-century urban working class as a whole. The Marxist model of the conditions which promote proletarian consciousness presumes not only permanency of membership in this class—the absence of upward mobility—but also, I suggest, some continuity of class membership *in one setting* so that workers come to know each other and to develop bonds of solidarity and common opposition to the ruling group above them. This would seem to entail a stable labor force in a single factory; at a minimum it assumes considerable stability in a community. One reason that a permanent proletariat along the lines envisaged by Marx did not develop in the course of American industrialization is perhaps that few Americans have *stayed* in one place, one workplace, or even one city long enough to discover a sense of common identity and common grievance. This may be a vital clue to the divergent political development of America and Western Europe in the industrial age, to the striking weakness of socialism here, as compared to Europe—though we can't be sure because we don't definitely know that the European working-class population was less volatile. I suspect that it was, to some degree, and that America was distinctive in this respect, but this is a question of glaring importance which no one has yet taken the trouble to investigate.

When I first stumbled upon this phenomenon in sifting through manuscript census schedules for nineteenth-century Newburyport, I was very doubtful that the findings could be generalized to apply to the big cities of the period. It seemed reasonable to assume that the laborers who drifted out of Newburyport so quickly after their arrival must have settled down somewhere else, and to think that a great metropolis would have offered a more inviting haven than a small city, where anonymity was impossible and where middle-class institutions of social control intruded into one's daily life with some frequency, as compared to a classic big-city lower-class ghetto, where the down-and-out could perhaps huddle together for protective warmth and be left to their own devices—for instance, those Irish wards of New York where the police made no attempt to enforce law and order until late in the century. Here if anywhere one should be able to find a continuous lower-class population, a permanent proletariat, and I began my Boston research with great curiosity about this point.

If Boston is any example, in no American city was there a sizable lower class with great continuity of membership. You can identify some more or less continuously lower-class areas, but the crucial point is that *the same people do not stay in them.* If you take a sample of unskilled and semi-skilled laborers in Boston in 1880 and look for them in 1890, you are not much more likely to find them still in the city than was the case of Newburyport.[9]

The bottom layer of the social order in the nineteenth-century American city was thus a group of families who appear to have been permanent transients, buffeted about from place to place, never quite able to sink roots. We know very little about these people, and it is difficult to know how we can learn much about them. You get only occasional glimpses into the part of this iceberg that appears above the surface, in the person of the tramp, who first is perceived as a problem for America in the 1870s and reappears in hard times after that—in the 1890s and in the great depression most notably. But what has been said here at least suggests the significance of the phenomenon.

So much for geographical mobility. What can be said about the people who come to the city and remain there under our microscope so that we can discern what happened to them? I have already anticipated my general line of argument here in my discussion of migration out of the city—which amounted to the claim that the city was a kind of Darwinian jungle in which the fittest survived and the others drifted on to try another place. Those who did stay in the city and make their way there did, in general, succeed in advancing themselves economically and socially. There was very impressive mobility, though not always of the kind we might expect.

In approaching this matter, we must make a distinction which is obscured by applying labels like "open" or "fluid" to entire whole social structures. There are, after all, two sets of escalators in any community; one set goes down. To describe a society as enormously fluid implies that there are lots of people moving down while lots of others are moving up to take their place. This would obviously be a socially explosive situation, for all those men descending against their will would arrive at the bottom, not with low horizons of expectation set in some peasant village, but with expectations established when they were at one of the comfortable top floors of the structure.

Downward mobility is by no means an unknown phenomenon in American history. There have been socially displaced groups, especially if you take into account rather subtle shifts in the relative status of such groups as professionals. [10] But the chief generalization to make is that the Americans who started their working life in a middle-class job strongly tended to end up in the middle class; sons reared in middle-class families also attained middle-class occupations in the great majority of cases. Relatively few men born into the middle class fell from there; a good many born into the working class either escaped from it altogether or advanced themselves significantly within the class. There is a well-established tradition of writing about the skilled workman, associated with such names as the Hammonds, the Lynds, Lloyd Warner, and Norman Ware, which holds the contrary, to be sure. [11] This tradition still has its defenders, who argue that with industrialization "class lines assumed a new and forbidding rigidity" and that "machines made obsolete many of the skilled trades of the antebellum years, drawing the once self-respecting handicraftsmen into the drudgery and monotony of factory life, where they were called upon to perform only one step in the minutely divided and automatic processes of mass production." [12] Rapid technological change doubtless did displace some skilled artisans, doubtless produced some downward mobility into semiskilled positions. But defenders of this view have built their case upon little more than scattered complaints by labor leaders, and have not conducted systematic research to verify these complaints.

Careful statistical analysis provides a very different perspective on the matter. Two points stand out. One is that as certain traditional skilled callings became obsolete, there was an enormous expansion of *other* skilled trades, and, since many of the craftsmen under pressure from technological change had rather generalized skills, they moved rapidly into these new positions and thus retained their place in the labor aristocracy. [13] Second, it is quite mistaken to assume that the sons of the threatened artisan were commonly driven down into the ranks of the factory operatives; they typically found a place either in the expanding skilled trades or in the even more rapidly expanding white-collar occupations. [14]

As for workers on the lower rungs of the occupational ladder, the unskilled and semiskilled, they had rarely drifted down from a higher beginning point. Characteristically, they were newcomers to the urban world. A substantial minority of them appear to have been able to advance themselves a notch or two occupationally, especially among the second generation; a good many of their sons became clerks, salesmen, and other petty white-collar functionaries. And the first generation, which had less success occupationally, was commonly experiencing mobility of another kind—property mobility. Despite a pathetically low (but generally rising) wage level, despite heavy unemployment rates, many were able to accumulate significant property holdings and to establish themselves as members of the stable working class, as opposed to the drifting lower class. [15]

It may seem paradoxical to suggest that so many Americans were rising in the world and so few falling; where did the room at the top come from? The paradox is readily resolved. For one thing, our attention has been fastened upon individuals who remained physically situated in one place in which their careers could be traced; an indeterminate but substantial fraction of the population was floating and presumably unsuccessful. By no means everyone at the bottom was upwardly mobile; the point is rather that those who were not were largely invisible. Furthermore, the occupational structure itself was changing in a manner that created disproportionately more positions in the middle and upper ranges, despite the common nineteenth-century belief that industrialization was homogenizing the work force and reducing all manual employees to identical robots. The homogenizing and degrading tendencies that caught the eye of Marx and others were more than offset, it appears, by developments which made for both a more differentiated and a more top-heavy occupational structure. Third, there were important sources of social mobility that could be attained without changing one's occupation, most notably the property mobility that was stimulated by the increases in real wages that occurred in this period. Finally, there was the so-called "demographic vacuum" created by the differential fertility of the social classes, best illustrated in the gloomy late nineteenth-century estimate that in two hundred years 1,000 Harvard graduates would have only 50 living descendants while 1,000 Italians would have 100,000. The calculation is dubious, but the example nicely clarifies the point that high-status groups failed to reproduce themselves, thus opening up vacancies which had necessarily to be filled by new men from below.

For all the brutality and rapacity which marked the American scene in the years in which the new urban industrial order came into being, what stands out most is the relative absence of collective working-class protest aimed at reshaping capitalist society. The foregoing, while hardly a full explanation, should help to make this more comprehensible. The American working class was drawn into the new society by a process that encouraged accommodation and rendered disciplined protest difficult. Within the urban industrial orbit, most of its members found modest but significant opportunities to feel that they and their children were edging their way upwards. Those who did not find such opportunities were tossed helplessly about from city to city, from state to state, alienated but invisible and impotent.

Notes

1. C. N. Glaab and A. T. Brown, *A History of Urban America* (New York, 1967), pp. 107-11.

2. Fred Shannon, "A Post Mortem on the Labor-Safety-Valve Theory," *Agricultural History*, XIX (1954), 31-37.

3. For general accounts, see Marcus L. Hansen, *The Atlantic Migration, 1607-1860* (paperback ed.; New York, 1961); Oscar Handlin, *The Uprooted* (Boston, 1951).

4. For discussion of the sociological concepts of reference groups and the theory of relative deprivation, see Robert K. Merton, *Social Theory and Social Structure*, rev. ed. (Glencoe, Ill., 1957) and the literature cited there. The problem of assessing the level of expectations of any particular migratory group in the past is extremely complicated, and it is obvious that there have been important differences between and within groups. But the generalizations offered here seem to me the best starting point for thinking about this issue.

5. *Boston Globe*, February 5, 1967.

6. Quoted in Oscar Handlin, *Immigration as a Factor in American History* (Englewood Cliffs, N.J., 1959), pp. 66-67.

7. For a convenient review of this literature, see Seymour M. Lipset and Reinhard Bendix, *Social Mobility in Industrial Society* (Berkeley, Cal., 1959), Ch. 4.

8. The main sources for the generalizations which follow, unless otherwise, indicated, are: Stephan

Thernstrom, *Poverty and Progress: Social Mobility in a Nineteenth Century City* (Cambridge, Mass., 1964); Merle E. Curti, *The Making of an American Frontier Community* (Stanford, Cal., 1959); Donald B. Cole, *Immigrant City: Lawrence, Massachusetts, 1845-1921* (Chapel Hill, N.C., 1963)—for my reservations about this work, however, see my review in the *Journal of Economic History*, XXIV (1964), 259-61; Herbert G. Gutman, "Social Status and Social Mobility in 19th Century America: Paterson, N.J., A Case Study," unpublished paper for the 1964 meetings of the American Historical Association; Howard Gitelman, "The Labor Force at Waltham Watch During the Civil War Era," *Journal of Economic History*, XXV (1965), 214-43; David Brody, *Steelworkers in America: The Nonunion Era* (Cambridge, Mass., 1960); Pauline Gordon, "The Chance to Rise Within Industry" (unpublished M.A. thesis, Columbia University); Robert Wheeler, "The Fifth-Ward Irish: Mobility at Mid-Century" (unpublished seminar paper, Brown University, 1967); and the author's research in progress on social mobility in Boston over the past century, in which the career patterns of some 8,000 ordinary residents of the community are traced.

9. Recent work suggesting that even the most recent U.S. Census serious undernumerated the Negro male population may make the critical reader wonder about the accuracy of the census and city directory canvases upon whch I base my analysis. Some elaborate directory canvases upon which I base my analysis. Some elaborate checking has persuaded me that these nineteenth-century sources erred primarily in their coverage—their lack of coverage, rather—of the floating working-class population. For a variety of reasons it seems clear that families which had been in the community long enough to be included in one of these canvases—and hence to be included in a sample drawn from them—were rarely left out of later canvases if they were indeed still resident in the same city. A perfect census of every soul in the community on a given day would therefore yield an even higher, not a lower, estimate of population turnover for men at the bottom, which strengthens rather than weakens the argument advanced here.

10. The assumption that discontent stemming from social displacement has been the motive force behind American reform movements has exerted great influence upon American historical writing in recent years. See for instance David Donald, "Toward a Reconsideration of Abolitionists," *Lincoln Reconsidered* (New York, 1956, pp.19-36; Richard Hofstadter, *The Age of Reform: From Bryan to F.D.R.* (New York, 1955). Donald's essay is easily demolished by anyone with the slightest acquaintance with sociological method. Hofstadter's work, while open to a very serious objection, is at least sufficiently suggestive to indicate the potential utility of the idea.

11. J. L. and Barbara Hammond, *The Town Labourer (1760-1832)* (London, 1917); Robert S. and Helen M. Lynd, *Middletown* (New York, 1929), and *Middletown in Transition* (New York, 1937); W. Lloyd Warner and J. O. Low, *The Social System of the Modern Factory* (New Haven, Conn., 1947); Norman J. Ware, *The Industrial Worker, 1840-1860* (Boston, 1924).

12. Leon Litwak, ed., *The American Labor Movement* (Englewood Cliffs, N.J., 1962), p. 3.

13. This is evident from aggregated census data and from my Boston investigation, but we badly need an American counterpart to Eric Hobsbawm's splendid essay on "The Labour Aristocracy in Nineteenth Century Britain," in *Labouring Men: Studies in the History of Labour* (London, 1964), pp. 272-315.

14. So, at least, the evidence from Boston and Indianapolis indicates; for the latter, see Natlie Rogoff, *Recent Trends in Occupational Mobility* (Glencoe, Ill., 1953).

15. The clearest demonstration of this is in Thermstrom, *Poverty and Progress*, Ch. 5. It might be thought, however, that the remarkable property mobility disclosed there depended upon the existence of an abundant stock of cheap single-family housing available for purchase. It could be that where real estate was less readily obtainable, laborers would squander the funds that were accumulated with such sacrifice in places where home ownership was an immediate possibility. It appears from Wheeler's unpublished study of nineteenth-century Providence, however, that the working-class passion for

property did not require an immediate, concrete source of satisfaction like a home and a plot of land. The Irish workmen of Providence were just as successful at accumulating property holdings as their Newburyport counterparts; the difference was only that they held personal rather than real property.

Middle-class families and urban violence

Richard Sennett

The American middle class constitutes the invisible people of our past. The economic growth of the late nineteenth century created an enormous class of urban dwellers of modest means, the white-collar workers, shopkeepers, and craftsmen. Little has been known of these middle-class Americans, least of all about their home and family lives. Only in recent years, as American scholars have moved beyond traditional notions of what constitutes the proper study of history, has interest begun to be directed at the bourgeoisie of the Gilded Age. And only with the development of new techniques of research have historians gained access to a group of people who left none of the personal, institutional, or public records that have normally been the basis for historical research. In his *Streetcar Suburbs*, as we have seen, Sam B. Warner showed the uses that could be made of a massive study of building permits to determine the housing patterns of the Boston middle class. Other historians have begun to employ surviving manuscript census records to study the middle class, utilizing statistical techniques and, sometimes, computers to analyze the data, and depending heavily on the social sciences for their conceptual frameworks.

Richard Sennett is one of the practitioners of the new scientific history. The following essay summarizes the findings of his study of the middle-class family structure of a Chicago neighborhood that he calls Union Park. Sennett discovers some significant correlations between types of family and family size on the one hand and social and geographic mobility on the other. The smaller nuclear families (i.e., father, mother, and children) experienced little upward mobility either in the occupations of the father or of the sons, and the families tended to stay in Union Park. In larger nuclear families and in extended families, the fathers tended to advance themselves in the job structure, and sons almost uniformly entered nonmanual occupations; and the families were more likely to leave Union Park. It was Sennett's thesis that the small nuclear family served as a haven against the turmoil of the city, but it acted also to inhibit its members in the urban scramble for economic opportunity.

Richard Sennett, "Middle Class Families and Urban Violence: The Experience of a Chicago Community in the Nineteenth Century," in *Nineteenth Century Cities: Essays in the New Urban History*, S. Thernstrom and R. Sennett, eds., New Haven: Yale University Press, copyright © 1969, by Yale University, pp. 386-418. Reprinted by permission of the publisher.

In the essay reprinted below, Sennett carries this analysis a step further. It is perhaps ironic that a sociologist, which Sennett is, should have felt the lack of historical texture and concreteness in the sociological analysis of the past—one of the major drawbacks of the scientific approach—and to have sought to remedy this, as well as to buttress his claim regarding the impact of the small nuclear family, by studying Union Park's reactions to two dramatic events of the 1880s. In 1886, the terrible Haymarket bombing occurred nearby; two years later a rash of burglaries hit the neighborhood, culminating in the murder of one of its leading citizens. The hysterical reaction in Union Park seemed to Sennett out of all proportion to the provoking events, and he concluded that the intense hostility really expressed deep frustration arising from the small nuclear family structure. This connection resides in the realm of hypothesis, since Sennett offers no hard evidence showing the connection and is depending on the psychological concept relating frustration to aggression. Assuming that Sennett is correct in his description of Union Park's reaction and in his analysis of the role of the small nuclear family (itself involving a heavy dose of hypothesis), then his conclusion would certainly hold much merit. Equally arresting from a methodological standpoint is Sennett's marriage of scientific and imaginative history, and the range of techniques which it suggests that historians will have to employ in pursuit of the middle-class America of the Gilded Age.

For further reading: Richard Sennett, *Families against the City* (1970); Henry David, *The Haymarket Affair* (1936); Arthur Calhoun, *A Social History of the American Family* (1917-1918), 3 vols.;* Sam B. Warner, *Streetcar Suburbs* (1962);* Bessie L. Pierce, *A History of Chicago* (1957), vol. 3; Ray Ginger, *Altgeld's America*, 1890-1905 (1958).*

Unlike the other writers in this volume, I have sought in this essay to make historical judgments that cannot be proved in a rigorous way. Historians using sociological tools find in quantitative methods and constructs the possibility of achieving great precision in describing the past; for sociologists like myself who turn to the historical frame, a rather opposite possibility exists. For us, the complexities and contradictions found in the "actual time" of human life suggest ways in which abstract concepts can be made more dense and more subtle, and so less precise, in their evocation of men's experience.

This study seeks the hidden connections between two seemingly disparate phenomena in a quiet middle-class neighborhood of Chicago in the late nineteenth century: the family patterns of the people of the community and the peculiar response made by men living there to the eruption of violence in their midst. In imagining how the structure of family life was related to the character of men's reaction to violence, I have tried to recapture some of the subtlety of what it was like to be a middle-class city dweller during this era of rapid urban growth.

In the years 1886 and 1888 an epidemic of violence broke out in this quiet neighborhood of Chicago. The striking feature of this epidemic lay not in the violent events themselves but in the reaction of shopkeepers, store clerks, accountants, and highly skilled laborers to the disorder suddenly rampant among their sedate homes. Their reaction to violence was impassioned to an extent that in retrospect seems unwarranted by events; indeed, it is the contrast between the limited character of the disorder and the sense residents had of being overwhelmingly threatened by anarchy that suggests that the response could have been a product of larger, seemingly unrelated social forces, such as the structure of family life.

The Community Setting

The scene of the disturbance, which I shall name Union Park, was an area centered on the near West Side of Chicago around a rather large park formally landscaped in the early 1850s. Like most of the middle and lower middle-class neighborhoods of American industrial cities in the later nineteenth century, the area was considered so nondescript that it was never given a special name, as were the richer and poorer sections of Chicago, Its people were the forgotten men of that era, neither poor enough to be rebels nor affluent enough to count in the affairs of the city. For a quarter century, from 1865 to 1890, Union Park epitomized that tawdry respectability of native born, lower middle-class Americans that Dreiser was to capture in the early sections of *Sister Carrie*, or that Farrell would later rediscover in the bourgeois life of Catholic Chicago.

The beginnings of Union Park, when Chicago was a commercial town rather than a diverse manufacturing city, were much grander. For in the 1830s and 1840s it was a fashionable western suburb on the outskirts of town, separated by open land from the bustle of the business district and the noisome, unhealthy river at the heart of the city. A change in the pattern of commercial land investment, the filling in of a swamp on the edge of Lake Michigan by Potter Palmer, and the growth of a manufacturing district to the south of Union Park in the years after the Civil War led fashionable people to desert the old suburb for newer, more magnificent residences along the lake shore of Chicago. In their place, in the 1870s, came people of much lesser means, seeking a respectable place to live where rents and land were becoming cheap. Union Park for these new people was a neighborhood where they could enjoy the prestige of a once-fashionable address, and even pretend themselves to be a little grander than they were. "The social Brooklyn of Chicago," Mayor Harrison called it; "a place where modest women became immodest in their pretensions," wrote another contemporary observer of the area. For twenty-five years, the old holdings were gradually divided up into little plots, and native-born Americans—who were the bulk of the migrants to the cities of the Midwest before the 1880s—rented small brick houses or a half floor in one of the converted mansions.

During the middle 1880s, it was in modest, cheerless Union Park that a series of unexpected events broke out. A bloody encounter between laborers and police took place on its borders during the Haymarket Riot of 1886, to be followed eighteen months later by a series of highly expert robberies in the community, a crime wave that culminated in the murder of a leading Union Park resident. Union Park reacted by holding a whole class—the poor, and especially the immigrant poor—responsible for the course of unique and rather narrow events.

The Haymarket Bombing

> Certain people, mostly foreigners of brief residence among us, whose ideas of government were derived from their experience in despotic Germany, sought by means of violence and murder to inaugurate a carnival of crime. *F. H. Head, official orator at the unveiling of the*

Haymarket Square Statue for policemen slain in the riot, reported in the Chicago Daily Tribune, *May 31, 1889, p. 5.*

During the 1870s and early 1880s the warehouse district of Chicago grew in a straight line west, across the Chicago River, up to the edge of Union Park. The haymarket constituted the farthest boundary of this district; it was the dividing line between the residences and neighborhood stores of Union Park and the warehouses of Chicago's growing central city. Haymarket Square itself was enclosed by large buildings and the Des Plaines Street Police Station was just off the Square. It was hardly a place to engage in clandestine activity, but, for a peaceful meeting, the Square was an ideal forum, since it could accommodate roughly 20,000 people.[1]

The common notion of what happened on May 4, 1886, is that a group of labor unionists assembled in Haymarket Square to listen to speeches and that, when the police moved in to break up the meeting, someone in the crowd threw a bomb, killing and wounding many policemen and bystanders. This account is true as far as it goes, but explains little of what determined the event's effect on the community and city in the aftermath.

The people who came to the meeting were the elite of the working class, those who belonged to the most skilled crafts;[2] they were hardly the "dregs" of society. The crowd itself was small, although it had been supposed that events in Chicago during the preceding days would have drawn a large gathering. On May 3, demonstrations had been organized in the southwestern part of the city against the McCormick Works, where a lockout of some union members had occurred. The police had responded with brutal force to disperse the crowd. Later that same night, at a number of prescheduled union meetings, it was resolved to hold a mass meeting at some neutral place in the city.[3]

A small group of Socialist union leaders, led by August Spies and Albert Parsons, decided the time was ripe for a mass uprising of laboring men; the moment seemed perfect for an expression of labor solidarity, when large numbers of people might be expected to rally to the cause as Spies and Parsons understood it—the growth of Socialist power. Haymarket Square was the obvious choice for a neutral site. Posters were printed in the early hours of the next day and spread throughout the city.

When Parsons and Spies mounted the speakers' rostrum the next night in Haymarket Square, they must have been appalled. Instead of vast crowds of militants, there were only a thousand or so people in the Square, and, as speaker after speaker took his turn, the crowd dwindled steadily. The audience was silent and unmoved as the explanations of the workers' role in socialism were expounded, though there was respect for the speakers of the kind one would feel for a friend whose opinions grew out of a different sphere of life. Yet as the meeting was about to die out, a phalanx of policemen suddenly appeared on the scene to disperse the crowd.

Why the police intruded is the beginning of the puzzle we have to understand. Their reaction was totally inappropriate to the character of what was occurring before their eyes; they ought rather to have breathed a sigh of relief that the meeting was such a peaceful fiasco. But, as the civil riots of a later chapter in Chicago's history show, it is sometimes more difficult for the police to "cool off" than the demonstrators. In any event, just as the Haymarket meeting was falling apart, the police moved in to disperse it by force, and thus brought back to life the temporary spirit of unity and of outrage against the violence at McCormick Works that had drawn crowd and orators together.

The knots of men moved back from the lines of police advancing toward the speaker's stand, so that the police gained the area in front of the rostrum without incident. Then, suddenly, someone in the crowd threw a powerful bomb into the midst of the policemen, and pandemonium broke loose. The wounded police and people in the crowd dragged themselves or were carried into the hallways of buildings in the eastern end of Union Park, drugstores, like Ebert's at Madison and Halstead and Barker's on West Madison, suddenly became hospitals with bleeding men stretched out on the floors, while police combed the residences and grounds of Union Park looking for wounded members of the crowd who had managed to find shelter, under stoops or in sheds, from the police guns booming in the Square.[4]

Reaction of the Middle Class

As the news spread, small riots broke out in the southwestern part of the city, with aimless targets, but they were soon dispersed. By the morning of May 5, the working-class quarters were quiet, though the police were not. They, and the middle-class people of Chicago, especially those living in Union Park, were in a fever, a fever compounded of fear, a desire for vengeance, and simple bewilderment.

It is this reaction that must be explored to gauge the true impact of the Haymarket incident on the Union Park community. The first characteristic of this reaction was how swiftly an interpretation, communally shared, was formed, the middle-class people of Union Park, and elsewhere in Chicago, were moved immediately by the incident to draw a defined, clear picture of what had happened, and they held onto their interpretation tenaciously. Today it is easy to recognize, from the location of the meeting next to a police station, from the apathy of the crowd, from the sequence of events that preceeded the bombing, that the Haymarket incident was not a planned sequence of disorder or a riot by an enraged mob, but rather the work of an isolated man, someone who might have thrown the bomb no matter who was there. The day after the bombing, these objective considerations were not the reality "respectable" people perceived. Middle-class people of Chicago believed instead the "the immigrant anarchists" were spilling out of the slums to kill the police, in order to destroy the security of the middle class themselves. "Respectable" people felt some kind of need to believe in the enormity of the threat, and in this way the community quickly arrived at a common interpretation.

The enormity of the perceived threat was itself the second characteristic of their reaction. The color red, which was taken as a revolutionary incitement, was "cut out of street advertisements and replaced with a less suggestive color."[5] On the day after the riot a coroner's jury returned a verdict that all prisoners in the hands of the police were guilty of murder, because Socialism as such led to murderous anarchy, and anyone who attended the meeting must have been a Socialist. Yet this same jury observed that it was "troublesome" that none of those detained could be determined to have thrown the bomb. Anarchism itself was generalized to a more sweeping level by its identification with foreign birth; the "agitators" were poor foreigners, and this fact could explain their lawlessness. For example, the *Tribune* reported that on the day after the Haymarket Riot police closed two saloons

that were the headquarters of the foreign-speaking population, which flaunts and marches

under the red flag, and heretofore they were the centers of a great throng of men who did
little but drink beer and attend the meetings in the halls above.[6]

On May 5 and 6, the police were engaged in a strenuous effort to determine where the
"anarchist" groups lived, so that the population as a whole might be controlled. On May 7,
and this was the view to prevail henceforward, they announced that the residences of
most anarchists must be in the southwestern portion of the city, the immigrant, working-
class area.[7]

The assigning of the responsible parties to the general category of "foreigner" excited
even more panic in Union Park. It was reported in the *Tribune* of May 7 that a fear
existed in the community that lawless marauders would again erupt out of the proletarian
sector of the city and terrorize people in the neighborhood of the riot.[8] These fears were
sustained by two events in the next week.

First were reports of the deaths, day after day, of policemen and innocent bystanders
who had been seriously wounded by the bomb on May 4, coupled with a massive newspaper campaign to raise money for the families of the victims. Second, and by far more
important, fear of renewed bombing was kept alive by the phantasies of a Captain
Schaack of the Chicago police who day by day discovered and foiled anarchist plots,
plans to bomb churches and homes, attempts on the lives of eminent citizens. Such were
the horror stories with which the middle-class people of Chicago scared themselves for
weeks.

Some kind of deep communal force engendered in the people of Union Park an
immediately shared interpretation of what objectively was a confused event; this same
communal force led men to escalate the metaphors of threat and challenge involved in
this one event. As events a year later were to show, the force that produced these two
characteristics of response was also to prevent the men of Union Park from being able to
deal with future violence in an effective way.

Burglaries and Murder

On Thursday, February 9, 1888, the *Chicago Tribune* gaves its lead space to the following
story:

Amos J. Snell, a millionaire who lived at the corner of Washington Boulevard and Ada
Street, was shot to death by two burglars who entered his house and made off with
$1,600 worth of county warrants and $5,000 in checks. The murder was committed at
about 2 A.M. and discovered by a servant at about 6:30 A.M.[9]

Snell had been a resident of the area since 1867, when he built a home in Union Park and
bought up many blocks of desirable real estate around it.

The murder of Snell climaxed a tense situation in Union Park that had existed since
the beginning of the year 1888. Since New Year's Day, "between forty and fifty burglaries have been committed within a radius of half a mile from the intersection of Adams
and Ashland Avenues," the Editor of the *Tribune* wrote the day after Snell's death. The
police counted half this number; it appears that the burglars had a simple and systematic
scheme: to loot any household goods, such as furs, silver plate, jewelry, or bonds left in

unlocked drawers. Occasionally some of the property was recovered, and occasionally a thief was arrested who seemed to have been involved, but the operation itself was remarkably smooth and successful.[10]

How did people in Union Park react to these burglaries, and what did they do to try to stop them? The reaction of the community was much like the reaction to the Haymarket bombing: they felt involved at once in a "reign of terror," as the *Tribune* said, [11] that was none of their doing—they didn't know when the danger would strike again or who would be threatened. Most of all, they didn't know how to stop it. [12] Once again, the level of fear was escalated to a general, sweeping, and impersonal level.

Before the Snell murder, the citizens of the community had tried two means of foiling the robbers, and so of quieting the fears within their families. One was to make reports to the police, reports which the Editor of the *Tribune* claimed the police did not heed. The citizens then resorted to fortifying their homes, to hiring elderly men as private night guards, but the thieves were professional enough to deal with this: "somehow or other the burglars evaded all the precautions that were taken to prevent their nocturnal visits."[13]

After the Murder: A Change in Communal Attitudes

The Snell murder brought public discussion of the robberies, and how to stop them, to a high pitch. Especially in Union Park, the vicinity of Snell's residence, the community was "so aroused that the people talked of little else than vigilance committees and frequent holdings of court . . . as a panacea for the lawless era that had come upon them." [14] Gradually, the small-town vigilante idea gave way to a new attitude toward the police, and how the police should operate in a large city. "It is no use," said one member of the Grant Club, the West Side club to which Snell himself had belonged, "to attempt to run a cosmopolitan city as you would run a New England village." He meant that the police had up to that time concentrated on closing down gambling houses and beer parlors as a major part of their effort to keep the town "respectable" and "proper." Thus they didn't deal effectively with serious crimes like robbery and murder because they spent too much time trying to clean up petty offenses; the main thing was to keep the criminal elements confined to their own quarters in the city. In all these discussions, the fact of being burgled had been forgotten. The search turned to a means of separatism, of protection against the threatening "otherness" of the populace outside the community.

Such views were striking, considering the position of Union Park. The community's own physical character, in its parks and playgrounds, was nonurban, designed in the traditions of Olmstead and Vaux; the people, as was pointed out repeatedly in the newspaper account, were themselves among the most respectable and staid in the city, if not the most fashionable. Yet here were the most respectable among the respectable arguing for abandoning the enforcement throughout the city of a common morality. The petty criminals outside the community's borders ought to be left in peace, but out of sight. Union Park existed in a milieu too cosmopolitan for every act of the lower classes to be controlled; the police ought to abandon the attempt to be the guardians of all morality and instead concentrate on assuring the basic security of the citizens against outbursts of major crime.

What Union Park wanted instead, and what it got, was a garrison of police to make the community riotproof and crimeproof. The police indeed abandoned the search for the killers, and concentrated on holding the security of Union Park, like an area under siege. In this way, the original totally suburban tone of the parks and mansions was transformed; this respectable neighborhood felt its own existence to be so threatened that only a state of rigid barriers, enforced by a semimilitary state of curfew and surveillance, would permit it to continue to function.

The effect of the riot and the train of burglaries and murder was to put the citizens in a frame of mind where only the closure of the community through constant surveillance and patrolling would reassure them. Indeed, the characteristics of their reaction to violence could only lead to such a voluntary isolation: everyone "knew" immediately what was wrong; and what was wrong was overwhelming; it was nothing less than the power of the "foreigner," the outsider who had suddenly become dominant in the city. Isolation, through garrisons and police patrols, was the only solution.

Union Park held onto its middle-class character until the middle of the 1890s; there was no immediate desertion by respectable people of the area in the wake of the violence: where else in a great city, asked one citizen, was it safe to go? Everywhere the same terror was possible.

The contrast between the limited character of civil disturbance and the immediate perception of that disturbance as the harbinger of an unnameable threat coming from a generalized enemy is a theme that binds together much research on urban disorders.

Until a few years ago, riots were taken to be the expression of irrational, and directionless, aggression. The "irrationality of crowds," and similar explanations of crowd behavior as an innate disorder, was first given a cogent interpretation in the industrial era in the writings of Le Bon, [16] for whom the irrational brutality of crowds was a sign of how the "psychology" of the individual becomes transformed when the individual acts in concert with other people. According to Le Bon, the crowd releases a man from the self-reflective, rational restraints that normally operate when a person is alone or with one or two other people. The anonymity of mass gatherings reinforces the desire each one has to cast off these rational, individual restraints, and encourages men to express more violent traits without fear of personal detection. It is the social psychology of the massive gathering to be unrestrained, Le Bon wrote, the psychology of the individual to prescribe rules for himself. [17]

This image of crowds was as congenial to many of the syndicalists on the Left (though not Sorel) as it was to the fears of bourgeois people like those in Union Park. The difficulty with the image is that, for the nineteenth century at least, it seems not to fit the facts of crowd behavior.

Thanks to the pioneering work of George Rudé and Charles Tilly, [18] it has been possible to ascertain that, in the urbanizing of English and French populations during the early nineteenth century, popular rebellions and crowd activities possessed a high degree of rationality; that is to say, the crowds acted to achieve rather well-defined ends, and used only as much force as was required to make their demands prevail. Though the work of Rudé and Tilly seems contradicted by the extensive researches of Louis Chevalier [19] on Parisian lower-class behavior during the nineteenth century, there are enough points of agreement, in looking at crowd behavior where violent coercion is involved, to rule out the "unrestrained frenzy" Le Bon saw in crowds that made them useless as a social tool to gain definite, common goals. [20] What is important in Le Bon's work, for the present purpose, was his *expectation* that this unrestrained frenzy would result from group action by the lower class.

For it is this same split between middle-class expectation of blind anarchy and the actual limitations on working-class disorder that characterized the Haymarket incidents, the same split between a reign of terror sensed during the later burglaries and the actual routine narrowness of these crimes.

The problem of the Union Park experience was the citizenry's inability to connect the facts seen to the facts as elements of what people knew was a correct interpretation. Expecting "seething passions" to erupt hysterically, the middle-class people of Chicago and their police were somehow immune to the spectacle they should have enjoyed, that of the workers becoming bored with the inflammatory talk of their supposed leaders. The expectations of a seething rabble had somehow to be fulfilled, and so the police themselves took the first step. After the shooting was over, the respectable people of Chicago became in turn inflamed. This blind passion in the name of defending the city from blind passion is the phenomenon that needs to be explained. A similar contradiction occurred in the series of robberies a half year later as well. As in the riot, the facts of the rationality of the enemy and his limited purpose, although acknowledged, were not absorbed; he was felt to be something else, a nameless, elusive terror, all-threatening. And the people reacted with a passion equal to his.

This mystifying condition, familiar now in the voices heard from the "New Right," is what I should like to explain, not through a sweeping theory that binds the past to the present, but through a theory that explains this peculiar reaction in terms of strains in the family life of the Union Park people. What I would like to explore—and I certainly do not pretend to prove it—is how, in an early industrial city, the fears of the foreign masses by a middle-class group may have reflected something other than the actual state of inter-action between bourgeoisie and proletariat. These fears may have reflected instead the impact of family life on the way the people like those in Union Park understood their places in the city society.

Studies of overreaction to limited stimuli have centered, for the most part, on the idea of a "frustration-aggression syndrome." This ungainly phrase was given a clear definition in one of the early classic works of American social psychology, *Frustration and Aggression* (1939). The authors wrote that

aggression is always a consequence of frustration. More specifically . . . the occurrence of aggressive behavior always presupposes the existence of frustration and, contrariwise, the existence of frustration always leads to some form of aggression. [21]

Applied in terms of social class, this frustration-aggression syndrome implies that when a group fails to achieve goals it desires, or when it is unable to maintain a position it covets, it becomes aggressive, and searches out objects on which it can blame its failure. This simple, clear idea Parsons [22] has applied to the formation of the Nazi party in Germany: the fall in status in the 1920s of fixed-income, middle-class groups breeding an aggressive desire to get back at their enemies, without knowing, or really caring, who they were. Lipset [23] has incorporated elements of the same idea in his essay on working-class authoritarianism in the United States after the Second World War. And of course the concept is now used to explain the hostility of lower middle-class whites toward blacks: the whites who have failed to rise high in the economic system they believe in are said to make blacks "aggression objects" of the frustration they themselves have suffered.[24]

If it is true, as this syndrome of frustration-aggression suggests, that in the character one ascribes to one's enemy lies a description of something in one's own experience, the nature of the fear of lower-class foreigners among Union Park families might tell something about the Union Park community itself. The Union Park men, during the time of the riot and robberies, accused their chosen enemies of being, first, lawless anarchists, which was transmuted, secondly, to being pushed by their base passions outside the bounds of acceptable behavior, which resolved itself, finally, to being emotionally out of control. If the poor were reasonable, if they were temperate, ran the argument, these violent things would not have come to pass.

What about the Union Park people themselves, then? Were they masters of themselves? A study I have recently completed on the family patterns of the Union Park people during the decades of the 1870s and '80s may throw some light on the question of stability and purposefulness in their lives: it is the dimension of stability in these family patterns, I believe, that shaped sources of the reaction to violence.

Intensive Family Life

In 1880, on a forty-square-block territory of Union Park, there lived 12,000 individuals in approximately 3,000 family units. These family units were of three kinship types: single-member families, where one person lived alone without any other kin; nuclear families, consisting of a husband, wife, and their unmarried children; and extended families, where to the nuclear unit was added some other relative—a brother or sister of the parents, a member of a third generation, or a son or daughter who was married and lived with his spouse in the parental home. The most common form of the extended family in Union Park was that containing "collateral kin," that is, unmarried relatives of the same generation as the husband or wife.

The dominant form of family life in Union Park was nuclear, for 80% of the population lived in such homes, with 10% of the population living alone in single-member families, and the remaining 10% living in extended family situations. A father and mother living alone with their growing children in an apartment or house was the pervasive household condition. There were few widowed parents living with their children in either nuclear or extended homes, and though the census manuscripts on which my study of the year 1880 is based were inexact at this point, there appeared to be few groups of related families living in separate dwellings but in the same neighborhood.

Is this nuclear-family dominance a special characteristic of middle-class life in this era? At the Joint Center for Urban Studies, I was fortunate in working with other researchers in this field to coordinate census measures of class and family form that could be used comparatively across different studies.[25] Comparison with these other studies, as well as within the limited range of social groups in Union Park, convinces me that this kind of family form was not a middle-class phenomenon. Within Union Park, the 80% dominance of the nuclear families held in lower social strata (of which enough existed to measure and test statistically, since the population as a whole was so large—about 25% of the community fell into a working-class category, excluding the servants in the homes of the other 75%) and throughout the range of middle-class groups. In Lynn Lees' data on an Irish working-class district in London in 1860, it similarly appeared that about 80% of her community's population lived in nuclear family configurations, 10% in single-member families, and 10% in extended families, virtually the same distribution as was found in Chicago's Union Park in 1880.

Again, the *outer* limits on the size of families in Union Park did seem to be the product of a special class condition. Contrary to the stereotype of the sprawling families of the poor, in Union Park the size of poor families was in its contours similar to the size of the wealthier ones: few families were larger than six members, among rich or poor. Similarly, comparison of family sizes in Union Park to the poor Irish of Lynn Lees' study or to the middle-class area of St. Pancras in London reveals the limits on family size in the three areas to have been the same.

Since family studies of nineteenth-century cities are at this date in a primitive stage, the body of future research may show these present examples to be "sports" or explainable by circumstances researchers do not now understand. Yet it does now seem more fruitful to concentrate on the *function* of nuclear families or on the *function* of families of restricted size in middle-class communities in the great cities of the nineteenth century, rather than to try to locate the conditions of peculiarly middle-class life in the *structural* existence of these family types.

What I did find to be true in Union Park was the following: over the course of time internal conditions of family structure and of family size tended to lead to similar family histories. Nuclear families had characteristic histories similar to the experience of smaller families having from two to four kin members in the 1870s and '80s. Extended families, on the other hand, had histories similar to the experience of the minority of families with four to six kin members during these decades. What made this process subtle was that nuclear families did not tend to be smaller, or extended larger. Family size and family kinship structure seemed rather to be independent structures with parallel internal differences in functioning.

Why and how this was so can be understood by assessing the patterns of the generations of the dominant group of nuclear, small-size families during the year 1880. These families were marked, in the relations between husbands and wives, parents and children, by strong patterns of family cohesion. Whether rich or poor, the young men and women from such homes rarely broke away to live on their own until they themselves were ready to marry and found families, an event that usually occurred when the man was in his early thirties. The families of Union Park, observers of the time note, were extremely self-contained, did little entertaining, and rarely left the home to enjoy even such modest pleasures as a church social or, for the men, a beer at the local tavern. The small family, containing only parents and their immediate children, resisted the diverse influences of either other kin associations or extensive community contacts. This was the mode of family life that dominated Union Park numerically. These families can be called "intensive families," and their life histories contrasted to families of larger size or more complex kinship. The intensive families would seem to epitomize a defined order of stability among the people of Union Park. Yet, Lynn Lees and I have found some functional differences between Chicago and London in families of this general character.

Instability through Separation or Desertion

In most census collections in the United States and Britain, the official tabulations of divorce are very low, because the formal breaking of the marital tie was considered a personal disgrace to both partners. But, as Talcott Parsons has demonstrated,[26] these official figures are misleading, since a great deal of unofficial divorce through separation or desertion occurred, at a higher rate, Parsons thinks, than in our own time. One means of detecting this hidden marital disorder in the census is to locate the individuals who were officially married but living without a spouse in the family. This measurement lets in a certain number of "beachhead migrants," men who have come to the city in advance of their families to establish a job and find a house, but in Union Park such men were less common in this category than spouses who were married, living with their children, but not with their husbands (or wives).[27]

In Union Park the number of families involved in such a break was about 10%. But in London, in the middle-class district of St. Pancras, the incidence of such marital separation was one-half of this, or 5%; in the lower-class Irish district Lynn Lees studied, there were less than a third as many marital separations of this type. In all three communities, of course, the official rate of divorce was nearly zero.

The explanation for this comparatively high incidence of marital break in Union Park is obscure, since there are now so few other comparative measures of family conditions behind the official statistics to use. In terms of these Chicago and London communities themselves perhaps the best thing to be said is the simplest: the higher incidence of marital break occurred in a city whose development was exclusively in the industrial era; the lower incidence of such a break occurred in a city for whom industrial production and large bureaucratic enterprises were but one chapter in a very long history.

Work Mobility and Family Stability

Added to this kind of family instability in the community as a whole, my study of intergenerational mobility in work and residence from 1872 to 1890 revealed a complicated, but highly significant pattern of insecurity in the dominant intensive families when compared to the smaller group of less intensive families.[28]

In the nuclear-family homes and in the smaller families the fathers were stable in their patterns of job holding, as a group, over the course of the eighteen years studied; roughly the same proportions of unskilled, skilled, and white-collar workers of various kinds composed the labor force of these nuclear fathers in 1890 as in 1872. Given the enormous growth of Chicago's industrial production, its banking and financial capital, retail trade volume, as well as the proliferation of the population (100% increase each ten years) and the greatly increasing proportion of white-collar pursuits during this time, such stability in job distribution is truly puzzling. Further, this pattern of job holding among the fathers of intensive families was not shared by the fathers in extended families or fathers of larger families living in Union Park. They were mobile up into exclusively bureaucratic, white-collar pursuits, so that by 1890 virtually none of these fathers worked with their hands. Within the range of white-collar occupations, the extended-family fathers and the large-family fathers gradually concentrated in executive and other lesser management pursuits and decreased their numbers in shopkeeping, toward which, stereotypically, they are supposed to gravitate.

Now the differences between fathers and sons in each of these family groups were even more striking. I found the sons in the dominant family homes to be, unlike their fathers, very unstable in their patterns of job holding, with as much movement down into manual pursuits over the course of the eighteen years as movement up within the white-collar occupations. Following the lead of Blau and Duncan, [29] we might be tempted to explain this pattern of dispersion simply as regression-toward-the-mean of higher status groups intergenerationally. But the sons of extended and large families did not move in this mixed direction. Rather, they followed in the footsteps of their fathers into good white-collar positions, with almost total elimination of manual labor in their ranks over the course of time. This pattern occurred in small-family sons versus large-family sons and in nuclear-family sons versus extended-family sons. The difference in the groups of sons was especially striking in that the starting distribution of the sons in the occupational work force was virtually the *same*, in the measure of family form and in those of family size. Thernstrom has pointed out in the conference discussions for this volume that economic aid between generations of workers ought to manifest itself more at the beginning point in the careers of the young rather than when the older generation has retired and the young have become the principal breadwinners. In Union Park, the fact that both extended-family and nuclear-family sons, both large- and small-family sons, began to work in virtually the same pursuits as their fathers, but then became distinctively different in their patterns of achievement, strongly suggests that something *beyond* monetary help was at work in these families to produce divergence in work experience in the city.

The residence patterns of the generations of the intensive and less intensive families also bears on the issues of stability and instability in the lives of the people of Union Park. Up to the time of violence in the Union Park area, the residence patterns of the two kinds of families, in both the parents' and the sons' generations, were rather similar. In the wake of the violence it appears that, within the parents' generation, there was significant movement back into the Union Park area, whereas for the half decade preceding the disturbances there was a general movement out to other parts of Chicago. It is in the generation of the sons that differences between the two family groups appeared. In the wake of the violence, the sons of large families and of extended families continued the processes of residential break from Union Park initiated during the early years of the 1880 decade. The sons from intensive families did not; in the years following the violence they stopped migrating beyond the boundaries of the community they had known as children, and instead kept closer to their first homes.

Two Theories of Intensive Family Stability

In my study of Union Park, [30] I tried to explain these differences in work experience and in residence in terms of patterns of family life and child nurturance for bourgeois people in a new, immensely dynamic, disordered city. In so doing, my researches led me into a debate that exists between the work of the sociologist Talcott Parsons and the cultural historian Phillippe Aries. [31] For Parsons has argued that the small nuclear family is an adaptive kinship form to the industrial order; the lack of extensive kin obligations and a wide kin circle in this family type means, Parsons has contended, that the kinship unit does not serve as a binding private world of its own, but rather frees the individual to participate in "universalized" bureaucratic structures that are urban-wide and dynamic. [32] Aries has challenged this theory by amassing a body of historical evidence to show that the extended kinship relationships in large families, at least during the period he studied, were actually less sheltering, more likely to push the individual out into the world where he would have to act like a full man on his own at an early age, than the intense, intimate conditons of the nineteenth-century home. In intensive homes, the young person spent a long time in a state of independence under the protection and guidance of his elders. Consequently, argues Aries, the capacity of the young adult from small nuclear homes to deal with the world about him was blunted, for he passed from a period of total shelter to a state in which he was expected to be entirely competent on his own. [33] Aries' attack has been supported for contemporary American urban communities by a variety of studies, the most notable being those of Eugene Litwak and Marvin Sussman, and it has been supported for English cities by the work of Peter Wilmott and Elizabeth Bott.[34]

The data I have collected on Union Park during the early stages of Chicago's industrial-bureaucratic expansion clearly are in line with the argument made by Aries. The young from homes of small scale or from homes where the structure of the family was nuclear and "privatistic," in Aries' phrase, had an ineptness in the work world, and a rootedness to the place of their childhood not found to the same degree among the more complex, or larger-family situations. (I have no desire to argue the moral virtues of this rootedness to community or failure to "make it" in the city; these simply happened to be the conditions that existed.) But the context of these Union Park families as new urbanites, in a new kind of city form, alters the meaning of stability and shelter leading to instability in the next generation among the intense family households. For it is clear that the nineteenth-century, privatistic, sheltering homes Aries depicts, homes Frank Lloyd Wright describes in his *Autobiography* for his early years in Chicago, homes that observers of the time pointed to as a basic element in the composition of the "dull respectability" of Union Park, could easily have served as a refuge themselves from the confusing, dynamic city that was taking shape all around the confines of Union Park. It indeed seems natural that middle-class people should try to hold onto the status position they had in such a disrupting, growing milieu, make little entrepreneurial ventures outside their established jobs, and withdraw themselves into the comfort and intimacy of their families. Here is the source of that job "freeze" to be seen in the mobility patterns of fathers in intense-family situations; the bourgeois intensive family in this way became a shelter from the work pressures of the industrial city, a place where men tried to institute some control and establish some comforting intimacies in the shape of their lives, while withdrawing to the sidelines as the new opportunities of the city industries opened up. Such an interpretation of these middle-class families complements, on the side of the home, the interpretation Richard Hofstadter has made of the middle classes politically, in the latter part of the nineteenth century. He characterizes them as feeling that the new industrial order was not theirs, but had passed them by and left them powerless. [35] It is this peculiar feeling of social helplessness on the part of the fathers that explains what use they made of their family lives.

Confusion in the Desire for Stability

What makes this complex pattern of family stability-instability significant for wider social orientations are the values about work to be found in the middle classes of this era. For here the idea of seizing opportunities, the idea of instability of job tenure for the sake of rising higher and higher, constituted, as John Cawelti has described it, [36] the commonly agreed-upon notion of how sure success could be achieved at this time among respectable people; in the same way, this chance-taking path was presented, in the Horatio Alger novels and the like, as the road into the middle class itself. One should have been mobile in work, then, for this was the meaning of "opportunity" and "free enterprise," but in fact the overwhelming dislocations of the giant cities seem to have urged many men to retreat into the circle of their own families, to try simply to hold onto what they knew they could perform as tasks to support themselves, in the midst of the upheaval of urban expansion.

This is deduction, to be sure, and perhaps it is characteristic of sociologists dealing with history that they speculate where historians would prefer to remain silent and let the ambiguities stand. Yet the body not only of Union Park data, but the memoirs, fictional portraits, and secondary studies of this period seem to me to indicate that such an internally contradictory response to urbanization among the heads of middle-class families is the means by which the differences in social mobility between kinds of families can be explained. Conditions of privacy and comfort in the home weakened the desire to get ahead in the world, to conquer it; since the fathers of the intensive families were retreating from the confusions of city life, their preparation of their sons for work in Chicago became ambiguous, in that they wanted, surely, success for their sons, yet shielded the young, and did not themselves serve as models of successful adaptation. The result of these ambiguities can be seen directly in the work experience of the sons, when contrasted to the group of sons from families which, by virtue either of family form or size, were more complex or less intense. Overlaid on these family patterns was a relatively high rate of hidden marital breakdown in Union Park—one in every ten homes—while the expectation was, again, that such breakdown must not occur, that it was a disgrace morally.

These contradictions in family process gave rise, I believe, to the characteristics of Union Park's reaction to violence during the years 1886 to 1888.

The Feeling of Threat Generated by the Family Experience

In the older version of the "frustration-aggression" syndrome it was assumed that if a social group failed to achieve a certain goal, it searched for an enemy to punish. But the goals of these middle-class people in Union Park were themselves self-contradictory: they wanted success in the work of the city and yet they didn't want it, given the definition of success at that time as an entrepreneurial grasping of opportunities rather than the fruit of plodding and routine service. The goals for the home were also contradictory: they wanted a stable shelter from the confusion and terror of the city, yet somehow they expected their sons, growing up sheltered, to be able to make it in that city world, and the sons of the dominant family groups seemed unable to do so. Divorce was a disgrace, yet there is evidence that one out of every ten of the neighborhood families were involved in a marital separation or desertion, a voluntary condition as opposed to the involuntary break of widowhood. Thus, because the goals of these middle-class people were bred of an equal desire to escape from and succeed in the city, the possibility of a wholly satisfying pattern of achievement for them was denied. The contradictory nature of the family purpose and products was innately frustrating so that a family impulse in one direction inevitably defeated another image of what was wanted. This meant that the sources of defeat were nameless for the families involved; surely these families were not aware of the web of self-contradictions in which in retrospect they seem to have been enmeshed; they knew only that things never seemed to work out to the end planned, that they suffered defeats in a systematic way. It is this specific kind of frustration that would lead to a sense of being overwhelmed, which, in this community's family system, led easily to a hysterical belief in hidden, unknown threats ready to strike at a man at almost any time.

Feeling of Threat and Perceptions of Violence

What I would like to suggest is that this complex pattern of self-defeat explains the character of the Union Park reaction to violence. For the dread of the unknown that the middle classes projected onto their supposed enemies among the poor expressed exactly the condition of self-instituted defeat that was the central feature of the family system in Union Park. And this dread was overwhelming precisely because men's own contradictory responses to living in such a city were overwhelming. They had defined a set of conditions for their lives that inevitably left them out of control. That fact that there was in Union Park a desire to destroy the "immigrant anarchists" or to garrison the neighborhood against them, as a result of the incidents of violence, was important in that it offered an outlet for personal defeats, not just for anger against lawbreakers. This response to violence refused to center on particular people, but rather followed the "path of hysterical reaction," in Freud's phrase, and centered on an abstract class of evildoers. For the fear of being suddenly overwhelmed from the outside was really a sign that one was in fact in one's own life being continually overwhelmed by the unintended consequences, or "latent consequences" as Merton calls them, of what one did. [37] By blaming the urban poor for their lawlessness, these middle-class people were expressing a passion for retribution that had little to do with riots or thefts. The retribution was rather in the nature of what Erikson calls a "cover object" for hostility, an expression of inability to deal with the issues of one's own life, of mobility and stability in the city: the fear in these middle-class people was that if they were to act entrepreneurially in the work world they might be destroyed, yet their desire was to make it big suddenly. The desire to escape to the safety of the simple home of father, mother, and children became, unexpectedly, a crippling shield when the sons went out into the world.

This dilemma, expressed in the terrible fear of attack from the unbridled masses, was also related to the fear of falling into deep poverty that grew up in urban middle-class families of this time. To judge from a wide range of novels in the latter half of the nineteenth century there was a dread among respectable people of suddenly and uncontrollably falling into abject poverty; the Sidwells in Thackeray's *Vanity Fair* plummet from wealth to disorganized penury in a short space of time; Lily Bart's father, in Edith Wharton's *Age of Innocence,* is similarly struck down by the symbol of entrepreneurial chance in the industrial city, the stock market. This feeling of threat from the impersonal, unpredictable workings of the city economy was much like the sense of threat that existed in the Union Park families, because the dangers encountered in both cases were not a person or persons one could grapple with, but an abstract condition, poverty, or family disorder that was unintended, impersonal, and swift to come if the family should once falter. Yet what one *should* do was framed in such a self-contradictory way that it seemed oneself and one's family were always on the edge of survival. In this way, the growth of the new industrial city, with its uncertainties and immense wastes of human poverty not all to be dismissed as personal failures, could surely produce in the minds of middle-class citizens, uneasy about their own class position, living out from the center of town, the feeling that some terrible force from below symbolized by the poor, the foreigner, was about to strike out and destroy them unless they did something drastic.

The demographic reaction among most of the families to the eruption of violence bears out this interpretation of events. With the exception of the upwardly mobile, extended-family sons, most family members did not try to flee the community as a response to the threats of riot and the organized wave of crime. The demographic movement mirrored a renewed feeling of community solidarity in the face of violence, a solidarity created by fear and a common dread of those below. Again, it is significant that the group that did not show this pattern of "sticking out the trouble" is the generation of young family members who lived in more complex family circumstances than the majority, and who achieved, on the whole, greater occupational gains than the majority.

The relations between family life and the perception of violence in this Chicago community could be formed into the following general propositions. These were middle-class families enormously confused in what they wanted for themselves in the city, considered in terms of their achievements in the society at large and in terms of their emotional needs for shelter and intimacy; their scheme of values and life goals was in fact formed around the issues of stability and instability as goals in a self-contradictory way. The result of this inner contradiction was a feeling of frustration, of not really being satisfied, in the activities of family members to achieve *either* patterns of stability or mobility for themselves. The self-defeat involved in this process led these families naturally to feel themselves threatened by overwhelming, nameless forces they could not control, no matter what they did. The outbreak of violence was a catalyst for them, giving them in the figure of the "other," the stranger, the foreigner, a generalized agent of disorder and disruption.

It is this process that explains logically why the people of Union Park so quickly found a communally acceptable villain responsible for violence, despite all the ambiguities perceived in the actual outbreaks of the disorders themselves; this is why the villain so quickly identified was a generalized, nonspecific human force, the embodiment of the unknown, the outside, the foreign. This is why the people of Union Park clung so tenaciously to their interpretation, seemed so willing to be terrorized and distraught.

If the complex processes of family and social mobility in Union Park are of any use in understanding the great fear of disorder among respectable, middle-class urbanites of our own time, their import is surely disturbing. For the nature of the disease that produced this reaction to violence among the industrial middle classes was not simply a matter of "ignorance" or failure to understand the problems of the poor; the fear was the consequence, rather, of structural processes in the lives of the Union Park families themselves. Thus for attitudes of people like the Union Park dwellers to change, and a more tolerant view of those below to be achieved, nothing so simple as more education about poor people, or to put the matter in contemporary terms, more knowledge about Negroes, would have sufficed. The whole fabric of the city, in its impact on staid white-collar workers, would have to have been changed. The complexity and the diversity of the city itself would need to have been stilled for events to take another course. But were the disorder of the city absent, the principal characteristic of the industrial city as we know it would also have been absent. These cities were powerful agents of change, precisely because they replaced the controlled social space of village and farm life with a kind of human settlement too dense and too various to be controlled.

And it comes to mind that the New Right fears of the present time are as deeply endemic to the structure of complex city life as was the violent reaction to violence in Union Park. Perhaps, out of patterns of self-defeat in the modern middle classes, it is bootless to expect rightwing, middle-class repression to abate simply through resolves of goodwill, "education about Negroes," or a change of heart. The experience of these bourgeois people of Chicago one hundred years ago may finally serve to make us a great deal more pessimistic about the chances for reason and tolerance to survive in a complex and pluralistic urban society.

Notes

1. Henry David, *The Haymarket Affair* (New York, 1936), p. 198.

2. See Foster Rhea Dulles, *A History of American Labor* (New York, 1949), passim.

3. *Chicago Daily Tribune,* May 4, 1886, pp. 1, 2.

4. See the full account in the *Chicago Daily Tribune,* May 5, 1886, p. 1.

5. David, p. 226

6. *Chicago Daily Tribune,* May 6, 1886, p. 3.

7. *Chicago Daily Tribune,* May 7, 1886, p. 8.

8. Ibid.

9. *Chicago Daily Tribune,* February 9, 1888, pp. 1-2.

10. Ibid., p. 4.

11. Ibid., pp. 1-2.

12. See the statements of the Union Park fathers in *Chicago Daily Tribune,* February 9, 1888, p. 2.

13. *Chicago Daily Tribune,* February 9, 1888, pp. 1-2.

14. Ibid.

15. Ibid.

16. G. Le Bon, *The Crowd: A Study of the Popular Mind* (London, 1909).

17. It is interesting that Le Bon was led by this route into looking later in his life for a different set of psychological "instincts" in crowds than in individuals.

18. George Rudé, *The Crowd in History, 1730-1840* (New York, 1954) and Charles Tilly, *The Vendée* (Cambridge, Mass., 1964).

19. L. Chevalier, *Classes Laborieuses et Classes Danguereuses* (Paris, 1958).

20. I understand Chevalier is now more convinced of the "rationality" hypothesis. See, as one indication of this, the writings on Belleville in L. Chevalier, *Les Parisiens* (Paris, 1967).

21. J. Dollard, L. Boob, J. Miller, E. Mower, J. Sears, et al., *Frustration and Aggression* (New Haven, 1939), p. 1.

22. See "Democracy and Social Structure in Pre-Nazi Germany" in Parsons, *Essays in Sociological Theory* (rev. ed., Gencoe, Ill., 1954).

23. See Seymour Martin Lipset, *Political Man,* Pt. I, Chap. 4 (New York, 1960).

24. This theory, widely expressed in the press by amateur sociologists, explains the phenomenon neatly as a whole, but explains nothing of the particulars of class jealousy or fear.

25. Stephan Thernstrom and Lynn Lees, work in progress (description to be found in Joint Center *Bulletin* of 1968). The measures are also relatable to the social class categories used by D. V. Glass in his study of intergenerational social mobility in Britain; Part III of *Social Mobility in Britain,* D. V. Glass, ed. (London, 1954).

26. Talcott Parsons and Robert Bales, *Family,* Chap. 1 (Glencoe, Ill., 1955).

27. See Charles Tilly, "Migration to an American City" (unpublished manuscript on file at Joint Center for Urban Studies) for an excellent discussion of migration patterns.

28. There were, of course, no two-generation households in the single-member families.

29. P. Blau and O. D. Duncan, *The American Occupational Structure* (New York, 1967).

30. *Families Against the City* (Cambridge, Mass., 1970).

31. Phillipe Aries, *Centuries of Childhood* (New York, 1965).

32. Parsons and Bales, Chap. 1.

33. Bernard Wishy, in *The Child and the Republic* (Philadelphia, 1967), has material relevant to this idea for America in the late nineteenth century.

34. See Sennett, *Families Against the City,* Chap. 9, for a review of this literature.

35. Richard Hofstadter, *The Age of Reform* (New York, 1958).

36. John Cawelti, *Apostles of the Self-made Man* (Chicago, 1965).

37. The Union Park situation was, in fact, a classic case of Merton's theory of latent consequences.

Anna Howard Shaw:
New approaches to feminism

James R. McGovern

The history of every social reform poses a central and intractable question: what
stimulated the movement into action? There are, of course, the real conditions to which
the movement objects and which it explicitly aims to rectify. But modern historians have
not been willing to settle for explanations that merely match the reform movements to
objective conditions of injustice. For one thing, there is the matter of timing. Why should
a long-term problem give rise to coherent opposition at one point rather than another?
There is, too, the question of motivation. Is the reform movement actuated strictly by
the existing inequities, or are other motives at work beneath the surface? Motivation
seems an especially acute question in studying reform leaders, those who show
single-minded zeal on behalf of a cause, usually at a high personal cost according to
contemporary measures of career and conventional life.

These questions seem to apply with particular force to the study of the American
women's rights movement that had its roots in the reform era before the Civil War,
developed an organizational base during the Gilded Age, and went on ultimately to
achieve the Women's Suffrage Amendment in 1920. For one thing, the absorbing concern
with voting rights seemed far out of correspondence with the range and depth of
disabilities under which American women labored. The struggle for women's suffrage,
moreoever, was not treated as a conventional political issue. For everyone, advocates and
opponents alike, deep emotions were touched relating to fundamental matters of morals,
sex roles, and family. And the feminist leaders themselves exhibited personal qualities
that placed them profoundly at variance with contemporary ideals of womanhood.

With questions such as these in mind, James R. McGovern has attempted in the
following essay to probe the mind of a leading feminist, Anna Howard Shaw, who left an
unusually full record of her childhood and personal life. The shaping forces McGovern
locates in the Gilded Age family—in the wife submissive and dependent, the father
dominant and authoritarian. The man's role seemed impregnable even when he failed
utterly—as Anna Shaw's father did—to live up to the responsibilities that went with

James R. McGovern, "Anna Howard Shaw: New Approaches to Feminism." © 1969 by The Regents
of the University of California. Reprinted from *Journal of Social History*, vol. 3, no. 2, pp. 135-153,
by permission of The Regents.

power. The marks of that unhappy and infuriating upbringing Anna Shaw carried into adulthood and into an unrelenting struggle for women's rights. Throughout her life, she exhibited a deep hostility to men and, simultaneously, an unmistakable masculinity in her own character and style of living; a disdain for the softer feminine qualities (and for marriage that demanded them) and, simultaneously, a profound sympathy for her sisters in marital and sexual bondage; and, finally, a driven quality in her career that bordered on the neurotic in McGovern's estimation. Nor was Anna Shaw at all unique. Her career formed a pattern among feminists, many of whom, in fact, experienced very similar childhoods.

In his presidential address to the American Historial Association in 1957, William L. Langer called on the historical profession to apply psychological analysis to the study of the past. Given the pitfalls and technical problems, not many have heeded Langer's advice. McGovern's essay suggests the exciting possibilities in a psychological approach for those skillful and daring enough to use it. In this instance, he has opened up a fresh prospect for understanding the impulse behind American feminism in the Gilded Age.

For further reading: Eleanor Flexner, *Century of Struggle: The Women's Rights Movement in the United States* (1959);* Aileen S. Kraditor, *The Ideas of the Women's Suffrage Movement, 1896-1920* (1965);* Andrew Sinclair, *The Better Half: The Emancipation of the American Woman* (1965);* Christopher Lasch, *The New Radicalism in America* (1965);* William L. Langer, "The Next Assignment," *American Historical Review,* LXIII (1958), 283-304; Cushing Strout, "Ego Psychology and the Historian," *History and Theory,* VIII (1968), 281-297.

This study of Anna Howard Shaw (1847-1919), a key figure in the American suffrage and feminist movements between 1890 and 1915, is designed to assess the nature of her leadership from the standpoint of her personal psychology. It shows that Miss Shaw's commitment to feminism and her achievements as one of its leaders are closely related to the circumstances of her childhood. These findings illustrate the social utility of Shaw's emotional problems in contributing to a valid social movement while they reveal her poignant and exaggerated personal qualities as a leader. Shaw's example raises the question whether she might be a model feminist in her time; a "sample survey" of the lives of numerous leaders in women's reform in the same period supports this hypothesis. It leads to the tentative conclusion that the feminist movement contained at least one prominent leadership type, like Miss Shaw, whose demonstrable fixity and tenacity, founded in psychic fantasy, nevertheless promoted the realistic goals of woman's social and political emancipation.

Historians are generally conservative about using "depth psychology"[1] to analyze historical figures and movements,[2] feminists and feminism, of course, included. Pleas for them to appropriate the tools of psychoanalysis have probably reached their widest audience through the vigorous advocacy of William L. Langer[3] and the psychoanalyst-social scientist Erik H. Erickson.[4] Pointing out that psychoanalysis and history have common interests in the understanding of men's motives, these advocates deplore historians' penchants for vague characterology instead of what Langer and Erikson regard to be the most scientific attempt yet devised to explain man's behavior.

New approaches, in line with depth psychology, would be useful to explore all phases of history, historical movements, and varieties of historical personality. Several reform movements lend themselves to this type of interpretation since they seem to attract large numbers of like-minded, "driven" people and thus permit psychological typing. What follows is primarily concerned with the deep, very personal reasons why Anna Shaw became a feminist. It will not deal with why feminism became a social movement in America in her lifetime, except to acknowledge that the social and intellectual factors precipitating the movement naturally influenced and reinforced her commitment.

The subject of American feminism is still one of the neglected areas of our history as far as depth psychology is concerned. Among the major treatments in recent years, Aileen S. Kraditor's *The Ideas of the Woman's Suffrage Movement, 1890-1920* covers the basic ground on women's justifications, rhetoric, and propaganda on behalf of suffrage, but it very seldom attempts to look behind the ideas.[5] Eleanor Flexner's *Century of Struggle: The Woman's Rights Movement in the United States* is an excellent general history, written from the standpoint of an advocate; like Andrew Sinclair's *The Better Half: The Emancipation of the American Woman,* it vigorously eschews all psychological interpretations.[6] While Sinclair criticizes the superficial use of psychology in history, he is, in fact, generally critical of any use of it at all. For him "good psychologists limited their treatment to the measurably insane" while "bad psychologists tried to allay the discontent of the sane by explaining that any questioner of majority rule was merely a sufferer from emotional or physical disturbance."[7] Flexner and Sinclair explain the feminist movement as primarily a consequence of the impact of the industrial revolution on women which freed them from home ties and expanded their opportunities for leisure, education, and work. Christopher Lasch devotes only a section of his important study, *The New Radicalism in America,* to feminism, but presents a very sophisticated treatment of the subject. Lasch detects in feminism "a sweeping assault on the male sex," "an enormous amount of sexual antipathy," and "envy." These feelings cannot be entirely explained by new sociological conditions.[8] For Lasch feminists belonged to a new breed of middle-class intellectuals of the 1890s and early 1900s who sought to live spontaneously and so revolted against the "stuffy" bourgeois norms of their elders. Yet Lasch himself questions: "Why did they persist in attributing their sufferings not to class but to sex, not to their being middle-class intellectuals in rebellion against what had come to seem a sterile and meaningless existence, but to the simple fact of being a woman?"[9] He answers that to the feminists being a woman was tantamount to a life of mere ceremonial futility. However, might not their vehemence have reflected discontent with their gender identity experienced as a child, while their later objections to woman's sex role have merely been rationalizations? In other words, there may be more sex and less intellect involved in feminism than Lasch perceives, and therefore good reason to employ a psychological approach to the subject.

The merit of Anna Howard Shaw for this type of investigation is established both by her importance to the feminist movement and by the abundance and nature of the source material about her.[10] Born in Scotland, the sixth of seven children, she moved to America at age four, and after living in Lawrence, Massachusetts, for eight years, moved to the Michigan frontier. Shaw attended Big Rapids High School and, in 1873, began at Albion College; in 1876 she entered Boston University Theological School and graduated two years later. While holding a pastorate in East Dennis, Massachusetts, as an ordained minister, she attended Boston University Medical School and was graduated in 1886. She then became a speaker for various woman's suffrage groups; this led to an appointment as lecturer for Susan Anthony's National American Woman's Suffrage Association in 1890. Shaw became its vice-president from 1892 until 1904 when she succeeded Susan Anthony as president; she held that post during a decisive period for woman's suffrage until 1915, and then became president emeritus. In April 1917, Shaw was appointed chairman of the Woman's Committee of the National Council of Defense to coordinate women's work on conservation and the sale of war bonds; for this she became the first American woman to win the Distinguished Service Medal. [11] While lecturing with President Taft and President Lowell of Harvard on behalf of the League of Nations, she contracted pneumonia and died 2 July 1919, at the age of seventy-two.

While she was president of the N.A.W.S.A., its membership multiplied from 17,000 to 200,000 and the number of states that adopted suffrage for women rose from four to twelve. [12] She led campaigns which secured the vote for women in the states of Washington (1910), Arizona, Kansas, and Oregon (1912), and Nevada (1914). An effective, colorful orator, Shaw contributed personally to these gains. It is probably that her speeches, delivered in civic centers, churches, or colleges in every state in the union, reached five million Americans. [13] By 1915 she may have outlived her usefulness as president of N.A.W.S.A. for she was most effective working on her own or with a few friends stirring up audiences for suffrage, not in the vast, complicated organization which was developing and which required even further elaboration.

This study is not so much concerned with the nature of Shaw's contributions to the feminist movement as with why she gave herself so completely to this cause. Most women of her period did not embrace the feminist ideology nor even desire to vote, let alone dedicate themselves as did Shaw. She felt keenly what other women experienced less intensely, or perhaps not at all—that men were lording over women—and she was more determined than most other women to eradicate these injustices.

Anna Howard Shaw's childhood was extremely unpleasant. She described it poignantly to a close friend:

I never could understand why I was born. That is the greatest mystery I have ever had to study over, and I have been at the problem ever since I can remember, and it is no nearer solution today than when I was a little girl, and in my misery used to ask God why He ever let me live. My childhood was very miserable, and I never had any girlhood. [14]

The household was dominated by her father, despite the fact that his ill-conceived plans and protracted absences disqualified him for the role and exposed his family to severe tensions and hardships. Despite his incompetence, he made the important decisions for the family, administered its corporal punishment—including regular spankings to Shaw for spelling errors—and determined a way of life for Shaw's mother which seriously jeopardized the support she could give her daughter. Shaw objected to his claims based on role rather than intrinsic worth. In *Story of a Pioneer* she sadly describes how he was responsible for a traumatic type of experience which emotionally felled her mother and led to her own deep anxieties. While staying behind in Lawrence, Mr. Shaw "sent my mother and five young children" to live in the Michigan woods near hostile Indians in a crude log cabin without flooring or plaster or provision for water and with food for only a few weeks. [15] Indeed, Anna Shaw wrote that he felt so justified in his role as husband and father remaining behind to earn wages and help the Abolitionists that "even if he had witnessed my mother's despair on the night of our arrival in our new home, he would not have understood it." [16] His later absences from home, notably during the Civil War when he and all his grown sons joined the Union Army leaving only a boy at home with the women of the family, made the discrepancies between his claims and reasonable authority even more incongruous. Although Shaw describes pleasantly in *Story of a Pioneer* this man whom she had known "to spend a planting season in figuring on the production of a certain number of kernels of corn, instead of planting the corn and raising it," [17] the family's needs for hard work and achievements could only have caused her to hold negative feelings toward him. She rapidly became her "father's most difficult daughter" [18] and the "family's black sheep." [19] When one day he criticized her for "idling" and not helping her mother, after she had made substantial economic contributions to the family, Shaw became indignant, announcing she would not be a domestic ("The soul within me refused to beat out its life against a barred door, and I rebelled.... I would live my life, not the life which had been urged as the destiny of women..), [20] but would become a minister. Anna became a minister for many of the same reasons she later led woman's suffrage. She was rebelling in each instance against what she perceived to be an extremely unjust social order in which men denied freedom to women and yet victimized or threatened to victimize them with impunity born of their conventional role supremacy.

Anna Shaw's pursuit of a male career and authority role as minister demonstrated not merely her identification with the authoritative male position, but her aversion to her mother's dependency and helplessness. Her handwritten recollection of the early years of her life presents her mother as an unenviable, self-sacrificing person whose work and troubles got in the way of the nurture which her daughter craved. Shaw writes how she was

born of an overworked mother burdened with the entire care of a family of six children at a time when even for the well-to-do there were but few conveniences . . . to lighten the drudgery of household toil. . . . So I came into being a tiny, underfed child robbed before birth of vigor and health. . . . [21]

Yet she notes how she was "saved from much unhappiness" by her mother's "sunny, hopeful disposition." Thus although crossing the Atlantic from Scotland caused her mother to become ill, "when we children were able to reach her, to cling to her for a blessed interval, she was still the sure refuge she had always been." [22] Her father's irresponsible venture in the Michigan wilderness threatened this bond with her mother. She describes her mother's reaction to the cabin and its primitive surroundings:

She could not realize even then, I think, that this was really the place father prepared for us, that here he expected us to live. When she finally took it in she buried her face in her hands, and in that way she sat for hours without moving or speaking. For the first time in her life she had forgotten us; and we, for our part, dared not to speak to her. . . . Our little world crumbled under our feet. Then she came to herself, but her face when she raised it was worse than her silence had been. She seemed to have died and returned to us from the grave. . . . [23]

Even after her mother's seeming "return," Anna Shaw felt that "we had lost our mother." For a time thereafter her mother was unable to stand up even as "she took up again the burden of her life, a burden she did not lay down until she passed away." [24] She reflects pathetically: "In some way which I did not understand the one sure refuge in our new world had been taken from us. I hardly knew the silent woman who lay near me, tossing from side to side and staring into the darkness." [25] Mother became "poor old Mother" whom Shaw longed to comfort in her later years. [26] Yet Shaw's need for that "one sure refuge" never disappeared. Throughout her life she attempted to recover, largely through identification with the feminist movement, as we shall see, the love and support which was denied her as a child.

The family backgrounds of a number of feminist leaders active in the period 1850-1900 suggest close parallels with Shaw's. There is reason to believe that they too may have perceived their father's style of life as preferable to their mother's, especially in terms of power and significance. They may have been predisposed therefore to agree with Shaw that it was better to be like a man than a woman. Charlotte P. Gilman and Margaret Sanger may have been aggrieved because they, like Shaw, found their father's claims unjustified by performance. Charlotte Gilman writes that her father, after divorcing her mother, dominated her family, though at a physical and emotional distance, by exposing it (apparently unconcernedly) to numerous hardships. [27] Margaret Sanger's father, while exacting and domineering, neglected his family just as Mr. Shaw did. Though often out of work, he insisted on all the privileges of an "artistic temperament." On one occasion he squandered all the family's winter coal money to pay for a lecture by Henry George; at another time he refused to defend his house from robbers. [28] The fathers of other feminist leaders were much more successful in supplying the physical needs of their families, but their daughters seem to have perceived in them by virtue of their overwhelming power in their families a preferable model for their own lives. Elizabeth Cady Stanton reveals that her father openly declared to her that he wished she had been a boy and concedes that she made every effort to fulfill his aspirations. [29] Susan Anthony's father also overshadowed her mother. Mary Livermore describes how her father dictated her choice of books, amusements, clothes, and education. [30] Lucy Stone concedes: "There was only one will in our home and that was my father's."[31]

Striking also are the similarities between Shaw and other leading women reformers in their attitudes toward their mothers and hence the feminine role. Susan B. Anthony, one of eight children born in her family in seventeen years, writes to her mother about her childhood: "my thoughts rest with dear mother, toiling unremittingly through the long day . . . and then reclining on her pillow with her consequent bodily suffering of overexertion." [32] Her judgment on marriage was that it "has ever been a one sided matter resting unequally upon the sexes. By it man gains all; woman loses all; tyrant law and lust reign supreme with him, submission and ready obedience alone befit her." [33] Lucy Stone's mother remarked at the time of Lucy's birth, "Oh, dear! I am sorry it is a girl. A woman's life is so hard!" [34] Abigail S. Duniway, a leading feminist in Oregon, records nearly identical remarks in her autobiography about her mother's reaction to the news of her birth. [34] Margaret Sanger in *An Autobiography* writes suggestively, "I was the youngest of six, but after me others kept coming along until we were eleven." [35] And, "Mother was everlastingly busy sewing, cooking, doing this and that. For so ardent and courageous a woman he [father] must have been trying. . . " Although Charlotte Gilman's family had only two children, her mother's separation from her father and consequent poverty provided her with an unusually poignant example of woman's sufferings at the hands of men.

It seems likely that several of Shaw's colleagues became feminists for many of the same reasons as Shaw. They probably experienced, as she surely experienced as a child, a "radical magnification of negative feelings toward the oppressors and of positive feelings toward the oppressed" to which psychologist Silvan S. Tomkins assigns the "major dynamic which powers the commitment of the individual reformer." [37] Anna Shaw's childhood served to limit the range of her alternatives as an adult. She was predisposed to see in feminism a system which would release the oppressed just as it would reduce the pretensions of men. It is reasonable to expect that as an adult she would conclude with marked emotional effect:

There is not a kind of father under the sun that we have not had; but like Topsy we never had a mother; and that is what is the matter with us. We have been pretty nearly fathered to death, and what we need is a little mothering to undo the evils of too much fathering. [38]

As the twig was bent, so was it strengthened by experiences of later youth. Shaw witnessed distressfully the inferior position of women while attending a coeducational college. She then suffered extreme hardship and almost continual hunger while studying at Boston University Theological School ("I realized that women theologians paid heavily for the privilege of being women" [39]) owing to regulations which prohibited women students in the divinity school from enjoying the same dining and living comforts as men. Her social life came to be exclusively woman-centered and led to a disproportionate focus on women's problems. The specific social context of the late nineteenth century which produced the feminist ideology attracted women with Shaw's education and ability by providing them with challenging opportunities and national prestige. [40] Shaw's views were undoubtedly reinforced as greater numbers of middle-class women became better educated and better informed about feminism in this country and Europe. Susan Anthony's charisma and their years of travelling together all over the country, often under adverse circumstances, added further ingredients. Shaw's oratorical skills were certain to be attractive to a movement which was just beginning to get a respectable hearing. But would any of these later circumstances have turned Anna Shaw into a leader of women's reform if she had not first found in feminism, in this age before personal therapy, a kind of situational therapy?

Shaw's system for coping with her emotional problems had two vital components. First, she sought to imitate men, thereby establishing that many of their "superior" qualities and skills were not particularly masculine but human. At the same time she pointed up the limitations of their abilities, thereby creating the impression that they were inferior to women's and to what she herself could do. Second, she sought to care for women and to strengthen them; in the process she hoped that they would look after her in return. This pattern—both her antagonism toward men by finding fault with them while seeking to deprive them of feminine companionship and also her extraordinary dependence on women—ultimately locked in her commitment to the woman's world.

Psychoanalysis offers many useful explanations for the masculine qualities which Shaw and other feminists seem to have possessed. Freud sees pronounced masculine behavior in women as resulting from incestuous ties between father and daughter. To avoid guilt which comes from a violation of this taboo, the girl develops a reaction formation and suppresses her feminine qualities. [41] Though the available source materials about Shaw do not parallel Freud's clinical experience, his interpretation opens the possibility of incestuous ties, especially as a reinforcement of Anna Shaw's personality. Neo-Freudian Karen Horney writes about the possibility that a woman's "masculine complex" might come from her witnessing that men enjoyed a superior type of life. [42] Clara M. Thompson, variously classified as neo-Freudian or post-Freudian, holds that a woman does not wish to be like a man "unless her life circumstances have made her feel that men are superior." [43]

Although Anna Shaw's remarks about men in her public speeches are not hostile because she felt this would hurt the cause of suffrage ("we will never win the battle by 'bullyragging' " [44]), it is very unusual to find complimentary references to men either as individuals or collectively in her vast correspondence. Her statement in a letter of 12 October 1905, praising George W. Catt, the deceased husband of Carrie Chapman Catt, represents both the exception and the rule. She writes: "Mr. Catt was a splendid man, and there are so few of them that we need every one." [45] It is common, however, to find such derisive remarks about men as "men know so much" [46] or they are "pious old frauds" or "so pompous." [47] She preferred that women receive her on her travels. "Give me one women rather than two men to meet me anytime." [48] When she was forced to deal with men, however, she said she could "take men as mass but not individually" [49] where a genuine personal relationship would prove distasteful. Surely she enjoyed criticizing individual men and defeating them. "I had larks with an editor who had been going for us. He was there and . . . I happened to look at him and just guyed him. It was fun." [50]

Shaw's critical views of marriage as well as her avoidance of intimate contacts with men suggest misanthropy as well. She lived almost entirely in a woman's world professionally and socially. Her correspondence is devoid of a single letter written to or from a man other than a member of her immediate family. "She employed women doctors when she was ill, women lawyers when she needed legal aid, and, of course, women secretaries and assistants on all occasions." [51] And she enjoyed the theater best when its comedies had been written by women. "Women need not marry"; indeed, she argued, woman's "highest crown of glory" was not motherhood, but a strong, independent type of womanhood. [52] She scorned the sturdy oak and clinging vine imagery, admonishing women: "They who observe more closely the sturdy oak about which the ivy clings, find it dead at the top." [53] Thus she advises her close friend Clara Osborne:

So you think it is better to be married and have companionship. I believe an ideal marriage is best for both men and women. But any other kind—Heaven deliver us! Just think of the men along your street beginning with old Dr. Whitney, Mr. Crawford, Mr. Wilson, Mr. Green, Mr. Robinson, and others. If a human being or a god could conceive of a worse hell than being the wife of any one of them I would like to know what it could be. In my long life of opportunities for observing, I have seen only six married people whose life would not have been perdition to me. I have seen nothing so far which does not make me say every night of my life, "I thank Thee for all good but for nothing more than I have been saved from the misery of marriage." [54]

The attitudes of several other feminist leaders toward men resemble Shaw's. They were critical of men and lacked any sustained, pleasurable sexual contacts with them. Jane Addams, Susan Anthony, Alice Blackwell, Anna Shaw, and Frances Williard were feminist leaders of first rank who did not marry. Elizabeth Blackwell's papers reveal how she as a young woman "condemned" attractions of sex "which made me uncomfortable and often very unhappy"; [55] so she decided to study medicine to place an "insuperable barrier" between herself and "those disturbing influences." The behavioral data on Charlotte P. Gilman suggests negative attitudes toward men: as a young woman she regarded herself in "infinite remoteness from physical affection for boys"; [56] her marriage to a supposedly ideal husband produced such emotional disturbance as to require separation as a means of recovering her mental health.

Apart from overt opinions and behavior which expressed directly or by implication her contempt for men, Anna Shaw like several other feminist leaders displayed a type of "mental masculinization." She adopted and preferred characteristics which, conventionally at least, are more identifiable with men than with women. She thereby made certain that most men would be deprived of the pleasure of complementary qualities in their dealings with her. Similar to Susan Anthony's quest for "perfect purity," [57] Elizabeth Stanton's desire to excel at everything boys attempted, [58] and Charlotte Gilman's and Margaret Sanger's intense period of physical culture and moral training [59] was Shaw's attempt to develop exceptional physical stamina and moral character. She extolled the virtues of power, strength, activity, and hard work, and she deprecated dependency on men, her personal appearance, "weak emotions" (indeed emotions in general), pleasure-seeking, fashionable socializing, and women who enjoyed these interests.

A woman in North Carolina fittingly complimented Shaw on a speech she delivered there: "There are just two things in which I have not been disappointed—Niagara Falls and Dr. Anna Shaw." [60] She enjoyed describing herself as having an "iron constitution" [61] or being a "tough specimen," [62] and in her campaigning for woman's suffrage she saw herself as a "hustler" and a "pioneer." [63] As her correspondence attests, she revelled in parading her remarkable feats of strength and endurance while speaking and travelling all over the country under often very difficult conditions. [64] Her strenuous efforts once caused her most respected adviser and companion, Susan B. Anthony, to criticize: "Oh, Anna, you might as well admit there are some things which you cannot do." [65] Her style on the lecture platform "took all captive," [66] her audience becoming "as soft and plastic as wax under her moulding hand." [67] Her quest for strength was unrelenting along other lines as well. She confessed failure would make her ill and wished forlornly that she "were wise enough to be right always, so that whatever does come might not be because I was wrong." [68] Shaw's work around her house consisted of puttering and fixing up things. She acknowledges fondly to her friend Henrietta Cooper that it was a man's work; "I will teach you to be a useful man about the house as I am." [69]

Anna Shaw's fondness for power and activity ruled out customary "lady-like" interests. She joked over her own appearance [70] and confessed herself "frightened" at the prospect of going to a dressmaker to select a dress without advice. [71] When she was presented with a hair brush as a Christmas present, she responds to the donor: "I won't know how to use so fine a brush. It is for a lady and alas, I shall never be a lady. I don't know how." [72] She took no interest in pleasurable social affairs and shunned "weak" romantic emotions above all. "It does seem to me," she informs Henrietta Cooper, "that when men and women get together on the sentimental side of life they can become nauciating [sic] fools."[73]

Shaw's negative attitudes toward men were offset by very positive ones on behalf of women. She demonstrated caring and protective feelings toward them in her professional role and private life. But she chose not only to give herself to women, but also to depend on them and accept their dependency on her. Her affection for them is obvious, of course, from her thousands of speeches and letters on their behalf and from the hard work and self-deprivation of her campaigns for suffrage. While evincing only a mild interest in progressive reforms outside woman's suffrage and temperance, she devoted her energies almost exclusively to woman's social and political amelioration. She confided woman's suffrage was her "all in all" and her "religion." [74]

Anna Shaw's relations with women in her private life resembled those in her suffrage work. She assumed a guiding, profoundly devoted, and protective role with a number of women, usually gentle, motherly women, from whom she sought attention and appreciation. Clara Osborne, a childhood companion, with whom Shaw remained friendly all her life was the first of these. A sickly girl who never left her home community or married, Clara Osborne received letters from Shaw addressed "My Dear Little One" and "My Dear Little Girl" and instructing her: "Now let me hear you are well soon. Good bye my darling. Do be good." [75] In one letter Shaw, then twenty-six, insists that she would leave college and help her secure the money to help her recover from an illness. Time may have diminished but did not destroy Shaw's affection. On 11 March 1917, she sent Clara Osborne a check for $100 "just for the things you want and enjoy." [76] Shaw lived in Boston and its vicinity between 1876 and 1878 with Persis Addy, a refined, well-to-do widow for whom she cared during the latter's sickness and time of death and with whom she remained tenderly joined in memory throughout her life. Fourteen years after Persis Addy's death, Shaw celebrates her friend for being "so gentle and so patient" [77] and in her diary on 8 March 1906, she writes: "This is the anniversary of Persis' death, twenty-eight years ago today. It does not seem so long. I wonder if she knows her picture is over my desk and I still wear her ring." [78] Henrietta Cooper, who had given up her own career to assist her mother's suffrage work and who was destined to kill her mother and commit suicide in 1896, was still another object of Anna Shaw's affection and source of the nurture she craved. Letters to Henrietta Cooper include such typical remarks as: "I send you a tender love thought and kiss," "I long to see your dear face," and "what more can I want except to go to California where my heart is," and also such greetings and addresses as "Dear Heart," "Sweetheart," and "My Girlie." [79] For a time Shaw looked forward to retirement with Henrietta on a ranch in California. Henrietta Cooper was apparently a self-sacrificing person who outwardly, at least, enjoyed administering to the needs of her mother and Anna Shaw. The imagery of the following, in a letter by Shaw to Cooper, tells as much about Shaw as it purportedly does about Cooper: "When you are with your mother and me I always think you act like a child playing with her dolls. You waltz us about, and wait on us and cuddle us up and mother us just as a child mothers a doll." [80]

In another letter Shaw compliments Cooper for being her very best "care taker" [81] and in still another when the relation between the two had begun to cool, apparently owing to Cooper's mother's displeasure, she expresses apprehension that Henrietta might "cease to care for me."[82]

The most intimate personal relationship of Anna Shaw's adult life was shared with

Susan Anthony's niece, Lucy E. Anthony, whom curiously she barely mentions in *Story of a Pioneer.*[83] Also a sickly girl,[84] Lucy Anthony became Shaw's private secretary and housekeeper in 1890 and kept house for her until Shaw's death. Shaw employed Lucy Anthony, then twenty-nine years old, for fifty dollars a month and the promise that she would give her half her savings if she needed the money during their work together.[85] Lucy Anthony, whom Shaw described as "my balance,"[86] was a perfect housekeeper and congenial friend. She kept track of Shaw's belongings,[87] kept her clothes clean, sewed on her buttons,[88] and advised on what clothes were appropriate—in short, as Shaw herself described, she would "look after me."[89] Most of all Shaw appreciated the quality of her companionship which was "so helpful and kind always"[90] and the fact that she kept a home for her. Her voluminous correspondence with Lucy Anthony is punctuated by frequent mention of the importance of home. When she was away on trips, remembering it was "like thinking of Paradise"[91] or "the happiest thought I have,"[92] and when there she declared it "makes me new."[93] Although Shaw spent more time travelling than living with Lucy Anthony, she maintained this characteristic balance of their relationship in her correspondence with her. She described for Lucy Anthony her prodigious feats of stamina and daring or the awful conditions of travel; these were usually accompanied by a reminder that it was difficult to do all this and by suggestions that she deserved sympathy and special attention as a reward.[94]

From Lucy Anthony, at least, Shaw obtained some of the feminine warmth and motherliness which her own home life had prevented. And Shaw appreciated Anthony extravagantly, as when she writes: "What should I have done without you this spring Heaven only knows, but then I think Heaven sent you to me...."[95] Anna Shaw once remarked in her middle age: "I would give years of my life and any celebrity which could come to know that in my later years I should have someone always with me who loved me."[96] She courted many women to fulfill her needs and of all of them Lucy Anthony came closest to restoring tolerable emotional stasis.

Shaw's commitment to feminism was so complete that it became irrational and compulsive. Indeed, she had lost her freedom to be anything but a feminist; as she herself concedes: "I hate to take a moment for anything else, to sleep, to eat or to do anything outside of work for suffrage."[97] In the words of Karen Horney:

the difference between spontaneous and compulsive [i.e., neurotic] is one between "I want" and I must in order to avoid some danger. Although the individual may consciously feel his ambition or his standards of perfection to be what he wants to attain, he is actually driven to attain it.[98]

As Shaw's friend Elizabeth Jordan describes: "It should not have been a hard task for any friend to understand Anna Howard Shaw. She was a woman with one consuming purpose in life—to win suffrage for her countrymen. It is not too much to say that never for a conscious, waking hour was this purpose out of her mind."[99] Occasionally Shaw expresses the wish that once in a while she "could take life easier and not feel keyed up all the time ... as if I were on a dead rush."[100] She began to sense late in her life that she was being driven, "a slave all my days,"[101] and yet she could not relent on her compulsive activity.

To understand the intensity of her commitment requires an analysis of the roots of her life and points up the utility of psychoanalysis for history. Most treatments of feminism, however sound technically, have been lifeless and intellectualized. Discussion and analysis of the socio-economic conditions of a period or a cataloging of the deprivations of women or their organized response to these forces, while valid and important for an understanding of feminism, do not do justice to the feminist movement. A new dimension is obtained through depth study of a model feminist, especially when it is possible, perhaps even likely, that the same influences, relatively speaking, prevailed among some other feminist leaders of the period. At the very least, this approach permits the historian to view the feminist movement in dynamic terms as a relationship between the drives of leaders and its social achievements. It also demonstrates the real role of fantasy in sustaining what for most followers of a movement are merely its "truths." But it underscores as well the important contributions of the neurotic personality to historical change and conversely illustrates how ideology and organization serve underlying needs and purposes of such personalities. In an age marked by determined leaders who espouse movements which aim at rapid social change, this type of analysis points up the need for discriminating followers, open to change yet mindful of the excesses to which leaders are easily committed.

Notes

1. As John Higham notes, American historians have hardly begun to use "depth psychology" (see Higham, Leonard Krieger, and Felix Gilbert, *History* [Englewood Cliffs, N.J., 1965], p. 229). For a perceptive, recent article on the subject which calls for judicious collaboration between ego psychology and historians, see Cushing Strout, "Ego Psychology and the Historian," *History and Theory* 8, no. 3 (1968): 281-297.

2. There are a few historians whose writings have shown psychoanalytic flavor in recent years, particularly in the form of applied social psychology: Emery J. Battis, *Saints and Sectaries: Anne Hutchinson and the Antinomian Controversy in Massachusetts* (Chapel Hill, 1962); William B. Wilcox, *Portrait of a General: Sir Harry Clinton in the War of Independence* (New York, 1964); Christopher Lasch, *The New Radicalism in America, 1889-1963* (New York, 1965); and Tilden G. Edelstein, *Strange Enthusiasm: A Life of Thomas Wentworth Higginson* (New Haven, 1968). An article which explores the utility of depth psychology on a reformer is my "David Graham Phillips and the Virility Impulse of Progressives," *New England Quarterly* 39 (Sept. 1966): 334-355.

3. "The Next Assignment," *American Historical Review* 63, no. 2 (Jan. 1958): 283-304.

4. *Young Man Luther: A Study in Psychoanalysis and History* (New York, 1962), pp. 35-36.

5. (New York, 1965).

6. Flexner (Cambridge, Mass., 1959); Sinclair (New York, 1965).

7. P. 360.

8. P. 56.

9. P. 60.

10. The Arthur and Elizabeth Schlesinger Library at Radcliffe contains the bulk of the extant manuscript materials on Shaw. While the collection is notably weak on her official correspondence, either because she did not make carbons or because her secretary, Lucy E. Anthony, destroyed this material, it is excellent on her personal life. Shaw was a prolific letter writer, her favorite correspondent being Lucy Anthony, to whom she sent several thousand letters. Anthony deposited copies of most of them

at the Schlesinger Library. Although there are unexplainable gaps in the correspondence and deletions as well, the letters are spontaneous in style and intimate in their disclosures. In addition, the Library contains other correspondence of Shaw to prominent women together with her diaries and appointment books, a large number of her pictures and newspaper clippings, and the texts of most of her speeches. The latter provide most of the material for Wilmer A. Linkugel, "The Speeches of Anna Howard Shaw," 2 vols. (Ph.D. diss. in speech, Univ. of Wisconsin, 1960). Schlesinger Library also holds Anna Shaw's unpublished, handwritten reminiscences of the first four years of her life which is more personal than the description in her helpful autobiography: *The Story of a Pioneer* (New York, 1916). Another good though small collection of 72 letters to Henrietta Cooper may be found in the John Olin Research Library, Cornell Univ. Small numbers of her letters are located at the Library of Congress in the Susan B. Anthony Collection, the Bancroft Library at Berkeley, the Kansas State Historical Soc. archives in Topeka, and the Laura Clay Collection at the Univ. of Kentucky. The merit for depth psychology of this vast collection is marred, unfortunately, by the fact that relatively few of her speeches or letters were preserved until 1888, when she was forty-one years old. Autobiographical materials and her recollections of the earlier period of her life are abundant, however. This information sometimes assumes, of course, a self-justificatory form, as it does with many feminists, but even when this is the case it is still useful for psychobiography, since it represents Shaw's perception of reality. Her writings about her childhood reveal an invariable pattern of feelings and identifications which serve, in approximation, the same function as a patient's recall to the analyst.

11. Wilmer A. Linkugel and Kim Griffin, "The Distinguished War Service of Dr. Anna Howard Shaw," *Pennsylvania History* 27 (Oct. 1961): 372-385.

12. *Story of a Pioneer*, p. 335.

13. Shaw's letters often report crowds of thousands of people in her audience. E.g., Shaw to Lucy E. Anthony (hereafter cited as Anthony), 9 May 1912 and 25 Aug. 1912, Shaw Papers, folder 18 (copy), Schlesinger Library (hereafter cited as S. L.).

14. Henrietta Cooper (hereafter cited as Cooper), 4 Sept. 1895, Sarah Cooper Papers, John Olin Library, Cornell Univ.

15. Pp. 27-31.

16. P. 28.

17. P. 43.

18. P. 178.

19. Anna Shaw described herself as a "black sheep" to her close friend Ida H. Harper (see Ida Husted Harper, Shaw Papers, folders 8, 31, S.L.)

20. Shaw Papers, folder 9.

21. Untitled in Shaw Papers, folder 27, S. L.

22. *Story of a Pioneer*, p. 8.

23. Ibid., pp. 25-26.

24. Ibid., p. 26.

25. Ibid.

26. Shaw to Anthony, 12 July 1892, Shaw Papers, folder 13, (copy), S. L.

27. *The Living of Charlotte Perkins Gilman* (New York, 1935), pp. 5-9.

28. *An Autobiography* (New York, 1936), pp. 11-32.

29. *Eighty Years and More: Reminiscences of Elizabeth Cady Stanton* (Rahway, N. J., 1897), pp. 20-33.

30. *The Story of My Life* (Conn., 1898), pp. 42, 122-126.

31. Alice Stone Blackwell, *Lucy Stone, Pioneer of Women's Rights* (Boston, 1930), p. 9.

32. 11 July 1844, Susan B. Anthony Collection, folder 11, S. L.

33. Stanton, *Eighty Years and More*, p. 217.

34. Blackwell, p. 3.

35. *Pathbreaking: An Autobiographical History of the Equal Suffrage Movement in Pacific Coast States* (Portland, Ore., 1914), p. 8.

36. P. 13.

37. "The Psychology of Commitment," in Martin Duberman, ed., *The Anti-Slavery Vanguard: New Essays on Abolitionists* (Princeton, 1965), p. 270.

38. Speech, 29 Oct. 1915, recorded in the *Lowell Courier-Citizen*, Shaw Papers, folder 45, S. L.

39. *Story of a Pioneer*, pp. 63-64.

40. In a previous period Shaw's activities would probably have been confined to local leadership in religious or charitable enterprises. Battis' book on Anne Hutchinson, *Saints and Sectaries*, is illustrative; see also Edelstein's *Strange Enthusiasm* for a skillful analysis of the interaction of personality and historical context. (see n. 2 above).

41. *New Introductory Lectures on Psychoanalysis and Other Works*, vol. 22 of *The Complete Psychological Works of Sigmund Freud* (London, 1964), pp. 112-135.

42. "The Flight from Womanhood: The Masculinity Complex in Women as Viewed by Men and Women," *International Journal of a Psycho-Analysis* 7 (1926): 338. Alfred Adler concurred when he wrote "If a girl . . . feels that the feminine position is worse or lower than the masculine, she will enter into some sort of competition with the man in her striving to show superiority" (*Problems of Neurosis* [New York, 1930] , p. 97).

43. *Interpersonal Psychoanalysis: The Selected Papers of Clara M. Thompson*, ed. Maurice R. Green (New York, 1964), p. 269.

44. Letters to Dr. Esther Phol-Lovejoy, 12 March 1914, Shaw Papers, folder 46, S. L.

45. To Mrs. Coonley Ward, Shaw Papers, folder 60, S. L.

46. Letter to Cooper, 21 Dec. 1895, Sarah Cooper Papers, Cornell Univ.

47. Letter to Anthony, 1 Feb. 1889, Shaw Papers, folder 12, S. L.

48. Letter to Anthony, 5 Feb. 1903, Shaw Papers, folder 16 (copy), S. L.

49. Letter to Anthony, 29 May 1917, Shaw Papers, folder 19 (copy), S. L.

50. Letters to Anthony, 11 Dec. 1904, Shaw Papers, folder 16 (copy), S. L., and also 16 Sept. 1890, Shaw Papers, folder 12 (copy)., S. L.

51. Elizabeth Jordan, "Anna Howard Shaw: An Intimate Study," in *Chicago Tribune*, 27 July 1919.

52. Linkugel, *Speeches*, 1: 380-381.

53. Kraditor, p. 122.

54. Letter, 19 Aug. 1902, Shaw Papers, folder 55, S. L.

55. Letter to Kitty B. Blackwell, 2 Jan. 1887, Blackwell Papers, folder 7, S. L.

56. *Living*, p. 63.

57. Ida Husted Harper, *The Life and Work of Susan B. Anthony* (Indianapolis, 1898), 1:29. Miss Shaw admired Susan Anthony's "superiority to purely human weakness' (*Story of a Pioneer*, p. 191).

58. *Eighty Years*, pp. 20-24.

59. Sanger, *Autobiography*, pp. 25-26.

60. Mary M. Petty to Shaw, 2 Jan. 1916, Shaw Papers, folder 154, S. L.

61. *Story of a Pioneer*, p. 163.

62. Letter to Anthony, 28 Nov. 1892, Shaw Papers, folder 13 (copy), S. L.

63. Letters to Anthony, 20 Jan. 1890, Shaw Papers, folder 12 (copy) and 5 Nov. 1908, folder 17 (copy), S. L.

64. Miss Shaw's statement in *Story of a Pioneer* is typical: "I rarely missed an engagement [lecturing], though again and again I risked my life to keep one" (p. 158). See also the quite typical statements in her letters to Anthony, 6 Oct. 1890, Shaw Papers, folder 13 (copy) and 24 Sept. 1891, S. L.

65. Letter to Anthony, 3 June 1895, Shaw Papers, folder 14 (copy), S. L.

66. Susan B. Anthony's Diary, 8 Dec. 1895, Library of Congress.

67. Nettie S. Thornburg, Anna Howard Shaw Memorial, Shaw Papers, folder 158, S. L.

68. Letter to Anthony, 27 March 1914, folder 18 (copy), S. L.

69. Letter, 4 Sept. 1895, Sarah Cooper Papers, Cornell Univ.

70. Letter to Cooper, 21 Aug. 1891, Sarah Cooper Papers, Cornell Univ. (see also 30 Aug. 1895).

71. Letter to Anthony, 28 June 1910, Shaw Papers, folder 17 (copy), S. L.

72. Letter to Cooper, 31 Dec. 1895, Sarah Cooper Papers, Cornell Univ.

73. Letter, 20 Jan. 1896. Shaw was a poor speller, perhaps on account of the regular spankings she received from her father for her spelling mistakes.

74. Letter to Harriet B. Laidlaw, 26 Nov. 1912, Harriet Burton Laidlaw Papers, folder 109, S. L.

75. 23 Sept. 1873, Shaw Papers, folder 55, and 26 Oct. 1875, S. L.

76. Letter, 11 March 1917.

77. Letter to Anthony, 6 March 1892, Shaw Papers, folder 13 (copy), S. L.

78. Shaw Papers, S. L.

79. 2 Oct. 1895 and 6 Oct. 1895, Sarah Cooper Papers, Cornell Univ.

80. 7 Nov. 1895.

81. 8 Nov. 1895.

82. 8 Oct. 1896.

83. Pp. 228-229.

84. Letter to Anthony, 15 April 1890, Shaw Papers, folder 12 (copy), S. L. References to her health and her "renal condition" are found in letters to Cooper, 22 Nov. 1895 and 26 Jan. 1896, Sarah Cooper Papers, Cornell.

85. Letter to Anthony, 15 April 1890, Shaw Papers, folder 12 (copy), S. L.

86. Letter to Anthony, 21 Oct. 1889.

87. Shaw's letter to Cooper, 14 Nov. 1895, Cornell Univ.

88. Shaw's letter to Anthony, 11 Feb. 1889, Shaw Papers, folder 12 (copy), S. L.

89. Letter to Anthony, Nov. 1918, folder 18 (copy).

90. Letter to Osborne, 23 April 1896, folder 55, S. L.

91. 11 Nov. 1904, Shaw Papers, folder 16 (copy), S. L.

92. 11 Nov. 1907, folder 17 (copy).

93. 11 August 1905, folder 16 (copy). Shaw was particularly fond of their home in Moylan, Pa., which she purchased in 1907 and gave to Anthony at the time of her death.

94. E.g.: "It is queer all the hard days come in a lump, but I will get through with them all right" (20 Jan. 1890, folder 12 [copy]). Again: "a few experiences such as mine of yesterday would make you and everyone else who knows nothing of my work and what it really is, realize what I have to endure. It just seems to me that I cannot bear anymore" (26 Jan. 1904, folder 16 [copy]).

95. Letter to Anthony, n.d., folder 12 (copy).

96. Mila Tuppard Maynard, n.d., Shaw Papers, folder 24, S. L.

97. Ida H. Harper, unpubl. biog. of Shaw, p. 163, Shaw Papers, folder 31, S. L.

98. *Neurosis and Human Growth: The Struggle Toward Self Realization* (New York, 1950), p. 29.

99. *Chicago Tribune*, 27 July 1919.

100. Letter to Anthony, 29 Oct. 1910, Shaw Papers, folder 17 (copy), S. L. Psychiatrist David Shapiro's lengthy chapter on obsessive-compulsive style in his book *Neurotic Styles* (New York, 1965), pp. 23-53, is especially illuminating for a study of Shaw's personality. Shaw's "dead rush" and similar statements to the same effect are indicative of a psychology in which "self-direction is distorted from its normal meaning of volitional choice and deliberate, purposeful action to a self-conscious directing of his every action, to the exercise, as if by an overseer, of a continuous willful pressure and direction on himself . . . (p. 36).

101. Letter to Anthony, 9 May 1916, folder 19, S. L.

Part V
Southerners and black men

Bourbonism in Georgia

C. Vann Woodward

The sectional conflict that led to the Civil War generated within the South a distinctive sense of identity. This stressed the virtues of agrarianism, a vigorous defense of slavery, and an open contempt for the money-grubbing capitalism of the North. The notion of a southern way of life was sustained and idealized by four years of war against the North and, perhaps even more, by the bitter resistance against the Radical Reconstruction, which southerners saw as essentially a struggle for self-determination. So it seemed logical to perceive the return to home rule, both by contemporaries and by historians, as the return to leadership by the old planter aristocracy and the resumption of the distinctively southern pattern of life (modified, of course, by the end of slavery). This conclusion was strengthened by the romanticism that infused the South and, indeed, the entire nation. Late nineteenth-century America idealized the Old South and glorified "the Lost Cause" and, in fact, seized on this nostalgia as a bridge to help bring about the reconciliation of North and South, as well as a shield behind which the black man might be shorn of his civil and political rights and shoved back down to the bottom of the southern social order.

In harsh fact, however, the New South was not the Old South restored. Not the old planter—the so-called Bourbons—took control of the Democratic party, but a new breed whose economic concerns were not essentially different from those of northern politicians. It may have been incumbent on the southern politicians to trace their lineage back to the Old South, to speak pridefully of their exploits in the late War Between the States, and to personify the courtly ways of the southern gentleman; but they were in truth men of the new industrial order, dedicated to railroad building, to the exploitation of the section's resources and, in general, to the pursuit of the almighty dollar. What was true of southern politics was true also of—indeed, mirrored—southern life in this era. There was an aggressive effort to make up for lost time and to emulate the North in the development of industries, trade and transportation. Nor was the South lacking in publicists—the most notable of whom was Henry W. Grady of the *Atlanta Constitution*— to celebrate the southern leap into industrialism. The degree of success actually fell a

C. Vann Woodward, "Bourbonism in Georgia," *North Carolina Historical Review*, XVI (January, 1939), pp. 23-35. Reprinted by permission of the publisher.

good deal short of Grady's aspirations. The South remained largely tied to its old agricultural base and to extractive industries. Much of its new economic activity held it in the kind of economic vassalage to the North that had been so bitterly resented before the Civil War. And the fruits of the new industrialism only very slowly raised the low standards of living in the South. Nevertheless, the direction after Reconstruction was clear: not backwards to the old order, but forward into industrial America.

No historian has been as instrumental in dispelling the myth of a Bourbon South than C. Vann Woodward. In a series of notable books (see below), he has traced the New South back into Reconstruction, studied closely its development in the late nineteenth-century, and showed its impact on southern politics and protest. The following essay on Georgia is one of Woodward's pioneer efforts. What it lacks in the sophistication of his later writings, the essay makes up for in the freshness of its perception and in the excitement of a young historian who has discovered his elders in fundamental error.

For further reading: C. Vann Woodward, *Reunion and Reaction* (1951);*—— The Origins of the New South: 1877-1913* (1951);* —— *The Burden of Southern History* (1960);* Paul H. Buck, *The Road to Reunion, 1865-1900* (1937);* Broadus Mitchell, *The Rise of Cotton Mills in the South* (1921); John F. Stover, *Railroads of the South, 1865-1900: A Study in Finance and Control* (1955); William I. Hair, *Bourbonism and Agrarian Protest: Louisiana Politics, 1877-1900* (1969).

As applied to that class of men who seized power in the South after Reconstruction, the term "Bourbon" has enjoyed a remarkable success as a political epithet. In this sense, in fact, it has become a part of the American language. Webster's *New International Dictionary* defines the word as, "A ruler or politician who clings obstinately to ideas adapted to an order of things gone by; sometimes applied to Democrats of the Southern United States." By implication the word suggests that these men belonged to the old ruling class, and further, that after overthrowing the Reconstruction regime, they obstinately sought to rehabilitate the ante-bellum order. Having caught the fancy of a suspicious North, and having been adopted by the South itself, this term "Bourbon" continues in use today. Only recently an eminent American historian used it. "Nevertheless," he writes, "the whole Reconstruction effort collapsed. By 1871 a number of Southern states had been 'redeemed'; their former Bourbon masters were again in the saddle."[1]

This article is limited to a consideration of "Bourbonism," or what has been called Bourbonism, in Georgia. Even within these limits, however, a little study of the period makes apparent the need for a thorough reëvaluation of the assumptions commonly made by laymen and historians alike in their thinking about Southern history after Reconstruction. Professor Arnett pointed out this need fifteen years ago in his excellent pioneer work on Populism.[2] Thus far his challenge has gone virtually unanswered. The two decades that lie between the restoration of home rule and the advent of Populism have received less attention, perhaps, than any period in Southern history. Where the Dunning school left off, no one has taken up, and it is the interpretation of that school that has largely colored the current attitude toward the period that follows Reconstruction.

In October, 1880, Joseph E. Brown applied the term "Bourbon" as an opprobrious epithet in a speech denouncing the ideas of Robert Toombs, who represented to him "the sentimentality of the South and the Bourbonism of the past." Because "the country must move forward," said Senator Brown, "we are obliged to leave him [behind] and let him cuss."[3] Hardly a more legitimate application of the word Bourbon could have been made than this. Example par excellence of the unreconstructed and unregenerate rebel, General Toombs was undoubtedly a member of the ante-bellum ruling class, the planter oligarchy, and he made no secret of his hatred of the new order. In 1870 Toombs had joined hands with Brown to overthrow the Bullock Reconstruction administration. "You know my rule," he wrote Stephens, "is to use the devil if I can do [no] better to save the country."[4] With that, Toombs' brief alliance with the new order came to a definite end. In 1872, he and Stephens made a fight to prevent Southern Democrats from joining with the Northern wing of the party in a "New Departure" to nominate Greeley for President. They were overwhelmingly defeated. Toombs' next defiance of the New Departure met with more success. In spite of powerful opposition by Brown and the corporation interests, Toombs was able to dominate the Constitutional Convention of 1877 and write into the new Constitution prohibitions against monopolistic combination of railroads, irrevocable franchises and immunities, state aid to railroads, and the purchase of railroad securities by the State.[5] "The great question is," said Toombs at the Convention, "shall Georgia govern the corporations or the corporations govern Georgia? Choose ye this day whom ye shall serve!" On the subject of railroads and corporations Toombs sounded very much like the Populists twenty years later.

Assisting the overthrow of Reconstruction and influencing the new Constitution were the last triumphs of the Bourbons of the old school. Of the ante-bellum triumvirate, Howell Cobb died in 1870; Alexander Stephens was subordinated to a minor place until he made common cause with the new rulers in the last years of his life; and Robert Toombs continued disfranchised, barred from holding federal office, and not even a citizen of the United States. These men whom Brown called "Bourbons," then, were not representative of the new order, and in the main were out of sympathy with the new rulers.

The nature of the new order in Georgia may be revealed in a number of ways: first, by a study of the new rulers themselves. During the interval between 1872 and 1890 either General John B. Gordon or Joseph E. Brown held one of Georgia's seats in the United States Senate, and after two terms as governor, General Alfred H. Colquitt occupied the other Senatorial seat. During the major part of the same period either Gordon or Colquitt occupied the governor's chair. So regularly were these offices bandied about among these three men that they came to be spoken of as the "triumvirate." It appears to have been the leaders of the Independent party, a small-farmer agrarian movement that made common cause with Toombs against the new order, who fastened upon the new rulers the epithet "Bourbon."[6] At any rate Brown, Gordon, and Colquitt were called "Bourbons" in the eighties, and "Bourbons" they have remained–"The Bourbon Triumvirate."

The facts of the early career of Joseph E. Brown, especially of his term as governor of Georgia before the war and of his service as war governor, are better known than his post-bellum career. Yet for a quarter of a century after the surrender, Brown's influence was powerfully exerted in Georgia and in the South. "The statesman, like the business man, should take a practical view of questions as they arise," wrote Governor Brown in his letter of resignation, June 29, 1865.[7] One of his admirers is responsible for the assertion that "We have never in the South had a more practical man than Governor

Brown."[8] Among the first to counsel Southern acquiescence toward Radical Reconstruction policy, Brown became a Republican himself temporarily and under the Bullock administration accepted the office of chief justice of the state supreme court. While holding that office he was closely associated with several men who were beneficiaries of the notorious bonds issued to railroad promoters by the Reconstruction administration. Some $4,450,000 worth of such bonds were later declared fraudulent and were repudiated.[9] In 1870 the Western and Atlantic Railroad Company, of which Brown was president, was awarded the lease of the state road by one of the last acts of the Reconstruction legislation just before Bullock left the State. Later investigation proved the obtaining of the lease and the formation of the company to be fraudulent, but the new legislature did not break the lease, in spite of the attempt led by Toombs.[10]

By his admirers Brown was said to be the wealthiest man in Georgia, and one of the largest railroad promoters in the South. During the next decade he was occupied with a multiplicity of industrial developments. At one and the same time he was president of the Western and Atlantic Railroad Company, the Southern Railway and Steamship Company, the Walker Coal and Iron Company, the Dade Coal Company, and the Rising Fawn Iron Works. His mineral interests alone were said to cover the greater part of three counties.[11] In his Dade County coal mines Brown employed a force of some 300 convicts for whose labor he paid about seven cents a working day to the State from which he leased them for twenty years. They were worked from ten to twelve hours a day, until those limits were removed by the legislature in 1876.[12]

At the time of Georgia's secession John B. Gordon, then a young and unknown man of twenty-nine, was in the extreme northwestern corner of the State engaged in the development of coal mines. Impetuously he dashed into the Confederate military service and in the next four years achieved fame as the most celebrated military figure in the history of his State.[13] In the South he became a folk hero, and for forty years after the war he was popularly regarded as the very incarnation of the Lost Cause. In 1872 Gordon defeated Alexander Stephens in a race for the Senate. At Washington the General served not the planter class, with which his aristocratic manner and his military fame associated him in the popular eye, but the rising capitalists and industrialists with whom he was identified both in personal fortune and in political alliance. Throughout the eighties and nineties Gordon was almost continuously engaged in a succession of promotions, schemes, and business ventures. To name only a few, there were the Southern Publishing Company, organized to print books "that will not slander our people," the Southern Insurance Company, which went bankrupt, the Georgia Pacific Railroad, of which he was president, and the International Railroad and Steamship Company, which he promised would make Florida "the great commercial center of the Western World."[14] The general was accustomed to speaking in terms of "millions" in discussing his plans. After the Florida venture collapsed he turned to still other schemes. Like Brown, Gordon employed convicts whom he leased from the State.[15]

In 1884 the publication of the Collis P. Huntington letters showed that Gordon willingly gave ear to the shady lobby of the Western railroad barons. The letters revealed that while Gordon was in the Senate he was in close contact with Huntington, introduced bills at his request, and organized senatorial tours of the West in his behalf.[16] As a comment upon the times it is interesting to note that Gordon was subsequently elected governor of Georgia, and later returned to the Senate. In 1888 he was spoken of as "the most popular man in the state, if not in the South." [17] The taste for irony was not cultivated in the Gilded Age, and Gordon's contemporaries saw nothing incongruous in electing him commander-in-chief of the United Confederate Veterans, an honor he held from 1890 to 1904.

Another military hero, though not so celebrated was General Alfred H. Colquitt. The third member of the triumvirate presents the most plausible claim to a logical application of the term "Bourbon." He was a gentleman of "family," the son of Walter T. Colquitt, the ante-bellum statesman. He was also the owner of one of the largest plantations in the State, and a prominent churchman, serving once as president of the International Sunday School Convention. [18] Governor Colquitt's connections with Brown and Gordon, however, were financial as well as political, for besides his planting interests, Colquitt was an industrial promoter. In one ambitious venture, the Georgia Pacific Syndicate, with a capital of twelve and one-half million dollars, he was associated with General Gordon, who was president of the syndicate. Like both of his colleagues Colquitt was especially cordial in welcoming Northern and Eastern financiers to the South. [19]

Certainly no one of these men "clung obstinately to ideas adapted to an order of things gone by." Nor, it seems, did the great majority of their associates, the lesser rulers of Georgia in the same period. Of the thirty-four Congressmen from the State in the seventies and eighties, three only were planters, and only one was a small farmer. Farmers were even relatively rare in the state legislature. "Before the Alliance was organized," observed the Macon *Telegraph,* a corporation paper, "it was a rare occurrence for a farmer, or a farmer's son to receive honor and recognition. The offices all went to the towns and to the lawyers. . . ." [20]

Restoration of home rule, then, did not mean restoration of the old order, or of the old rulers. Willing hands were speedily found in the South to carry forward the work of economic revolution that Reconstructors began. These willing hands were not all recruited in Georgia. The fact that some of them are associated in legend and history with the old order does not alter the case, but merely confuses the unwary. "Governor Colquitt and General Gordon," writes one historian in perfect good faith, "stood as striking types of the most cherished sentiments and practices of our ante-bellum civilization." [21] It would seem that behind this term "Bourbon" lies a confusion more fundamental than a mistaken terminology, and that a golden voice and a courtly manner have been accepted at face value for "the cherished sentiments and practices."

The year 1880 marks the consolidation of power by the new rulers in Georgia. Brown then stepped from his place as a "hidden power" behind the scenes into the open. That year Gordon suddenly resigned his seat in the Senate, only three weeks before the end of the session. He explained that a pressing, though vaguely described, railroad offer in Oregon, necessitated the resignation. [22] Colquitt immediately appointed Brown to fill the vacancy, and a few months later the legislature elected him in his own right. Colquitt became governor in 1886. In a speech supporting his candidacy in October, 1880, Brown voiced the dominant mood of the eighties. "If the people of Georgia think that a man should be sent to the Senate to represent that sentiment of the old ruling class . . ." declared Brown, "then I admit my honorable opponent [Lawton] is a fit representative." If on the other hand they agreed with him that "we live in a new era, and the New South must adopt new ideas, must wake up to new energy," he was their choice. As to the class he represented he left no doubt. I seek "to build up the manufacturing interest of the country . . . we have in future no Negroes to buy; we are making money; we shall want investments." He promised to tell Northern capitalists of "our advantage in cheap labor," and of "the profits made by our Augusta mills."[23]

The International Cotton Exposition that opened in Atlanta in October, 1881, might be regarded as the inaugural ceremony of the New South—of the industrial revolution. Senator Brown was the first president of the exposition, Governor Colquitt the second. Senator Zebulon B. Vance, in an address at the opening ceremony, extended a "soulful Southern welcome," inviting visitors "to see that we have renewed our youth at the fountains of industry." Out of the enthusiasm engendered the *Industrial Review* was founded; the very exposition buildings were converted into a cotton factory; between 1880 and 1885 the number of cotton spindles in the Southern states doubled. Between 1879 and 1894 the value of cotton factories in Georgia increased ninefold, and the value of railroad property shot up from nine millions to thirty-nine millions.[24]

Hailed widely as the cultural capital of the New South, Atlanta was appropriately selected host of the exposition. Atlantans were pleased to describe their city as "the Chicago of the South," or "the city of self-made men."[25] A. K. McClure, in 1886, described Atlanta as "the Legitimate offspring of Chicago," with "not a vestige of the old Southern way about it." "Here the most advanced leaders of the whole South have their homes," he discovered, men who were contemptuous of "effete pride," who had learned that "hardness ever of hardiness is mother," who had "revolutionized Georgia," and were overrunning the South. "There are more potent civilizers in Georgia than I have met with in any portion of the South," he declared. They were "the foremost missionaries of the new civilization in the South."[26] William D. (Pig-Iron) Kelley of Pennsylvania was equally enthusiastic, and was especially delighted with "the elegant residences of Atlanta's millionaires."[27]

Other cities and would-be cities of Georgia, and throughout the urban South, strove to keep step to the new music. Augusta, which took pride in the millions that Jay Gould invested in its factories and railroads, boasted of being "the Lowell of the South." Columbus aspired to be "the Pittsburg of the South." "Sandersville is fast assuming 'big city' proportions," it was said. "Capitalists are invited to investigate." "That booming town of Wadley. . . ." "Even Odum booms. . . ."[28] A present-day writer has caught the attitude in an inimitable phrase: " 'Yes sir-ree, it's a regular little old metropolis—New York of the South we call it, 89,000 people in the last census—and *Progress?* Gen-tle-men, *Progress? I'll say Progress!* "[29] At Vanderbilt University, then recently endowed by the Commodore, a professor rejoiced in the triumph of the new spirit and blandly prophesied that "Southern millionaires there will yet be, and not a few, who will use their wealth, righteously gotten by their own honest labor, to develop their land and bless the race."[30] Patrick Calhoun proclaimed that "The future of the South is commercial and manufactural. She will exchange the modest civilization of the country gentleman for the bustling civilization of the towns." Calhoun was the grandson of the great Carolina statesman. He was also a wealthy railroad lawyer in the employment of Jay Gould, and he was spoken of as "Wall Street's biggest representative in the South."[31] Henry Watterson most accurately expressed the spirit of his times by saying, "The South, having had its bellyfull of blood, has gotten a taste of money, and is too busy making more of it to quarrel with anybody."[32]

"For four hundred years," observes Professor Preserved Smith, "law, divinity, journalism, art, and education have cut their coats, at least to some extent, in the fashion of the court of wealth." [33] This generalization seems to apply as well to the Industrial Revolution as it did to the Reformation. Deploring the rise of commercial greed and acquisitiveness in the South, Sidney Lanier wrote in 1872: "Our religions, our politics, our social life, our charities, our literatures, nay, by Heavens! our music and our loves almost, are all meshed in unsubstantial concealments and filthy genitures by it." [34] Poets, novelists, preachers, educators, journalists, historians—professionals once in the service of an agrarian state—swung rapidly into procession behind the new leaders. Paul Hamilton Hayne, in "The Exposition Ode," written in 1881, rejoiced that he had been "Set by the steam-god's fiery passion free." [35] A novelist, through thinly disguised fiction, celebrated the exploits of Joseph E. Brown, and proclaimed him "the most representative man of our new civilization," and "perhaps the richest man in the state." [36] Historians echoed with chapters upon the "splendid demonstration of individual management, and formidable coalitions of capital and genius," "dramatic audacities of railway enterprise," "enterprise full of romantic eventfulness." [37] Fifteen religious institutions of five denominations in the South were recipients of gifts from Joseph E. Brown ranging from $500 to $53,000. His smaller charities were said to be "simply innumerable." [38]

The regimentation of opinion was not, of course, complete. But many sincere and intelligent men, who had resisted the new spirit in the past or came to denounce it in the future, were temporarily confused and swept along with the tide. Sidney Lanier, whose sentiments on the New South have already been noted, could also write enthusiastically of:

> The South whose gaze is cast
> No more upon the past.
> But whose bright eyes the skies of promise sweep,
> Whose feet in paths of progress swiftly leap;
> And whose fresh thoughts like cheerful rivers run
> Through odorous ways to meet the morning sun.

A Georgia novelist of the period begins a supposedly autobiographical story with a voluntary exile in France, after service in the Confederate Army. There he joined the French communists and shed blood on the barricades of the Paris Commune. Deported from France he returned to Atlanta, where he was met at the station by cheering admirers. "Citizens!" he proclaimed, "I have fought two months in Paris for what many in this crowd fought four years [for] in Virginia and the West." He forthwith plunged into the work of the Ku Klux Klan, and followed that exploit by joining Joseph E. Brown in the work of "civilizing" the South, as he put it. [39]

Another confused young man was Thomas E. Watson. Though he entered politics in 1880 as a bitter opponent of the new order, one discovers him writing in 1883: "In the name of the future let the dead past bury the dead. The world moves, let us move with it. Let us get out of our Egypt." Prophets are not wanting, and "Should our path be blocked by the sea, the master will divide it. Should our lips grow parched with famine the rock will give forth water, the desert manna." The South must prepare for prosperity. "It will come by the stream where the factory moves. It will come through the streets busy with hurrying feet." [40] Though temporarily deflected from his course, Tom Watson was one of the first to regain his poise, and later headed the movement of revolt against the New South.

Most pathetic was the confusion of the agricultural masses, who took up the slogans handed down from the city industrialists and repeated them with something like despair. Speaking before the State Agricultural Society in Atlanta in 1883, a man who described himself as a dirt farmer exclaimed:

We must get rich! Let the young South arise in their might and compete with them [Yankees] in everything but their religion and morals. Don't mind old fogies like myself and others of the same age who are sulking in their tents.

> *Life is real, life is earnest;*
> *In this modern fight of life,*
> *Be not like your old ancestors,*
> *But let money be your strife. . . .*

Get rich! Sell everything marketable and live on the culls. Let every yellow-legged chicken, dozen of eggs and pound of butter look in your eyes as fractions of a dollar, and act accordingly. Get rich! If you have to be mean! The world respects a rich scoundrel more than it does an honest poor man.
Poverty may do to go to heaven with. But in this modern times. . . .
Get rich! and the south will no more beg for settlers; the sails of your vessels will whiten every sea; emigrants will pour in; capitalists will invest. . . .[41]

The presiding genius of the New South, and the most eloquent spokesman of its rulers (though always with a word for the "Heroes in Gray") was Henry W. Grady. At the attractive young editor's side, though keeping always shyly in the background, was the most lovable literary figure in the South, Joel Chandler Harris, chief editorial writer of the *Constitution*. There was no resisting this partnership of major prophet of the New South and tenderest chronicler of the Old South. Southerners generally quite lost their hearts to the two of them.

Grady's services to the new order were manifold. He contributed much to its ethos by glorifying the new way of life, and surrounding it with a romantic appeal. In his newspaper and in his speeches he was wont to dwell upon the obscure stories of the self-made men, the industrialists and capitalists, telling of their rise to wealth, polishing their histories till they took on the lustre of his imagination. "They have sunk the corner-stone," he declared, "of the only aristocracy that Americans should know."[42] A more tangible service, perhaps, was the perfect flood of publicity that Grady gave to Southern resources for industrial development. His oratorical poems picturing "mountains stored with exhaustless treasures, forests, vast and primeval, and rivers that, tumbling or loitering, run wanton to the sea" were one long hymn of invocation to preëmption and exploitation. From Boston to Dallas thousands were enchanted by his vision of the New South. "I see a South the home of fifty millions of people; her cities vast hives of industry; her countrysides the treasures from which their resources are drawn; her streams vocal with whirring spindles. . . ."[43] "Every train brings manufacturers from East and West seeking to establish themselves or their sons near the raw material in this growing market," he told eager Southerners, and he added: "Let the fullness of the tide roll in."[44]

Henry Grady, it is held by some, was chiefly significant as a prophet of reconciliation—reconciliation between sections, between classes, and between races. In a certain sense that is true. In the last year of his life Grady addressed a letter to the leaders of the

Farmers' Alliance movement in Georgia marked "Strictly confidential." "Let me give you an idea," he said. "Put yourself in line with the movement to bring about peace between the agricultural and commerical interests of the state which is now threatened by the Alliance. . . . The man who does it will be master of the situation."[45] Addressing a convention of Alliancement Grady said: "There is no room for divided hearts in the south . . . without regard to class." [46] No division was possible because of the threat of "Negro Domination." The only "hope and assurance of the South," thought Grady, was "the clear and unmistakable domination of the white race. . . . What God hath separated let no man join together. . . . Let no man tinker with the work of the Almighty." [47] Finally, Grady preached reconciliation between sections—that is, between the industrial East and the New South.

Here in substance was the political philosophy of the new order in Georgia: the enthronement of business enterprise as the ideal of the good life; the reconciliation of classes; that is, reconciliation of the farmers and laborers to the continuation of the business man's regime, in the name of "White Supremasy"; reconciliation of the Negro race to the domination of the white race; reconciliation between sections; that is, an alliance—cultural, financial, and political—between industrial East and New South; and finally, a type of reconciliation about which Grady had nothing to say, reconciliation of the workers in the new factories to their lot—whatever that might be.

This philosophy is better understood in contrast with the creed of the Populists—who challenged every one of its tenets. The Populists, of course, glorified the farmer and his way of life; they preached reconciliation between sections; that is, between agrarian South and agrarian West; reconciliation between races; that is, between Negro farmer and white farmer, between Negro worker and white worker, on a basis of equal political rights for both races and support by both of the Populist platform. But the new prophet of reconciliation, Tom Watson, came not to send peace but a sword, and to set brother against brother—that is, farmer and laborer against capitalist and industrialist.

Notes

1. Hacker, Louis M., "Why Reconstruction Failed," *New Republic*, LXXXII (Oct. 27, 1937), 346.

2. Arnett, Alex M., *The Populist Movement in Georgia*, especially Chap. I.

3. Quoted in Fielder, Herbert, *The Life and Times of Joseph E. Brown,* pp. 536-537, especially p. 550.

4. Quoted in Phillips, Ulrich B., *The Life of Robert Toombs*, p. 264.

5. Small, Samuel W., *Stenographic Report of the Proceedings of the Georgia Constitutional Convention . . . 1877*, pp. 407-409 and *passim*; Phillips, *Life of Toombs*, pp. 269-272: Stovall, Pleasant A., *Life of Robert Toombs*, pp. 337-352; Avery, Issac W., *History of Georgia, 1850-1881,* pp. 528-530.

6. Felton, Rebecca L., *Memoirs of Georgia Politics, passim.*

7. Quoted in Avery, Issac W., *History of Georgia* p. 340.

8. *Ibid*., p. 339.

9. Thompson, C. Mildred. *Reconstruction in Georgia.* Chap. IV; Fielder, *Life of Brown*, pp. 465-480; Avery. *History of Georgia* pp. 495-497.

10. For differing views on the fairness of the lease see Thompson. *Reconstruction in Georgia* pp. 251-254: Pearce, Haywood, Jr., *Benjamin H. Hill*, pp. 218-230; Arnett, *Populist Movement in Georgia* pp. 26-27; Fielder *Life of Brown*, pp. 480-483; Felton, *Memoirs*, pp. 62-63, 68-78.

11. Avery, *History of Georgia*, p. 606; Fielder, *Life of Brown*, pp. 448-490.

12. "Report of the Investigating Committee on Convict Lease," Georgia Legislature, in *Georgia Laws, 1908*, pp. 1059-1091; Felton, *Memoirs*, pp. 583-596: Cable, Georgia W., "The Convict Lease System in the South," *Century Magazine*, V (1884), pp. 582-599.

13. Gordon, John B., *Reminiscences of the Civil War*, I, 40, 65.

14. Augusta *Chronicle*, July 6, 1883; Felton, *Memoirs*, pp. 484-485, 494-495, 502.

15. *Ibid.*, pp. 498-501.

16. "Report and testimony taken by U.S. Pacific Railway Commission," *Senate Executive Document No. 51, 59th Cong., I Sess.*, Vols. II, IV, V. See also, Felton, *Memoirs*, pp. 82-83, 89, 100, 115.

17. Field, H. M., *Bright Skies and Dark Shadows*, pp. 102-103.

18. Avery, *History of Georgia* p. 535; Knight, L. L., *Standard History of Georgia*, II, 880.

19. Avery, *History of Georgia*, p. 635.

20. Macon *Telegraph*, March 22, 1891; Arnett, *Populist Movement in Georgia*, p. 31.

21. Avery, *History of Georgia*, p. 604.

22. *Ibid.*, pp. 560-561: Knight, *Standard History of Georgia*, II, 898-900.

23. Fielder, *Life of Brown*, pp. 536-559.

24. Atlanta *Constitution*, October-November, 1881; Appleton's *Annual Cyclopedia*, 1881, pp. 260-271; Avery, *History of Georgia*, p. 650; Wilson, P. M., *Southern Exposure*, pp. 141-143; Howell, Clark, *History of Georgia*, II, 677.

25. Clarke, E. Y., *Atlanta Illustrated* (Atlanta, 1881), *passim*.

26. McClure, A. K., *The South: Industrial, Financial, Political*, pp. 58-76.

27. Kelley, W. D., *The Old South and the New*, pp. 13-14, 162.

28. Augusta *Chronicle*, Nov. 3, 1891: Macon *Telegraph*, Aug. 21, 1888, Apr. 3-9, 1890.

29. Wade, John D., "Old Wine in New Bottles," *Virginia Quarterly Review*, XI, 239-252.

30. Tillett, W. F., "The White Man of the New South," *Century Magazine*, XXXIII (March, 1887), 769-776.

31. Atlanta *Constitution*, May 23, 1883.

32. Quoted in Nevins, Allan, *Grover Cleveland*, p. 323.

33. Smith, Preserved, *Age of the Reformation*, p. 552.

34. Sidney Lanier to Paul Hamilton Hayne, April 17, 1872, quoted in Starke, Aubrey, *Sidney Lanier*, p. 201.

35. Atlanta *Constitution*, Oct. 6, 1881.

36. Trammell, William Dugas, *Ca Ira, passim*, especially pp. 303-304.

37. Avery, *History of Georgia*, pp. 630-637; Fielder, *Life of Brown*. There are also numbers of allied writings, among them the following: Edmonds, Richard H., *The South's Redemption;* Cowan, George B., *The Undeveloped South:* Atkinson, Edward, *The Future Situs of the Principal Iron Production of the World; South Carolina in 1884. . . . A Brilliant Showing;* McKissick, E. P., *A Story of Spartan Push, the Greatest Manufacturing Centre in the South* (pamphlet): Newton, J. C. C., *The New South and the Methodist Episcopal Church, South.*

38. Avery, *History of Georgia*, pp. 568-587.

39. Trammell, *Ca Ira*, pp. 239-240. "I think," says the protagonist, "the reasoning of the Commune itself ought to be satisfactory to everybody—except 'divine right and lilies of Bourbon' people." *Ibid.*, p. 264.

40. MS. Journal 2, pp. 317-331, Watson MSS., University of North Carolina Library, Chapel Hill, N.C.

41. Atlanta *Constitution*, Aug. 16, 1883.

42. *Ibid.*, Mar. 24, Aug. 15, 1880, and generally the articles and editorials in this paper from 1880 to 1889.

43. Harris, Joel C., *Henry W. Grady*, p. 182.

44. *Ibid.*, p. 82.

45. Henry W. Grady to William J. Northern, Mar. 4, 1889, MS. in Northern Scrapbooks, III, 164 (Atlanta).

46. Atlanta *Constitution*, Oct. 25, 1889.

47. Harris, Joel C., *Henry W. Grady*, pp. 99-101.

Populist dreams and Negro rights: East Texas as a case study

Lawrence C. Goodwyn

The Solid South developed a one-party system in the wake of Republican Reconstruction. But, if southern politics after 1877 was oriented to economic interests and came thoroughly under conservative control, as C. Vann Woodward has demonstrated, then it followed that a political opposition was possible based on the economic groups suffering at the hands of conservative rule. This was precisely the significance that Woodward found in Populism in the South, where the farmers' movement developed as much vitality as it did in the West. The emergence of class politics, in turn, opened a channel for racial reconciliation. From a strictly economic standpoint, the interest of poor whites and blacks coincided, and their common enemy was the entrenched conservatives who controlled the Democratic party. This was the plea made by Tom Watson and other leaders, and in Georgia and elsewhere (but not everywhere) white Populists joined with blacks in a common struggle and, in the process, championed black political rights. This venture, so pregnant with possibilities for a different southern future, quickly came to grief. The southern Populists went down to defeat in the mid-1890s and poor whites turned viciously on the blacks. The price paid was painfully stiff—a virulent racism became a prime ingredient of southern politics, and the deprivation of black civil and political rights, hitherto largely informal and partial, now became fully legalized and rigidly enforced.

In the following essay, Lawrence C. Goodwyn tests this line of analysis against the specific experience of an East Texas county. On the whole, Woodward's thesis comes off well, but with several noteworthy variations. The white Populists did develop a viable alliance with the blacks of Grimes County, but the latter came in more nearly as equal partners than has usually been thought, for in Grimes County the black Republican organization had survived as a political force from Reconstruction days, and had given the local black community a measure of political power even before the advent of Populism. The collapse of the coalition likewise had some distinctive features: it occurred after the general failure of southern Populism, and it resulted directly from the use of terror by

Lawrence C. Goodwyn, "Populist Dreams and Negro Rights: East Texas as a Case Study," *American Historical Review*, vol. 76 (December, 1971), pp. 1435-1456. Copyright © 1971, by Lawrence C. Goodwyn. Reprinted by permission of The Sterling Lord Agency.

Democratic conservatives. Normally cast in a more benign light, the middle-class whites seemed in Grimes County to have been wholly instrumental in the destruction of the local racial coalition, and to have employed the kinds of extralegal methods usually associated with southern rednecks.

The essay is important also for its methodology. It is a fine example of the use of local study, especially for a subject that has suffered from generalized and abstract analysis. The principal pitfall of the case-study approach is evident also: how much was distinctive to Grimes County, how much characteristic of the larger movement? The essay demonstrates, too, the value of oral history, even for an event all of whose actors are long dead. By shrewd use of oral tradition, Goodwyn is able to reconstruct a story that was never fully committed to the written record. Finally, Goodwyn displays the healthy new sensitivity presently developing against the racial bias of sources and shows concretely how that bias may be neutralized both by a conscious awareness of its existence and by weighing the white perception of events against the black perception. It may yet be possible, if this essay is a sign, to write a true history of race relations in America.

For further reading: C. Vann Woodward, *Tom Watson, Agrarian Rebel* (1938);*——, "Tom Watson and the Negro," *Journal of Southern History*, IV (1938), 14-33; Alfred D. Kirwan, *Revolt of the Rednecks* (1951);* Jack Abromovitz, "The Negro in the Agrarian Revolt," *Agricultural History*, XXIV (1950), 89-95;——, "The Negro in the Populist Movement," *Journal of Negro History*, XXXVIII (1953), 257-289; Robert Saunders, "Southern Populists and the Negro, 1893-1895," *Journal of Negro History*, LIV (1969), 240-261; William H. Chafe, "The Negro and Populism: A Kansas Case Study," *Journal of Southern History*, XXXIV (1968), 402-419.

Nearly a century later the Populist decade lingers in historical memory as an increasingly dim abstraction. The very word "Populism" no longer carries specific political meaning. It is now invoked to explain George Wallace, as it was used to explain Lyndon Johnson in the sixties, Joe McCarthy in the fifties, and Claude Pepper in the forties. Though afflicting principally the popular mind, this confusion is at least partly traceable to those historians who have insisted on concentrating on Populism as exhortation, so that Ignatius Donnelly's utopian novels or Mary Lease's pronouncements on the respective uses of corn and hell become the explanatory keys to agrarian radicalism. For scholars who mine political movements with a view to extracting cultural nuggets, the focus has been chiefly upon the word, not the deed; in the process the agrarian crusade has become increasingly obscure.[1]

Much of the difficulty centers on the subject of race. There is essential agreement that, on economic issues, Populists were men of the Left, primitive to some, prophetic to others, but leftists to all. But did their banner indicate a highly selective nativist radicalism for whites only, or did they grapple with the inherited legacies of the caste system as part of an effort to create what they considered a more rational social and economic order? The analysis of Populist rhetoric has left us with contradictory answers.

While party platforms can be useful tools in determining professed attitudes, the gap between asserted ideals and performance is sufficiently large to defeat any analysis resting on the implicit assumption that political manifestos have an intrinsic value apart from the milieu in which they existed. In America the distance between assertion and performance is especially evident in matters of race; as a result on this issue above all, the context of public assertions is central to the task of their political evaluation.[2] An inquiry into the murkiest corner of Populism, interracial politics, should begin not merely with what Populists said but what they did in the course of bidding for power at the local level. What was the stuff of daily life under Populist rule in the rural enclaves where the third party came to exercise all the authority of public office, including police authority? What can we learn not only about Populist insurgency but also about the orthodoxy the third party opposed?

Grimes County, Texas, was one of many counties scattered across the South and West where the People's party achieved a continuing political presence in the latter part of the nineteenth century. Located some sixty miles north of Houston in the heart of what the natives call the Old South part of Texas, Grimes County displayed the cotton-centered economy typical of rural East Texas in 1880. Its largest town, Navasota, contained 1,800 persons in 1890 and its second largest town, Anderson, the county seat, only 574 persons as late as 1900. Farms in Grimes County ranged from plantation size in the rich bottomland country of the Brazos River on the county's western border to small, single-family agricultural units on the poorer land of the northern part of the county.[3] The 1890 census revealed a county population of 21,312, of which 11,664 were black.[4]

Populism in Grimes County is the story of a black-white coalition that had its genesis in Reconstruction and endured for more than a generation. In time this coalition came to be symbolized by its most enduring elected public official, Garrett Scott. The Scotts had roots in Grimes County dating back before the Civil War. Their sons fought for the Confederacy and returned to face a postwar reality by no means unique in the South; possessing moderately large holdings of land but lacking necessary capital to make it productive, the Scotts did not achieve great affluence. During the hard times that continued to afflict undercapitalized Southern agriculture through the 1870s Garrett Scott became a soft-money agrarian radical.[5] His stance was significant in the political climate of Grimes County in the early 1880s. During Reconstruction Negroes in the county had achieved a remarkably stable local Republican organization, headed by a number of resourceful black leaders. When Reconstruction ended and white Democrats regained control of the state governmental machinery in Texas, Grimes County black retained local power and sent a succession of black legislators to Austin for the next decade.[6] The local effort to end this Republican rule took the usual postwar Southern form of a political movement of white solidarity under the label of the Democratic party. In supporting the Greenback party Garrett Scott not only was disassociating himself from the politics of white racial solidarity, he was undermining it.

In 1882 a mass meeting of various non-Democratic elements in Grimes County nominated a variegated slate for county offices. Among the candidates were black Republicans, "lily-white" Republicans, and Independent Greenbackers. Garrett Scott was on the ticket as the Independent Greenback candidate for sheriff.[7] Not much is known about the racial climate in Grimes County in 1882, but it must not have been wholly serene, because the "lily-white" nominee for county judge, Lock MacDaniel, withdrew from the ticket rather than publicly associate with black candidates.[8] Garrett Scott did not withdraw, and in November he was elected. Also elected, as district clerk, was a black man who became a lifelong political ally of Scott, Jim Kennard.[9] Thus began an interracial coalition that endured through the years of propagandizing in Texas by the increasingly radical Farmers Alliance and through the ensuing period of the People's party. The success of the coalition varied with the degree of white participation. After the collapse of the Greenback party in the mid-eighties visible white opposition to the Democratic party declined for several years before Grimes County farmers, organized by the Alliance, broke with the Democracy to form the nucleus of the local People's party in 1892. Scott and Kennard were the most visible symbols of the revitalized coalition, but there were others as well. Among them were Morris Carrington, a Negro school principal, and Jack Haynes, both staunch advocates of Populism in the black community, as well as J. W. H. Davis and J. H. Teague, white Populist leaders. These men led the People's party to victory in the county elections of 1896 and again in 1898.[10]

A subtle duality creeps into the narrative of events at this point. To the world outside Grimes County in the 1890s, to both Populists and Democrats, Garrett Scott was simply another Populist officeholder, distinguished for his antimonopoly views and his generally radical approach to monetary policy. To his white supporters within Grimes County he was doubtless respected for the same reasons. But to the Democrats of Grimes County the sheriff symbolized all that was un-Southern and unpatriotic about the third party. Under Populist rule, it was charged, Negro school teachers were paid too much money; furthermore, in Scott's hands the sheriff's office hired Negro deputies. The two Democratic newspapers in Navasota were fond of equating Populist rule with Negro rule and of attributing both evils to Scott. The Navasota *Daily Examiner* asserted that "the Negro has been looking too much to political agitation and legislative enactment. . . . So long as he looks to political agitation for relief, so long will he be simply the means of other men's ambition."[11] To the Navasota *Tablet* Scott was simply "the originator of all the political trouble in Grimes County for years."[12] Both these explanations oversimplify Grimes County politics. The political presence and goals of blacks were definite elements of local Populism, as was, presumably, the personal ambition of Garrett Scott. But the Populists' proposed economic remedies had gained a significant following among the county's white farmers, and this was of crucial importance in inducing white Populists to break with Democrats and ally themselves with blacks. Garrett Scott was a living embodiment of white radicalism; he did not cause it.[13] Beyond this the political cohesion of blacks was a local phenomenon that had preceded Scott's entry into Grimes County politics and had remained relatively stable since the end of the war. The ease with which Democratic partisans saw the fine hand of Garrett Scott in Negro voting was more a reflection of their own racial presumptions than an accurate description of the political dynamics at work in the county.

Through the election of 1898 Democrats in Grimes County had labored in vain to cope with the disease of Populism among the county's white farmers. Finally, in the spring of 1899, the Democrats moved in a new direction. The defeated Democratic candidate for county judge, J. G. McDonald, organized a clandestine meeting with other prominent local citizens and defeated Democratic office seekers. At this meeting a new and—for the time being—covert political institution was created: The White Man's Union. A charter was drawn providing machinery through which the Union could nominate candidates for county offices in elections in which only White Man's Union members could vote. No person could be nominated who was not a member: no person could be a member who did not subscribe to these exclusionary bylaws; in effect, to participate in the organization's activities, so adequately expressed in its formal title, one had to support, as a policy matter, black disfranchisement. [14] Throughout the summer and fall of 1899 the white Man's Union quietly organized.

Writing years later McDonald explained that care was taken to launch the organization publicly "until the public attitude could be sounded." [15] By January 1900 the covert organizing had been deemed sufficiently successful to permit the public unveiling of the White Man's Union through a long story in the *Examiner*. During the spring the *Examiner's* political reporting began to reflect a significant change of tone. In April, for example, the *Examiner's* report of a "quiet election" in nearby Bryan noted that friends of the two mayoral candidates "made a display of force and permitted no Negroes to vote. All white citizens went to the polls, quietly deposited their ballots for whom they pleased and went on about their business." [16] The *Examiner* had progressed from vague suggestions for disfranchisement to approval of its forcible imposition without cover of law.

The first public meetings of the White Man's Union, duly announced in the local press, [17] occupied the spring months of 1900 and were soon augmented by some not-quite-so-public night riding. The chronology of these events may be traced through the denials in the local Democratic press of their occurrence. In July the *Examiner* angrily defended the county's honor against charges by the Negro Baptist State Sunday School Conference that the county had become unsafe for Negroes. The Austin *Herald* reported from the state's capital that the Sunday School Board, "after mature thought and philosophical deliberation," had decided to cancel its annual meeting scheduled for Navasota. [18] The *Examiner* cited as "irresponsible slush" the charge that Negroes were being threatened and told to leave the county, but within weeks reports of just such events began cropping up in the *Examiner* itself. [19] One example of terrorism left no one in doubt, for it occurred in broad daylight on the main street of the county seat: in July Jim Kennard was shot and killed within one hundred yards of the courthouse. his assailant was alleged to be J. G. McDonald. [20]

Intimidation and murder constituted an even more decisive assault on the People's party than had the ominous bylaws of the White Man's Union. The Populist leadership recognized this clearly enough, and Scott went so far as to attempt to persuade Southern white farmers to shoulder arms in defense of the right of Negroes to vote. [21] Beyond this we know little of the measures attempted by the local Populist constabulary to contain the spreading terrorism. A well-informed member of the Scott family wrote a detailed account of these turbulent months, but the manuscript was subsequently destroyed. In the early autumn of 1900 members of the White Man's Union felt sufficiently strong to initiate visits to white farmers with a known allegiance to the People's party. Under such duress some of these farmers joined the White Man's Union. [22]

In August the Union, aided by a not inconsiderable amount of free publicity in the local press, announced "the Grandest Barbecue of the Year," at which the "workings of the White Man's Union" would be explained to all. The leadership of the People's party objected to announced plans to include the local state guard unit, the Shaw Rifles, in the program. After some discussion the Texas adjutant general, Thomas Scurry, placed at the discretion of the local commander the question of the attendance of the Shaw Rifles in a body. The commander, Captain Hammond Norwood, a leading Navasota Democrat and a member of the White Man's Union, exercised his option, and the Shaw Rifles appeared en masse at the function. Populist objections were brushed aside. [23]

Shortly after this well-attended barbecue had revealed the growing prestige of the White Man's Union as well as the inability of the People's party to cope with the changing power relationships within the county, a black exodus began. People left by train, by horse and cart, by day and by night. The *Examiner*, with obvious respect for the new political climate its own columns had helped engender, suggested elliptically that the exodus could produce complications. Some citizens, said the *Examiner*, "are beginning to feel a little nervous as the thing progresses, and lean to the idea that the action will bring on detrimental complications in the labor market."[24]

The next day, however, the paper printed a public address that it said had been "ordered published by the executive committee of the White Man's Union in order to combat the many reports that are calculated to injure the Union." After reaffirming the Union's intent to end "Negro rule" in the county, the report concluded with a message "to the Negroes":

Being the weaker race, it is our desire to protect you from the schemes of those men who are now seeking to place you before them. . . . Therefore, the White Man's Union kindly and earnestly requests you to keep hands off in the coming struggle. Do not let impudent men influence you in that pathway which certainly leads to trouble. . . . In the future, permit us to show you, and convince you by our action, that we are truly your best friends.[25]

Fourteen days later a black Populist leader, Jack Haynes, was riddled with a shotgun blast by unknown assailants. He died instantly in the fields of his cotton farm. [26]

The White Man's Union held a rally in Navasota two nights later that featured a reading of original poetry by one of the Union's candidates, L. M. Bragg. The verse concluded:

> *Twas nature's laws that drew the lines*
> *Between the Anglo-Saxon and African races,*
> *And we, the Anglo-Saxons of Grand Old Grimes,*
> *Must force the African to keep his place.*[27]

Another White Man's Union rally held in Plantersville the same week displayed other Union candidates whose conduct won the *Examiner's* editorial approval: "They are a solid looking body of men and mean business straight from the shoulder." [28] Apparently this characterization of the Plantersville speakers was not restricted to approving Democrats; Populists, too, responded to events initiated by the men who "meant business." In October, the Plantersville school superintendent reported that only five white families remained in his local district and that all the Negroes were gone. The superintendent stated that twelve white families had left that week and "the end is not in sight."[29]

Amid this wave of mounting terror the People's party attempted to go about its business, announcing its nominating conventions in the local press and moving forward with the business of naming election judges and poll watchers. But there were already signs of a fatal crack in Populist morale. The People's party nominee for county commissioner suddenly withdrew from the race. His withdrawal was announced in the *Examiner*, and no explanation was offered.[30]

Throughout the late summer and autumn of 1900 the demonstrated power of the White Man's Union had protected McDonald from prosecution in the Kennard slaying. Nothing short of a war between the Populist police authority and the White Man's Union could break that extralegal shield. An exasperated and perhaps desperate Garrett Scott angrily challenged a White Man's Union official in October to "go and get your Union force, every damn one of them, put them behind rock fences and trees and I'll fight the whole damn set of cowards." [31] That Scott had to use the first person singular to describe the visible opposition to the Union underscores the extent to which terror had triumphed over the institutions of law in Grimes County. By election eve it was clear that the Populist ticket faced certain defeat. The third party had failed to protect its constituency. White Populists as well as black were intimidated. Many would not vote; indeed, many were no longer in the county.[32]

Over 4,500 votes had been cast in Grimes in 1898. On November 6, 1900, only 1,800 persons ventured to the polls. The People's party received exactly 366 votes. The Populist vote in Plantersville fell from 256 in 1898 to 5 in 1900. In the racially mixed, lower-income precinct of south Navasota the Populist vote declined from 636 to 23. The sole exception to this pattern came in a geographically isolated, lower-income precinct in the extreme northern part of the county that contained few Negroes and thus, presumably fewer acts of terrorism.The Populist vote in this precinct actually increased from 108 to 122 and accounted for one-third of the countywide vote of 366. In north Navasota, also almost all white but not geographically isolated from the terror, the Populist vote declined from 120 to 3. [33] An additional element, nonstatistical in nature, stamped the election as unusual. The underlying philosophy of the South's dominant political institution, the Democratic party, has perhaps never been expressed more nakedly than it was in Grimes County in 1900 when "the party of white supremacy," as C. Van Woodward has called the Southern Democracy, appeared in the official ballot as the White Man's Union.[34]

On the way to its landslide victory the Union had grown more self-confident in its willingness to carry out acts of intimidation and terrorism in defiance of the local Populist police authority. Now that that authority had been deposed and a sheriff friendly to the White Man's Union had been elected, would terrorism become even more public?

On November 7, 1900, the morning after the election, a strange tableau unfolded on the streets of Anderson, the tiny county seat. [35] Horsemen began arriving in town from every section of the county, tied their horses all along the main street, and occupied the second floor of the courthouse. In a nearby house Garrett Scott's sister, Cornelia, and her husband, John Kelly, watched the buildup of Union supporters on the courthouse square, not fifty yards from the sheriff's official residence on the second floor of the county jail. They decided the situation was too dangerous to permit an adult Populist to venture forth, so the Kellys sent their nine-year-old son with a note to warn Scott not to appear on the street.

At about the same time that this mission was carried out Garrett Scott's younger brother, Emmett Scott, came into town from the family farm, rode past the growing clusters of armed men, and reined up in front of the store belonging to John Bradley, his closest friend in town. Bradley was a Populist but, as befitting a man of trade, a quiet one. His store was adjacent to the courthouse.

Cornelia Kelly's son found the sheriff at Abercombie's store across the street from the jail and delivered the warning note. As Scott read it an outbreak of gunfire sounded from the direction of Bradley's store. Scott stepped to the street and peered in the direction of the fusillade. Rifle fire from the second floor of the courthouse immediately cut him down. Upon hearing the gunfire Cornelia Kelly ran out of her house and down the long street toward the courthouse. The gunsights of scores of men tracked her progress. Seeing her brother's body in the street she turned and confronted his attackers. "Why don't you shoot me, too," she yelled, "I'm a Scott." She ran to her brother and, with the assistance of her son, dragged him across the street to the county jail. He was, she found, not dead, though he did have an ugly wound in his hip. Inside Bradley's store, however, three men were dead—Emmett Scott, Bradley, and Will McDonald, the son of a Presbyterian minister and a prominent member of the White Man's Union. McDonald had shot Scott shortly after the latter had entered the store; the two men grappled for the gun, and the fatally wounded Scott fired one shot, killing McDonald. Bradley was killed either by a shot fired from outside the store where Union forces had gathered near the courthouse or by a stray bullet during the struggle inside.[36]

The siege of Anderson continued for five days, with the wounded sheriff and his deputies—black and white—in the jail and the White Man's Union forces in the courthouse. Shots crossed the fifty yards between the two buildings intermittently over the next several days. On the evening of the fatal shooting another member of the Scott clan, Mrs. W. T. Neblett, had left Navasota for Austin to plead with the governor, Joseph D. Sayers, for troops. On Friday she returned, accompanied by the adjutant general of the State of Texas, Thomas Scurry—the same official who had earlier acquiesced in the participation of the state guard in the White Man's Union barbecue. After conferring with the contending forces Scurry pondered various methods to get the wounded Scott out of town and into a hospital; gangrene had set in. For protection, Scurry suggested that he be authorized to select a group of twenty prominent citizens of Navasota to escort the sheriff from the jail to the railroad station. Since most of the "prominent citizens" of Navasota were members of the White Man's Union, it is perhaps understandable that Scott declined this offer. The adjutant general then suggested that the Shaw Rifles be employed as an escort. This idea was respectfully declined for the same reason. Asked what he would consider a trustworthy escort, the wounded sheriff suggested a state guard unit from outside the county.[37]

On Saturday, four days after the shooting, a company of Houston light infantry of the Texas Volunteer State Guard detrained at Navasota and marched the eleven miles to Anderson. On Sunday morning Garrett Scott was placed on a mattress, the mattress put in a wagon, and the procession began. In the wagon train were most of the members of the large Scott clan—Emmett Scott's widow and children, the Kelly family, and the Nebletts, all with their household belongings piled in wagons. A file of infantrymen marched on either side as the procession formed in front of the jail, moved past hundreds of armed men at the courthouse and onto the highway to Navasota, and then boarded a special train bound for Houston.[38]

Thus did Populism leave Grimes County. From that day in 1900 until well after mid-century Negroes were not a factor in Grimes County politics. J. G. McDonald regained his judgeship and served for many years. The White Man's Union continued into the 1950s as the dominant political institution in the county. None of nominees, selected in advance of the Democratic primary, was ever defeated.[39] The census of 1910 revealed the extent of the Negro exodus. It showed that Grimes County's Negro population had declined by almost thirty per cent from the 1900 total.[40] School census figures for 1901 suggest an even greater exodus.[41]

To this day the White Man's Union, as a memory if no longer as an institution, enjoys an uncontested reputation among Grimes County whites as a civic enterprise for governmental reform. In this white oral tradition the general events of 1900 are vividly recounted. Specific events are, however remembered selectively. The exodus of Negroes from the county is not part of this oral tradition, nor is the night riding of the White Man's Union or the assassination of the Negro Populist leaders.

As for Garrett Scott, he endured a long convalescence in a San Antonio hospital, regained his health, married his nurse, and moved to a farm near Houston. He retired from politics and died in his bed. He is remembered in the oral tradition of the black community as the "best sheriff the county ever had." Kennard and Haynes were killed because they "vouched" for Scott among Negroes.[42] In this black oral tradition the Negro exodus plays a central role. It is perhaps an accurate measure of the distance between the races in Grimes County today that two such contradictory versions of famous events could exist side by side without cross-influence.

To these two oral traditions a third must be added—the Scott tradition. The Scotts were, and are, a proud family. One by one, as they died, they were brought home to be buried in the family plot in the Anderson cemetery, little more than a mile from the site of the bloody events of 1900. Tombstones of female members of the clan bear the Scott middle name, defiantly emblazoned in marble. Edith Hamilton of Richards, Grimes County, was ten years old in November 1900 and remembers vividly the day her nine-year-old brother carried her mother's message to Garret Scott. She remembers the defiance of her mother, the political commitment of her father, the acts of intimidation by the White Man's Union, the Negro exodus, and what she calls the "intelligence of Uncle Garrett." "They said that Uncle Garrett was a nigger-lover," recalls Mrs. Hamilton. "He wan't a nigger-lover, or a white-lover, he just believed in being fair to all, in justice."[43]

The Scott oral tradition—similar to the black oral tradition and at odds with the white tradition—is virtually the only legacy of the long years of interracial cooperation in Grimes County. Beyond this the substance of political life that came to an end in Grimes County in 1900 cannot be measured precisely from the available evidence. Very little survives to provide insight into the nature of the personal relationship that existed between Garrett Scott and Jim Kennard, between any of the other Populist leaders of both races, or between their respective constituencies. Scott and his third-party colleagues may have been motivated solely by personal ambition, as the White Man's Union charged; on the other hand, the impulses that made them Populists in the first place may have led them toward public coalition with blacks. It is clear that such stridently white supremacist voices as the Navasota *Tablet* were unable to project any reason other than personal ambition to explain the phenomenon of white men willingly associating themselves politically with black men. To what extent this attitude reflected Populist presumptions is another question. White Populists and black Republicans shared an animosity toward the Southern Democracy that grew in intensity during the bitter election campaigns of the 1890s. Democratic persistence in raising the cry of "Negro domination" to lure Populist-leaning voters back to the "party of the fathers" was effective enough to keep white Populists on the defensive about the race issue throughout the agrarian revolt in the South. The circumstance of a common political foe nevertheless provided Populists and Republicans with a basis for political coalition that was consummated in a bewildering variety of ways—and sometimes not consummated at all. The stability of local black organizations and their demonstrated capacity to withstand Democratic blandishments or acts of intimidation were only two of the factors governing the complex equation of post-Reconstruction interracial politics. A stable, local black political institution existed in Grimes County, and its enduring qualities obviously simplified the organizational task confronting Garrett Scott. What might be regarded as "normal" Bourbon efforts to split blacks from the Populist coalition—mild intimidation, petty bribery, campaign assertions that the Democrats were the Negroes' "best friends," or a combination of all three—failed to achieve the desired results in Grimes county in the 1890s. The precise reasons are not easily specified. The Navasota *Tablet*, seeing the world through lenses tinted with its own racial presumptions, ascribed the credit for Negro political cohesion solely to the white sheriff. In the face of all Democratic stratagems, the third party's continuing appeal to Negroes was, in the *Tablet's* view, a thing of "magic." A white supremacist view does not automatically exclude its holder from rendering correct political analyses on occasion, and it is possible that the *Tablet's* assessment of the cause of Negro political solidarity was correct; however, such an analysis does not explain how the Negro Republican organization was able to send a succession of black legislators to Austin in the 1870s and 1880s, before Garrett Scott became politically active. It seems relevant that when Grimes County Democrats decided upon an overt campaign of terrorism, the men they went after first were the leading black spokesmen of Populism in the county rather than the third party's white leadership. To this extent the actions of Democratic leaders contradicted their public analysis of the causal relationships inherent in the continuing Populist majorities.

Before they indulged in terrorism the Democrats already possessed another method of splitting the Populist coalition: regaining the loyalty of white Populists. Against the historic Democratic campaign cry of white supremacy, the People's party had as its most effective defense the economic appeal of its own platform. The persuasiveness of Populism to white farmers in Grimes County was confirmed by newspaper accounts of the public reaction to the Populist-Democratic debates that occurred during the years of the agrarian uprising. While the reports in the *Examiner* were uniformly partisan and invariably concluded that Democratic spokesmen "won" such debates hands down, the papers conceded that Populist speakers also drew enthusiastic responses from white residents. The absence of reliable racial data by precincts renders a statistical analysis of the Populist vote in Grimes County impossible; however, the fragmentary available evidence suggests that the People's party was generally able to hold a minimum of approximately thirty per cent of the county's white voters in the four elections from 1892 to 1898 while at the same time polling approximately eighty to ninety per cent of the Negro electorate. The inability of the Democratic party to "bloc vote" the county's white citizenry, coupled with the party's failure to win black voters by various means or, alternatively, to diminish the size of the Negro electorate, combined to ensure Democratic defeat at the polls. The fact merits emphasis: both the cohesion of black support for the People's party and the maintenance of substantial white support were essential to the local ascendancy of Populism.

This largely deductive analysis, however, reveals little about the internal environment within the third-party coalition during the bitter struggle for power that characterized the decade of Populist-Democratic rivalry. However scrutinized, the bare bones of voting totals do not flesh out the human relationships through which black and white men came together politically in this rural Southern county. In the absence of such crucial evidence, it seems prudent to measure the meaning of 1900 in the most conservative possible terms. Even by this standard, however, a simple recitation of those elements of Grimes County politics that are beyond disputes isolates significant and lasting ramifications.

An indigenous black political structure persisted in Grimes County for thirty-five years following the Civil War. Out of his own needs as a political insurgent against the dominant Southern Democratic party, Garret Scott decided in 1882 to identify his Greenback cause with the existing local Republican constituency. Once in office as sheriff he found, among other possible motives, that it was in his own self-interest to preserve the coalition that elected him. It is clear that the style of law enforcement in Grimes County under Scott became a persuasive ingredient in the preservation of black support for the People's party. The presence of black deputy sheriffs and Scott's reputation within the black community seem adequate confirmation of both the existence of this style and its practical effect. The salaries paid Negro school teachers constituted another element of third-party appeal. Comparisons with white salaries are not available, but whatever black teachers received, partisans of the White Man's Union publicly denounced it as "too much." It is evident that Grimes County Negroes supported the People's party for reasons that were grounded in legitimate self-interest—an incontestable basis for political conduct. The point is not so much that the county's Negroes had certain needs, but that they possessed the political means to address at least a part of those needs.

From this perspective the decisive political event of 1900 in Grimes County was not the overwhelming defeat of the local People's party but the political elimination of that part of its constituency that was black. Scott was valuable to Negroes in short-run terms because he helped to translate a minority black vote into a majority coalition that possessed the administrative authority to improve the way black people lived in Grimes County. In the long run, however, it was the presence of this black constituency—not the conduct of a single white sheriff nor even the professed principles of his political party— that provided the Negroes of the county with what protection they had from a resurgent caste system. As long as Negroes retained the right to cast ballots in proportion to their numbers they possessed bargaining power that became particularly meaningful on all occasions when whites divided their votes over economic issues. Disfranchisement destroyed the bargaining power essential to this elementary level of protection. Arrayed against these overriding imperatives for Negroes such questions as the sincerity of Garrett Scott's motives fade in importance. Whatever the sheriff's motives, both the political realities that undergirded the majority coalition and Scott's ability to respond to those realities shaped a course of government conduct under the People's party that was demonstrably of more benefit to Negroes than was the conduct of other administrations before or since. The permanent alteration of those realities through black disfranchisement ensured that no other white administration, whether radical, moderate, or opportunistic, would be able to achieve the patterns in education and law enforcement that had come to exist in the county under Populism. Stated as starkly as possible, after 1900 it was no longer in the interest of white politicians to provide minimal guarantees for people who could not help elect them.

Beyond this crucial significance for the county's black people, disfranchisement also institutionalized a fundamental change in the political environment of whites. More than a third party passed from Grimes County in 1900; in real political terms an idea died. Though a new political idea invariably materializes in democratic societies as an expression of the self-interest of a portion of the electorate, the party that adopts the idea in the course of appealing for the votes of that sector of the electorate inevitably is placed in the position of having to rationalize, defend, explain, and eventually promote the idea. If the concept has substance, this process eventually results in the insinuation of the idea into the culture itself. In this sense it is not necessary to know the precise depth of the commitment to Negro rights of the Grimes County People's party to know that the *idea* of Negro rights had a potential constituency among white people in the county as long as black people were able to project its presence through their votes. Given the endurance of this real and potential constituency, one could reasonably intuit that twentieth-century politics in Grimes County would have contained one, or a dozen, or a thousand Garrett Scotts—each more, or less, "sincere" or "ambitious" than the Populist sheriff. Disfranchisement destroyed the political base of this probability. A political party can survive electoral defeat, even continuing defeat, and remain a conveyor of ideas from one generation to the next. But it cannot survive the destruction of its constituency, for the party itself then dies, taking with it the possibility of transmitting its political concepts to those as yet unborn. It is therefore, no longer possible to speak of two white political traditions in Grimes County, for the White Man's Union succeeded in establishing a most effective philosophical suzerainty. Seventy years after disfranchisement Mrs. Hamilton can recall the racial unorthodoxy of Uncle Garrett; she cannot participate in such activity herself. "The Negro people here don't want this school integration any more than the whites do." she now says. "They're not ready for it. They don't feel comfortable in the school with white children. I've talked to my maid. I know."[44]

While Garrett Scott's memory has been preserved, the local presence of the creed of this political party died with the destruction of that party.There has been literally no political place to go for subsequent generations of Scotts and Teagues, or Kennards and Carringtons. This absence of an alternative political institution to the Democratic party, the party of white supremacy, has been a continuing and unique factor in Southern politics. [45] The circumstance is based on the race issue, but in its long-term political and social implications it actually transcends that issue.

The Populist era raises a number of questions about the interaction of the two races in the South, both within the third party and in the larger society. It is widely believed, by no means merely by laymen, that after the failure of Reconstruction meaningful experiments with the social order were finished in the South and that the aspirations of blacks were decisively thwarted. The example of Grimes County suggests, however, the existence of a period of time—a decade perhaps, or a generation—when nascent forms of indigenous interracial activity struggled for life in at least parts of the old Confederacy. Was some opportunity missed and, if so, how? How widespread through the South, and the nation, was this opportunity?

The White Man's Union was organized and led by men who considered themselves the "best people" of the South. If this attitude was typical, major adjustments must be made in our understanding of precisely how, and for what reasons, the antebellum caste system, in altered form, was reinstitutionalized in Southern society a generation after the formal ending of slavery. Was the "red-neck" the source of atrocity, or was he swept along by other stronger currents? And what of the Populist role? To what extent was agrarian racial liberalism in Texas traceable to an overall philosophy within the third-party leadership? Through what intuition of self-interest did the radical organizers of the Farmers Alliance, the parent institution of the People's party, accept the political risks of public coalition with blacks? What were their hopes and fears, and where did they falter? And, finally, what does the substance of their effort tell us about the Democrats in the South and the Republicans in the North who opposed them?

Answers to these questions rest, in part, on detailed knowledge of such events as those in Grimes County, but they require more than compilations of local histories, just as they assuredly require more than cultural assessments based on novels, speeches, and party manifestoes considered apart from their organic milieu. These answers will not provide much of a synthesis—Populism was too diverse, too congregational, and too ideologically thin—but they should tell us more about the larger society that, along with the Populists, failed to erect the foundations for a multiracial society in the nineteenth century. As the inquiry proceeds, it should be remembered that Populism perished before developing a mature philosophy—on race, on money, or on socialism. One must generalize, therefore, not only from contradictory evidence but, more important, from incomplete evidence. An analogy, doubtless unfair, could be made with the plight that would face modern historians of Marxism had that movement been abruptly truncated at the time, say, of the Brussels Conference in 1903. Who could have predicted on the evidence available to that date the Stalinist reign of terror that evolved from the mature, victorious revolutionary party of 1917? By the same token sweeping generalizations about what Populist radicalism could have become are not only romantic but historically unsound.

It should be sufficient to observe that in the long post-Reconstruction period—a period not yet ended—during which the social order has been organized hierarchically along racial lines, Populism intruded as a brief, flickering light in parts of the South. For a time some white Southerners threw off the romanticism that has historically been a cover for the region's pessimism and ventured a larger, more hopeful view about the possibilities of man in a free society. Under duress and intimidation this public hope failed of persuasion at the ballot box; under terrorism it vanished completely.

The Grimes County story dramatically illustrates this failure, but in the insight it provides into the underlying politics of black disfranchisement and the achievement of a monolithic one-party political environment in the American South it is not unique. Other Populists in East Texas and across the South—white as well as black—died during the terrorism that preceded formal disfranchisement. In Texas the extraparliamentary institutions formed by white Democrats to help create the political climate for disfranchisement bore a variety of local names: the Citizens White Primary of Marion County; the Tax-Payers Union of Brazoria County; the Jaybird Democratic Association of Fort Bend County; and the White Man's Union of Wharton, Washington, Austin, Matagorda, Grimes, and other counties."[46] The available historical material concerning each of these organizations comes largely from the founders themselves, or their descendants, reflecting an incipient or a mature oral-tradition—one oral tradition.[47] The secondary literature based on these accounts, including scholarly works used in graduate schools as well as primary and secondary textbooks, is correspondingly inadequate.[48]

A surprising amount of uninterpreted material from violently partisan white supremacist sources has found its way into scholarly literature. One example from the Grimes experience pertains directly to the scholarly characterization of Negro political meetings during the Populist era. It is worth attention as an illustration of the impact of white supremacist modes of thought on modern scholarship. The sunup-to-sundown work routine of Southern farm labor obviously precluded daytime political meetings. Accordingly, Kennard, Haynes, and Carrington campaigned among their black constituents by holding political meetings in each of the towns and hamlets of the county at night. Democratic partisans termed these rallies, "Owl Meetings" and characterized black Populist leaders as " 'fluence men." Drawing upon their own party's time-honored campaign technique with Negroes, Democrats further asserted that owl meetings were more concerned with sumptuous banquets and whisky than with politics. If partisans of white supremacy had difficulty finding reasons for white acceptance of political coalition with blacks, they were culturally incapable of ascribing reasons for Negro support of the third party to causes other than short-run benefits in terms of money and alcohol. The point is not that Democrats were always insincere in their descriptions (as white supremacists they were quite sincere), but that scholars have subsequently accepted such violently partisan accounts at face value. The darkly sinister picture of " 'fluence men" corrupting innocent blacks with whisky at surreptitious owl meetings served to justify, at least to outsiders, the use of terrorism as the ultimate campaign technique of Democratic interracial politics. This sequential recording of events has found its way into scholarly monographs that otherwise demonstrate no inherent hostility to the Populistic inclinations of Southern farmers, black or white. In *The People's Party in Texas* Roscoe Martin precedes his brief allusion to the White Man's Union with a resumé of owl meetings and " 'fluence men" that reflects in detail the bias of white supremacist sources. [49] Other scholars writing broadly about Gilded Age politics have routinely drawn upon such monographs as Martin's, and by this process " 'fluence men" have materialized as an explanation of Negro political insurgency in the nineties. [50] In the heat of local political combat, however, Democratic leaders often were able to face a wholly different set of facts in the course of persuading their followers, and the citizenry as a whole, to adjust to the necessity of terrorism. As the time approached for actual precinct campaigning in Grimes County in the autumn of 1900, the executive board of the White Man's Union published a notice of the Union's intentions, climaxed by a "fair distinct warning" to the county's Negro leadership. The statement is revealing—not only of the transformation visited upon normal campaign practices when they were viewed through the cultural presumptions of white supremacy but also of the dangers of uncritical acceptance of such perspectives by scholars relying upon monoracial sources. The notice read in part:

The Union is largely composed of the best citizens of the county. . . . They are the tax payers, representing the worth, the patriotism, the intelligence, and the virtues of the county. . . . We are not fighting any political party or individuals, but only those who band together under any name, who seek to perpetuate negro rule in Grimes County. [Good citizens] are astounded at the manner in which the children's money has been expended. Colored teachers with fat salaries and totally incompetent have been appointed for political "fluence." Our white teachers, male and female, enjoy no such fat salaries as these colored politicians or these sweet colored girls. . . . One of the most corrupting practices in the past has been the system of Owl Meetings which has been in vogue for years. . . . This is the school and hot bed where the negro politician received his inspiration, and riding from one end of the county to the other as an apostle of his race, corrupting his own people who may be in the honest pathway of duty. We give fair warning that any effort to continue these Owl Meetings—by the appointment of special deputies sheriffs to organize and carry them on—will be prevented. No threat of shotguns will deter us from the discharge of this duty. [51]

Even without recourse to other perspectives this view of the existing political situation in Grimes County contains serious internal contradictions. Black Populist leaders were "incompetent" but as "apostles of their race" they had been so effective that their efforts needed to be stopped. Black teachers were paid "fat salaries" solely for political reasons, but among those receiving such gross patronage were "sweet colored girls," who obviously were not conducting owl meetings. The assertion that black teachers were actually paid more than white teachers must be rejected out of hand. In addition to the compelling fact that such an arrangement would have constituted poor political behavior on the part of a third party strenuously endeavoring to hold a substantial portion of the white vote and the further reality that such expenditures were unnecessary since parity for blacks in itself would have represented a notable accomplishment in the eyes of Negro leaders, Democrats had access to the records of all county expenditures and no such charge was ever leveled, much less documented, at any other time during the Populist decade. Whites complained that Negro teachers received "too much," not that they received more than white teachers. In any case, it seems necessary only to observe that American political parties have routinely utilized night gatherings without having their opponents characterize them as owl meetings and that persons who benefited from incumbency were not presumed to be acting in sinister ways when they campaigned for their party's re-election. The only thing "special" about Garrett Scott's deputies was that some of them were black. Viewed as some sort of black abstraction Jim Kennard might appear convincing as a shadowy " 'fluence man," but as an intelligent and determined voice of the aspirations of Negro people he merits scholarly attention from perspectives not bounded by the horizons of those who murdered him. To an extent that is perhaps not fully appreciated, decades of monoracial scholarship in the South have left a number of Jim Kennards buried under stereotype of one kind or another. They sometimes intrude anonymously as " 'fluence men," but they simply do not appear as people in books on Southern politics.

This circumstance suggests that not only the broad topic of interracial life and tension but the entire Southern experience culminated by disfranchisement needs to be tested by a methodology that brings both black and white sources to bear on the admittedly intricate problem of interpreting a free society that was not free. At all events, evidence continues to mount that monoracial scholarship, Northern and Southern, has exhausted whatever merit it possessed as an instrument of investigating the variegated past of the American people. The obvious rejoinder—that written black sources do not exist in meaningful quantity—cannot, of course, be explained away; at the same time this condition suggests the utility of fresh attempts to devise investigatory techniques that offer the possibility of extracting usable historical material from oral sources. The example of the erroneous report in the Navasota *Examiner* of Morris Carrington's death [52] illustrates, perhaps as well as any single piece of evidence, not only the dangers inherent in relying on such "primary sources" for details of interracial tension in the post-Reconstruction South but also the value of received oral traditions in correcting contemporary accounts. Nevertheless, the problem of evaluating such source material remains; white and black versions of the details of racial conflicts are wildly contradictory. When they are measured against other contemporary evidence, however, the interpretive problem becomes considerably less formidable; indeed, the task of penetrating the substance behind partisan contemporary accounts may be lessened through recourse to available oral sources, as I have attempted to demonstrate.

Since much of the *Realpolitik* of the South, from Reconstruction through the modern civil rights movement, rests on legal institutions that, in turn, rest on extralegal methods of intimidation, the sources of political reality may be found less in public debate than in the various forms of intimidation that matured in the region. However determined a historian may be to penetrate the legal forms to reach this extralegal underside of the political culture of the South he is, in our contemporary climate, blocked off from part of his sources by his skin color. For black scholars there are limits to the availability both of courthouse records in the rural South and of responsive white oral sources. There are corresponding limits to the information scholars can gain from interviews in black communities. Here, then, is fertile ground for scholarly cooperation. Methods of achieving this cooperation need to be explored. In its fullest utilization the subject is not black history or Southern history but American history.

Notes

1. Such careful inquiries as C. Vann Woodward, *Origins of the New South* (Baton Rouge, 1951); Woodward, *Thomas Watson, Agrarian Rebel* (New York, 1938); and Walter T. K. Nugent, *The Tolerant Populists* (Chicago, 1963), demonstrate how regional and state studies can reconstruct the milieu within which men performed their public political labors. Both historians are careful to set the words of Populists, Democrats, and Republicans against their respective acts. In contrast Richard Hofstadter and Norman Pollack, though in healthy disagreement in their assessment of the quality of Populist agitation, both rest their analysis on elusive cultural and ideological categories that often seem far removed from the inner workings of the agrarian crusade. In *The Populist Response to Industrial America* (Cambridge, 1962), Pollack strains to find an authentic socialist basis for Populist criticisms of American capitalism. The attempt has the effect of diminishing the provincial generosity and innocence of Populism as well as socialist claims to ideological consistency; it also carries Pollack's inquiry toward the upper reaches of the party hierarchy in a manner frequently unrelated to the substance of third-party survival at the local level. The scholarly assault on Hofstadter's *The Age of Reform* (New York, 1955), has been both telling and recurring—the recurrence a testament to the vitality of this creative and persuasively written book. The criticism that Hofstadter selected a small number of Populist writings as a basis for sweeping generalizations about the nature of the agrarian crusade remains as true as ever.

2. For example, a central aspect of race relations in the South concerns the question of which classes in Southern society took the lead in the successive processes—black disfranchisement being one of the more essential ones—by which the antebellum caste system, in altered form, was reinstitutionalized after Reconstruction. Analysis of rhetoric that is not intimately related to these processes as they occur cannot be expected to produce evidence that bears on the crucial causal relationships involved. In this connection a recent study by William I. Hair touches directly on one of these processes—the violent suppression of black trade unionism. Hair asserts that the gentry "embraced the kind of Negrophobia elsewhere usually attributed to ignorant poor whites." When Louisiana planters crushed a Knights of Labor strike in the lower delta parishes in 1887 casualties among cane field workers "ran into the hundreds." *Bourbonism and Agrarian Protest: Louisiana Politics, 1887-1900* (Baton Rouge, 1969), 184.

3. The author wishes to acknowledge the assistance of Marcus Mallard of Navasota, chairman of the Grimes County Historical Society. Mr. Mallard provided social, economic, and genealogical information on the county and many of its prominent families.

4. Bureau of the Census, *Thirteenth Census of the United States, Abstract with Supplement for Texas* (Washington, 1913), 620; *Texas Almanac, 1910* (Dallas, 1910), 133.

5. Galveston *News*, Sept. 10, 1882; *Navasota Tablet*, Nov. 11, 1900.

6. Harrell Budd, "The Negro in Politics in Texas, 1877-1898" (master's thesis; University of Texas, 1925), 83; J. Mason Brewer, *Negro Legislators of Texas* (Dalls, 1935), 64, 74-75, 81.

7. Galveston *News*, Sept. 10, 1882.

8. *Ibid.*, Sept. 21, 1882.

9. *Ibid.*, Nov. 11, 1882.

10. Carrington and Haynes as well as Kennard had been active in the county Republican organization prior to the emergence of the third party. The information from contemporary sources on the political lives of Negro leaders in Grimes County that was used in this paper was augmented by oral interviews with their descendants. The author wishes to express his gratitude to Maurice Lyons and B. T. Bonner, both former students at the University of Texas, for their assistance in the conduct of oral interviews in the black communities of Navasota, Anderson, Plantersville, and Richards in Grimes County. Largely through the efforts of Mr. Lyons and Mr. Bonner, the author was able to locate the descendants of every known black leader of the People's party in Grimes County. With respect to the third party's white leadership, the political histories of Teague, Davis, and Scott, traced through both oral interviews and contemporary sources, stand as examples of the diverse sources of Southern Populism. Teague, like Scott, spent his entire political life in opposition to the Democratic party—but as a Republican rather than as an agrarian radical. Quietly progressive on the race issue, Teague possessed considerable administrative talents and eventually became chairman of the third party for the first congressional district of Texas. He was elected county judge in 1896 and was reelected in the local third-party sweep of 1898. Davis, a Democrat, became quite radical on economic issues, broke with his party, and became a third-party editor. He displayed an ambivalent stance on the race issue and was not prominent in the events described in this paper.

11. Navasota *Daily Examiner*, Oct. 13, 1898.

12. *Tablet*, Nov. 11, 1800.

13. The characterization of third-party rule as "Negro rule" was common in the Democratic press in counties where Populism was strong. Such accounts must be weighed against other stories, appearing in the same newspapers, that acknowledged the strong appeal of the People's party among white farmers. In this connection, see the *Examiner*, Nov. 4, 1898.

14. The bylaws of the White Man's Union were published in the *Examiner*, Jan. 6, 1900.

15. J. G. McDonald to E. L. Blair, July 10, 1928, in E. L. Blair, *Early History of Grimes County* (Austin, 1930), 197.

16. *Examiner*, Apr. 4, 1900.

17. *Ibid.*, Apr. 2, 3, June 4, 6, 11, July 17, 18, 19, 20, 30, 1900.

18. Austin *Herald* reprinted in *Examiner*, July 17, 1900.

19. *Examiner,* Sept. 4, 13, Oct. 19, Nov. 5, 1900.

20. Carrie Meacham, private interview near Plantersville, Texas, Aug. 12, 1970. Mrs. Meacham is the daughter of the slain Populist leader. W. F. McGowan, private interview in Navasota, Apr. 14, 1970.

Mr. McGowan, now ninety-four years old, was a personal friend of Jim Kennard. A. P. Wickey, private interview in Anderson, May 14, 1970. Mr. Wickey is the source of statement attributing Kennard's death to Judge McDonald. Mr. Wickey's stepfather was a prominent member of the White Man's Union; the younger Wickey, now in his eighties, was present in Anderson the day of the slaying. His account is supported by Mrs. Meacham: "Judge McDonald shot my father off his horse on the main street of Anderson."

21. The Navasota *Tablet* accused Scott of attempting to rally Populists in defense of Negro voting rights, describing his public appeals as "raving speeches." *Tablet,* Nov. 11, 1900.

22. Edith Hamilton, private interview in Richards, Texas, May 24, 1970. Though specific information about the night-riding activities of the White Man's Union can occasionally be found in the local Democratic press, that source cannot be characterized as zealous in its reporting of extraparliamentary aspects of the campaign of 1900. Accounts of intimidation of Negro Populists have been preserved in the oral tradition of Grimes County Negroes; accounts of intimidation of white Populists have been preserved in the oral tradition of the Scott family. Mrs. Hamilton, now eighty years of age, is the niece of Garrett Scott. Richards, Texas, is located in Grimes County, a few miles from the county seat of Anderson. The lost "Populist history" of Grimes County was written by Mrs. Hamilton's father. It was destroyed after his death by his wife, Cornelia Kelly, because, says Mrs. Hamilton, "my mother felt we had all suffered enough and no purpose would be served by keeping my father's manuscript."

23. *Examiner* July 30, Aug. 8, 17, 18, 24, 1900. The affair of the Shaw Rifles was described in the *Examiner*, Aug. 21, 1900. The *Examiner* had by this stage become quite committed to the cause of extraparliamentary disfranchisement. On August 24 the paper described the White Man's Union picnic in terms of triumph, asserting that five thousand people had feasted at "1500 feet of tables . . . laden with well-turned and thoroughly seasoned barbecue, pork and mutton." Replying a week later to out-of-town dispatches that Grimes County politics had become complicated by the presence of four political tickets (Democratic, Republican, Populist, and White Man's Union), the paper replied: "Grimes County is in better shape politically than most counties in Texas. There is only one ticket and one piece of a ticket in the field. Anyone who viewed the Anderson picnic parade last week would have left little room for doubt as to which side would win." *Examiner*, Aug. 31, 1900.

24. *Ibid.*, Sept. 13, 1900.

25. *Ibid.*, Sept. 14, 1900. The promptness of the reply by the White Man's Union to the *Examiner's* gentle admonition may be taken as an indication of the confidence and aggressiveness of the organization's leadership.

26. Jack Haynes, Jr., private interview, Navasota, Texas, Apr. 14, 1970. Mr. Haynes is the son of the slain Populist leader. W. F. McGowan, interview, Apr. 14, 1970. The *Examiner*, Sept. 27, 1900, carried a one-paragraph story on Haynes's murder without, however, attributing to it any political implications. Haynes was not identified as a Populist leader. The murder of another black Populist leader, Morris Carrington, was also reported in the same issue, again without specifying Carrington's role in the People's party. This report had no foundation in fact and was printed either through error or by design to frighten the county's black population. Mr. Carrington died in 1923. The value of received oral traditions in correcting primary—and partisan—sources is briefly discussed at the conclusion of this paper.

27. *Examiner*, Sept. 29, 1900.

28. *Ibid.*

29. *Ibid.*, Oct. 24, 1900.

30. *Ibid.*, Oct. 30, 1900.

31. *Tablet*, Nov. 11, 1900.

32. The *Examiner's* pre-election issue foresaw a "quiet election" despite "some unmistakable bitterness in some quarters." The paper reported that "everything points to the success of the White Man's Union ticket." *Examiner*, Nov. 5, 1900.

33. *Examiner*, Nov. 10, 1898, Nov. 9, 1900. Official Texas election returns are available in the state archives only on a countywide basis.

34. The twenty-five percent decline in the Democratic vote showed that not everyone was wholly content with the climate of violence that had developed. The *Examiner* somewhat opaquely expressed this anxiety. After noting that the Negro exodus was not confined to Grimes County, the White Man's Union and its tactics having spread to other counties, the newspaper felt constrained to add: "Yet there is a positive indication that something deep is at the bottom of the removal–some source for the frightful, unchristian and willful fabrications circulated." *Examiner*, Nov. 5, 1900. The *Examiner* can perhaps be pardoned for its failure to comment on its own role as a "source" if not of fabrications then of the advantages of the exclusionary administration of the ballot.

35. The ensuing account of the events of November 7-11 is derived from a variety of sources. Both Navasota newspapers published versions of the Anderson affair, the *Tablet*, in a lengthy story on November 11 and the *Examiner* on November 8-10. The Galveston *News* carried increasingly detailed accounts on November 8-12. In addition to those persons cited elsewhere herein, a number of Grimes County residents supplied information on a basis not for attribution. In the black community the effect of the terrorism of 1900 has not yet run its course. The adjutant general's account, which is available in the Texas State Archives, Austin, is quite brief. *Report of the Adjutant General, 1899-1900* (Austin, 1900).

36. The *Tablet* leaves open the question of how Bradley's death occurred. White oral tradition holds that Scott killed Bradley. This is disputed by the Scott family oral tradition, supplied by Mrs. Hamilton, that Bradley was Scott's "best friend." The Galveston *News* supports Mrs. Hamilton's version: "As a result of some words, McDonald emptied his revolver into Emmett Scott, killing him, hitting him every time. He grabbed Scott's pistol, and the two began scuffling when a shot rang out and Bradley fell." *News*, Nov. 8, 1900. A subsequent bulletin, also printed in that issue, revises the story: "It was first thought Bradley received an accidental shot from Scott's pistol but later reports say he was shot by someone else. It is claimed Bradley had nothing to do with the fight between Scott and McDonald." The *News* described all three victims as men "prominent in the county."

37. *Report of the Adjutant General*, 12. Both the *Tablet*, November 11, 1900, and Mrs. Hamilton agree in principle on this summation of the conversation between Garrett Scott and the adjutant general.

38. Galveston *News*, Nov. 12, 1900; *Tablet*, Nov. 11, 1900; *Report of the Adjutant General* says that eight men and six women had taken refuge in the jail (p. 12).

39. On this point all oral traditions in Grimes County correspond.

40. *Thirteenth Census*, 822. The Negro population declined from 14,327 in 1900 to 9,858 in 1910. In 1890 the black population of Grimes had been 11,664.

41. *Scholastic Population and Apportionment of Available School Fund for 1901* (Austin, 1901), 7. While school census figures are available for 1901, I have been unable to locate comparable data for 1900. Nearest available figures prior to 1901 are for 1889. The 1901 school census, though taken a year after the exodus and presumably reflecting the return of some Negroes in addition to in-migration encouraged by the labor shortage, reveals a decline in the number of Negro pupils of fifteen per cent from the 1889 total, despite the fact that census returns show an increase of almost twenty per cent in

Negro population between 1890 and 1900. This comparison suggests that the thirty per cent decline in Negro population evident from the census returns for 1900 and 1910 probably substantially minimizes the actual exodus that occurred in the late summer and fall of 1900. An exodus in the range of from forty to fifty per cent probably would be a reasonable estimate.

42. W. F. McGowan, interview, Apr. 14, 1970.

43. Edith Hamilton, interview, May 13, 1970.

44. *Ibid.*, May 24, 1970.

45. V. O. Key, *Southern Politics* (New York, 1949), is an authoritative study of the forms of Democratic orthodoxy in the various states of the old Confederacy, including the dominating orthodoxy of white supremacy; Vincent P. DeSantis, *Republicans Face the Southern Question* (Baltimore, 1959), summarizes the Republican failure to cope with the same imperatives.

46. J. A. R. Moseley, "The Citizens White Primary of Marion County," *Southwestern Historical Quarterly*, 49 (1946): 524-31; Pauline Yelderman, "The Jaybird Democratic Association of Fort Bend County" (master's thesis, University of Texas, 1938); Millie L. Kochan, "The Jaybird Woodpecker Feud: A Study in Social Conflict" (master's thesis, University of Texas, 1929); Ira Brandon, "The Tax Payers Union in Brazoria County," *Texas History Teachers Bulletin* 14 (1926): 86-92. Roscoe Martin reflects a knowledge of these extraparliamentary institutions, though the closest the author comes to exploring the topic is the following footnote: "One who is willing to undergo the hardships involved may learn many interesting things concerning the White Man's Party from those who have a first hand knowledge of the organization. Practically nothing, however, has been written on the subject." *The People's Party in Texas* (2d ed.; Austin, 1970), 236n. Other than accounts reflecting the perspective of the founders of these institutions the statement is as true in 1971 as when Martin wrote in 1933.

47. J. A. R. Moseley is the son of the founder of the Marion County Citizens White Primary. Both the Yelderman and Kochan manuscripts on the Jaybird Democratic Association rest on versions supplied by founders, as does the Brandon article on Brozoria County. The following extract from Brandon may be taken as indicative of the style of this genre: "On the night before the returns were canvassed, a comparatively small band of determined, conservative, honest, white, Christian, representative men of the county assembled . . . and the result of their deliberations was the creation of the present Tax Payers' Union of Brazoria County. . . . According to the rules, only white men can be members of this union and . . . vote in the Tax Payer's Primary.' " "Tax Payers Union," 37. Douglas G. Perry makes no inquiry into the structure of the party at the local level, in Grimes or any other Texas county, nor does he investigate the politics of black disfranchisement as it affected the People's party. "Black Populism: The Negro in the People's Party" (master's thesis, Prairie View Agricultural and Mechanical College, 1945).

48. Dewey Grantham, *The Democratic South* (Athens, Ga., 1963), is but one of the more recent manifestations of a long scholarly tradition in the South reflecting an unconscious assumption that reform politics is a function of white Southerners and that the observable victims of "Negrophobia" are Southern white progressives who are forced to employ race-baiting demogoguery in order to prevail at the polls. In this context see also Grantham's *Hoke Smith and the Politics of the New South* (Baton Rouge, 1958), 178: "The publicity given [Smith's] anti-Negro measures during the years 1905-1909 stamped him in the eyes of the nation as a Southern demagogue. It was unfortunate for his reputation as a Progressive leader that his work should have been marred in this respect." The failure of this kind of monoracial Southern scholarship rests less in its detail than in its underlying perspective on the qualifications for being "Southern" and the criteria upon which progressive "reputations" are based. Negroes lived desperately "political" lives during the period covered by Professor Grantham's books, though the substance of this politics, after disfranchisement, rarely took the form of decisions made at a ballot box.

49. Martin, *People's Party* 179-83, 236.

50. See, for example, H. Wayne Morgan, *From Hayes to McKinley* (New York, 1969), 382.

51. *Examiner*, Sept. 13, 1900. Jack Haynes was murdered two weeks after publication of this statement.

52. See note 26 above.

Booker T. Washington in biographical perspective

Louis R. Harlan

In the years following Reconstruction, the early promise of freedom for the black man was betrayed by repression, including lynching, and legally imposed inequality. What response could the black community fashion to the increasingly harsh treatment at the hands of white America? The Answer was accommodation. On this, there has been little historical dispute. In his famous Atlanta Exposition address of 1895, Booker T. Washington spelled out the ingredients of accommodation: and acceptance of segregation; the abandonment of political protest; the stressing of economic progress through self-help and practical education; the celebration of the bourgeois virtues of hard work and property accumulation; and reconciliation with the South (the Negro's "best friend"). This statement so perfectly matched the needs of the time, as perceived both by whites and blacks, that it catapulted Washington into national prominence and made him the country's preeminent black spokesman at the turn of the century. The deceptive simplicity of this analysis, which went on unquestioned for many years, has begun to crumble under recent research in Washington's papers and in the study of black protest of the late nineteenth century.

For one thing, Booker T. Washington himself turns out to be far from the one-dimensional figure that emerges from his autobiography *Up from Slavery*—which expressed the very quintessence of the qualities that Washington celebrated in the Atlanta address. If he was deferential in the circle of his white patrons, Washington was a stern taskmaster at Tuskegee and a national leader who insisted on absolute loyalty from his followers. If Washington stood for the acceptance of segregation and political quiescence, he was himself the most effective black politico of his generation and a man who moved with utmost ease in northern white society. Despite his public stance on accommodation, moreover, Washington worked in secret to defend his people's civil and political rights in the courts and legislative halls. To some degree, these facts of Washington's career are what one would normally expect of any leader of his stature; and it is a measure of white insensitivity to the black experience that Washington was so readily perceived as the benign figure portrayed in *Up from Slavery*.

Louis R. Harlan, "Booker T. Washington in Biographical Perspective," *American Historical Review*, vol. 75 (October, 1970), pp. 1581-1599. Reprinted by permission of the publisher.

But the complexity and tensions evident in Washington's career also suggest that his qualities were part of the Negro patterns of response to white oppression. In a brilliant analysis of black thought, August Meier (see below) has argued that the main strands—protest, accommodation, and separatism—should not be seen as separate and distinct, but rather as intertwined, with elements of all three incorporated in the thinking of the entire black community of this era. Meier further argued that the relative dominance of either protest or accommodation was a function of the treatment at the hands of the larger white society. This was cyclical in character, and when the cycle reached its oppressive phase, as it did in the 1890s, the black response would stress accommodation—hence the significance of Washington's Atlanta Compromise.

⟨In the following essay, Louis R. Harlan, who is writing the major biography of Washington, tests this thesis through a closer examination of Washington's life. Himself a leading discoverer of the crosscurrents in Washington's career, Harlan finds a continuity going back to Washington's early days, and emphasizes those shaping experiences rather than external conditions as the prime determinant of the way Washington functioned. Failing to find the shifts of emphasis that Meier's analysis would have indicated, Harlan suggests that the intensity of oppression may not have varied in the decades of the late nineteenth century, at least not in the perception of black men. From a methodological standpoint, Harlan's essay also is valuable as an example of the uses of biography. Where a man's life intersects a major historical development, the study of the former may well provide the key to the latter.⟩

For further reading: August Meier, *Negro Thought in America, 1880-1915: Racial Ideologies in the Age of Booker T. Washington* (1963);* Rayford W. Logan, *The Negro in American Life: The Nadir, 1887-1901* (1954)* Samuel R. Spencer, *Booker T. Washington and the Negro's Place in American Life* (1955);* Charles Wynes, *Race Relations in Georgia, 1870-1902* (1961); G. G. Johnson, "Southern Paternalism toward Negroes after Emancipation," *Journal of Southern History*, XXIII (1956), 483-509; Clarence A. Bacote, "Negro Proscriptions, Protests, and Proposed Solutions in Georgia. 1880-1908," *Journal of Southern History*, XXV (1959), 471-498; Elsie M. Lewis, "The Political Mind of the Negro, 1865-1900," *Journal of Southern History*, XXI (1955), 189-202.

In the current vogue of black history Booker T. Washington has been a figure to ignore rather than to grapple with, an anomaly, an embarrassment. This is partly because his methods were too compromising and unheroic to win him a place in the black pantheon, but it is also because he was so complex and enigmatic that historians do not know what to make of him. We have lost the thread we used to believe would guide us through his labyrinth. When his rich private collection of papers was opened to scholars two decades ago, historians had to abandon the simpler picture of Washington presented in his auto-biography. They generally seized upon the concept that Washington was a symbol of his age in race relations, a representative figure whose actions and philosophy were pragmatically adjusted to the demands of an era of sharply worsening race relations. He was the type of Negro leader that the age of Jim Crow would throw to the top. There is something to be said for this view, and certainly Washington was delicately attuned to his age.

From the biographical perspective, however, Washington seems thoroughly consistent throughout a life that spanned from the slavery era into the twentieth century. In the period of his leadership after 1895 he followed the lessons he had learned at Hampton Institute in the seventies and practiced at Tuskegee in the eighties.

In his mature years Washington's life became extremely complex. There was first of all the public image, that of a race leader who told his people to accommodate themselves to the realities of white power, and whose own personal success illustrated that such a course could be personally rewarding. In the Atlanta Address in 1895, the year the old militant leader Frederick Douglass died, Washington stated the formula: "In all things that are purely social we can be as separate as the fingers, yet one as the hand in all things essential to mutual progress." Put down your buckets where they are, make peace and common cause with your white neighbor, seek a white patron, but also improve yourself slowly through education and property, through "severe and constant struggle rather than . . . artificial forcing."[1] A few years later Washington's success story, *Up from Slavery*, a worldwide best seller, further buttressed the accommodation formula. It described, somewhat mythically, his rise from a slave cabin to the middle class, the inculcation at Hampton Institute of Puritan virtues, and their practice through a useful and successful life. It was a comforting witness that even the American race system could not keep a good man down. Tuskegee Institute, which he founded in a Negro church and a henhouse and built into one of the largest and best-endowed schools in the South, was a monument to the effectiveness of his approach.

Though Washington never made another speech of the significance of the Atlanta Address nor wrote another book equal to *Up from Slavery*, he remained throughout his life a popular platform speaker and magazine article writer. He expressed what John Kenneth Galbraith calls "the conventional wisdom" of his day in race relations and social thought. He was the apostle of things as they were. He had to employ a series of ghost writers to meet the demand for books and articles. Unfortunately, however, under his instructions the ghost writers merely paraphrased Washington's earlier utterances, thus freezing his public thought in outmoded patterns. His mind as revealed in formal public expression became a bag of clichés.

Washington's mind or psyche as the directing force of his private actions, on the other hand, was kaleidoscopic in its changing patterns and apparent lack of a central design. The source of this complexity, no doubt, was being a black man in white America, with the attendant dualism and ambivalence that black people feel. Washington's life and thought were layered into public, private, and secret and also segmented according to which subgroup of black or white he confronted. For each group he played a different role, wore a different mask. Like the proverbial cat, Washington lived nine lives, but he lived them all at once. Yet there were so few slips of the mask that it is no wonder his intimates called him "the wizard."

One of Washington's private roles was that of master of the Tuskegee plantation. From his big house, "The Oaks," Washington ran his school without delegation of authority and with infinite attention to detail. Even during his absences in the North, he continued to direct affairs closely though the confidential reports of his brother, private secretary, and other informers. He saw the sparrow's fall. Faculty members dreaded the crunch of carriage wheels that signaled his return, for each morning he toured the campus on horseback and noted every scrap of trash, every stray chicken, every dirty plate, every evidence of student waste or neglect. It all went into his little red notebook,[2] from which flowed a thousand memoranda reminding errant faculty members of their high duty to make of Tuskegee a black utopia, a proof that Negroes were capable of the petit bourgeois life.

In the radically different world of the white philanthropists Washington showed his appealing mask, deferential but dignified. At first, following the example of Hampton Institute, he made Boston his Northern headquarters and the church and Sunday-school philanthropy of New England small towns his principal philanthropic target. At the turn of the century, however, he began spending his winters and summers in New York, center of the new wealth of industry and finance. Showing that there can be a subtlety even in platitudes, Washington gradually modified his rhetoric from the style of Puritan homiletics to that of the "gospel of wealth." His principal appeal to businessmen, however, was that he seemed so much like them, not only in his attitude toward labor, property, public order, and other questions but in the earnestness, diligence, and energy with which he conducted his school. What struck Andrew Carnegie, when he gave Tuskegee a library, was Washington's ability, through the cheap labor of students, to get so much building for so little money. He was a safe, sane, self-made man who could be trusted with one's money. Moving freely in the offices, homes, and summer resorts of the wealthy, Washington constantly crossed the color line in the North, riding first-class cars and staying at first-class hotels. Though he had dinner at the White House only once, that was no measure of his dining habits among the Northern elite, who accepted him on perhaps more completely equal terms that any other black American in history.

Among Southern whites Washington was more circumspect. He made a point of not crossing the color line while in the South. He sought to reduce social friction by what Southerners called keeping his place. Washington divided white Southerners into two classes: employers who were the benefactors of Negroes and fit allies of Northern philanthropists, and poor whites, who were enemies of the black people and of a harmonious social order. Washington's strategy of partnership with the Southern white elite was notably unsuccessful in halting the tide of white racial aggression, violence, disfranchisement, discrimination, and segregation in his day. The white planters and businessmen turned out to be not as benevolent as expected and nowhere near as powerful, and the Southern political system and to some extent its economy fell into the hands of whites in whose lives of hardship and disappointment in a depressed Southern economy the Negro served as a convenient scapegoat. Washington refused to face this worsening of race relations realistically, refused to doubt the viability of his Atlanta Compromise. In 1908, after a tour of Mississippi, then in the throes of Vardaman's demagoguery, he wrote to Oswald Garrison Villard: "I was surprised to find a large number of white men and women who, close down in their hearts, I am sure are all right, but only need encouragement and help to lead them to the point where they will speak out and act more bravely." When a white mob at Lula, Mississippi, hanged two Negroes where Washington could see them as his train passed, he assured Villard that this episode was not significant "outside of the ordinary disgraceful lynchings that so frequently occur in that state."[3]

Among Southern blacks Washington presented a fatherly image. He was of the same rural Southern peasant origins and could speak to them in their own language. They responded also to the peasant conservatism of his economic program, with its emphasis on the basic needs of a rural people—small property accumulation, education of a practical sort, recognition of the dignity of toil, doing the common, everyday things of life "uncommonly without a murmur." Washington conceived of Tuskegee as "a school built around a social problem." He thought that all his compromises would be justified if his industrial school, located like a settlement house in the middle of a rural slum, could transform the lives of the black sharecroppers of Macon County, Alabama, and the surrounding Black Belt. So he not only trained teachers and skilled farmers and tradesmen to return to these communities, but he offered them schemes to improve their lives. The Jesup Wagon, an agricultural classroom on wheels, toured the back roads; an annual Negro Conference brought farmers from Alabama and neighboring states for lessons in scientific agriculture and the economics of landownership. Tuskegee managed several loan funds to aid local farmers to buy their land.[4] It is easy to see now that Washington's plan for economic progress was bound to fail because he sought to build through small business institutions in a day when big business was sweeping all before it. Worse yet, it was in agriculture, the sickest industry in America, and in the South, the nation's sickest region, and in certain obsolescent trades such as blacksmithing that Washington sought to work his economic wonders. All that was less clear in his day, however, and besides he had an emotional commitment to "keep them down on the farm," for he hated and feared the city.

Despite his Southern rural distrust of the city and particularly the Negro intellectuals and professional men of the Northern cities, Washington used the power that white approval and financing gave him to dominate also the Northern black ghetto-dwellers. As August Meier has shown so convincingly, he even bound a large segment of the "talented tenth," the professional-class elite, to him by patronage and mutual interest rather than common ideology.[5] He was the founder and president of the National Negro Business League, an organization he shrewdly used to create a nucleus of conservative blacks in all the Northern cities. He could not completely control Negro journalistic expression, but he did dominate it by a combination of ownership of some newspapers and advertising subsidies to others, and by paying a Negro syndicated columnist to follow the Tuskegee line. Black professors were kept under control by college presidents who recognized that Washington could reward or punish them when philanthropists asked his advice. His smile or frown could govern the fate of a college library, and he personally dispensed much of the Negro philanthropy of Carnegie, Schiff, and Rosenwald. His white friends patronized the black painters, singers, and writers whom he favored. His friends infiltrated the leading black church denominations and even the Negro Odd Fellows and Prince Hall Masons in his interest. In all the activity of this Tuskegee Machine was a determination to crush rash militants who were more and more openly denouncing him as a traitor to his race.

Despite his public advice to Negroes to abandon voting and officeholding as a solution of their problems, Washington became the leading Negro political broker in the era of Theodore Roosevelt and Taft. The constituency of black politicians was dissolving in those years because of disfranchisement in the South, while the Northern ghetto populations were still too small to have much political weight. The trend in Negro patronage positions, therefore, was downward, and Washington could do little to reverse its course. He simply secured places for his friends, particularly Negro businessmen in the South and well-trained lawyers in the North. He also helped Roosevelt pick white Southerners as judges, revenue collectors, and marshals who gave evidence of conservatism and a paternalistic sympathy for Negroes. Washington used his position as a Negro political boss to try to curb the lily-white Republican movement in the South, to moderate the Republican platforms and presidential utterances on racial matters, and to dampen Negro protest against the wholesale dismissal of Negro troops accused of rioting in Brownsville, Texas, in 1906. Although Washington supported Taft in 1908, he was subsequently dismayed by the president's rapid removal of nearly all Southern Negro officeholders. The Wilson administration continued this trend and increased segregation in the federal civil service. By the end of his life Boss Washington's political machine was in a state of nearly complete breakdown.

Finally, Washington had an elaborate secret life. In his civil rights activity he presented himself publicly as a social pacifist and accommodationist, while secretly he financed and generaled a series of court suits challenging the grandfather clause, denial of jury service to Negroes, Jim Crow cars, and peonage. Working sometimes with the Negro lawyers of the Afro-American Council, sometimes through his own personal lawyer Wilford H. Smith, and sometimes with sympathetic Southern white lawyers, Washington took every precaution to keep his collaboration a secret. He used his private secretary and a Tuskegee faculty member as go-betweens, and in the Alabama suffrage cases that were carried to the United States Supreme Court he had his secretary and the lawyer corresponding using the code names R. C. Black and J. C. May.[6]

It cannot be said that Washington's secret militancy had much effect against the downtrend of race relations. Another secret activity, however, that of espionage against his Negro enemies, sometimes had devastating effect. When the Boston black radical William Monroe Trotter began openly to denounce Washington and created a disturbance known as the Boston Riot, Washington employed a spy named Melvin J. Chisum to infiltrate Trotter's New England Suffrage League. Chisum acted as a provocateur and informed Washington of secret meetings so that Washington could counter their strategy. Washington also planted a Boston lawyer, Clifford Plummer, in the Trotter organization and arranged with a Yale student to sue Trotter's paper for libel. When W. E. B. Du Bois and some thirty of his friends met at Niagara Falls in 1905 to found the Niagara Movement, Washington paid Plummer to go there and spy on the meeting and to stop the Associated Press from giving it publicity. The following year Washington used a distinguished old Negro, who hoped Washington would help him regain his political appointment, to infiltrate the Niagara Movement at Harper's Ferry. Washington had many other agents, including Pinkerton detectives and paid and unpaid Negro informers. Melvin Chisum worked for years as Booker Washington's spy in New York and Washington, infiltrating the Niagara Movement and the NAACP, holding meetings with Washington on park benches to disclose his findings, and obviously enjoying his work. "I am your obedient humble servants, Chisum," he roguishly ended one letter, "your own property, to use as your Eminence desires, absolutely."[7]

In each of these compartmentalized worlds Washington displayed a different personality, wore a different mask, played a different role. At Tuskegee he was a benevolent despot. To Northern whites he appeard a racial statesman; to Southern whites he was a safe, sane Negro who advised blacks to "stay in their place." To Southern Negroes he was a father, to Northern blacks a stepfather; to politicians he was another political boss. In his paradoxical secret life he attacked the racial settlement that he publicly accepted, and he used ruthless methods of espionage and sabotage that contrasted sharply with his public Sunday-school morality.

Perhaps psychoanalysis or role psychology would solve Washington's behavioral riddle, if we could only put him on the couch. If we could remove those layers of secrecy as one peels an onion, perhaps at the center of Booker T. Washington's being would be revealed a person single-mindedly concerned with power, a minotaur, a lion, fox, or Br'er Rabbit, some frightened little man like the Wizard of Oz, or, as in the case of the onion, nothing, a personality disintegrated by the frenzied activity of being all things to all men in a multifaceted society. He "jumped Jim Crow" so often that he lost sight of the original purposes of his motion.

It is possible to explain many of the seeming contradictions in Washington's mature life by examining his biography. A biographical approach may counter-balance a slight distortion introduced by the historical approach. Historians have tended to see Washington's accommodationist behavior as of its time, that is, of the period of his leadership after 1895, and as a deliberate, realistic, pragmatic response to the black man's "time of troubles." While C. Vann Woodward, for example, recognizes that Washington "dealt with the present in terms of the past," he says that "it is indeed hard to see how he could have preached or his people practiced a radically different philosophy in his time and place."[8] The biographical evidence, on the other hand, shows that all the hallmarks of Washington's style of leadership—his conservative petit bourgeois social philosophy, his accommodation to white supremacy and segregation, and his employment of secret weapons against his adversaries—were well developed prior to the 1890's. They were a response to precepts and pressures of the 1870's and 1880's. These decades turn out on close examination to have been not as different from the period after 1890 as some historians have assumed. Perhaps we have too sharply periodized the history of American race relations and have exaggerated the differences between one decade and another. This is not to say that the Progressive era was not characterized by racial violence, disfranchisement, and segregation, but so were the seventies, the age of the Ku Klux Klan and the abandonment of Reconstruction, and the eighties, the era of reversal of civil rights legislation.

Knowledge of Washington's early life is based primarily on his two autobiographies. *Up from Slavery* is more detailed and better written but distorted by its success-story formula. *The Story of My Life and Work*, written a year earlier primarily for the Negro subscription book market, reveals facets of his career ignored in *Up from Slavery*. These works are supplemented, however, by other contemporary evidence and the reminiscences of a number of close associates of Washington's youth.

Washington was born on a small Virginia farm, the child of a slave cook and a white man of the neighborhood. His birth occurred prior to his mother's marriage to Washington Ferguson, the slave of a neighboring farmer, and prior to the birth of the darker half-sister Amanda. It was a common pattern of slavery that house servants, because of higher status, lighter work load, closeness to the master class, and, sometimes, lighter color often identified themselves in attitude as well as mutual interest with the master and his family. They learned by daily study to interpret and respond to the whims and desires of the white owners. Because he had the softer life and better food of a house servant's child, because he was only five when his master died and only nine when he was freed, because he lived on a small farm instead of a large plantation, Washington never experienced slavery in its harshest forms. He later recalled his horror at seeing a grown man whipped for a minor infraction, but he also recalled "Christmas Days in Old Virginia" with a curious sentimentality, telling how grown slaves hung their stockings on Christmas Eve on the mantel of the master's or mistress' bedroom, and came in next morning shouting "Christmas gift," singing, and bearing the Yule log.[9] One day in 1909, while speaking to the Republican Club at the Waldorf-Astoria, Washington saw in the audience the grandson of his former owner and recalled:

He and I played together as children, fought and wept, laughed and sobbed together. He was the white boy, I was the black boy, on that old plantation.

He liked me then and he likes me yet. I liked him then and I like him now. But until this week I have not met Abe Burroughs since one day away back in 1863 it came to my frightened ears that old "Massa" Burroughs, his grandfather and my owner, had been killed.

There was a skirmish and the Federal troops, I was told, had shot him. I was frightened. I rushed home and told Abe and he and I cried together. Our hearts were broken. That is a long while ago.[10]

Washington probably exaggerated the hardness of his early life for purposes of contrast in conformity with a literary convention of the success-story genre. He recalled in *Up from Slavery* the hard physical work of the salt furnace and coal mine, and he rejected both the work and the exploitative black stepfather who forced him into it, probably within a few months of his arrival in the little West Virginia town of Malden. He moved out of the home occupied by his mother, stepfather, half-brother, and half-sister. He moved into the mansion of General Lewis Ruffner, the leading citizen of the village and perhaps its richest man. "Booker Washington came to me about 1865 as servant," the general's wife Viola later recalled, "and as there was little for him to do, he had much spare time which I proposed he should use by learning to read, which he readily accepted." If Mrs. Ruffner was a godsend to Booker Washington, so was he to her. A Yankee schoolteacher who had married the widowed general after teaching his younger children, Mrs. Ruffner was ostracized by the general's family because of her alien background and sharp tongue, and she threw all the frustrated energies of a New England do-gooder into the training of Booker Washington. She as well as he later recalled his strenuous efforts to meet her exacting demands. "I would help and direct, and he was more than willing to follow direction," she remembered. "There was nothing peculiar in his habits, except that he was always in his place and never known to do anything out of the way, which I think has been his course all thru life. His conduct has always been without fault, and what more can we wish?" And yet there was something more. "He was ever restless, uneasy, as if knowing that contentment would mean inaction. 'Am I getting on?'–that was his principal question."[11] A neighbor similarly recalled: "The reported hard times that he underwent never really occurred. He lived a thoroughly easy life with General Ruffner."[12]

The general himself was a prototype of those Southerners "of the better class" whom Washington later sought as allies. Of a distinguished Virginia family that owned the Luray Caverns and pioneered in the salt industry of West Virginia, General Ruffner has owned slaves and worked them in his mines and furnaces but believed slavery retarded Southern economic growth and therefore opposed it. He supported the Union and the new state of West Virginia and became a militia general and Republican leader. One day the young houseboy Booker witnessed a riot that dramatized the struggles of race and class with which he would have to live for the rest of his life. A group of whites, largely of the working class, began meeting in the hills at night and called themselves Gideon's Band or the Ku Klux Klan. One day General Ruffner heard the shots of a melee between the Klansmen and the black workers of Malden. The Klansmen were trying to prevent the blacks from testifying about the Klan's activities. Running past the blacks, the general shouted, "Put down that revolver you scoundrel," and was obeyed. When he moved on to reason with the whites, however, a brick one of them had hurled hit him on the back of the head. Relatives dragged the general away unconscious as the battle resumed, and the old man never completely recovered. "It seemed to me as I watched this struggle between members of the two races that there was no hope for our people in this country," Washington later recalled. [13] That there were dangers in transgressing white racial codes was certainly one of the lessons of this incident, but another was that the white paternalist was the black man's only friend, albeit never a perfect one and in this case an ineffectual one.

Not many black boys had an early life as full of generals as Booker T. Washington. He found his beau ideal in General Samuel Chapman Armstrong, the principal of Hampton Institute in Virginia, the Christian soldier, the great white father for whom Washington had long been searching. He began to model his own conduct and thought on Armstrong's. Washington described him as "the most perfect specimen of man, physically, mentally and spiritually" that he had ever seen, and he considered the best part of his education to have been the privilege of being permitted to look upon General Armstrong each day. [14] The general was the child of missionaries in Hawaii, a graduate of the Williams College of Mark Hopkins, and a commander of black troops in the Civil War. One of the war's youngest generals, Armstrong had a quick, nervous, but unhesitating manner, what might appropriately be called a commanding presence; he was the very model of a modern major general. Washington had the opportunity of observing the general closely, for throughout the black youth's three years at Hampton he was janitor in the academic building. Close to the general and the white teachers, picking up all they had to teach, he impressed them as ingratiating, ambitious, and quick to learn.

It was from Hampton and General Armstrong that Washington borrowed what became known in his day as "the Tuskegee idea." Armstrong seems sincerely to have believed that the Polynesians among whom he had grown up and the Negroes and Indians at Hampton were lower on the evolutionary scale than the white race, not so much inferior as "backward." [15] They were children who must crawl before they could walk, must be trained before they could be educated. Their moral training was much more important than their intellectual instruction, for it was only after the backward people, as individuals and races, put away childish things, stilled their dark laughter, and learned self-discipline through the imposition of the morning inspection and close-order drill that they would be ready for higher things. Armstrong would not discourage a bright young man from higher education, but he believed that the black race should abstain from politics and civil rights agitation until industrial education should have done its work. Industrial education as Armstrong conceived it was not so much technical as moral, a training in industriousness, abstinence, thrift, in short, the Protestant ethic, the virtues that helped a man get ahead, mankind progress, and the world turn. The bluff General Armstrong was unaware of the cultural and racial arrogance of his faith and program. He was benevolent and earnest, toiling all his life amid the alien corn, a missionary to the benighted blacks. He slept well because his soul was daily cleansed by good works. [16] The contradictions and inner tensions came when one of his black pupils, Booker T. Washington, eager to please and eager to learn all that it took to be a General Armstrong, incorporated not only the

method but the rationale and values of this benevolent white racist, and then went forth
to preach the gospel of industrial education.

It would be difficult to find in Booker T. Washington's own writings a better statement of his philosophy than the following advice of General Armstrong to Southern
black people:

*Be thrifty and industrious. Command the respect of your neighbors by a good record and
a good character. Own your own houses. Educate your children. Make the best of your
difficulties. Live down prejudice. Cultivate peaceful relations with all. As a voter act as
you think and not as you are told. Remember that you have seen marvellous changes in
sixteen years. In view of that be patient—thank God and take courage.*[17]

General Armstrong's conservative influence on Washington extended far beyond these
conventional homilies, however. When the Civil Rights Act of 1875 was passed, for
example, the school's magazine, the *Southern Workman*, repeatedly warned blacks "to
raise no needless and ill-considered issue under the present law," to use integrated facilities
only when none were provided for black people separately.[18] Armstrong openly endorsed the Compromise of 1877 by which Reconstruction was ended, accommodated his
school to the new Southern conservative regime, and urged Negroes to do the same.[19]
Washington along with the other readers of the *Southern Workman* were told not only
that the requisites of a gentleman's dress were "cleanliness, quiet colors, and well brushed
boots," they were also told that labor unions were conspiracies to defy the laws of
economics and get something for nothing.[20] As for federal aid to education in the Blair
Bill, Armstrong thought its "fatal error" was that "it is opposed to the doctrine of
self-help."[21]

In the graduation exercises of 1875, Washington took the negative in a debate on the
annexation of Cuba. It may have been merely accidental that Washington had the conservative role in the debate, but his skill at presenting that side and the warm response from
his audience prefigured his later career. His arguments were so terse and vigorous that he
carried with him the whole audience, white and black. He argued that Spain had a right to
Cuba by discovery and colonization, that the United States should wait until the Cubans
were more capable of self-government, that annexation would flood the country with
ignorance and crime, that it would increase the power of the Roman Catholic Church,
"already so degrading to the great masses of white voters." This sentiment was roundly
applauded. "As to helping their ignorance, we have enough of that article already," he
said. "Wouldn't it be wise, before we risk a war for Cuba, to redeem ourselves from the
meshes of the last war?"[22]

To what extent did Booker T. Washington, Armstrong's aptest pupil, Hampton's most
distinguished son, internalize the teachings, values, and example of his master, his teacher? "I require all to keep their clothes neat and clean, and their hair combed every
morning, and the boys to keep their boots cleaned," he reported back to Hampton from
his first teaching position. "To see that this is done I have a morning inspection, as we did
at Hampton." He also began military drill for the boys, marching them up and down the
surrounding hills to his shrill "hip! hip! hip!"[23]

"Can we not improve?" Washington asked in a letter to a newspaper in 1877, "I mean
the colored people, for I am a colored man myself, or rather a boy." (He was then
twenty-one.) He found some things to praise in their first decade of freedom, but the

time was coming when bondage could no longer be an excuse for ignorance. Parents should prepare their children by education for the duties of citizenship, but above all Negroes should improve their use of leisure time. "I think there are many who, if they would count up the time spent by them in vain and idle street talk, would find it to amount to hours and days enough in which they might have obtained for themselves a valuable and respectable education," he said.[24]

When Washington was invited back to Hampton to give the postgraduate commencement address in 1878, he entitled it "The Force That Wins." He referred to a "tide in the affairs of men" and announced that the key to success was "not in planning but in *doing*."[25] His reward was a teaching position at Hampton, first with the night school students whom he called "The Plucky Class" and then as supervisor of the dormitory for Indian boys, "The Wigwam." The reasoning behind this apparently was that Indians would learn better the white man's values and style of life from a black man who had internalized them. Washington taught them how to make their beds, exhorted them to learn how to farm, and carefully observed the extent of their "enlightenment." For almost a year he wrote a monthly column in the *Southern Workman* on the Indians. In studying the five races of mankind they had to be told that they were the red men, but when reciting the "four conditions of mankind," Washington could hear their subdued whispers, "We savages, we savages."[26]

When Washington established his own school in 1881 in Alabama, he deliberately followed the Hampton model not only in educational philosophy and industrial features but in accommodation to the conditions of Southern life. Samuel R. Spencer, Jr., has pointed out that in his first major national speech, before the National Education Association at Madison, Wisconsin, in 1884, Washington clearly foreshadowed the Atlanta Compromise address in all of its major elements.[27] He was so complimentary of the local white people that a member of the audience, a white woman teacher in a Tuskegee female seminary, wrote a glowing report of it back to her girls. "He represented things as they are at the South, and said some nice things of the Tuskegee citizens," she said.[28] The Civil Rights Act of 1875 had been declared unconstitutional only a year before Washington's speech, but he took the complacent view that good schoolteachers and money to pay them "will be more potent in settling the race question than many civil rights bills." "Brains, property, and character" were the forces that would win, he said. At the bottom of everything "for our race, as for all races, an economic foundation, economic prosperity, economic independence."[29]

That nothing could shake this faith was illustrated in 1885, when a wedding party of Tuskegee teachers of "brains, property, and character" tried to ride a first-class railroad car through Alabama. They were insulted, physically assaulted, and twice forced into the Jim Crow car. Finally they were ejected from the train in a small town where they were arrested and fined. They completed their journey on horseback.[30] Washington wrote a letter of protest to the state's leading newspaper, the Montgomery *Advertiser*, but his first sentences were: "I wish to say a few words from a purely business standpoint. It is not a subject with which to mix social equality or anything bordering on it. To the negro it is a matter of dollars and cents." Washington's complaint was not against separation itself but against the crowded, old, uncarpeted cars, in which drunken or slovenly whites felt free to slouch when ostracized from the white first-class cars. If railroad officials did not want blacks in the first-class cars occupied by whites, said Washington, "let them give us a separate one just as good in every particular and just as exclusive, and there will be no complaint." "If the railroads will not give us first-class accommodations," he added, "let them sell us tickets at reduced rates." He expressed doubt that national legislation or outside attempts would succeed and agreed to wait with "a wise patience" for an equitable adjustment from within the South that would end what he called "these jars in our business relations." He concluded the letter with a remarkable anticipation of the Atlanta Address: "We can be as separate as the fingers, yet one as the hand for maintaining the right."[31]

Acquiescence in segregaton was, then, one of the prices Washington believed he had to pay for peace with his white neighbors, in 1885 as in 1895. Another concession was a rather sweeping abandonment of the First Amendment guarantee of free speech. On at least three occasions white opinion in Tuskegee became inflamed by the speeches or writings of those whom the local newspaper called the "dusky Romeos" at the normal school. In 1885 a speech by a Tuskegee graduate was "misunderstood by the whites who heard it."[32] In 1887 Hiram H. Thweatt, a graduate, published in his newspaper, *The Black Belt*, what were alleged to be "incendiary articles against the white race." Booker Washington, "seeing the natural results that would follow from his unwise course, requested Thweatt, so rumor has it, to suspend publication, which he had the good sense to do," said a white reporter. "Washington is a sensible negro," he added, "averse to any intrusion upon our social welfare, and emanations of an agitating character from these senseless babblers, will meet his condemnation."[33] A year later George W. Lovejoy, a young employee and graduate, wrote an indiscreet letter during Washington's absence to a Mississippi Negro paper saying that the recent effort of a mob to take a Negro from the county jail was proof that the white people of Macon County had "caught the spirit of the lynch-law." Readers of the usually drab Tuskegee *News* were startled to read the following headline: "Lying Lovejoy is His Name, Of Ginger Cake Color, The Third Dusky Romeo Turned out to Roam From the Tuskegee Normal School That Has Ventilated his Spleen and Hate of the White Race. Is it the Purpose of the School to Breed Such Whelps?" The newspaper warned him to leave town as the other two had done. The Tuskegee teachers hastily sent one of their number to say that they "rebuked Lovejoy for his folly and advised him to leave the school." On his return to the school Washington sent a card to the newspaper. "It has always been and is now the policy of the Normal School to remain free from politics and the discussion of race questions that tend to stir up strife between the races, and whenever this policy is violated it is done without the approbation of those in charge of the school." Washington reminded the critics that among three of four hundred students and teachers over a seven-year period there had not been "a half dozen acts performed or utterances made at which any one took offense."[34]

All through the eighties, both locally and regionally, Washington made common cause with the Southern conservative establishment. He exchanged letters with Henry Grady, the principal spokesman of the New South, in which they agreed that "there need be no hostility between the white and the colored people in the South," their interests being "identical."[35] In his solicitation for funds in the North, he carried letters of endorsement from a succession of Alabama governors and superintendents of education, and he seems to have mesmerized the local bankers, businessmen, and planters, for whom Tuskegee Institute was both an economic stimulant and a social tranquilizer. Local white approval constantly soothed him like a balm, and when he said, as he frequently did, that the race problem had been solved in the city of Tuskegee, he generalized from his own experience. He was "one of the best men in the United States," said a visiting legislator. "His influences have all been for the best interest of his own race," said the Montgomery *Advertiser*, "and for peace and good feeling between the whites and blacks." [36] It was not merely that Washington was circumspect, that the mask he turned to Southern whites was a mirror. In many cases Washington not only seemed to agree with those whites who were moderate in their racial views and conservative in their economic views, he actually did agree with them, and they correctly sensed his response.

Washington was a circumspect man, however, full of covert goals and secret devices that would not bear the light of day. Just how far back in his life this habit of secrecy went it is impossible to say, perhaps back to the days of slavery and the saving art of fooling the master, perhaps back to the inevitable deceptions of the house servant. We can be sure, however, that the practice of secrecy was fully developed in Booker T. Washington in the 1880's, when he carried on an elaborate clandestine intrigue against another Negro school. In 1887, after a student riot between the white Marion Institute cadets and State Colored University students, the president of the latter asked the state to move his school to another city. Montgomery, only forty miles from Tuskegee, was the probable new site, and a move there would threaten an important source of Tuskegee students. Washington tried to prevent this in an astonishing variety of ways. He secretly encouraged a Marion Negro grocer to try to keep the school in Marion and asked a Negro doctor friend in Montgomery to pretend to be friendly to the move only to spy on the enemy's councils. He secured the confidential support of a Negro editor in Montgomery, who subsequently complained to Washington that he was being accused of being "bought off" by Washington. He sent a Tuskegee faculty member to prevent the Negro Baptist state conventions and the state Labor party convention from endorsing the Montgomery site. He paid a Tuskegee white lawyer to lobby against Montgomery with the legislature, governor, and superintendent of education, and to go to Birmingham to persuade both whites and Negroes there to invite the school to their town. Washington also secretly paid the state's leading Negro radical, William J. Stevens of Selma, to seek to secure the school for his town, a safe distance to the west of Montgomery. Stevens was the leader of the "Black and Tan" faction that allied with the white Greenbackers, Independents, and Labor party members rather than with the Black Belt Conservatives. But he was at least as opportunistic as Washington. Stevens promised to "leave no stone unturned" and asked in return that Washington place "as liberal 'ad' as possible" in Stevens' paper, the Selma *Cyclone*. Washington suddenly panicked, however, at the thought that his secret bargain with Stevens might come to light and embarrass his relations with white conservatives. "I have come to the conclusion that we had better have nothing more to do with him in this matter," he wrote privately to Tuskegee's treasurer. "I have just written him a letter asking him to do no more in our interest. Whether the school goes to Montgomery or elsewhere I intend to do nothing that I would be ashamed to have the public know about if necessary and this should be our rule in all actions." [37] The Montgomery school question was actually a tempest in a teapot. Despite all Washington's secret maneuvers the school moved to Montgomery, but it did no appreciable harm to Tuskegee's prosperity or standing. The significance of the episode is in what it reveals about Washington—the insecurity at the threat of even so petty a competitor, his employment of secret aggressive tactics, and the astonishing vigor and complexity of his countermoves.

There were other illustrations of Washington's secret forays and of his separate peace with the conservative white establishment, such as his sub rosa campaign among Negroes in the early nineties in behalf of Thomas G. Jones, who was running for governor against the quasi-Populist Rueben F. Kolb.[38] The clearest illustration of Washington's predicament as a Negro spokesman in the South occurred when, only a few months before the Atlanta Compromise, a wounded black militant, Thomas A. Harris, sought refuge on the Tuskegee campus from a lynch mob.

Tom Harris' problem stemmed from his decision in middle age to practice law in Tuskegee, a town that took pride in its toleration of black farmers, teachers, and businessmen but could not accept black lawyers or editors. Formerly a slave and a Confederate officer's body servant, during and after Reconstruction he was a Republican politician. The local white newspaper described him as "rather a seditious character," "a very ambitious and rather an idle negro man, extremely unpopular with his own race on account of his airs of superiority" and obnoxious to whites because of his "impudent utterances and insolent bearing." Booker T. Washington called him "worthless and very foolish." Yet he appeared before the Alabama bar in 1890 with testimonials to his character and probity from the leading conservative lawyers of Tuskegee, was admitted to the bar, practiced for a time in Birmingham, and then returned to Tuskegee.[39] He had the temerity to entertain an itinerant white preacher in his home. A white mob forced the minister to leave and then sent a note to Harris giving him a deadline for leaving town.

By the time Harris received the note the deadline had already passed. As Harris crossed the street to ask his white neighbor's advice, the lynch mob came down the road with blazing torches. "There they are now, coming to kill me!" Harris shouted, entering John H. Alexander's front yard in an attempt to escape by running through the house and out the back door. Fearful for his daughters seated on the porch, Alexander wrestled with Harris at his front gate until the lynch mob arrived. As Harris frenziedly burst into the yard, one of the mob rushed behind him in the light of the moon put his pistol within a foot of Harris and fired with intent to kill. The black man squatted in time to avert the shot, which struck Alexander in the throat and lodged in his spinal column. Other shots rang out, one wounding Harris in the leg as he ran down the road toward his own house. His leg bone shattered, Harris lay in the dirt road within a few feet of his gate, screaming for help. Several white physicians in the crowd rushed past the black man to render Alexander all the assistance in their power. Though first thought mortally wounded, he recovered after the lead ball was found and removed.

Since Tom Harris needed medical attention, his son Wiley brought him in the dead of night to Booker T. Washington's home, "where however he was not received," according to the local newspaper, "for Booker T. Washington . . . has ever conducted himself and his school in the most prudent manner, and learning that a mob was in pursuit of Harris he told him that he could not be admitted there."[40]

The report that Washington had turned away Harris pleased local whites but brought much criticism from the Negro press all over the country. In a debate on the Atlanta Compromise at the Bethel Literary and Historical Society in Washington, an important forum of black expression, the Harris affair was characterized as "hypocritical and showing the natural bent of the man." The house roared its approval when a speaker said: "Mr. Washington, the negro head of a negro institute refused a fellow negro admittance to his negro college, thereby denying the right of medical assistance."[41]

The Reverend Francis J. Grimké, pastor of the Fifteenth Street Presbyterian Church, left the Bethel Literary meeting very disturbed at the conflict the incident created between his friendship for Washington and his commitment to Negro rights. Writing a letter of inquiry, he received from Washington a detailed explanation:

After the man was shot his son brought him to my house for help and advice, (and you can easily understand that the people in and about Tuskegee come to me for help and advice in all their troubles). I got out of bed and went out and explained to the man and his son that . . . I could not take the wounded man into the school and endanger the lives of students entrusted by their parents to my care to the fury of some drunken white men. Neither did I for the same reason feel that it was the right thing to take him into my own house. For as much as I love the colored people in that section, I can not feel that I am in duty bound to shelter them in all their personal troubles any more than you would feel called on to do the same thing in Washington.

Washington then told Grimké what he said he had told no one else:

I helped them to a place of safety and paid the money out of my own pocket for the comfort and treatment of the man while he was sick. Today I have no warmer friends than the man and his son. They have nothing but the warmest feelings of gratitude for me and are continually in one way or another expressing this feeling. I do not care to publish to the world what I do and should not mention this except for this false representation. I simply chose to help and relieve this man in my own way rather than in the way some man a thousand miles away would have had me do it.[42]

Washington was, of course, a genius at self-justification, but his other correspondence confirms his statements to Grimké. In September 1895, about ten days after the Atlanta Address, Tom Harris wrote him from Selma: "Dear friend, I remember all of your kindnesses to me, I will not take time to mention them, as you know them all." He was getting well. "I think I will be able one day to walk on my leg as well as ever," he reported. "It will be a little shorter than the other."[43]

A chastened Tom Harris was eventually allowed to return to Tuskegee, George Lovejoy became a successful lawyer in Mobile, and Hiram Thweatt became the head of an industrial school modeled after Tuskegee. In a physical sense at least, none of these men was victimized by Washington's conservative approach. On the other hand, it is also clear that in his years of power Washington was neither a fragmented personality pursuing contradictory and unclear goals nor an illusion-free pragmatist coolly adjusting his program to a realistic view of a worsening racial situation. He confronted a threatening social environment in 1895, but so did he in 1875 and 1885.

If we read Washington's life from front to back, we find that his life was of a peice. Perhaps the clearest characterization of his program would be "Uncle Tom in his own cabin," peasant conservatism, originating in the experience of slavery—the central life experience being emancipation itself—and practiced in a nation and by a race still overwhelmingly rural and agricultural. Perhaps because there were few black models in his life with the charisma of success, Washington from early life became inordinately attached to a succession of fatherly white men, white racists all, but mild and benevolent in their racism: General Ruffner, General Armstrong, William H. Baldwin, Jr., Theodore Roosevelt. All his life Washington followed the precepts that Hampton Institute taught and all these men subscribed to: a nineteenth-century faith in individual initiative and self-help, and accommodationist strategy toward Southern and American white racism that Armstrong believed to be the lesson taught by Reconstruction, and a faith that men like these could be his effective partners in counteracting Southern proscription and discrimination. Whenever his identity with the black community or his own interest impelled him to actions of which these white counselors and benefactors would not approve, he resorted to secrecy. Some complexities and inner tensions inevitably resulted. Washington's experiences in the 1880's and his responses to them suggest that historians have generally exaggerated the cyclical pattern of race relations in the period after Reconstruction or that Washington's life was more consistent and in a way more principled than we have assumed. If by 1895 he had become a "white man's black man," considering his background it is hard to see how he could have been anything else.

Notes

1. "The Atlanta Exposition Address," Sept. 18, 1895, in Booker T. Washington (hereafter BTW), *Up from Slavery* (Bantam ed., New York, 1963), 153-58.

2. See, for example, the red notebook of 1887, Booker T. Washington Papers, Library of Congress, Container 949 (hereafter these papers will be cited as BTW Papers, LC, with container number in parentheses).

3. BTW to Oswald Garrison Villard, Oct. 30, 1908, BTW Papers, LC (42).

4. These included the Dizer, Cockran, and Milholland Funds, the Southern Improvement Company, and Baldwin Farms.

5. See particularly the chapter "Booker T. Washington and the 'Talented Tenth,' " in August Meier, *Negro Thought in America, 1880-1915: Racial Ideologies in the Age of Booker T. Washington* (Ann Arbor, 1963), 207-47.

6. *Ibid.*, 100-18.

7. See the author's forthcoming article, "The Secret Life of Booker T. Washington," in *Journal of Southern History*.

8. C. Vann Woodward, *Origins of the New South, 1877-1913* (Baton Rouge, 1951), 367.

9. BTW, "Christmas Days in Old Virginia," *Suburban Life*, V (1907), 336-37.

10. Quoted in New York *Age*, Feb. 18, 1909, BTW Papers, LC, clipping (1052). James Burroughs actually died of "lung disease" in 1861, but several of his sons died in Confederate service.

11. See letters of William Henry Ruffner to his wife written in 1865-66 from the home of his uncle Lewis Ruffner, in Ruffner Family Papers, Presbyterian Historical Foundation, Montreat, N.C.; Viola Ruffner to Gilson Willets, May 29, 1899, in Willetts, "Slave Boy and Leader of His Race," *The New Voice*, XVI (June 24, 1899), 3. It was actually in 1867 or later, rather than in 1865, that Washington became the Ruffners' houseboy.

12. William A. MacCorkle, *Recollections of Fifty Years* (New York, 1928), 569. A Democratic governor of West Virginia, MacCorkle knew Washington well in his mature years.

13. Charleston *West Virginia Journal*, Dec. 15, 22, 1869, Mar. 30, 1870; BTW, *Up from Slavery*, 54-55. Washington concluded, from the perspective of 1900: "There are few places in the South now where public sentiment would permit such organizations to exist."

14. BTW, *Up from Slavery*, 37-40; BTW, *The Story of My Life and Work* (rev. ed., Naperville, Ill., 1915), 41-42. BTW said of Armstrong: "I shall always remember that the first time I went into his

presence he made the impression upon me of being a perfect man: I was made to feel that there was something about him that was superhuman." *Up from Slavery*, 37.

15. Samuel C. Armstrong, "Lessons from the Hawaiian Islands," *Journal of Christian Philosophy*, III (1884), 200-29.

16. On Armstrong's thought and attitudes, see Suzanne Carson [Lowitt], "Samuel Chapman Armstrong: Missionary to the South," Ph.D. dissertation, The John Hopkins University, 1952; Meier, *Negro Thought in America, 1880-1915,* 88-90, 95-99; Samuel C. Armstrong, *Armstrong's Ideas on Education for Life* (Hampton, Va., 1940); Edith Armstrong Talbot, *Samuel Chapman Armstrong* (New York, 1904).

17. *Southern Workman*, VI (1877), 10, editorial presumably written by Armstrong.

18. *Ibid.*, IV (1875), 26, 43.

19. Sir George Campbell, *White and Black: The Outcome of a Visit to the United States* (New York, 1879), 277.

20. *Southern Workman*, IV (1875), 26, 43; series of articles by T. T. Bryce, "Labor," *ibid.*, VII (1878), 76-78, "Capital," *ibid.*, 85. "Strikes and Lockouts," *ibid.*, IX (1880), 57. Bryce was a Hampton Institute faculty member who employed hundreds in his private oyster cannery.

21. Quoted in Daniel W. Crofts, "The Blair Bill and the Elections Bill: The Congressional Aftermath to Reconstruction," Ph.D. dissertation, Yale University, 1968, p. 150.

22. Reports of Hampton Institute commencement in New York *Times*, June 15, 1875; Springfield *Daily Republican*, June 26, 1875; *Southern Workman*, IV (1875), 50-51.

23. Letter of "W" in *Southern Workman*, VII (1878), 52; Max B. Thrasher, *Tuskegee: Its Story and Its Work* (Boston, 1900), 19.

24. Letter of "B. T. W." to the editors of Charleston *West Virginia Journal*, reprinted in *Southern Workman*, VI (1877), 62.

25. Natalie Lord, "Booker Washington's School Days at Hampton," *Southern Workman*, XXXI (1902), 258.

26. BTW, "Incidents of Indian Life at Hampton," *ibid.*, X (1881), 43. This was one in a series of articles of the same title.

27. Samuel R. Spencer, Jr., *Booker T. Washington and the Negro's Place in American Life* (Boston, 1955), 91-94; reprint of speech in *Selected Speeches of Booker T. Washington*, ed. E. Davidson Washington (New York, 1932), 1-11.

28. "M. A. O.," letter in Tuskegee *Macon Mail*, July 23, 1884.

29. *Selected Speeches*, ed. Washington, 3.

30. Samuel E. Courtney, interview, Boston *Journal*, Mar. 29, 1896, BTW Papers, LC, clipping (6).

31. Letter in Montgomery *Advertiser*, Apr. 30, 1885.

32. BTW to J. F. B. Marshall, Dec. 22, 1885, BTW Papers, LC (91).

33. Tuskegee Special, Montgomery *Advertiser*, Aug. 21, 1887.

34. Tuskegee *News*, Aug. 2, 1888; Montgomery *Advertiser*, Aug. 4, 1888; BTW to the editor, and editorial, Tuskegee *News*, Aug. 16, 1888; George W. Lovejoy to BTW from Olustee Creek Post Office, Ala., Aug. 12, 1888, BTW Papers, LC (89).

35. Henry W. Grady to BTW. Jan. 10, 1887, in Montgomery *Advertiser*, Jan. 15, 1887.

36. Montgomery *Advertiser*, Nov. 22, Dec. 13, 1890.

37. Stephen Childs to BTW, Feb. 26, 1887 (85), Cornelius N. Dorsette to BTW, Jan. 11, 1887 (99), J. C. Duke to BTW, Jan. 20, 1887 (85), BTW to Warren Logan, July 15, 1887 (86), all in BTW Papers, LC; Montgomery *Advertiser*, Mar. 24, 1888; Warren Logan to BTW, May 3, 1887 (86), L. H. Watkins to BTW, May 14, 1887 (86), Arthur L. Brooks to BTW, June 14, 1887, and undated letter (85, 86), BTW to Logan, July 17, 1887 (86), Logan to BTW, July 20, 1887 (86), BTW to Logan, July 22, 1887 (86), William J. Stevens to BTW, May 18, 24, 1887 (86), all in BTW Papers, LC; J. K. Jackson to Stevens, May 16, 1887, Booker T. Washington Papers, Tuskegee Institute, Container I (hereafter these papers will be cited as BTW Papers, Tuskegee, with container number in parentheses); BTW to Warren Logan, June 15, 1887, BTW Papers, Tuskegee (I).

38. Account of Washington's campaign for Jones, in Jacksonville (Fla.) *Citizen*, Apr. 22, 1897, BTW Papers, LC, clipping (1029).

39. Tuskegee *News*, May 8, 1890, June 13, 1895; BTW to Rev. Francis J. Grimké, Nov. 27, 1895, Booker T. Washington Collection, Moorland Foundation, Howard University, Container I (hereafter this collection will be cited as BTW Collection, Howard, with container number in parentheses); Montgomery *Advertiser*, Apr. 30, May 13, 1890.

40. Tuskegee *News*, June 13, 1895; Birmingham *Age-Herald*, June 10, 1895; Montgomery *Advertiser*, June 11, 13, 1895.

41. George W. Lovejoy to BTW, July 17, 1895, BTW Papers, LC (862); Washington *Bee*, Oct. 26, 1895.

42. BTW to F. G. Grimké, Nov. 27, 1895, BTW Collection, Howard (I).

43. Thomas A. Harris to BTW, Sept. 29, 1895, BTW Papers, LC (862). See also Harris to Warren Logan, Dec. 18, 1895, from Okolona, Miss., BTW Papers, Tuskegee (7); Harris to BTW, Oct. 27, 1902, from Anniston, Ala., BTW Papers, LC (229).

Part VI
Citizens and politicians

The New York Mugwumps of 1887: A profile

Gerald W. McFarland

In an age explosive with social and economic change, political reform in America expended itself on such relatively sterile issues as civil-service reform. As the post-Civil War system of party politics emerged, and with it the rampant venality evident in Boss Tweed's New York and President Grant's Washington, reform-minded Americans rallied in opposition, first in the Liberal Republican Party of 1872 and later with greater effect in the Mugwump movement that broke from the Republican party to support Grover Cleveland in 1884. In the single-minded pursuit of an honest, disinterested politics, the reform elements quickly turned against radical Reconstruction (although many had been identified with the antislavery cause before the Civil War) and abandoned the Negro to his fate in the South. The Mugwumps, moreover, stood foursquare against social reform: they believed in laissez faire and the gold standard; they heartily detested the trade unions; they were indifferent to the plight of the farmer and opposed the movements of agrarian protest. And they barely concealed the elitist, antidemocratic bias of their political thinking. The history of Gilded Age liberal reform is well known, partly because the reformers themselves were literate men who left an ample historical record and partly because succeeding generations of historians operated in the same genteel framework. It may well be, indeed, that the emphasis on liberal reform has diverted attention from more important issues raised by the political history of this era. Yet, for all that is known of the history of reform, important questions remain unanswered. For one thing, given their small numbers and their obvious alienation from contemporary standards, how did the Mugwumps manage, as they did, to define the terms of political debate that prevailed during the Gilded Age? And for another thing, who were the liberal reformers and what motivated them?

The second question has received a good deal of recent attention, although directed mainly at the next generation of progressive reformers. In his stimulating book *The Age of Reform* (1955), the late Richard Hofstadter advanced his arresting thesis of a status revolution. He suggested that certain middle-class groups had suffered a relative decline in social standing as a result of economic and organizational advances, and expressed their

Gerald W. McFarland, "The New York Mugwumps of 1884: A Profile." Reprinted with permission from the *Political Science Quarterly*, vol. 78 (March, 1963), pp. 40-58.

sense of grievance through an identification with reforms. This notion seemed applicable to the Mugwump experience as well as to such other groups as the abolitionists. Although Hofstadter's specific thesis has not stood up well against closer analysis, his focus on reform motivation has been taken up to good advantage by others.

One excellent example is the following essay by Gerald McFarland. His study of the New York Mugwumps does not sustain the notion of a status revolution. These reformers seemed not to be acting out of psychological response to social decline. They were, on the contrary, a strongly entrenched and confident elite whose reformism was a self-conscious application of a set of principles inculcated by family background, education, and sense of civic responsibility. But if McFarland rejects the status thesis, he employs the promising empirical and statistical mode of analysis that Hofstadter's work helped to stimulate.

McFarland has no explicit explanation for the profound influence of liberal reform in defining the political discourse of this era. But there is a good deal in his picture of the New York Mugwumps—strategically located in the urban world, sitting astride the journals and newspapers that shaped public opinion, and confidently asserting their right to leadership—that would help explain how this small group made so large an imprint on Gilded Age politics.

For further reading: Ari Hoogenboom, *Outlawing the Spoils: A History of the Civil Service Reform Movement, 1865-1883* (1961);* Geoffrey T. Blodgett, *The Gentle Reformers: Massachusetts Democracy in the Cleveland Era* (1966);—, "The Mind of the Boston Mugwump," *Mississippi Valley Historical Review*, L (1962), 614-634; Henry Adams, *Democracy a Novel* (1880); Gerald W. McFarland, "Partisanship of Nonpartisanship; Dorman B. Eaton and the Genteel Reform Tradition," *Journal of American History*, LIV (1968), 806-822.

In an era when party regularity was regarded with more than ordinary reverence, the Mugwumps displayed remarkable political independence. Between 1870 and 1896, the Mugwumps, most of whom were members of the Republican party's reform faction, frequently engaged in protests against "unsuitable" party candidates. Their only attempt to organize a reform party was the abortive Liberal Republican party of 1872, and after its failure they resorted to temporary associations for particular campaigns such as the anti-Grant movements of 1876 and 1880 and the anti-Blaine bolt of 1884. Believing it their duty to educate the public to its civic responsibilities, they filled such Mugwump journals as the *Nation* and *Harper's Weekly* with scathing denunciations of the laxity in public morals which permitted the Boss Tweeds, Jay Goulds and Roscoe Conklings to flourish in post-Civil War America.

Aside from their efforts as bolters and critics, the Mugwumps seem most improbable reformers. Well-educated men of comfortable circumstances, their intellectual protest against the spoils politics of the Gilded Age had little appeal for the majority of their contemporaries. Gentlemen reformers, they denied that labor unions should serve as vehicles from social reform, and they resisted every effort to expand the government's economic and social functions on behalf of farmers. The Mugwumps' program was limited to economy in government, civil service reform, tariff reduction, the gold standard and honesty in politics. Their political hero was Grover Cleveland, an honest man although somewhat less than an ardent reformer, and the high point of their reform crusade came in 1884 when they bolted the Republican party and its nominee, James G. Blaine, to support Cleveland's successful campaign for the presidency. In 1896, even those Mugwumps who were nominally Democrats shrank from the "free silver mania" and voted for the thoroughly conservative Republican candidate, William McKinley.

I

The phenomenon of Mugwump reform has been explained as a status revolution, as a moral crusade and as patrician reform. While each of these interpretations contains some elements of the others, they have distinctly different perspectives, each describing one characteristic of Mugwump reform particularly well.

The status revolution thesis appears to have broad significance for middle class reform movements from 1820 to 1920. It was first applied to Progressivism and Abolitionism, and was recently employed by Ari Hoogenboom in his treatment of the early agitation for civil service reform, a movement related to, but not identical with, Mugwump reform.[1] The status revolution thesis describes reform as the response of an established leadership group to the deterioration of its position of influence in the community. In the nineteenth century the "old élite" was composed of lawyers, clergymen, merchants, and bankers whose careers were associated with the commercial-mercantile economy of pre-industrial America. In the post-Civil War period community leadership was assumed more and more frequently by men whose rise to prominence was based on the emergence of an industrial economy. The old élite's status did not decline in absolute terms. They held respected positions and were moderately wealthy, but they were no longer the most influential men in the community. Sensing this fact, they turned to political reform as a means of reasserting their leadership.

A feature of the old élite's decline was their estrangement from majoritarian politics. Believing that the crudely acquisitive "new men" joined with the "politicians" to undermine high standards of civic morality, the old élite found any connection with regular party politics distasteful. They became convinced that principled men such as themselves were a beleagured minority exiled from political power because of their independent spirit. The classical expression of this feeling among the Mugwumps was Henry Adams' protest that there was no place for young men of talent in the political life of the Gilded Age. Richard Watson Gilder, editor of *Century Magazine*, echoed this sentiment: "There seems to be a feeling that an honest man is an impertinent intruder if he expresses any dissent from the management of politics by murderers, liquor dealers, and selfish and vulgar politicians generally."[2]

Gilder's statement contains a suggestion of the "moral crusade" thesis, an interpretation which treats reform as the effort of "honest men" to wrest power from the "selfish and vulgar politicians" who possess it. Reform aligns the forces of good against the forces of evil, or, as Professor Nevins observes in his biography of Cleveland, "the health of the nation requires, from time to time, a far-reaching moral movement to awaken men from old lethargies."[3] The quality of a moral crusade was unmistakably present in the Mugwump bolt of 1884. The leaders of the bolt stressed the moral aspect above all others.

According to George William Curtis, editor of *Harper's Weekly*, "The paramount issue of the Presidential election this year is moral rather than political. It concerns the national honor and character and honesty of administration rather than general policies of government, upon which the platforms of the two parties do not essentially differ."[4] While this thesis provides a good account of the Mugwumps' moral intensity, it does not explain why some men were reformers and others were not.

Noting the Mugwumps' tendency to look upon themselves as the "best men," several scholars have treated Mugwumpery as "patrician reform."[5] Their thesis is that the Mugwumps' reform urge stemmed mainly from a belief that the "best men" must accept civic responsibility. George William Curtis spoke of this obligation in a commencement address entitled "The Public Duty of Educated Men": "By the words 'public duty' . . . I mean simply that constant and active participation in the details of politics without which, on the part of the most intelligent citizens, the conduct of public affairs falls under the control of selfish and ignorant or crafty and venal men."[6] No doubt the Mugwumps' class attachments contributed to their conviction that they were an élite, and to their belief that reform must originate from men such as themselves; nevertheless, their class status also seems to have circumscribed severely their reform program. More work needs to be done on the relationship between the Mugwumps' reform drive and their élitist assumptions about the proper origins of reform.

II

An examination fo the socio-economic characteristics of the Mugwumps has led me to an interpretation somewhat different from those mentioned above. Unlike the status revolution theorists, I do not believe that "displacement" was the primary stimulus for the Mugwumps' reform efforts. As I will attempt to show in my conclusions, the Mugwumps' moral intensity and élitist feelings were in large part the outgrowth of their family tradition, educational background and professional status. Their familial, educational and professional experiences led them to feel a personal responsibility for the preservation of civic morality. When the standards to which they adhered were threatened by the spoilsmen in the post-Civil War period, the Mugwumps' reactions were natural, even habitual responses: demands for moral reform.

The basis for my analysis of the Mugwumps' socio-economic characteristics will be a close study of the membership of the New York Mugwump bolt of 1884. Some of the traits which I will discuss here (such as club membership, religion and great wealth) were clearly less important in shaping the Mugwumps' reform drive than were their education, occupation and family tradition. I have included these traits in my findings because they indicate the remarkable consistency of what I will call the Mugwumps' socio-economic profile.

Although based on a large sample of the New York Mugwumps, the statistics which I will present should not be taken too literally. For example, the fact that one-fourth of my sample were lawyers does not necessarily mean that one-fourth of all Mugwumps were lawyers. Nor am I advancing the thesis that all men of a certain socio-economic group were Mugwumps. The Mugwumps were a minority within a minority; most of the members of their class did not support the Mugwump movement. The validity of a social interpretation, however, is demonstrated by reversing the case. The point is not that all men of a certain class were Mugwumps—such class solidarity not being characteristic of American political life—but that nearly all the Mugwumps were members of one class.

My chief source of Mugwump names was the *New York Times* for 1884. The *Times* published lists of Republican bolters from all over the state. Mention of a man in its columns meant that he had actively supported the bolt by signing protests, walking in anti-Blaine demonstrations, or attending Mugwump gatherings. Supplementing the *Times* lists with the *New York Tribune, Harper's Weekly*, the *Nation* and historical monographs, I collected the names of 410 Mugwumps of whom I identified 396 (96.6%). The amount of information I was able to gather about these men varied greatly from category to category. For instance, I ascertained the occupational background of 379 Mugwumps (92.4% of the total sample), but discovered the religious identification of only eighty-two of them (20% of the total sample).[7]

III

The fact that the Mugwump leaders—Carl Schurz, E. L. Godkin, George William Curtis and Henry Ward Beecher—were all more than fifty years old in 1884 may give a false impression of the age of the majority of the Mugwumps. Table I indicates that approximately half of the Mugwumps were in their twenties or thirties at the time of the bolt; by far the largest ten-year age group is the category for men in their thirties.

Table I
The Mugwumps' Age in 1884

Age group	Individuals in group
21-29	24
30-39	49
40-49	35
50-59	28
60-69	13
70-	6

The Mugwumps in their twenties and thirties were members of a political generation which came of age after the Civil War. The young Mugwumps found it hard to identify with the same issues of union and disunion which had excited their fathers and which continued to be of great importance to the Republican party. Henry L. Stoddard, a reporter, voted for Blaine but expressed a Mugwump-like despair with the Republican party: "For me the Republican party had overplayed the war. I had no desire to vote as others had shot."[8] Another journalist, Richard R. Bowker, asserted, "Parties have lost their significance, . . . our young men who have come into political life since the Civil War find nothing to fight for."[9] To these young men, Blaine, who had a reputation as a spoilsman and rebel-baiter, did not offer any hope for a change in the politics of the day. Cleveland, on the other hand, had demonstrated his incorruptibility as Governor of New York, and seemed to promise something better in the attitude of politicians towards their duties. One contemporary wrote, "There was nothing in the ideals, practices, or leaders of either party which commanded my admiration . . . till the nomination of Grover Cleveland."[10]

The experience which distinguished the men over forty from the young Mugwumps was their service to the party. Not only could they remember the party of Lincoln, but they could recall their efforts in its behalf. Francis Barlow had been a Lincoln elector in 1860. Edward Salomon, a refugee from the German revolution of 1848, had been wartime governor of Wisconsin. Daniel Chamberlain had been Governor of South Carolina during reconstruction. Benjamin Bristow had served as one of Grant's secretaries of the Treasury. Carl Schurz was another ex-cabinet member.[11] These men felt that the Republican party has "sprung from a moral sentiment. It was the party of political morality and of personal liberty."[12] This idealism was no longer present in the Republican organization of 1884. The nomination of Blaine, whose public record was marred by his involvement in a questionable railroad bond deal, seemed intolerable to the Mugwumps. Their efforts had been betrayed, and, they felt, "We have not left the party; it is fairer to say that the party has left us."[13]

While the Mugwump spokesmen were older Republicans, much of the organizational drive behind the bolt was supplied by younger men. Frederic Bancroft, later a noted historian, was a Columbia graduate student when he volunteered for the Independent Committee's office staff. Six men under thirty-five were members of this executive committee and handled many of the organization's projects: Richard R. Bowker; three lawyers, Frederick Whitridge, Horace Deming, George W. Green; the publishers, Charles Scribner and J. Henry Harper. Some of the foremost Mugwump journalists were in their forties: Richard Watson Gilder; George Haven Putnam, son of George Palmer Putnam; Henry Holt, author and publisher; Thomas Nast, cartoonist for *Harper's Weekly;* and Edward Cary, editorial writer for the *New York Times.*

Table II
Occupations of Mugwumps

Occupation*	Individuals
Lawyer	101
Businessman	97
Financier	57
Journalist	27
Physician	25
Teacher	25
White collar	22
Clergyman	13
Miscellaneous	12

*For my purposes these general categories were specific enough. A more detailed break-down of four of the categories is as follows: Businessman: merchant 66, manufacturer 24, miscellaneous 7. Financier: banker 15, broker 25, insurance agent 9, investor 8. White collar: clerk 4, secretary 6, agent 10, manager 2. Journalist: editor 15, publisher 10, author 2.

Occupationally, the vast majority of the bolters were professionals or entrepreneurs.

From the figures summarized in Table II, it appears that approximately one-fourth of the New York Mugwumps were lawyers, that another fourth were businessmen, that one--eighth were financiers and that most of the rest were professionals: journalists, physicians, teachers or clergymen.

Exceptions to this upper middle class economic pattern were few and not especially striking. Only one labor leader and one farmer were found in the sample. Of the white collar category, ten were clerks or secretaries associated with law firms and stock brokerages. Others were agents for various types of firms. One man was listed as a "cashier." Of the miscellaneous category, only William Webster a "railroad engineer," Owen Torrington a "painter" and Andrew W. White a "polisher," do not seem to be professionals or entrepreneurs.

As well as being drawn from a relatively narrow segment of the occupational spectrum, the Mugwumps were men in comfortable circumstances. Many of them were owners of mercantile or manufacturing establishments; others were partners in the larger law firms of their cities. Those who worked in Brooklyn or Manhattan lived in the better residential districts of those cities or commuted from homes in Flushing, Yonkers, Tarrytown and New Jersey. Many were men of considerable affluence such as Pascal P. Beals, the Buffalo steel and hardware manufacturer, William Childs, a well-to-do roofing manufacturer, and Alfred T. White, fur importer and housing reformer, whose estate exceeded $300,000. [14] Undoubtedly many of the ninety-six businessmen were not as wealthy as Beals or Childs, but they were owners of their business establishments, and, as such, largely independent, if not completely self-employed.

Along with the moderately well-to-do majority of the Mugwumps were a few men of great wealth. Twenty-six of the sample were millionaires. [15] Three of them—James Stokes, a real estate investor, George Jones, owner of the *New York Times* and Thomas C. Sloane, a prominent Manhattan merchant—served on the Independent Executive Committee. [16] Three others—the leather goods manufacturer Jackson S. Schultz and two publishers, Joseph W. Harper, Jr. and J. Henry Harper—attended Mugwump meetings from the start of the bolt. Eleven of the Mugwump millionaires inherited their fortunes. Twelve of the other fifteen appear to have reached the millionaire level well before the 1880's. Ten were in merchandizing, three in publishing, five each in importing and real estate and one each in contracting, banking and manufacturing. Their attitude toward wealth was expressed by the ever-trenchant Godkin, "Who knows how to be rich in America? Plenty of people know how to get money; but . . . to be rich properly is, indeed, a fine art. It requires culture, imagination, and character." [17]

Two further indexes of the Mugwumps' social status are their representation in the *Social Register* and in the exclusive clubs of New York City. The *Social Register* listed the foremost families of New York City. One hundred Mugwumps achieved this pinnacle of social prominence. [18] This was in part a reflection of their membership in the city's most exclusive social clubs. Four of the more prestigious organizations in which they participated were the Union Club, the Union League Club, the Century Association and the University Club.

The Union Club and the Union League were social clubs with quasi-political functions. Writing in the twentieth century one author said, "So far as the aristocartic clubs enter into politics they are defense-units against reform criticism." [19] Although in the 1880's some members of these groups rebelled against these anti-reform tendencies, Peel's description was almost as applicable in 1884 as in 1935. The Union Club was the oldest organization of this type. For many years after its founding in 1836, it was "the wealthiest and most exclusive" [20] social club in New York. In the post-Civil War period it remained the "representative organization of the 'old families'." [21] Sixteen Mugwumps were among its members.

The Union League was a patriotic organization founded in 1863 to "strengthen love and respect for the Union." [22] In the post-Civil War period "this wealthy club tended . . . toward extreme conservatism." [23] In 1884, however, a "large element in the club opposed Blaine's nomination." [24] The *Nation* reported that at an October meeting about thirty per cent of the members present voted against endorsing the Blaine ticket. [25] The thirty-eight Mugwumps who belonged to the club were undoubtedly the core of this number. Some of them, such as Jackson S. Schultz, who was an ex-president of the League, must have used their prestige to gather the large vote against Blaine.

Although the Mugwumps were members of and even leaders in these conservative organizations, their presence was felt more fully in the Century Association and the University Club of New York City. These two organizations were literary and intellectual rather than political in their aims. Both were select, but neither were the bellicose Republican club which the Union League epitomized. The tenor of the Century Association and University Club was humorously portrayed by Samuel Clemens:

By permission, I visited the Century Club last night—the most unspeakably respectable club in the United States, perhaps. . . . The reading and supper rooms were crowded with the distinguished artists, authors, and amateurs of New York. I averaged the heads, and they went three sizes larger than the style of heads I have been accustomed to. In one of the smaller rooms they averaged best—thirteen heads out of the twenty-seven present were what I choose to call prodigious. I never felt so subjugated in my life. And I was never so ashamed of wearing an 8¼ before. [26]

The Century Association limited its membership to seven hundred. Fifty-five Mugwumps were members. The University Club had somewhat over a thousand members of whom sixty-seven participated in the Mugwump movement. The Mugwumps were often prominent in the governing councils of these bodies. In 1884 the University Club had four Mugwumps on its Executive Committee. [27] This included Henry Holt who was one of the club's founders.

The Mugwumps' remarkable record of college, professional and graduate education contrasts strikingly with the educational experience of most of their contemporaries. In 1880 only 2.72 per cent of the Americans between eighteen and twenty-one years of age were enrolled in institutions of higher learning. [28] The median number of years in school for people born in 1865 was eight. [29] The Mugwumps far exceeded both these figures. Of the 188 individuals whose educational background is known, 164 had received some college or professional training, 14 had done high school or academy work and 10 had attended elementary school or were largely self-educated. One hundred and twenty-five had received A.B. or B.S. degrees: 32 from Harvard, 24 from Columbia, 22 from Yale, 11 from Cornell and the rest from other colleges. Fifty-three Mugwumps were graduates of law schools, all but 8 receiving their LL.B's from Columbia or Harvard. During their lifetimes the Mugwumps amassed 35 M.A.'s, 11 M.D.'s, 3 D.D.'s, 27 LL.D.'s and 11 Ph.D.'s.

One outgrowth of the Mugwumps' educational background and occupational status was an interest in professional standards and in organizations promoting these standards. A few outstanding examples suffice to illustrate that the Mugwumps were prominent in the development of professional societies. Two presidents of the American Medical Association, Abraham Jacobi (1912-13) and Lewis Sayre (1880-81), were Mugwumps. Benjamin Bristow was the second president (1879-80) of the American Bar Association. Moses Coit Tyler and Herbert Tuttle were organizers of the American Historical Association. Josephus N. Larned was president of the American Library Association from 1893 to 1894. Mugwumps also figured prominently in the founding of the Association of the Bar of the City of New York in 1870. By 1884 fifty-three Mugwumps belonged to the Association; James C. Carter was its president, and five other bolters were on its Executive Committee. It is not difficult to see that such devotion to personal and professional standards was related to the Mugwump demand for the implementation of a civil service merit system and the election of "honest" men.

The Mugwumps were predominately natives of New York and New England. Eighty-two were born in New York State, thirty-three in the New England states, fourteen in other parts of the United States and eighteen in foreign countries.

Both at birth and in 1884, the Mugwumps were much more likely to be city-dwellers than were their fellow Americans. The year 1860 may serve as a reference point for assessing the Mugwumps' urban background. In that year only fifteen per cent of the American people lived in cities having over ten thousand residents;[30] whereas, as Table III indicates, at birth (most Mugwumps were born well before 1860) slightly over half of the Mugwumps lived in cities. By 1884 nearly all the Mugwumps lived or worked in the more populous areas of New York—Manhattan, Albany, Brooklyn, Buffalo and Syracuse—the smallest of which was Syracuse with 51,792 inhabitants.[31] Thirty bolters lived in Flushing (population, 6,683), but many of these men worked in Manhattan. Most of the nineteen Ithaca Mugwumps were associated with Cornell. (Ithaca's population was 9,105.) Only R. H. Palmer whose farm was near Walden (population 1,254) lived in a rural environment.

Table III
The Mugwumps' Residential Environment at Birth

Type of Environment	Individuals
City (urban area with more than 10,000 residents)	69
Town (urban area with between 500 and 10,000 residents)	40
Rural (farms or urban areas with less than 500 residents)	16

It is not surprising that upper middle class men born in New England and New York should have many ties with colonial America. David Allerton (a produce merchant) and Ethan Allen Doty and Charles E. Tracy (lawyers) claimed to have Mayflower ancestors. The Reverend Alfred P. Putnam was descended from Governor John Endicott of Massachusetts Bay Colony. The editor of *Harper's Monthly*, Henry Mills Alden, was a descendant of John Alden. There were also old New York names among the Mugwump ranks for which two lawyers serve as examples. Edmund L. Baylies was descended from the original patroon of Rensselaerswyck, and the ancestor of George W. Verplanck arrived in New Netherland in 1647. Eighteen Mugwumps belonged to the St. Nicholas Society, a club which required each member to have an ancestor who had lived in New York before 1785.[32]

In direct contrast to the colonial roots of most of the bolters, eighteen of the Mugwumps were foreign-born. Germany supplied the most with nine. England, Scotland, Ireland and Canada followed with two each. One man came from Denmark. Although this group was small, some of the most prominent Mugwumps were foreign-born. E. L. Godkin and George Haven Putnam emigrated from England. Six of the Germans had been driven out of Germany for supporting the revolution of 1848. Of these, Carl Schurz, Thomas Nast, Dr. Abraham Jacobi and ex-Governor Edward Salomon have already been mentioned. Of the other two, Sigismund Kaufmann was a prominent lawyer, an influential member of the New York Turnverein and the Republican candidate for Lieutenant Governor of New York in 1870. Hugo Wesendonck was a former member of the German Diet, and upon arriving in America he became a banker. He was a militant free-thinker and a leader in the movement to set up German schools for immigrants from the old country.

While information on the religious identification of the Mugwumps was not available in abundance, that which is summarized in Table IV reflects the Mugwumps' high social status and New York-New England origins. Almost two-thirds of the Mugwumps belonged to the Episcopalian, Unitarian, or Congregational Churches, denominations which had figured prominently in American religious life during the colonial and early national periods. The Congregational and Episcopal Churches were the old, established denominations of New York and New England, and the Unitarian Church was the intellectual offspring of Congregational New England. By far the largest single church affiliation shown in Table IV is Episcopalian, a denomination which drew the bulk of its membership from the upper classes of the community.

Table IV
The Mugwumps' Religious Affiliations

Denomination	Individuals
Episcopalian	34
Unitarian	11
Congregational	10
Presbyterian	8
Jewish	5
Methodist	4
Baptist	3
Catholic	2
Miscellaneous	5

Evangelical creeds such as the Methodist and the Baptist which had spread over frontier America, and which, with Roman Catholicism, were the largest denominations in America by the post-Civil War period, were lightly represented in the Mugwump ranks. As shown by Table V, the distribution of Mugwumps in various denominations was almost an inverse proportion to the percentage of their contemporaries in these faiths.[33]

Table V
The Percentage of Americans, New Yorkers and
Mugwumps in Various Religious Denominations

Denomination	Americans	New Yorkers	Mugwumps
Roman Catholic	30%	53%	2%
Methodist	22	12	5
Baptist	18	7	4
Presbyterian	6	8	10
Episcopal	3	6	41
Congregational	2	2	12
Jewish	.6	2	6
Unitarian	.3	.2	13

IV

Every aspect of the Mugwump profile—religion, education, wealth, occupation, club membership—indicates that the Mugwump reformers came from a narrow segment of the socio-economic spectrum. I demonstrated earlier that the reform tradition with which these men were associated was notable for its moral fervor, élitist tendencies and alienation from regular party politics. It now remains to show some connections between the Mugwumps' socio-economic profile and their interest in reform.

Consider how the environment in which the Mugwumps were raised formed the basis for their view of themselves as an élite of principled men with public responsibilities. The family tradition of the Mugwump men was community leadership. Typical biographical statements about the Mugwumps' fathers were: "leading politician," "diplomat," "president of Wesleyan College," "country storekeeper, farmer, and justice of the peace," "elected reform mayor of New York in 1844," and "a noted publisher." These biographical descriptions imply another characteristic of the Mugwump families, for the statements might be collectively paraphrased, "His father was a man of high principle who taught his son these values." The Mugwump families were pillars of respectable society; they assumed that their sons would carry on this tradition.

The importance of education to the Mugwumps' reform instinct can scarcely be overemphasized. The college education which so many of the Mugwumps sought was far more than preparation to enter the law, business, or medicine. Their college years were also an experience which shaped their attitude toward themselves and their civic role. The young men who listened to George William Curtis discuss the "Public Duty of Educated Men" could not fail to perceive the implication of the speaker's words: that college graduates were an educated élite and that because the maintenance of public standards necessarily lay with such men, they had an obligation to prevent the control of public affairs from falling into the hands of "selfish and ignorant or crafty and venal men."

By virtue of their professional duties the Mugwumps' private pursuits were closely tied to the public life of the community. As professional men and owners of businesses, they were particularly sensitive to any deviation from responsible conduct of public affairs and were likely to react to such deviations by calling for reform. Mugwump clergymen ministered to the spiritual needs of the community and denounced any lapse of public morals. Doctors such as Jacobi and Sayre treated victims of crowded tenements and poor sanitation and agitated for more effective government regulations and services. Journalists informed the public of the misconduct of public affairs. Businessmen protested the evil effects of the irregular business practices and favoritism fostered by political bosses. The lawyers of the Association of the Bar of the City of New York stated that because Blaine "had sold his official power and influence for railroad bonds ... the rights of every citizen, even the humblest, would be endangered by his election." [34] Such sentiments were not the outgrowth of professional attachments alone, but the Mugwumps' occupational duties did reinforce the civic role previously imposed by their family and educational backgrounds.

The Mugwumps' high economic status contributed to their reform response in a variety of ways. First, although it would be incorrect to characterize them as an élite of wealth alone, wealth must be counted as one of the characteristics which set them apart from their contemporaries and supported their élitist assumptions. Secondly, their economic security enabled them to put off working until they finished college and later provided them with the leisure for political activity. Finally the fact, so evident from their club memberships and *Social Register* listings, that they were an established élite, was conducive to an interest in public affairs. To men who were born into well-to-do families, the acquisition of more money did not always seem an adequate source of personal distinction. Some of the most energetic of these talented men turned to public affairs as a means of self-fulfillment. Henry L. Stimson voiced his sentiment in his memoirs:

The profession of the law was never thoroughly satisfactory to me, simply because the life of the ordinary New York lawyer is primarily and essentially devoted to the making of money. ... There had been an ethical side to it [public service] which has been of more interest to me, and I have felt that I could get a good deal closer to the problems of life than I ever did before, and felt that the work was a good deal more worth while. And one always feels better when he feels that he is working in a good cause. [35]

The reaction of individual Mugwumps to situations which threatened the public good can be illustrated by a few examples. John Sloane protested the open thievery practiced by the Customs House officials; George Jones refused a one million dollar bribe to end the *Times'* anti-Tweed campaign; Benjamin Bristow would not stop his prosecution of the Whiskey Ring case even though the President's closest associates were implicated by his findings; the president of the Bar Association, James C. Carter, led the Association's campaign against Blaine; Thomas Nast slashed away at politicos such as Tweed and Blaine in his cartoons.

In their various campaigns against "venal politicians" the Mugwumps acted out a civic role to which they were committed by their career pattern. This pattern (or profile) of educational, family and professional associations educated them to a life of conscientious citizenship. They instinctively defended this tradition of public morality against any threat to it. Their reform was not so much the reaction of a displaced élite to their own displacement as it was the response of self-appointed trustees of public morality to the irresponsible ways of the spoilsmen. Their "exile" from public office was in large part self-imposed because they refused to subordinate their principles to the party's interest.

The rigidity of this stand irritated many of their contemporaries and often made the Mugwumps seem foolish, pharisaical and vain; yet, this stubborn adherence to principle was also their most notable group characteristic.

If Mugwumpery is viewed from the perspective of its socio-economic origins, the Mugwumps do not seem "improbable reformers" at all. There was no contradiction between the fact that they were reformers and the fact that they were a self-conscious élite. The intense awareness of class attachments which limited the Mugwumps' reform program also shaped their belief that men whose education and status made them fit arbiters of civic standards were an élite which should act as moral stewards for the rest of society. Without the conviction, largely derived from their socio-economic background, that the "best men" should accept civic responsibilities, these essentially conservative men would not have felt the need to attempt "the education of all classes in the community in their duties of citizenship."[36]

Notes

1. David Donald's essay, "Toward a Reconsideration of the Abolitionists," is found in his *Lincoln Reconsidered* (New York, 1956), 19-36. Richard Hofstadter treats the progressives in *The Age of Reform: From Bryan to F.D.R.* (New York, 1955). See also Ari Hoogenbloom, *Outlawing the Spoils: A History of the Civil Service Reform Movement 1865-1883* (Urbana, Illinois, 1961).

2. Rosamond Gilder (ed.), *Letters of Richard Watson Gilder* (Boston, 1916), 222.

3. Allan Nevins, *Grover Cleveland, A Study in Courage* (New York, 1932), 156. This interpretation of Mugwumpery is typical of narrative accounts of the campaign such as Carleton Putnam's *Theodore Roosevelt, the Formative Years, 1858-1886* (New York, 1958), I, 494-496, and David S. Muzzey, *James G. Blaine, A Political Idol of Other Days* (New York, 1934), 269-71, 287-325.

4. Address published by the National Committee of Independents and Republicans, Pamphlet I, July 30, 1884.

5. Eric Goldman's chapter, "Thrust from the Top," in *Rendezvous with Destiny* (New York, 1952), 10-28, is a suggestive essay on the "patrician dissidents." Harrison C. Thomas also notes the élitist quality of Mugwumpery in *The Return of the Democratic Party to Power in 1884* (New York, 1919), 27-28, as does Geoffrey T. Blodgett in a perceptive analysis of Massachusetts Mugwumpery, "The Mind of the Boston Mugwump," *Mississippi Valley Historical Review*, March, 1962.

6. Charles Eliot Norton (ed.), *Orations and Addresses of George William Curtis* (New York, 1894), I, 266.

7. For identifying these names I utilized biographical directories of all types, from the *Dictionary of American Biography, Who Was Who*, and other sources stressing biographies of prominent men, to city directories for Brooklyn, Buffalo, Ithaca, and New York City which included all heads of families living or employed in the city and listed men with occupations such as "laborer," "driver" and "shoeshine."

8. Henry L. Stoddard, *As I knew Them* (New York, 1927), 52.

9. E. McClung Fleming, *R. R. Bowker, Militant Liberal* (Norman, Oklahoma, 1952), 95. Bowker was known as the "original Mugwump" because he organized a "Young Scratcher" movement to oppose Alonzo Cornell's campaign for Governor of New York in 1879. He was aided by Horace E. Deming and George H. Putnam, both later Mugwumps.

10. David F. Houston, *Eight Years with Wilson's Cabinet* (New York, 1926), I, 1, 2.

11. Because of their efforts to maintain high standards of official responsibility, the Mugwump politicians were ostracized by regular party politicians. Barlow was twice elected New York's Secretary of State, but in reporting the 1876 Florida election returns he was the only investigator to report against his party's candidate. This ended his political career. Grant dismissed Bristow because the Secretary's vigorous prosecution of the Whiskey Ring case pointed clearly to duplicity on the part of the President's crony, Orville E. Babcock.

12. George William Curtis, *Address* (National Committee of Republicans and Independents), Pamphlet I, July 30, 1884, 2.

13. The *New York Times*, October 26, 1884.

14. A little known fact about the Mugwumps is the leading role some of them took in tenement house reform. White was exceptionally active in this field. He built model tenements and advocated government enforcement of better housing standards as early as 1877. No effective legislation was passed until the Tenement House Commission Investigations of 1894–95 under the chairmanship of another Mugwump, Richard Watson Gilder. R. R. Bowker, A. P. W. Seaman, Richard W. G. Welling and R. F. Cutting also participated in "model tenement" ventures.

15. Sidney Ratner (ed.), *New Light on the History of Great American Fortunes* (New York, 1953).

16. The Mugwumps who engaged in importing were angered by the extortionist policies of the Republican-controlled New York Customs House, a notorious center of spoils politics. Sloane protested this graft (*New York Tribune* January 3, 1872) in a petition signed by several other importers including two other Mugwumps.

17. Edwin L. Godkin, "Waste," *The Nation* (March 8, 1866), II, 302.

18. *Social Register*, New York, 1890 (New York 1935), IV, No. I.

19. Roy V. Peel, *The Political Clubs of New York* (New York, 1935), 316.

20. Francis G. Fairfield, *The Clubs of New York* (New York, 1873), 154.

21. *Ibid.*, 155.

22. Union League Club of New York, *Report* (New York, 1887), 9.

23. Will Irwin, *A History of the Union League Club of New York City* (New York, 1952), 125.

24. *Ibid.*, 155.

25. *The Nation*, October 16, 1884, 322.

26. The Century Association, *The Century 1847-1947* (New York, 1947), 27.

27. University Club, *Report 1884-85* (New York, 1885).

28. U.S. Department of Commerce, *Historical Statistics of the United States from Colonial Times to 1957* (Washington D.C., 1960), 211.

29. *Ibid.*, 214.

30. U.S. Department of Commerce, *Historical Statistics*, 9.

31. See Departmetn of the Interior, Census Office, *Compendium of the Tenth Census,* Part I (Washington, D.C., 1882) for population statistics. All figures in the paragraph are for 1880.

32. St. Nicholas Society, *Constitution and List of Members* (New York, 1895), 22.

33. These figures are for 1890. Bureau of the Census, *Religious Bodies, 1906* (Washington D.C., 1906), I, 25. Eight of the Episcopalians were identified by their membership in the Church Club, an exclusive Episcopalian society. Even without the names found by this "ready-made" device the percentage of Episcopalians among the Mugwumps is double that of the next most representative denomination.

34. Everett P. Wheeler, *Sixty Years of American Life* (New York, 1917), 127.

35. Henry L. Stimson and McGeorge Bundy, *On Active Service in Peace and War* (New York, 1948), 17.

The political revolution of the 1890s: A behavioral interpretation

Paul Kleppner

American political history has become an innovative subject in recent years. No longer are historians willing to explain political behavior solely on the basis of formal issues and rational economic interests. They have increasingly emphasized social and psychological factors, and in so doing have generated some exciting proposals about American political behavior. But their work has also tended to suffer from an inadequacy of solid evidence. As it happens, the Gilded Age is one period for which, thanks to the arduous work of a group of young historians, statistical evidence has been developed from voting records and census data to show correlations between party affiliation and social characteristics.

In the following essay, Paul Kleppner summarizes the findings of his research in mid-western politics in the second half of the 19th century. (The statistical underpinnings are laid out in great detail in his recent *The Cross of Culture* [1970], and may be studied there at the student's leisure). Kleppner's most significant discovery, since borne out in the work of Richard Jensen (see below), reveals a line of political cleavage, in the Midwest at any rate, not along class or occupational lines but rather by ethnic and religious identification. Kleppner perceives two large groupings: the pietists, those belonging to the Protestant denominations connected especially to the Revivalist tradition, voted Republican; and the ritualists, heavily Catholic and German Lutheran, who voted Democratic. The religious identifications carried over into politics because of the inclination of the pietists to use government as a mechanism of social control. Their objective was to force the ritualists to conform to pietistic notions of public morality especially by means of temperance, sabbath observance and public education. These explosive issues go a long way toward explaining why the Gilded Age saw a level of voter participation higher than at any time in the 20th century. The size of these groups, however, was such as to make midwestern politics a stalemate (and, since the Midwest was the swing area nationally, a stalemate in national politics as well).

The break in this stalemate occurred during the 1890's, and the Republicans emerged as the majority party for the next 40 years. The thrust of Kleppner's essay, given the

This essay appears for the first time in this collection. An earlier version was printed in Joel H. Sibley and Samuel T. McSeveney, ess. *"Voters, Parties and Elections: Quantitative Essays in the History of American Popular Voting Behavior"* (Lexington, Mass: Xerox Publishing).

existing configuration of cultural politics, is to explain the revolution of the 1890's. Kleppner discerns two forces at work. First, the severe depression injected an economic factor, especially pronounced in the 1894 elections, that operated against the Democrats as the party in power and in favor of the Republican Party—"the party of prosperity." Overlaying this was a resurgence of the cultural factor in the campaign of 1896, but not in a way that restored old party allegiances. On the contrary, Kleppner discovers a shift of ritualist support into the Republican column, pietistic into the Democratic column. This he explains essentially by the kind of leadership given by Bryan and McKinley, neither of whom adhered to the cultural stance normal to his own party.

These findings testify to the fruitfulness of the new political history that stresses statistical method and rigorous analysis. By so doing, Kleppner has been able to establish a pattern of cultural politics hitherto overlooked by historians of the late nineteenth century. When it comes to explaining his findings, however, Kleppner must abandon the high standards of scientific history. Having ascertained by statistical analysis the shifts in voting patterns in the 1890's, Kleppner proceeds to an explanation that is plausible, but that is no more rigorous than those of conventional historians. The connection that he draws between voting shifts and party leadership (assuming his characterization to be correct) depends on the garden variety of impressionistic evidence, with a strong dash of hypothesis. The new history does not eliminate these conventional modes of analysis; it merely provides more solid ground from which to launch an interpretation. And, if anything, the new historians engaged in the exacting measurement of historical data seem unusually daring in the interpretation of their findings.

For further reading: Paul Kleppner, *The Cross of Culture: A Social Analysis of Midwestern Politics, 1851-1900*; Richard Jenson, *Winning of the Midwest: Social and Political Conflict, 1885-1896* (1971); J. R. Hollingsworth, *The Whirligig of Politics: The Democracy of Cleveland and Bryan* (1963); Horace S. Merrill, *Bourbon Democracy in the Middle West: 1865-1896* (1953); Walter D. Burnham, *Presidential Ballots: 1836-1892* (1955); Paul Glad, *The Trumpet Soundeth: William Jennings Bryan and His Democracy, 1896-1912* (1960);* Robert Marcus, *Grand Old Party: Political Structure in the Gilded Age, 1880-1896* (Oxford, 1971).

Probably no sphere of historical investigation is more ripe for "new directions" than political history. Standard explanations of past political action need critical reexamination. That unique fascination with which political historians have consistently approached presidential contests needs to be expanded into a concern for the systematic analysis of party strength in all types of elections. Even more importantly, the conceptual framework within which political history has been analyzed needs to be broadened. Political parties have to be conceived as more than static institutions struggling for control over patronage and the direction of national policy. They are heterogeneous coalitions of disparate social groups. Accordingly, "politics" should be thought of as that sphere of human activity in which a wide variety of conflicts among social groups seeks resolution. To attempt to understand political history without first understanding that range of conflict becomes an exercise in futility.

The numerous and glaring inadequacies of the "old directions" of political history have been perceptively catalogued elsewhere.[1] Here, however, it is useful to draw attention to three common analytical weaknesses.

First, political historians have frequently attempted to explain the outcome of an election without first assessing its relationship to those which preceded and followed it. This has resulted in a focus on the episodic, but for no better reason than its intrinsic drama. It has resulted, too, in *ahistorical explanations* of past events. Only by using that dimension of analysis which is uniquely the historian's, analysis over time, can political historians discern those elections in which major changes in the balance of political forces have occurred and provide *historical* explanations.

Second, political historians have displayed relatively little interest in *systematically* determining the social bases of support of the contesting parties. All too frequently, they have accepted as factual the descriptions of social support emanating from partisan contemporaries. For example, following the claims of Carl Schurz, political historians have described the movement of German voters into the Republican ranks in 1860, and have attributed this shift to their antipathy to slavery.[2] Or, since farmers somehow appeared to have been "conservative," it has been assumed that they provided a solid phalanx of support for the "conservative" Republican party in the 1870s and 1880s.[3] No basis in fact exists for either of these assertions. Only a systematic comparison of election and demographic data can provide historians with solid answers to *factual* questions concerning the social bases of political support.

Third, political historians have used inadequate models of explanation. Indeed, rarely have they made their design of proof explicit. But there is a pattern of implicit assumptions which is common to most historical explanations. Underlying these, is the notion that the stands taken by parties on public issues somehow or another serve as determinants of popular voting behavior. Thus, when the party of "tariff reform" wins over that of "tariff protection," historians explain the result in terms of public receptivity to this tariff position. The explanation assumes that the voter perceives the relationship between his own economic position and the tariff; that the voter further perceives the relationship between his tariff attitude and party positions on that question; and that the voter minimizes all other factors and makes his decision on the basis of these perceived relationships. In short, the explanation assumes that the voter translates a policy belief into a partisan selection. This is an adequate explanation of the behavior of the highly issue-oriented voter. When a voter is aware of an issue or has an opinion about it, when that issue arouses at least a minimal intensity of feeling, and when he perceives that one party represents his position better than others, he is likely to react in this way. But these are highly specific conditions which must be present in order to elicit an issue-oriented response.[4] There is no reason to assume, as historians generally have, that such conditions are always and everywhere satisfied.

Traditional View

The combined impact of these shortcomings has been to produce a grossly inadequate view of the politics of the 1890s. Accepting the notion that a "dramatic" election must be a "significant" one, historians have seen the 1896 contest as the focal point of the decade.[5] According to the prevailing view, in that contest, for the first time since the Civil War, there were "real" differences between the two major parties. Until then both parties had subserved the business interests and had remained oblivious to the interests of "the people". In 1896 William Jennings Bryan, the admixture of the Jacksonian Democrat and Populist yeoman, emerged as the standard bearer of the Democratic party. Its espousal of free silver placed that party and its candidate squarely on the side of "the people" in the battle against the very personification of the business interests, the political puppet of Mark Hanna, William McKinley. But as a result of a combination of manipulation, corruption, and coercion, "the people" lost and McKinley was elected to the Presidency.

Imbedded in this view of the 1890s are all of the shortcomings which characterize historical political analysis generally. Failure to view the 1896 results in the context of a series of elections obscures the changes in voting behavior which had taken place prior to that election. Furthermore, the omission of a systematic description of the social bases of partisan support prior to and after the 1896 election makes it impossible to determine *who*, i.e., what social groups, were responsible for the political change. Was it upper and middle class voters, repelled by Bryan's "radicalism," who shifted away from his brand of Democracy? Or, was it working class urban voters, fearful of monetary inflation and the decreased purchasing power of their wages, who offered greater-than-usual support to the Republican party? The social identification of those voter groups responsible for the realignment is a logical prerequisite to any explanation of its causes. Finally, traditional political analyses focus on free silver exclusively as a substantive economic issue and thereby overlook its broader, non-economic implications as a voter mobilization ideology.

Rather than concentrating further on the negative aspects of past analysis, I want to suggest here an alternative hypothesis.[6] This hypothesis stems from a research design which explicitly attempts to overcome the weaknesses of the usual approach. The design borrows heavily from work in political science, sociology, and social psychology. It attempts to combine a quantitative analysis of election and demographic data across time with a social analysis of the usual historical sources. Specifically, I have analyzed county-level voting and demographic data for five states, Illinois, Indiana, Michigan, Ohio, and Wisconsin, from 1848 through 1936, and minor civil division data for three states, Michigan, Ohio, and Wisconsin, from 1870 to 1900. Through a systematic, multivariate analysis of these data, it is possible to describe the social bases of party support in terms of class, ethnic, and religious factors. It is possible, too, to determine *when* political realignment began and *which groups* were responsible for it.

I

Between 1860 and 1892 the gap between Republican and Democratic party percentages in the Midwest narrowed considerably. As the data in Table 1 illustrate, by the mid-1880s election results were much closer than they had been for at least two decades, and *neither* major party could command the loyalty of a majority of the region's voters.[7] However, these perceptible changes in the levels of major party support were not the result of a political realignment of social groups. Analysis of minor civil division voting and demographic data affirms the fact that, in general, those groups which had been "very strongly" Republican in the 1860s remained so in 1892, and to about the same degree. The same was true of those social groups which had offered disproportionate support to the Democracy.[8]

Two independent trends operative in the Midwest in the 1870s and 1880s produced the increasingly close balance of political forces. First, the size of the strongly Democratic social groups within the electorate increased at a faster rate than that of the anti-Democratic groups. The resulting increase in the number of Democratic voters *did not* involve the recruitment of converts from the Republican ranks.[9] The second trend ac-

Table 1
Regional Party Mean Percentages

	Democratic	Republican
1860	43.3	53.5
1864	44.7	55.1
1868	45.1	54.7
1872	43.1	55.9
1876	47.5	50.3
1880	43.9	51.7
1884	45.1	49.4
1888	46.1	49.4
1892	46.9	46.6

counts for the declining Republican strength in the region. The emergence of the Prohibition party as a persisting and persevering force in midwestern politics affected the levels of Republican support. Disproportionately, the Prohibitionists drew their voters from the Republican lists. The combined and simultaneous impact of both trends resulted in the narrowed differences between the levels of support drawn by the two major parties.

The crucial point, however, is that the political alignment of social groups was the same at the end of the period as it had been at the beginning. What was the pattern of political behavior that characterized the period 1860 to 1892? The distribution of political support across social groups was not a random one. The social basis of politics had a clear and discernible central tendency. Regardless of degree of economic prosperity or occupational category, irrespective of rural or urban place of residence, those *religious* groups interested in a moral reconstruction of society offered disproportionate support to the Republican party. These *pietistic* religious groups included native born Methodists, Congregationalists, and Presbyterians, acting in unison with Norwegian and Swedish Lutherans, Dutch Reformed voters, and Germans who were Methodists, United Brethren, or members of the Evangelical Association. The Democracy was a social coalition of Catholic voters, of all types of ethnicity, a small majority of German Lutherans, and voters with southern kin-group connections.

This polarization of religious groups can most conveniently be illustrated by making *relative* estimates of each group's voting percentages. Table 2 presents the relevant information.[10]

What cohesive force enabled such disparate groups to cooperate politically within each of the major parties? More than any other, that force was a general attitude toward *social control*; and that attitude, in turn, derived from religious perspectives.

The Republican support groups shared in common a pietistic religious perspective which impelled them to *re-form* society, to purge it of godlessness. These were groups whose religious values inclined them to activism, predisposed them to reach out and try to change the world, to bring it into conformity with their conception of the good and moral society. They aimed at extending their own canons of social behavior to the broader society through measures such as prohibitory legislation and laws keeping holy the Sabbath. Collectively, they could support the Republican party as the "party of great moral ideas."

The groups supporting the Democracy shared in common the status of "reformee." It

Table 2
Estimated Party Percentages, 1870-1892
by Ethnocultural Groups

	"Immigrants"			*"Natives"*	
	Dem.	*Rep.*		*Dem.*	*Rep.*
Irish Catholic	95.0	5.0	Methodist	10.0	90.0
Polish Catholic	95.0	5.0	Congregational	10.0	90.0
German Catholic	85.0	15.0	Presbyterian	30.0	70.0
Bohemian Catholic	80.0	20.0	Baptist	45.0	55.0
German Lutheran	55.0	45.0			
German Reformed	55.0	45.0			
			Southern Stock		
German Sectarians	35.0	65.0	Presbyterian	55.0	45.0
Dutch Reformed	30.0	70.0	Baptists	60.0	40.0
Norwegian Lutheran	30.0	70.0	Disciples	60.0	40.0
Swedish Lutheran	10.0	90.0			
Irish Protestant	5.0	95.0			

was *their* social customs and mores which the pietists sought to change. They also shared a ritualistic religious perspective, one which emphasized intellectual assent to formal doctrine and traditional confessions. Their religious values imbued them with a passive social orientation, one which saw the world as sinful, but accepted it as such. It was to conserve this religious value system that they turned to the Democracy as "the party of personal liberty."

It was not the events of the 1870s or 1880s which had produced these political coalitions of social groups. The functional realignment of the 1850s had been responsible for that.[11] The political contests of the three subsequent decades served to reactivate latent party loyalties and to reinforce these partisan commitments. Whether the battle was over a Sunday-closing law, a local option measure, laws aimed at closing the parochial schools, Bible reading in the public schools, or the election of Catholics to local school boards, the effect was to perpetuate a partisan division of social groups which accorded, not with class differences or differences in ethnicity, but with differing religious perspectives.

This was the political division of social groups at the beginning of the 1890s. By 1900 the social bases of politics differed markedly from that which had persisted for nearly half a century. The voting shifts of the 1890s altered the political juxtaposition of social groups. Those which had been strongly Democratic prior to 1892 were less strongly so, or even mildly anti-Democratic, eight years later. Conversely, groups which had been steadfastly anti-Democratic showed a greater propensity to move in the direction of the Democracy than the party's usual supporters.

The political realignment of social groups which occurred during the 1890s was not solely the product of the Bryan-McKinley confrontation. It was produced by two different types of political change.

The first of these shifts began under the impact of an urban-industrial depression.

What started as a financial panic on Wall Street in the late spring of 1893 broadened, by the early summer, into a major depression. Indices of factory employment began to drop in June, and the rate of decline increased in July and August. During the winter of 1893-94 unemployment hovered around three million, and was sustained at that level throughout most of the following year.[12]

This economic downturn depressed the political fortunes of the Democracy. In the 53rd Congress, elected in 1892, 61.2% of the members of the House of Representatives were Democrats. In the 1894 Congressional elections the Democrats lost 113 seats in the House, and were reduced to only 29.4% of the membership in the 54th Congress.[13] Democratic losses in the Midwest were diffused throughout the region. The 1894 Democratic regional mean vote was 9.9 percentage points below its 1892 level, and 6.1 percentage points lower than the previous nadir in 1872. The party suffered declines among all types of social groups. Regardless of ethnic group or religious orientation, irrespective of place of residence, type of occupation, or degree of economic prosperity, voters reacted negatively to the "party of hard times".[14]

This was the political context in which Bryan and McKinley contested for the Presidency in 1896. Bryan was the standard bearer of a party which had already been reduced to a minority position, and McKinley was the nominee of a party which had benefited from the negative reaction of voters to the "party of depression." But the 1896 voter movement was not simple continuation of that which had characterized the 1894 elections. As the data in Table 3 indicate, the distributions of the changes in the two adjacent pairs of elections correlate negatively. Thus, the 1894-96 changes in the percentage strength of the contesting parties did not generally occur in the same units as had the 1892-94 changes.

Table 3
Intra-Party First Difference Correlations,
1892-94 with 1894-96

	Michigan	Ohio	Wisconsin
Democratic	−.548	−.773	−.088
Republican	−.075	−.644	−.261

Midwestern Democratic percentage strength in 1896 increased over the disastrously low levels of 1894. The party's regional mean rose from 37.0% to 43.6%. But the spatial distribution of the Democratic gains displays an unexpected pattern. The sharpest gains came in areas which had been traditionally anti-Democratic. In Michigan, for example, the most pronounced Democratic gains, 21.6 and 15.5 percentage points, came in Republican strongholds in the Old Stock and Dutch counties. In Ohio the Democracy registered its strongest gains in the counties which constituted bastions of Republicanism; the party gained 15.7 percentage points in the Western Reserve, and 14.4 percentage points in the counties of the Ohio Land Company Purchase. At the same time, Bryan's Democracy continued to lose support in areas populated by normally strong Democratic voter groups. Even the steadfast who had resisted the 1893-94 movement shifted away from the "new Democracy."

The 1896 movement was a bi-polar one. One set of social groups moved towards

Bryan's Democracy; and another moved away from it. That observation is not very arresting in itself, but it becomes so when one realizes that the movement was precisely what would *not* have been expected on the basis of a knowledge of previous partisan identifications. The groups reacting most negatively to Bryan were precisely the ones which had been consistently loyal to the Democracy, the party of "personal liberty," for half a century; and the groups offering new support to Bryan were the ones which had been most strongly anti-Democratic. Expressed in specific terms, those groups which offered lower levels of support to the Democrats in 1896 than they had in either 1894 *or* 1892 included German Lutherans and Catholics of all ethnic varities, except the Irish. Bryan drew greater support than had any nineteenth-century Democratic candidate among native Methodists, Norwegian and Swedish Lutherans, Dutch Reformed voters, and German Evangelicals.[15] The correlational data for Michigan in Table 4 provide a clear illustration of the changed nature of the Democracy's social coalition.[16]

Table 4
Correlations of Democratic Percentage Strength with
Selected Demographic Characteristics: Michigan, 1892 and 1896

	1892	*1896*
Percent Lutheran	+.592	−.067
Percent Catholic	+.600	−.289
Percent Norwegian	−.618	+.052
Percent Protestant	−.312	+.443

Contrary to the usual "explanations," the outcome of the 1896 election cannot be understood in terms of conflicting class, or economic, identifications among voter groups. While Bryan's campaign strategy and rhetoric were designed to unite the "toiling masses" into a political coalition against the Republicans, this attempt to attract urban workers and farmers as *economic* groups, to produce a class polarization in politics, failed.

The political configuration which Bryan envisaged did not involve an *extension* of the old social bases of political action, but the creation of an entirely new one. Late nineteenth-century voting behavior was not significantly determined by differences in relative degrees of economic prosperity. To polarize voting behavior along economic lines required that large numbers of voters not only accept a new set of priorities, one which placed economic considerations above ethnic and religious ones, but that they structure entirely new political perspectives. Essentially, Bryan was asking Democrats to view their party, not as a preserver of their religious value system, not in the way in which they had seen it since the 1850's, but as a vehicle through which they could implement class objectives. His aim was to orient traditional Democrats to a pattern of values and a basis of party identifications which was specifically in conflict with their time-honored political perspective and its attendant values and definitions. In formal terms, such rhetoric was disruptive rather than reactivating.[17]

Instead of polarizing politics along class lines, the Bryan-McKinley confrontation elicited a voter response along *cultural lines*, but in a way that cut across long-standing partisan *identifications*. While depression and unemployment had shaken the loyalty of large numbers of Democratic voters in 1893 and 1894, those least affected had been the

German Lutheran and Catholic voters. As long as the Democracy remained a political vehicle through which to defend religious values, these groups remained committed. It was only when they perceived that the Democracy had ceased to fulfill that function, when they perceived that it was no longer the defender of "personal liberty," that they broke away from their political allegiance, rejected the "Democracy of Bryan," and turned to the Republicanism of McKinley.

II

Any realistic model designed to explain the results of the 1896 election must take into account three significant findings. First, voter groups which had been anti-Democratic for over fifty years offered *greater than usual* support to Bryan. Second, strong Democratic voter groups gave *lower levels of support* to Bryan than they had to earlier Democratic candidates. Third, these usually Democratic voter groups opted, not for a third party or non-voting, but for the Republicanism of William McKinley.

Partially, these findings can be explained by the fact that in 1896 the two major parties each projected an image which was at variance with its historical role. In the hands of William Jennings Bryan, the Democracy was not the "traditional Democracy," not the party of the "saloon interests" and the Catholics, but a vehicle through which those groups interested in a moral reconstitution of society would pursue their goals. The Republican party of McKinley was not the agency of rabid evangelical Protestantism that had housed the temperance, sabbatarian, and abolitionist crusaders of the 1850's; instead, it was an integrative mechanism whose leaders sought to minimize latent cultural animosities in order to broaden its social base of support.[18] To a major extent, these "new departures" mirrored the political and social backgrounds and commitments of each party's nominee.

Bryan had been born and reared in Salem, in Marion county, Illinois. His perspective, especially his religious outlook, was rooted in this small-town, evangelical Protestant background. That religious perspective was one which focused on the integral connection between *right belief* and *right behavior*. The Christian did not compartmentalize his behavior, he did not demarcate between the secular and the spiritual; rather, he evaluated all activities in terms of their consonance with God's maxims.

From the blending of the emotionalism of the Methodist with the Calvinistic doctrine of man's natural depravity, Bryan's religious perspective attained social relevance. He viewed "progress" as the establishment of a truly religious relationship between God and man. Society would steadily march toward "progress" but for man's depravity and the plethora of the devil's temptations in the world about him. The Christian's duty was to abolish these temptations, to create a "safe" atmosphere for the religious and the potentially religious. This was not a passive orientation which accepted the world as it was, but an imperialistic one which sought to change man's behavior, to bring it into conformity with religiously sanctioned norms. It was not that those whose behavior was to be circumscribed would in this way be "saved," but that a pure social atmosphere would be created in which the righteous would not be led astray from the path of "progress." Bryan's religious zeal did not concern itself with uplifting the down-trodden, but with safeguarding and exhaulting the righteous.[19]

This type of perspective, with its emphasis on the "oneness" of all human activity, did not permit Bryan to distinguish readily between "political" and "religious" activities. To him these were two aspects of the same battle, the battle between good and evil, between the Christian and the sources of temptation which abounded in his social environment. Thus, because he did not compartmentalize his behavior, because his religious perspective led him to see the connection between the power of government and the purification of society, Bryan could enter a political battle with the same righteous self-assurance, the same rhetoric, and the same goals, as when he did battle for the literal integrity of Holy Writ against the assaults of the evolutionists. "From the fight against gold to the fight against the ape," there had been no change in Bryan's religious perspective.[20]

Bryan's commitment to the pietistic canons of right behavior stood in sharp contrast to the political attitudes of William McKinley. While of Scotch-Irish ancestry and a communicant in the Methodist Episcopal Church, McKinley did not perceive the same type of inexorable relationship between religious attitudes and secular activity that characterized Bryan's perspective. Bryan's experiences had reinforced his religious values; McKinley's had exerted a cross-pressuring influence.

In Salem, Illinois, a community whose population was a mixture of Baptists, Methodists, and Cumberland Presbyterians, Bryan's personal religious values had found social reinforcement. McKinley spent his early years in Niles, in Trumbull county, and in Poland Village, in Mahoning county. Both of these communities were heterogeneous ones in which there was no commonly shared religious outlook.

Nor did McKinley's involvement in Stark county politics reinforce his religious commitment. The county's voting population included a relatively large proportion of German Lutheran, and German and Irish Catholic voters. As McKinley learned from his successful race for the office of prosecuting attorney in 1869, and his unsuccessful reelection bid in 1871, political success for a Republican in the county depended upon preventing the coalescence of Catholic and German Lutheran voters into a solid voting bloc. This, in turn, meant that Republican politicians had to minimize the pietistic goals with which the party was publicly identified. The party had to be used not as an ideological vehicle though which pietistic groups could seek the implementation of their norms of right behavior, but as an integrative one enlisting the support of a broad range of social groups.

That pietistic voters frequently perceived themselves to be Bryan's "kind of people," while religious ritualists rejected him for McKinley's Republicanism, can only be partially explained by the social and political backgrounds of the candidates, the perspectives to which these gave rise, and the personal images which they projected. These were important elements, but they were relatively less important in evoking a voter response than other considerations.

That Bryan could draw new support from normally anti-Democratic voter groups was due, not merely to his personal image, but to the functional affinity and organizational relationships which existed between the Bryan movement and older norm-oriented movements. The movement of former Prohibition party voters and the "1892 Populists" into the Democratic ranks accounted for the major portion of the new strength which Bryan brought to the Democracy. These were voters who shared a common pietistic religious perspective, and who sought to implement their religious values through political action. Precisely because they had perceived relatively little hope of realizing their goals through the major political parties, they had earlier rejected them and turned instead to minor party organization. In 1896 the Bryan candidacy gave them new hope. They turned to

Bryan because they saw in his evangelism their best hope for reconstituting the social order to conform to their religious norms. They were responsive to Bryan because he, as they, did not seek to structure a *new* set of social values, but to restore an older one. He, as they, sought the restoration of the moral society.[21]

In 1896 there was more than inchoate affinity among "reform" groups. Organizations and leaders who had endorsed the "cold water" cause and had long been identified with it came to the support of Bryan's Democracy. Of greater consequence in the actual mobilization of voters was the fusion not only between the Democrats and Populists, but at the county-level between Democrats and Prohibitionists.[22] This enabled Prohibition party voters who were attracted to Bryan to cast a straight ticket for him and at the same time to give support to their own local leaders. It also meant that the local Prohibitionists could cooperate with the Democrats in enlisting support for Bryan without weakening their own local party structure.

While later historians have concentrated on the economic nature of the Bryan crusade, his contemporary supporters showed a greater interest in its moral aspects. Populist and Prohibition papers in the Midwest, which supported Bryan, identified him with pietistic virtues; denounced the "saloon power," with which they claimed McKinley was identified; and argued that Bryan's election would guarantee the advent of "a grander civilization," of the "moral society." The party which they had characterized in 1894 as the "party of corruption," the "Catholic party," in 1896 they hailed as the "party of piety."

While enlisting new supporters from the ranks of the pietists, Bryan was uniquely unsuccessful in holding the loyalties of normally Democratic voter groups. For over fifty years Catholic and German Lutheran voters, religious ritualists, had been steadfastly Democratic. This commitment was the political expression of their religious perspective. From that perspective, one which concentrated on *right belief* as opposed to *right behavior*, they did not regard as sinful those social customs which pietists, in the name of morality, sought to eradicate. The repeated conflicts between the two types of religious groups, although occurring over a variety of substantive issues, were ones between two divergent sets of religious values. Each group sought to use the political·structure of society to resolve the conflict in its favor. As the pietists sought government *action* to create the moral society, the anti-pietists espoused government *inaction* as a means of resisting such encroachments. The old personal liberty theme of the Democracy was at once an apt political expression of the religious perspective of the ritualists and a voter mobilization ideology through which that perspective could be translated into a partisan commitment. In 1896 it was precisely because ritualists perceived that the Democracy had ceased to be the "old Democracy," had ceased to be the defender of "personal liberty" and negative government, that they rejected it.

Because they were relatively more concerned with conversion than with reinforcement of old commitments, both Bryan and his midwestern supporters deemphasized their Democratic lineage and their connections with the old Democratic ideology. The image they projected of themselves was not that of "negative government," but of a government dedicated to the use of *positive action* to remedy social inequalities. This was not the Democracy whose usual program was a litany of "thou shalt nots," but a Democracy espousing that very type of government which for over half a century had repelled religious ritualists.[23]

Democratic voters were not very likely to expose themselves to campaign propaganda emanating from Prohibition and Populist sources. It is reasonable to assume that their exposure was to partisan Democratic sources. Most of the regular Democratic papers in the Midwest opposed Bryan in 1896. The fact that they devoted a significant proportion of their symbolism to projecting basically the same *kind* of image of Bryan as did those organs which supported him is highly important. It suggests that the old-line Democratic strategists, aware of the underlying reasons for the commitment of voter groups to their party, saw in the pro-Bryan themes much that would repel normally Democratic voters. It suggests that the very causes which led pietistic voters to respond favorably were the ones which induced religious ritualists to reject Bryan.

When anti-Bryan Democratic papers set out to attack the candidate's free silver program, they did not deal solely with economic arguments. Instead, they argued that Bryan was not a "real" Democrat, and that free silver was not a Democratic doctrine. This line of attack implies that these strategists were relatively less concerned with the appeal of free silver as an economic ideology to normally Democratic voters than they were with that of party identification. Since they aimed at defeating Bryan, they concentrated on undermining his identification *as a Democrat.* The specific line of argument which they used for that purpose is revealing. Stripped of its hyperbolic allusions, these anti-Bryan Democratic papers presented an argument with whose essence the Bryanites could have agreed. Bryan was not a Democrat, and his Democracy was not the "old Democracy," they argued, because his program would magnify the regulatory power of government. This was a violation of the "personal liberty" for which the Democratic party had always stood.

That the image of the Democratic party and its nominee in 1896 differed from the traditional image of the party can account both for its ability to attract new support from pietistic groups and its inability to win the usual levels of strength among ritualistic voters. But when religious ritualists were repelled by Bryan's Democracy, they had more than one available alternative. The third important finding derived from the relevant empirical evidence is that these normally Democratic voter groups not only rejected Bryan, but chose the alternative of voting for McKinley. The anti-Bryan Democratic leaders, or "gold bugs" as they were labeled by Bryanites, organized a separate party as a haven for "real" Democratic voters. But despite being provided with this "safe" third party haven, most of the Catholic and German Lutheran voters who abandoned Bryan's Democracy chose to cast a ballot for the Republican party. The decision to support the Republicans was ultimately contingent upon the voter's perception of that party and its image. Two years earlier, in 1894, Democratic Catholic and German Lutheran voters had been the groups least likely to shift to the Republicans. When they defected in 1894, they more often than not sought a third party as a means through which to express their dissatisfaction with the Democracy while not giving a stamp of approval to the Republicans. That they did not react in the same way in 1896 suggests that their perception of the Republican party then was different than it had been in 1894.

Republican party strategists recognized the discontent of these voter groups with Bryan's candidacy and sought to recruit them to support McKinley. Since the 1850s the Republicans had had the support of a strong majority of pietistic voters. The strength of party identification, despite the appeals of the Bryanites, could be counted on to assure that the majority of these would remain loyal. In addition, Republicans attempted to attract Catholic and German Lutheran voters. This type of coalition was possible only if the party's strategists were willing to tolerate a high degree of ideological non-congruence among its subcoalitional elements. This "price" McKinley Republicans were certainly willing to pay.

Throughout the Midwest, and probably elsewhere as well, Republican leaders employed precisely the strategy which McKinley had used successfully in earlier elections in Ohio. They avoided identification with those cultural symbols with which the party had usually identified itself. They presented to defecting Democrats an image of the party as a culturally safe vehicle through which they could express their dissatisfaction with Bryan. Democrats need not reject the Republican party as the "party of pietism." If they could not vote for it as the "party of personal liberty," they could support it as the "party of prosperity." In the hands of McKinley, the Republican party was a much different social organism than it had been in 1892. It was no longer the vehicle of pietism; but an integrative mechanism which sought to avoid subcoalitional conflicts by minimizing cultural questions and addressing itself to a commonly shared concern with "prosperity."

III

The movement of voter groups which characterized the 1896 election was not an ephemeral phenomenon. The change in the social base of support of the two major parties which that movement produced constituted a *persisting* alteration of the preexisting balance of political forces. [24] Since the 1850's pietistic groups had used the Republican party as an agency through which to attain their social goals. Ritualistic religious groups had resisted pietism's encroachments by mobilizing in the ranks of the Democracy. The structure of politics, the pattern of the distribution of partisan support, accorded with this pietistic-ritualistic scale.

The realignment of social groups in the mid-1890s changed the structure of American politics. Pietists were attracted by the strident evangelism and the moral fervor of Bryan's brand of Democracy, and repelled by McKinley's willingness to compromise true morality for the sake of mere votes. The very feature of McKinley Republicanism which led to pietistic disaffection proved attractive to anti-pietistic religious groups. What emerged as a result was a new structure of politics, a new social basis of political action.

But the political realignment of social groups is never accomplished without intraparty pain. This was especially the case for the Republican party. That party's newly won support shared a value system which conflicted with the one held by its old stock leadership. To preserve the social coalition that had produced its electoral majority, the party had to avoid those public issues, such as prohibition, Sunday closing, the school and language questions, which could convert potential conflict into election losses.

Much of the internal combat and political schism that marked the Republican party in the early twentieth century can be traced to this strategy. In Ohio, for example, the Republicans, sensitive to the need for continuing support among German voters in Cincinnati and Cleveland, handled the prohibition question by supporting a local option law favorable to the state's urban centers. Disenchanted with this vacillation on the key moral issue of the day, the state's Anti-Saloon League, between 1904 and 1906, began attaching itself to the Democracy. Ultimately, that party responded to the League's moral overtures by nominating a "dry" for governor.

The subsequent voter shifts and countershifts usually have been explained, in the rhetoric of the alleged "Progressive Era," as public responses to "regulator legislation." Instead, they were the culmination of the realignment of the 1890s, the product of the Republican party's attempts to harmonize its new with its old support groups.

Notes

Author's Note: An earlier version of this essay was presented at the 1968 annual convention of the Midwest Political Science Association. The study was completed on a Social Science Research Council Fellowship.

1. Although it was written over thirteen years ago, Lee Benson's perceptive critique is still relevant; see Benson, "Research Problems in America Political Historiography," in Mirra Komarovsky [ed.], *Common Frontiers in the Social Sciences* (Glencoe, Ill., 1957), pp. 113-183.

2. For early examples of what might be termed the "Schurz syndrome," see W. Hense-Jensen, "Influence of the Germans in Wisconsin," *Proceedings of the Wisconsin State Historical Society* (1902), p. 145; and F. I. Heriott, "The Germans of Chicago and Stephen A. Douglas in 1854," *Deutsch-Amerikanische Geschichtsblatter*, XII (1912), 381. For an empirically based corrective, see Paul Kleppner, "Lincoln and the Immigrant Vote: A Case of Religious Polarization," *Mid-America*, XLVIII (July, 1966), 176-195.

3. See, for example, the claim by Gilbert G. Fite, "Republican Strategy and the Farm Vote in the Presidential Campaign of 1896," *American Historical Review*, LXV (July, 1960), 804-805. For the relevant empirical data which refute such intuitively derived claims, see Paul Kleppner, "The Politics of Change in the Midwest: The 1890's in Historical and Behavioral Perspective" (unpublished Ph.D. dissertation, University of Pittsburgh, 1967), pp. 35-44. For conceptual clarification of the problem of agrarian political involvement, see Ronald P. Formisano and William G. Shade, "The Concept of Agrarian Radicalism," *Mid-America*, LII (January, 1970), 3-30.

4. For the conditions requisite to issue-oriented voting, see Angus Campbell, Philip E. Converse, Warren E. Miller, and Donald E. Stokes, *The American Voter* (New York, 1960), pp. 169-171.

5. The concept of a "critical," or realigning, election was first developed by V. O. Key, Jr., "A Theory of Critical Elections," *Journal of Politics*, XVII (February, 1955), 3-18.

6. For a much more detailed demonstration and discussion of the matters dealt with here, see Paul Kleppner, *The Cross of Culture: A Social Analysis of Midwestern Politics, 1850-1900* (New York, 1970).

7. The election and demographic data used in this study are from the Historical Data Archives, Inter-University Consortium for Political Research, University of Michigan.

8. For the relevant data demonstrating the point, see Kleppner, "The Politics of Change," pp. 54-105. Operationally, the term "very strongly" Republican (or Democratic) is defined here as 65.0%, or more, Republican (or Democratic); for an elaboration of this type of operational definition as applied to varying levels of party percentage strength, see Lee Benson, *The Concept of Jacksonian Democracy: New York as a Test Case* (1st Atheneum ed.; New York, 1964), p. 138.

9. Samuel T. McSeveney, "The Politics of Depression: Voting Behavior in Connecticut, New York, and New Jersey, 1893-1896" (unpublished Ph.D. dissertation, University of Iowa, 1965), pp. 34-42, documents a similar demographic trend in three eastern states.

10. These estimated party percentages have been arrived at by systematically examining minor civil division voting and demographic data, and by taking into account contemporary estimates of partisan

support. Such figures, however, should not be construed literally. An estimate, for example, of 90.0% Democratic does not mean that 9 of 10 members of the group invariably voted Democratic; but it does mean that the group was more Democratic than one to which an estimate of 70.0% is assigned. For a discussion of this point and of the utility of making such estimates, see Benson, *Jacksonian Democracy*, pp. 167 and 184-185.

The estimated party percentages assigned to the German Lutheran group conceal a very wide range of variation within the group; see Kleppner, *Cross of Culture*, pp. 42-49.

11. On the realignment of the 1850's, see Ronald P. Formisano, "Egalitarians and Evangelicals: Voters and Parties, Michigan, 1835-1861" (unpublished ms, 1969), Sandra Alexandra McCoy, "The Political Affiliations of American Economic Elites: Wayne County, Michigan, 1844, 1860, as a Test Case" (unpublished Ph.D. dissertation, Wayne State University, 1965), and Roger D. Petersen, "A Revolution in Political Preferences: The North, 1848-1860" (unpublished Ph.D. dissertation, University of Pittsburgh, 1970).

12. On the extent and severity of the depression, see Charles Hoffmann, "The Depression of the Nineties—An Economic History" (unpublished Ph.D. dissertation, Columbia University, 1954) and Douglas W. Steeples, "Five Troubled Years: A History of the Depression of 1893-1897" (unpublished Ph.D. dissertation, University of North Carolina, 1961).

13. In the 52nd Congress, elected in 1890, 70.8% of the members of the House of Representatives were Democrats, as were 48.9% of the House members in the 51st Congress. Prior to 1894 the Democrats had failed to elect 30.0% of the House membership only in 1860, 1864, 1866, and 1868. The data on party affiliation in Congress are from U.S. Bureau of the Census, *Historical Statistics of the United States, Colonial Times to 1957* (Washington, D.C., 1960), pp. 691-692.

14. Not all social groups moved away from the Democracy *at the same rate*; nor did all defecting voters select the *same* political alternative. For the empirical data which specify the variations in rate of change among social groups, see Kleppner, "The Politics of Change," pp. 283-394.

15. This does not mean to imply that such voting units necessarily gave Bryan a majority of their vote; or even that *all* such units gave him a higher percentage than they had given Democratic candidates in 1892. It is simply a description of the *central tendency* of the voting behavior of these groups.

16. These are Pearson product-moment correlations of county level data. For the computation and interpretation of the statistic, see Hubert M. Blalock, Jr., *Social Statistics* (New York, 1960), pp. 273-325. For the problems which inhere in the substantive interpretation of correlational data, see W. S. Robinson, "Ecological Correlations and the Behavior of Individuals," *American Sociological Review*, XV (June 1950), 351-357; and especially Paul F. Lazarsfeld and Herbert Menzel, "On the Relation Between Individual and Collective Properties," in Amitai Etzioni (ed.), *Complex Organizations: A Sociological Reader* (New York, 1961), pp. 422-440, and W. Phillips Shively, " 'Ecological' Inference: The Use of Aggregate Data to Study Individuals," *American Political Science Review*, LXIII (December, 1969), 1183-1196.

17. I am adapting here the distinctions which Talcott Parsons makes among propaganda which is revolutionary, disruptive, or reinforcing, to the analytical categoreis which political scientists and sociologists have used to describe political propaganda. It is important to emphasize that this is primarily a semantic adaptation of an analytical typology which has far more extensive application than to campaign rhetoric. See Parsons, *Essays in Sociological Theory* (Free Press ed.; New York, 1964), pp. 142-176; also see James O. Whittaker, "Cognitive Dissonance and the Effectiveness of Persuasive Communications," *Public Opinion Quarterly*, XXVIII (Winter, 1964), 547-555.

18. On the coalitional concept of party, see Samuel J. Eldersveld, *Political Parties: A Behavioral Analysis* (Chicago, 1964).

19. This type of perspective parallels that which Joseph R. Gusfield, *Symbolic Crusade: Status Politics and the American Temperance Movement* (Urbana, 1963), pp. 87-117, attributes to the "coercive reformer." That congruence is extremely significant in accounting for Bryan's attractiveness to prohibition groups.

20. The phrase is quoted from Richard Hofstadter, *The American Political Tradition and the Men Who Made It* (Vintage Books ed.; New York, n.d.), p. 205; his essay, "William Jennings Bryan: The Democrat as Revivalist," pp. 186-205, is a highly perceptive one.

21. For the affinity among participants in norm-oriented movements which share a common value system, see Neil J. Smelser, *Theory of Collective Behavior* (New York, 1963), pp. 270-312; for the affinity among these particular norm-oriented movements, see Gusfield, *Symbolic Crusade*, pp. 111-165.

22. For the details of this county level fusion, see the local reports which appeared in the *Detroit Free Press, Milwaukee Sentinel, Milwaukee Journal,* and *Cleveland Plain Dealer*, August-October, 1896. The requisite data are not extant to make possible a *systematic* assessment of the extent of this local fusion.

23. These conclusions derive from content analysis of the relevant national and state platforms for 1892, 1894, and 1896, the texts of Bryan's midwestern campaign addresses, and the campaign propaganda disseminated by party organs.

24. For the data which establish the point, see Kleppner, *Cross of Culture*, pp. 269-279, and especially Table 34, p. 278.

The new empire

Walter LaFeber

After its early decades of aggressive continental expansionism, the United States after the Civil War lapsed into the status of a "satisfied" power, without evident interest in further territorial acquisition and disinclined to take an active part in world affairs. Then, in the late 1890s, the country suddenly embarked on a new period of expansion, annexing Hawaii and, in the aftermath of the war with Spain, acquiring Puerto Rico and the Philippines, and making Cuba a virtual dependency. The reasons for this imperial adventure have been puzzling to historians. The Marxist line of analysis seemed not to fit the American situation. In his *Expansionists of 1898*, Julius Pratt demonstrated that American business on the whole opposed the war with Spain. And it was not, in any case, clear precisely what economic benefits were to be derived from the new possessions. So historians turned to noneconomic explanations, stressing public opinion, the tensions generated by urbanism and economic depression, the revival of Mainifest Destiny in a new guise, and the application of social Darwinian ideas to racial thinking and to world affairs.

In the following selection from his recent book *The New Empire*, Walter LaFeber returns to an economic analysis, but of a new and more subtle kind. LaFeber argues that American imperialism was not (and is not) "colonialist" in character, that is, it was not aimed at the acquisition of territory for its own sake, but rather as a means to gain access to foreign markets for American goods. Nor were the new possessions important as markets in themselves, but as strategic points necessary for penetrating Asia and Latin America. As for the fact that foreign trade was relatively unimportant to the American industrial economy at this period, LaFeber finds that American interest was in *future* markets, and that what made this concern compelling was a widespread anxiety over social instability at home. The American economy had fallen periodically into depression, which in turn triggered strikes and social unrest. Since unemployment was the cause, the solution seemed to be assured access to foreign markets for American production. This line of reasoning, LaFeber claims, influenced a small circle of American expansionists from the 1870s onward. Then, in the 1890s, with the discovery that the American

Reinterpreted from Walter LaFever, *The New Empire: an Interpretation of American Expansion, 1860-1898*, pp. 407-417. Copyright © 1963 by the American Historical Association. Used by permission of Cornell University Press.

frontier had ended and with the onset of another severe depression and its attendant troubles, the expansionist argument gained a wide vogue and led directly to the imperial adventure of 1898. LaFeber does not deny the existence of other varieties of expansionist thinking, but he skillfully demonstrates that power strategists such as Admiral Mahan and moralistic imperialists such as Josiah Strong actually incorporated the economic analysis in their own advocacy of expansionism. In fact, LaFeber argues that even the anti-imperialists shared the economic assumptions of the imperialists in the late 1890s. The only difference was over strategy: the anti-imperialists rejected the necessity of territorial expansion as a means of gaining access to overseas markets.

LaFeber reflects the current New Left interest in exploring the dark side of the American past, but his work is exceptional for the subtlety of its argument and its sensitivity to the nuances of historical reality. What remains open to question is whether LaFeber is describing a central cause of American expansionism or a peripheral one. His analysis rests on an assumption of widely felt anxiety about the stability of the American social order in the Gilded Age. And, given the sense of optimism and progress that other historians have perceived in this era, that thinly explored claim demands further investigation.

For further reading: Julius Pratt, *The Expansionists of 1898* (1964);* Ernest R. May *Imperial Democracy* (1961); Foster R. Dulles, *Prelude to World Power: American Diplomatic History, 1860-1900* (1965); D. M. Pletcher, *The Awkward Years: American Foreign Relations under Garfield and Arthur* (1961); Robert L. Beisner, *Twelve Against Empire: the Anti-Imperialists, 1898-1900,* (1968);* Lee Benson, "The Historical Background of Turner's Frontier Essay," *Agricultural History*, XXIV (1951), 59-82; Dorothy R. Muller, "Josiah Strong and American Nationalism: A Reevaluation," *Journal of American History*, LIII (1966), 487-403.

In his classic autobiography, Henry Adams recalls sitting at John Hay's table and discussing "the Philippines as a question of balance of power in the East" with members of the British cabinet. Adams suddenly realized "that the family work of a hundred and fifty years fell at once into the grand perspective of true empire-building, which Hay's work [in the Far East] set off with artistic skill." In less than a century and a quarter the United States had developed from thirteen states strung along a narrow Atlantic coastline into a great world power with possessions in the far Pacific.

Until the middle of the nineteenth century this had been, for the most part, a form of landed expansion which had moved over a large area of the North American continent. The Louisiana Purchase in 1803 had been followed by further important acquisitions in 1819, 1848, 1853, and 1867. But when William H. Seward entered the State Department in 1861, the nature of American expansion had begun to change. Under the impact of the industrial revolution Americans began to search for markets, not land. Sometimes the State Department seized the initiative in making the search, as in the Harrison administration. Frequently the business community pioneered in extending the interests of the United States into foreign areas, as in Mexico in the 1870's and in China in the 1890's. Regardless of which body led the expansionist movement, the result was the same: the growth of economic interests led to political entanglements and to increased military responsibilities.

Americans attempted to build a new empire, an empire which differed fundamentally from the colonial holdings of European powers. Until 1898 the United States believed that its political institutions were suitable only for the North American continent. Many policy makers and important journalists warned that extra-continental holdings would wreck the American republic just as they had ruined the Roman republic. Such sentiment helped to prevent the acquisition of Hawaii in 1893.

In 1898, however, the United States annexed Hawaii and demanded the Philippines from Spain. These acquisitions were not unheralded. Seward had pushed his nation's claims far out into the Pacific with the purchase of Alaska and the Midway islands. Fish, Evarts, Bayard, Blaine, and Cleveland had maintained a tight hold on Pago Pago in Samoa, although they strongly disliked the political entanglements with England and Germany which were necessarily part of the bargain.

One striking characteristic tied these acquisitions to the new territory brought under American control in 1898 and 1899, immediately after the war with Spain. The United States obtained these areas not to fulfill a colonial policy, but to use these holdings as a means to acquire markets for the glut of goods pouring out of highly mechanized factories and farms.

The two acquisitions which might be considered exceptions to this statement are Alaska and Hawaii. It is most difficult, however, to understand the purchase of "Seward's Icebox" without comprehending the Secretary of State's magnificent view of the future American commercial empire. This view did not premise a colonial policy, but assumed the necessity of controlling the Asian markets for commercial, not political, expansion. As the chairman of the House Foreign Affairs Committee commented in 1867, Alaska was the "drawbridge" between the North American continent and Asia.

Hawaii had become an integral part of the American economy long before Harrison attempted to annex it in 1893. Missionaries had forged strong religious and secular links between the islands and the mainland, but of much more importance were the commercial ties. After the reciprocity treaty of 1875 the United States possessed a virtual veto power over Hawaii's relations with foreign powers. American capital, especially attracted by the islands' fertility during the depression years that plagued the mainland in the 1870's and 1880's, developed sugar plantations whose prosperity depended upon the American consumer. Exports of finished industrial goods left United States ports in increasing amounts for Hawaiian consumers. When the 1890 tariff severely retarded the export of Hawaiian sugar, American exports moved without abatement into the islands. The economic expansion of the United States, in terms of both capital and goods, had tied Hawaii irrevocably to the mainland.

By 1893 only the political tie remained to be consummated. The United States enjoyed the benefits of Hawaiian trade without the burdens of governmental responsibilities. But in five years the situation changed. Regaining confidence in American political institutions as the depression lessened in severity, and fearful of Japanese control, the McKinley administration attempted to annex the islands in 1897-1898. But one other factor was also of prime importance. American interests in Asia suddenly assumed much significance. And in this new framework, the Isthmian canal project gained added importance and support, for many expansionists believed the canal to be absolutely necessary if the eastern and Gulf states hoped to compete in Asian markets. As Senator John T. Morgan, Alfred Thayer Mahan, and Senator Cushman Davis noted, Hawaii was essential if the United States was to safeguard the Pacific approaches to the canal. When the Senate Foreign Relations Committee issued its majority report in March, 1898, which advocated annexation by joint resolution, the committee argued that the strategic position of Hawaii was "the main argument in favor of the annexation" plan. This, the report explained, meant not only the shielding of the western coast of the United States, but the "efficient protection" of American commerce as well. This report also noted the irrelevance of one of the antiannexationist arguments, then combined the strategic factor with the fear of Japanese encroachment as reasons for annexation: "The issue in Hawaii is not between monarchy and the Republic. That issue has been settled. . . . The issue is whether, in that inevitable struggle, Asia or America shall have the vantage ground of the control of the naval 'Key of the Pacific,' the commercial 'Cross-roads of the Pacific.' "[1]

The administration forces finally won their objective during the summer of 1898. By July both the business community and policy makers had fully realized the value of Asia as a potential area for American financial and commercial expansion. The operations of Admiral George Dewey in the Philippines had, moreover, taught Americans that Hawaii was absolutely essential as a coaling station and naval base if the United States hoped to become a dominant force in the Far East.

The Philippines marked the next step westward. In 1899 the Secretary of the American Asiatic Association analyzed the reason for the annexation of these islands in a single sentence: "Had we no interests in China, the possession of the Philippines would be meaningless." Mark Hanna, a somewhat more objective observer of the Far East than the gentleman just quoted, also desired "a strong foothold in the Philippine Islands," for then "we can and will take a large slice of the commerce of Asia. That is what we want. We are bound to share in the commerce of the Far East, and it is better to strike for it while the iron is hot." The interests of missionaries and of investors who believed the islands had great natural wealth no doubt encouraged McKinley to demand the Philippines. But it should be noted that, when the President first formulated his peace terms, he wanted the islands to "remain with Spain, except a port and necessary appurtenances to be selected by the United States." He changed this view only when convinced that Manila would be insecure and indefensible unless the United States annexed the remainder of the islands. Mahan had followed similar reasoning to reach the same conclusion. The key to the Philippine policy of both men was their view of Manila as a way station to the Orient.[2]

Throughout the 1890's, debate had raged around the desirability of annexing yet another outlying possession. The growing desire for an American-controlled Isthmian canal partially explains the interest Hawaii held for some Americans. But it should be emphasized that in the 1890's, at least, Americans did not define their interests in a future canal as military; they termed these interests as economic. Policy makers viewed the control of strategic areas such as Hawaii or Guantánamo Bay in the same light as they viewed the Philippines, that is, as strategic means to obtaining and protecting objectives which they defined as economic. Few persons discussed the military aspects of the canal, and to interpret American expansion into the Pacific and the Caribbean as expansion for *merely* strategic objectives distorts the true picture. Most of those who were concerned with a canal agreed with McKinley's statement in his annual message of 1897: the Nicaragua canal would be of "utility and value to American commerce." The foremost advocate of a Central American passageway, Senator Morgan, constantly discussed the canal's value in economic terms.[3]

American control of these areas followed logically if two assumptions were granted: first, the general consensus reached by the American business community and policy makers in the mid-1890's that additional foreign markets would solve the economic, social, and political problems created by the industrial revolution; and, second, the growing belief that, however great its industrial prowess, the United States needed strategic bases if it hoped to compete successfully with government-supported European enterprises in Asia and Latin America. The *Journal of Commerce* summarized opinion on the first point when it remarked in early 1895 that "within the last half century" the industrial and transportation revolutions had made it a fact that "we are a part of 'abroad.' " Commenting upon one aspect of the frontier thesis, this journal warned that the nation was no longer "a vast public domain awaiting agriculture"; as a result of this transformation, Americans could not afford "to imagine that we can maintain ourselves in isolation from the rest of the commercial world."[4]

Almost all Americans agreed on this first assumption. It was only on the second (how the United States could best protect its commercial interests abroad), that important disagreement flared. Walter Quintin Gresham, Edward Atkinson, and Carl Schurz were three of the leaders of the antiannexationist cause, but they were also strong advocates of increased commercial expansion. This point became evident when Atkinson and Schurz had to defend their ideals after the Spanish-American War. Atkinson presented his case through the pages of his periodical, *The Anti-Imperialist*. He admitted at the outset that "the export demand is the balance-wheel of the whole traffic of this country," but he believed that the largest demand would be found in Europe, not in the Pacific area. He had to face the fact, however, that many Americans did believe the Far East to be of great importance, and he attempted to destroy their premises by pointing out that the Philippines bought only $100,000 worth of goods from the United States each year. This was quite beside the point as far as the new empire expansionists were concerned. Atkinson began to see the weakness of his argument and countered with an attack which struck closer to the annexationists' theme: the Philippines, Atkinson remarked, could be maintained as a "sanctuary of commerce" without American involvement. Once he had gone this far, however, he had granted the McKinley forces their major assumption.[5]

Schurz developed his case in more detail. In a speech of August 19, 1898, he noted a report from the Foreign Commerce desk of the State Department which demanded more foreign markets. "I fully agree," Schurz said. "We cannot have too many. But can such markets be opened only by annexing to the United States the countries in which they are situated?" This was his first mistake. Few people, other than some missionaries, viewed the Philippines as a great market. Certainly the McKinley administration did not. Schurz then made his second mistake when he repeated his staple argument that if the Philippines remained neutral, "we shall not only be able to get coaling-stations and naval depots wherever we may want them, but we shall qualify ourselves for that position which is most congenial to our democratic institutions." Other Americans were not as certain that such naval bases could be protected in the face of European encroachment, and this doubt had become stronger since the continental powers had shown their hands in China in late 1897 and early 1898. Annexationists could legitimately ask Schurz what power the United States could use if other nations used force or disciminatory methods to exclude Americans from Asian markets. Schurz replied in a letter to McKinley on June 1, 1898, that the nation could use the immense moral power inherent in posing as "the *great neutral Power of the world*." He could find no better answer, and to these policy makers, schooled in the theories of Mahan, the answer was insufficient. In their eyes Schurz had granted the common premise of the necessity for commercial expansion, and then had made the two crucial errors of, first, utterly confusing the strategic, new empire policies of McKinley with the colonial policies of European powers; and, second, believing that such commercial expansion could be continued without defensible strategic bases.[6]

Thus when the debates began on the annexation of Hawaii and the Philippines, the antiannexationists had ironically undercut their own argument. When the minority of the House Foreign Affairs Committee declared that "political dominion" over Hawaii "is not commercially necessary," the majority report replied that a continuation of a protector- ate meant responsibility without control, but by annexation the United States "would assume no more responsibilities, and would acquire absolute control." Under a protector- ate, Hawaii would still remain an incubator of international friction. And when Senator Vest introduced a resolution condemning the annexation of the Philippines, probably the most important of the antiannexationist moves in the Senate, he made the mistake of saying that the federal government could not annex a whole area as a colony, "except such small amount as may be necessary for coaling stations." The McKinley administra- tion could accept this argument and then ask how the coaling station of Manila, for example, could be useful without Luzon, and how Luzon could be defended or main- tained without the remainder of the Philippines.

The principal antiannexationist argument, that the Constitution and traditional Ameri- can society would be ruined by expanding to noncontiguous areas, was, in fact, quite irrelevant granted the common assumption of the need for commercial expansion. By agreeing that a constantly expanding trade was also vital to the economic and political well-being of the nation, the antiannexationists had opened themselves to the devastating counterargument that this trade could not find the crucial markets in Asia and Latin America without the security which the Philippines and Hawaii would provide.[7]

As for the annexationist forces, Lodge could espouse "large policies," but correctly argue, "I do not mean that we should enter on a widely extended system of coloniza- tion." When Alfred Thayer Mahan urged the State Department to demand only Manila in the summer of 1898, he differed little from many antiannexationists. His studies had convinced him, however, that a naval base could be strong and secure only when the hinterland of the base was strong and secure. He would accept the political burdens of the hinterland if this was necessary in order to safeguard the naval base and the trade which depended upon that base. McKinley apparently arrived at the same conclusion in much the same way. The President actually occupied a middle-of-the-road position on the issue, for by the early summer of 1898 some business periodicals, military experts, and such politicians as "Fire Alarm Joe" Foraker of Ohio urged the annexation of other Pacific islands and wanted to renege on the Teller Amendment in order to annex Cuba.[8] The administration's Cuban policy is one of the best examples of the new empire approach. Not wanting the political burdens or the economic competition inherent in annexation, the problem was neatly solved by the Platt Amendment, which gave the Cubans their independence; but the measure also gave to the United States the Guantànamo Naval Base as a safeguard for American interests in the Caribbean, created a Cuban tariff which opened the island to American agricultural and industrial products, and recognized the right of American military intervention in the event that Cuban political life became too chaotic.

It may be suggested that one fruitful way to approach the "imperialist versus anti-imperialist" clash in the 1890's is to view the struggle in terms of a narrow and limited debate on the question of which tactical means the nation should use to obtain commonly desired objectives. Schurz's view of overseas empire differed from that of Mahan's in degree, not in kind. Few Americans believed that the Latin-American and Asian markets were of little importance to the expansive American industrial complex. On the other hand, few agreed with Foraker's intimation that the United States should claim and occupy every piece of available land in the Pacific. The mass opinion fell between these two views, and within that consensus the debate was waged. The fundamental assumptions of the consensus were never fought out. The grace note to this was appropriately supplied by William Jennings Bryan, who first successfully urged that the Philippine annexation measure be passed by Congress, and then tried to use the Philippine issue in the 1900 presidential campaign. He discovered on election night that, whatever the effect of other issues in the campaign, the issue of "imperialism" was apparently of little importance to the voters. McKinley, having solved this problem during the two previous years, had moved so far ahead of Bryan that the distance could be measured in political light years.

By 1899 the United States had forged a new empire. American policy makers and businessmen had created it amid much debate and with conscious purpose. The empire progressed from a continental base in 1861 to assured pre-eminence in the Western Hemisphere in 1895. Three years later it was rescued from a growing economic and political dilemma by the declaration of war against Spain. During and after this conflict the empire moved past Hawaii into the Philippines, and, with the issuance of the Open-Door Notes, enunciated its principles in Asia. The movement of this empire could not be hurried. Harrison discovered this to his regret in 1893. But under the impetus of the effects of the industrial revolution and, most important, *because of the implications for foreign policy which policy makers and businessmen believed to be logical corollaries of this economic change*, the new empire reached its climax in the 1890's. At this point those who possessed a sense of historical perspective could pause with Henry Adams and observe that one hundred and fifty years of American history had suddenly fallen into place. Those who preferred to peer into the dim future of the twentieth century could be certain only that the United States now dominated its own hemisphere and, as Seward had so passionately hoped, was entering as a major power into Asia, "the chief theatre of events in the world's great hereafter."

Notes

1. *Senate Report No. 681*, 55th Cong., 2nd Sess. (serial 3627), 1-119, especially 31; Stevens, *American Expansion in Hawaii*, 297-299; James Harrison Wilson, "America's Interests in China," *North American Review*, CLXVI (February, 1898), 140; *Commercial Advertiser*, Feb. 8, 1898, 6:3; clipping of London *Times*, June 17, 1897, enclosed in Hay to Sherman, June 17, 1897, Great Britain, Despatches, NA, RG 59.

2. Campbell, *Special Business Interests*, 16; memorandum of McKinley's terms, Day to Day, June 4, 1898, copy in Box 185, and Hay to Day, May 18, 1898, Box 185, J. B. Moore MSS; *Economist*, June 11, 1898, 877; F. F. Hilder, "The Philippine Islands," *Forum*, XXV (July, 1898), 534-545; Truxtun

Beale, "Strategical Value of the Philippines," *North American Review*, CLXVI (June, 1898), 759-760; Livermore, "American Naval-Base Policy in the Far East, 1850-1914," 116-117; Philadelphia *Press*, June 29, 1898, 6:3.

3. *Public Opinion*, May 26, 1898, 646; *Congressional Record*, 55th Cong., 2nd Sess., 6 and 3222; Melville, "Our Future on the Pacific," 293-294. There is a good discussion of the canal issue in Campbell, *Special Business Interests*, 14-15.

4. *Journal of Commerce*, Jan. 22, 1895, 4:2-3; also Chapter IV, above.

5. *The Anti-Imperialist*, I, 16, 26-32, 45-46.

6. *Speeches, Correspondence and Political Papers of Carl Schurz*, edited by Frederic Bancroft (New York, 1913), V, 489-490, 473, 476. The same anti-imperialist approach may be found in Oscar Straus to A. D. White, Aug. 1, 1898, papers of Andrew Dickson White, Ithaca, New York.

7. Fred Harvey Harrington, "The Anti-Imperialist Movement in the United States, 1898-1900," *Mississippi Valley Historical Review*, XXII (September, 1935), 211-212; *House Report No. 1355*, part 2, 55th Cong., 2nd Sess. (serial 3721), 1-2; *Senate Report No. 681*, 55th Cong., 2nd Sess. (serial 3627), 1-119. *Congressional Record*, 55th Cong., 3rd Sess., 20, contains Vest's resolution.

8. Lodge's statement is given in Stevens, *American Expansion in Hawaii*, 279; on Mahan, see Chapter II, above; on the business views, see Pratt, *Expansionists of 1898*, 274-275.

Part VII
Culture bearers

William Graham Sumner, social Darwinist

Richard Hofstadter

Every age has need of rationalizers, and none more so than the late nineteenth century. In an era of freewheeling enterprise and fantastic economic growth, how could America justify the amassing of huge fortunes by a few and the spread of misery and insecurity for the many? How could it justify a public policy that gave no guidance to the economic process nor made any sustained effort to minimize the social costs? The classical economics, standard doctrine by now in America's academics produced one set of justifying ideas, but not of such force as to carry the full burden of an intellectual defense of the status quo. The classical economics was too formalistic—too dependent on *a priori* assumptions and on abstract reasoning—for the scientific spirit of the age. And it described an economic world of perfect competition and self-regulating markets far removed from the reality of pools and combinations. At the very time when the need for intellectual defense was most pressing, the persuasiveness of the classical economics was, as Richard Hofstadter suggests, very much on the wane. What filled the breach, and did so with awesome success, was Social Darwinism. The evolutionary theory that Charles Darwin had advanced in his *The Origin of Species* (1859) had at once opened up a new perspective for the study of society. Evolutionary progress through the struggle for life and the survival of the fittest seemed to make remarkably good sense when it was shifted from the world of nature (which alone had concerned Darwin) to the nineteenth-century world of business enterprise; still better, these ideas offered the sturdiest intellectual defense of the status quo. In England, Herbert Spencer was the preeminent exponent of Social Darwinism, and his books and ideas were eagerly accepted in America, in sharp contrast to the fierce opposition that *The Origin of Species* itself engendered among conservative scientists and theologians.

The foremost American exponent of Social Darwinism was the dour Yale professor William Graham Sumner, about whom Richard Hofstadter has written the following essay. There is no question of Sumner's enormous success as a popularizer of Social Darwinism, but the reasons for that success are less clear. Hofstadter suggests two native sources for the power of Sumner's advocacy: first, the Puritan zeal and moral fervor that

Richard Hofstadter, "William Graham Sumner, Social Darwinist," *The New England Quarterly*, XIV (September, 1941), pp. 457-477. Reprinted by permission of the publisher.

he brought to it; and, second, his deep personal identification with "the forgotten man" celebrated in his essays. But there are also puzzling crosscurrents: a dark pessimism and fatalism in contrast to the American sense of optimism and mastery; an open rejection of American equalitarian and democratic traditions; and an uncompromising insistence on pushing arguments to their logical conclusions at a time when American business exhibited an easygoing disregard for principles when profits were at stake. How can one explain Sumner's effectiveness in the face of these atypical qualities? Or can it be argued that these qualities actually contributed to his effectiveness? Sumner may, indeed, be one key to an understanding of a darker side—an antidemocratic strain and a deep pessimism—that other historians have recently perceived in American thinking during the Gilded Age.

Hofstadter's treatment of Sumner also suggests a major methodological problem. Intellectual history seeks to show the relationship between the ideas and conditions of an era. Clearly Social Darwinism was brilliantly matched to the age of enterprise. But how did William Graham Sumner come to his advocacy of Social Darwinism? Assuredly not—given the man's independent and uncompromising cast of mind—out of any desire to defend the status quo or to truckle to the men of power. Hofstadter suggests the complex roots of Sumner's thinking in terms of background and personal experience. It follows that no satisfactory explanation of how ideas shaped themselves to the needs of an age will arise from a facile analysis of self-interest or conscious choice.

For further reading: Richard Hofstadter, *Social Darwinism in American Thought: 1869-1915* (1945);* Robert G. McCloskey, *American Conservatism in the Age of Enterprise* (1951);* Joseph Dorfman, *The Economic Mind in American Civilization* (1949), vol. 3; Sidney Fine, *Laissez Faire and the General-Welfare State: a Study of Conflict in American Thought, 1805-1901* (1956);* Chester M. Destler, "The Opposition of American Businessmen to Social Control during the 'Gilded Age,' " *Journal of American History*, XXXIX (1953), 641-672; Bert J. Loewenberg, "Darwinism Comes to America, 1859-1900," *Mississippi Valley Historical Review*, XXVIII (1941), 339-368.

In the years that followed the Civil War, one of the major problems facing American intellectuals was the assimilation of the new science into their patterns of thought. Especially important was the rise of evolutionism in biology. The tide of Darwinism, sweeping upon our shores in the three decades after the publication of *The Origin of Species* in 1859, washed away many familiar landmarks of the intellectual scene, and necessitated a long and painful rebuilding. One of the curious features of the reception of Darwinism, however, was the fact that it was as acceptable to many thinkers in economics and sociology as it was repugnant to theologians. It was popularized at a time when the authority of classical economics was waning, and when social legislation was being rapidly extended. Alarmed conservatives welcomed Darwinism as a fresh substantiation of an old creed. To some of them the Darwinian struggle for existence seemed to provide a new sanction for economic competition, and the survival of the fittest a new argument in opposition to state aid for the weak.[1]

The most vigorous and influential apostle of American social Darwinism was William

Graham Sumner. Sumner was born in Paterson, New Jersey, on October 30, 1840. His father, Thomas Sumner, was a hard-working, self-educated English laborer who came to America because his family's trade had been disrupted by the growth of the factory system. He brought up his children with respect for the traditional Protestant economic virtues, and left a deep impress upon his son William, who came in time to acclaim the savings bank depositor as "a hero of civilization."[2] "His principles and habits of life," Sumner later wrote, "were the best possible. His knowledge was wide and his judgment excellent. He belonged to the class of men of whom Caleb Garth in *Middlemarch* is the type. In early life I accepted, from books and other people, some views and opinions which differed from his. At the present time, in regard to these matters, I hold with him and not with the others."[3]

The economic doctrines of the classical tradition which were current in his early years strengthened Sumner's paternal heritage. He learned to think of pecuniary success as the inevitable product of diligence and thrift, and to see the lively capitalist society that was growing up around him as the fulfillment of the classical ideal of an automatically benevolent, free, competitive order. At fourteen he had read Harriet Martineau's popular little volumes, *Illustrations of Political Economy*, whose purpose was to propagandize for *laissez faire* through a series of parables. There he became acquainted with the wages fund doctrine, and its corollaries: "Nothing can permanently affect the rate of wages which does not affect the proportion of population to capital"; and "combinations of laborers against capitalists . . . cannot secure a permanent rise of wages unless the supply of labour falls short of the demand—in which case, strikes are usually unneccessary." There also he found fictional proof that "a self-balancing power being . . . inherent in the entire system of commercial exchange, all apprehensions about the results of its unimpeded operation are absurd," and that "a sin is committed when Capital is diverted from its normal course to be employed in producing at home that which is expensive and inferior, instead of preparing that which will purchase the same article cheaper and superior abroad." Charities, whether public or private, Miss Martineau had shown, would never reduce the number of the indigent, but would only encourage improvidence and nourish "peculation, tyranny, and fraud."[4] Later Sumner declared that his conceptions of "capital, labor, money and trade were all formed by those books which I read in my boyhood."[5] Wayland's standard text in Political Economy, which he recited in college, seems to have impressed him but little, perhaps because it only confirmed well-fixed beliefs.

In 1859, when he matriculated at Yale, young Sumner devoted himself to theology. During his undergraduate years, Yale was a pillar of orthodoxy, dominated by its versatile president, Theodore Dwight Woolsey, who had just turned from classical scholarship to write his *Introduction to the Study of International Law*, and by the Reverend Noah Porter, Professor of Moral Philosophy and Metaphysics, who as Woolsey's successor would some day cross swords with Sumner over the new science in education. Sumner, a somewhat frigid youth who could seriously question, "Is the reading of fiction justifiable?", repelled many of his schoolmates, but his friends made up in munificence what they lacked in numbers. William C. Whitney persuaded his elder brother, Henry, to supply funds for Sumner's further education abroad; and Sumner liberalized his theology at Geneva, Göttingen, and Oxford while a substitute procured with Whitney's money filled his place in the Union Army.[6] In 1866 Sumner was elected to a tutorship at Yale, where he opened a lifelong association, broken only by a few years spent as editor of a religious newspaper and rector of the Episcopal Church in Morristown, New Jersey. In 1872 he was elevated to the post of Professor of Political and Social Science in Yale College.

Despite personal coldness, and a crisp, dogmatic classroom manner, Sumner had a wider following than any other teacher in Yale's history.[7] Upper classmen found unique satisfaction of his courses; lower classmen looked forward to promotion chiefly as a means of becoming eligible for them.[8] William Lyon Phelps, who took all Sumner's courses as a matter of principle, without regard for his interest in the subject matter, has left a memorable picture of Sumner's dealings with a student dissenter:[9]

> *"Professor, don't you believe in any government aid to industries?"*
> *"No! it's root, hog, or die."*
> *"Yes, but hasn't the hog got a right to root?"*
> *"There are no rights. The world owes nobody a living."*
> *"You believe then, Professor, in only one system, the contract-competitive system?"*
> *"That's the only sound economic system. All others are fallacies."*
> *"Well, suppose some professor of political economy came along and took your job away from you. Wouldn't you be sore?"*
> *"Any other professor is welcome to try. If he gets my job, it is my fault. My business is to teach the subject so well that no one can take the job away from me."*

II

The religious stamp of his early upbringing marked all Sumner's writings. Although clerical phraseology soon disappeared from his pages, his temper remained that of a proselyter, an espouser of causes with little patience for distinguishing between error and iniquity in his opponents. "The type of mind which he exhibited," writes his biographer, "was the Hebraic rather than the Greek. He was intuitive, rugged, emphatic, fervently and relentlessly ethical, denunciatory, prophetic."[10] He might insist that political economy was a descriptive science divorced from ethics,[11] but his strictures on protectionists and socialists resounded with moral overtones. His faith in the superiority of the industrious, prudent, economical citizen, his background in Ricardian economics, and his distrust of the shibboleths of an uncritical democracy,[12] prepared Sumner for the acceptance of social Darwinism; his crusading zeal and talent for popularization made him an ideal standard-bearer.

Sumner's life was not entirely given to crusading. His intellectual activity passed through two overlapping phases, distinguished less by a change in his thought than a change in the direction of his work. During the seventies, eighties, and early nineties, in the columns of popular journals and from the lecture platform, he waged a holy war against the rising tide of reformism, protectionism, socialism, and government interventionism. In this period he published *What Social Classes Owe to Each Other* (1883), "The Forgotten Man" (1883), and "The Absurd Attempt to Make the World Over" (1894). By the early nineties, however, Sumner showed an increasing interest in academic sociology. It was during this period that the manuscript of "Earth Hunger" was written and the monumental *Science of Society* projected. When Sumner, always a prodigious worker, found himself with a 200,000-word chapter on human customs, he decided to publish it as a separate volume. Thus, almost as an afterthought, *Folkways* was published in 1906.[13] Although Sumner's tone changed from the deep ethical feelings of his youth to the sophisticated moral relativism of his social science period, his underlying philosophy always remained the same.

The major premises of this philosophy Sumner derived from Herbert Spencer. For years, since his graduate residence at Oxford, Sumner had had "vague notions floating in my head" about the possibility of creating a systematic science of society. In 1870, when Spencer's *Study of Sociology* was running serially in the *Contemporary Review*, Sumner seized upon his ideas, and the evolutionary viewpoint in social science took root in his mind. It seemed that Spencer's proposals were but a flowering of his own germinal ideas. The young man who had been impervious to Spencer's *Social Statics*, because "I did not believe in natural rights or in his 'fundamental principles,' " now found *The Study of Sociology* irresistible. "It solved the old difficulty about the relations of social science to history, rescued social science from the dominion of cranks, and offered a definite and magnificent field to work, from which we might hope at last to derive definite results for the solution of social problems." In a few years Professor O. C. Marsh's researches in the evolution of the horse fully convinced Sumner of the development hypothesis. Plunging into Darwin, Haeckel, Huxley, and Spencer, he saturated himself with evolutionism.[14]

Like Darwin before him, Sumner went back to Malthus for the first principles of his system. In many respects his sociology simply retraced the several steps in biological and social reasoning which ran from Malthus to Darwin and through Herbert Spencer to the modern social Darwinist. The foundation of human society, said Sumner, is the man-land ratio. Ultimately men draw their living from the soil, and the kind of existence they achieve, their mode of getting it, and their mutual relations in the process, are all determined by the proportion of population to the available soil.[15] Where men are few and soil is abundant, the struggle for existence is less savage and democratic institutions are likely to prevail. When population presses upon the land supply, earth hunger arises, races of men move across the face of the world, militarism and imperialism flourish, conflict rages, and in government aristocracy dominates.

As men struggle to adjust themselves to the land, they enter into rivalry for leadership in the conquest of nature. In Sumner's popular essays, he stressed the idea that the hardships of life are incidents of the struggle against nature, that "we cannot blame our fellow-men for our share of these. My neighbor and I are both struggling to free ourselves from these ills. The fact that my neighbor has succeeded in this struggle better than I constitutes no grievance for me."[16] He continued:[17]

> Undoubtedly the man who possesses capital has a great advantage over the man who has no capital at all in the struggle for existence. . . . This does not mean that one man has an advantage against the other, but that, when they are rivals in the effort to get the means of subsistence from Nature, the one who has capital has immeasurable advantages over the other. If it were not so capital would not be formed. Capital is only formed by self-denial, and if the possession of it did not secure advantages and superiorities of a high order men would never submit to what is necessary to get it.

Thus the struggle is like a whippet race; if one hound approaches the mechanical hare of pecuniary success, he sets up no barrier to a similar movement by the others.

Sumner was perhaps inspired to minimize the human conflicts in the struggle for existence by a desire to dull the resentment of the poor for the rich. He did not at all times, however, shrink from a direct analogy between animal struggle and human competition. [18] While Sumner was forming his sociological system, Walter Bagehot in England and Gustav Ratzenhofer and Ludwig Gumplowicz on the Continent were at work applying the concept of the struggle for existence to human affairs, predicating the survival of certain kinds of human societies or the selection of individual types upon the presence of special survival values. [19] In America the ideas of Spencer were occasionally being used to oppose legislation to ease the condition of the poor, on the grounds that it would limit the selective effect of competition. [20] In this intellectual atmosphere it was natural for conservatives to see the economic contest in a competitive society as a reflection of the struggle in the animal world. It was easy to argue from natural selection of fitter organisms to social selection of fitter men, from organic forms with superior adaptability to citizens with a greater store of economic virtues. The competitive order was now supplied with a cosmic rationale.

Competition was glorious. Just as survival was the result of strength, success was the reward of virtue. Sumner could find no patience for those who would lavish compensations upon the virtueless. Many economists, he declared in 1879, in a lecture on the effect of hard times on economic thinking,[21]

seem to be terrified that distress and misery still remain on earth and promise to remain as long as the vices of human nature remain. Many of them are frightened at liberty, especially under the form of competition, which they elevate into a bugbear. They think it bears harshly on the weak. They do not perceive that here "the strong" and "the weak" are terms which admit of no definition unless they are made equivalent to the industrious and the idle, the frugal and the extravagant. They do not perceive, furthermore, that if we do not like the survival of the fittest, we have only one possible alternative, and that is the survival of the unfittest. The former is the law of civilization; the latter is the law of anti-civilization. We have our choice between the two, or we can go on, as in the past, vacillating between the two, but a third plan—the socialist desideratum—a plan for nourishing the unfittest and yet advancing in civilization, no man will ever find.

The progress of civilization depends upon the selection process; and that in turn depends upon the workings of unrestricted competition. Competition is a law of nature which "can no more be done away with than gravitation," [22] and which men can ignore only to their sorrow.

III

The fundamentals of Sumner's philosophy had been set forth in his magazine articles before his sociological works were written. The first fact in life is the struggle for existence. The greatest forward step in this struggle is the production of capital, which increases the fruitfulness of labor and provides the necessary means of an advance in civilization. Primitive man, who long ago withdrew from the competitive struggle and ceased to accumulate capital goods, must pay with a backward and unenlightened way of life. [23] Social advance depends primarily upon hereditary wealth. For wealth offers a premium to effort, and assures the enterprising and industrious man that he may preserve in his children the virtues which have enabled him to enrich the community. Any assault upon hereditary wealth must begin with an attack upon the family and end by reducing men to "swine."[24] The operation of social selection depends upon keeping the family intact. Physical inheritance is a crucial part of Darwinian theory; society substitutes for it the instruction of the children in the necessary economic virtues.[25]

If the fittest are to be allowed to survive, if the benefits of efficient management are to be available to society, the captains of industry must be paid for their unique organizing talent.[26] Their huge fortunes are the legitimate wages of superintendence; in the struggle for existence, money is the token of success. It measures the amount of efficient management that has come into the world and the waste that has been eliminated.[27] Millionaires, then, are the bloom of a competitive civilization:[29]

The millionaires are a product of natural selection, acting on the whole body of men to pick out those who can meet the requirement of certain work to be done. . . . It is because they are thus selected that wealth—both their own and that entrusted to them—aggregates under their hands. . . . They may fairly be regarded as the naturally selected agents of society for certain work. They get high wages and live in luxury, but the bargain is a good one for society. There is the intensest competition for their place and occupation. This assures us that all who are competent for this function will be employed in it, so that the cost of it will be reduced to the lowest terms. . . .

In the Darwinian pattern of evolution, animals are unequal; this makes possible the appearance of forms with finer adjustment to the environment, and the transmission of such superiority to succeeding generations brings about progress. Without inequality the law of survival of the fittest could not operate. Accordingly, in Sumner's evolutionary sociology inequality was at a premium.[29] The competitive process "develops all powers that exist according to their measure and degree." If liberty prevails, so that all may exert themselves freely in the struggle, the results will certainly not be everywhere alike: those of "courage, enterprise, good training, intelligence, perseverance" will come out at the top.[30]

Sumner concluded that these principles of social evolution negated the traditional American ideology of equality and natural rights. In the evolutionary perspective equality was ridiculous, and no one knew so well as those who went to school to nature that there are no natural rights in the jungle. "There can be no rights against Nature except to get out of her whatever we can, which is only the fact of the struggle for existence stated over again."[31] In the cold light of evolutionary realism, the eighteenth-century idea that men were equal in a state of nature was wrong side up; masses of men starting under conditions of equality can never be anything but hopeless savages.[32] Rights to Sumner were simply evolving folkways crystallized in laws. Far from being absolute or antecedent to a specific culture—an illusion of philosophers, reformers, agitators, and anarchists—they are properly understood as "rules of the game of social competition which are current now and here."[33] In other times and places other *mores* have prevailed, and still others will emerge in the future:[34]

Each set of views colors the mores *of a period. The eighteenth-century notions about equality, natural rights, classes, and the like produced nineteenth-century states and legislation, all strongly humanitarian in faith and temper; at the present time the eighteenth-century notions are disappearing, and the* mores *of the twentieth century will not be tinged by humanitarianism as those of the last hundred years have been.*

Sumner's power to resist the catchwords of the American tradition is also evident in his skepticism about democracy. The democratic ideal, which was so alive in the minds of men diverse as Eugene Debs and Andrew Carnegie, as a thing of great hopes and tears, warm sentiments, and vast friendly illusions, was to him a transient stage in social evolution, determined by a favorable quotient in the man-land ratio and the political necessities of the capitalist class.[35] "Democracy itself, the pet superstition of the age, is only a phase of the all-compelling movement. If you have abundance of land and few men to share it, the men will all be equal."[36] Conceived as a principle of advancement based on merit, democracy met his approval as "socially progressive and profitable." Conceived as equality in acquisition and enjoyment, he thought it unintelligible in theory, and thoroughly impractical.[37] "Industry may be republican; it can never be democratic so long as men differ in productive power and in industrial virtue."[38]

In a brilliant essay which he never published, but which was written some time before the studies of J. Allen Smith and Charles A. Beard, Sumner divined the intentions of the founding fathers in the making of the American Constitution. They feared democracy, Sumner pointed out, and attempted to fix limitations upon it in the federal structure. But since the whole genius of the country has inevitably been democratic, because of its inherited dogmas and its environment, the history of the United States has been one of continual warfare between the democratic temper of the people and their constitutional framework.[39]

IV

One idea in the evolutionary philosophy which Sumner borrowed from Spencer and employed with great effect in his fight against reformers was its social determinism. Society, the product of centuries of gradual evolution, cannot be quickly refashioned by legislation:[40]

The great stream of time and earthly things will sweep on just the same in spite of us. . . . Every one of us is a child of his age and cannot get out of it. He is in the stream and is swept along with it. All his science and philosophy come to him out of it. Therefore the tide will not be changed by us. It will swallow up both us and our experiments. . . . That is why it is the greatest folly of which a man can be capable to sit down with a slate and pencil to plan out a new social world.

To Sumner and Spencer society was a super-organism, changing at geological tempo. Because of the bewildering complexity of the body politic and its naturally slow rate of growth, Spencer had argued, attempts at legislative reform seldom have the desired effect; the causal sequences at work in society are too elaborate to be traced. A scientific sociology, accepting the multiple relations of social life, would discourage state interventionists.[41] Hence Sumner's eager welcome of *The Study of Sociology*. In his view, the social tinkers had been laboring under the delusion that since there are no natural laws of the social order, they might make the world over with artificial ones.[42] But Spencer's new science would dissolve these fantasies.

With the evolutionist's characteristic scorn for all forms of meliorism and voluntarism, Sumner dismissed Upton Sinclair and his fellow socialists as puny meddlers, social quacks, who would break into the age-old process of societal growth at an arbitrary point and remake it in accordance with their petty desires. They started from the premise that "everybody ought to be happy" and assumed that therefore it should be possible to make them so. They never asked: In what direction is society moving? or What are the mechanisms which motivate its progress? Evolution would teach then that it is impossible to tear down overnight a social system with roots centuries deep in the soil of history. History would teach them that revolutions never succeed—witness the experience of France, where the Napoleonic period left essential interests much as they had been before 1789.[43]

Every system has its inevitable evils. "Poverty belongs to the struggle for existence, and we are all born into that struggle."[44] If poverty is ever to be abolished, it will be by a more energetic prosecution of the struggle, and not by social upheaval or paper plans for a new order. Human progress is at bottom moral progress, and moral progress is largely the accumulation of economic virtues. "Let every man be sober, industrious, prudent and wise, and bring up his children to be so likewise, and poverty will be abolished in a few generations."[45]

Thus the evolutionary philosophy provided a powerful argument against legislative meddling with natural events. Sumner's conception of the proper limits of state action, although not so drastic as Spencer's, was radical in the extreme. "At bottom there are two chief things with which government has to deal. They are the property of men and the honor of women. These it has to defend against crime."[46] Outside of the field of education, where Sumner's influence was always progressive, there were few reforms proposed in America during his active years which he did not attack. In a series of essays written for the *Independent* in 1887 Sumner assailed several current projects as tools of rampant pressure groups. The Bland Silver Bill he called an irrational compromise, set up by a few public men, without substantial promise of aid for debtors, silver miners, or any other part of the population. State laws on convict labor he damned as hasty and pointless legislation in response to partisan clamor. The Interstate Commerce Act lacked philosophy or design. The railroad question "is far wider than the scope of any proposed legislation; the railroads are interwoven with so many complex interests that legislators cannot meddle with them without doing harm to all concerned."[47] The free silver movement he attacked with the arguments of orthodox economics.[48] "All poor laws and all eleemosynary institutions and expenditures" he stigmatized as devices which protect persons at the expense of capital and ultimately lower the general standard of living by making it easier for the poor to live, increasing the number of consumers of capital while lowering incentives to its production.[49] With trade unions he was more indulgent, conceding that a strike, if carried on without violence, might be a means of testing the market conditions for labor. All the justification a strike required was success; failure was ample grounds for its condemnation. Trade unions might also be useful in maintaining the *esprit de corps* of the working class, and of keeping them informed. The conditions of labor—sanitation, ventilation, the hours of women and children—might better be controlled by the spontaneous activity of organized labor than by state enforcement.[50]

Aside from anti-imperialism, the one great reform of his age which attracted Sumner was free trade. But free trade was not, in his mind, a reform movement; it was an intellectual axiom. Although he wrote a short tract elaborating the classical arguments against protection—*Protectionism, The Ism that Teaches that Waste Makes Wealth* (New York, 1885)—he felt the subject hardly open to dispute by enlightened men—"that it ought to be treated as other quackeries are treated."[51] Sensing that protectionism and other forms of government intervention in economic life might culminate in socialism, he identified the doctrines on principle, defining socialism as "any device whose aim is to save individuals from any of the difficulties or hardships of the struggle for existence and the competition of life by the intervention of 'the state.' "[52] The tariff, he admitted, never ceased to arouse his highest moral indignation. He once wrote angry protests to the newspapers because women employed in sweatshops stitching corsets for fifty cents a day had to pay a tariff on their thread.[53]

V

In arms against abuses of the right or left, Sumner drew bitter cross-fire from both sides. Upton Sinclair, in *The Goose Step*, called him, long after his death, "a prime minister in the empire of plutocratic education";[54] and another socialist accused him of intellectual prostitution.[55] Such critics showed little comprehension of Sumner's character or the governing motives of his mind. He was at times doctrinaire only because his ideas were bred in his bones. He was not a business hireling, nor did he feel himself to be the spokesman of plutocracy, but rather of the lower middle classes. If he attacked economic democracy, he had no sympathy for plutocracy as he understood it; he thought it responsible for political corruption and protectionist lobbies.[56] Significantly, he had praise for Jeffersonian democracy, at least in so far as it practised abnegation of state power and decentralization in government.[57] Sumner's unforgettable "Forgotten Man," the hero of most of his popular essays, was simply the lower middle-class citizen, who, like Sumner's father, went quietly about his business, providing for himself and his family without making demands upon the state.[58] The crushing effect of taxation upon such people gave him his most anxious moments and explains in part his opposition to state interventionism.[59] It was his misfortune that this class had moved on to the support of reform while he was still trying to fight its cause with the intellectual weapons of Harriet Martineau and David Ricardo.

On the rare occasions when Sumner's thought ran counter to the established verities, he would stand his ground even though the heavens fall. His famous fight with President Porter over the use of *The Study of Sociology* as a textbook might have cost him his position at Yale. Constantly under criticism from the press for his outspoken stand on the tariff, he never faltered. The New York *Tribune*, in the course of a denunciation of his articles on protection, once likened his manners to those of "the cheap Tombs shyster."[60] The Republican press and the Republican alumni periodically urged his dismissal, and the demand became general when he announced his opposition to the Spanish-American War.[61] Although one old-fashioned benefactor of Yale doubled his donation because Sumner's presence had convinced him "that Yale College is a good and safe place for the keeping and use of property and the sustaining of civilization when endangered by ignorance, rascality, demagogues, repudiationists, rebels, copperheads, communists, Butlers, strikers, protectionists, and fanatics of sundry roots and sizes,"[62] Sumner was always suspect to a large part of the community of wealth and orthodoxy because of his independence.

Sumner's reputation has come to rest upon his *Folkways*, and in lesser measure upon his historical writings, while his many social Darwinist essays have shrunk into compara-tive obscurity. [63] Natural selection in the realm of ideas has taken its toll upon his life work. The ideas which have been most esteemed in *Folkways* were never reconciled with the rest of his thought. The great contribution of that work was its treatment of folkways as products of "natural forces," as evolutionary growths, rather than artifacts of human purpose or wit. [64] Critics have often suggested that Sumner's denial of the intuitive character of morals, his insistence upon their historical and institutional foundations, undermined his own stand against socialists and protectionists. [65] By a thoroughly consis-tent evolutionist, prepared to carry out the amoral and narrowly empirical approach to social change laid down in *Folkways*, the decline of *laissez faire*, which was so disturbing to Sumner's mature years, might have been accepted in a mellow and complaisant spirit as a new trend in the development of the *mores*. But on the subject of *laissez faire* and property rights Sumner was an uncompromising absolutist. There is no complaisance in *Protectionism, the Ism that Teaches That Waste Makes Wealth*, no mellowness in "The Absurd Attempt to Make the World Over." As a recruit from the theological life who had always been absorbed in his own Yankee-puritan culture, Sumner found the effort of a completely consistent relativism too great. It was easier for an unacclimated alien like Thorstein Veblen to treat American society with the loftiness of a cultural anthropolo-gist. For Sumner, the marriage customs of the Wawanga and the property relations of the Dyaks were always in a separate universe of discourse from the like institutions of his own culture.

As a defender of the *status quo* Sumner was an effective figure in American life. In the few independent efforts which earned for him the reputation of a radical, he was frus-trate. It was not merely that he chose lost causes; his philosophy and the qualities of his mind were ill adapted to the ends of reform. His attacks upon the tariff were too dogmatic to be convincing. His stand against imperialism was nullified by his pessimism about the future of international relations. In 1898 he joined other New England intellec-tuals in the Anti-imperialist League and spoke in a forthright way against the Spanish war and imperialist ambitions, [66] but his allegiance must have been accepted with mixed feelings when it became clear that his own analysis of the roots of war implied the futility of resistance. What could one say of a man who four years later calmly remarked, "It is the competition of life . . . which makes war, and that is why war has always existed and always will," who stressed the human virtues nourished in battle, and concluded: "There is only one thing rationally to be expected, and that is a frightful effusion of blood in revolution and war in the century now opening"?[67]

This prophecy, with its somber realism, characterizes Sumner's prevailing mood and his role in the history of American thought. Since the Revolution, the dogmas of the Enlightenment had been traditional ingredients of the American faith. American social thought had been optimistic, confident of the special destiny of the country, humani-tarian, democratic. Its reformers still relied upon the sanctions of natural rights. It was Sumner's function to take the leadership in a critical examination of these ideological fixtures, using as his instrument the early nineteenth-century pessimism of Ricardo and Malthus, now fortified with the tremendous prestige of Darwinism. He set himself the task of deflating the philosophical speculation of the eighteenth century with the science of the nineteenth. He tried to show his contemporaries that their optimism was a hollow defiance of the realities of social struggle, that their "natural rights" were nowhere to be found in nature, and that their humanitarianism, democracy, and equality were not found in nature, and that their humanitarianism, democracy, and equality were not eternal verities, but the passing *mores* of a stage of social evolution. In an age of helter-skelter reforms, he tried to convince men that their confidence in their ability to will and plan their destinies was unwarranted by history or biology or any of the facts of experience; that the best they could do was to bow to natural forces. Like some latter-day Calvin, he came to preach the predestination of the social order and the salvation of the economically elect through the survival of the fittest.

Sumner's cold criticism of ossified beliefs and his broad evolutionary perspective on the tempo of social change must be counted among the critical contributions of the Gilded Age. The old ideals were, if not obsolete, certainly in need of more solid foundation. But adept as Sumner was in attacking the sometimes sweeping assumptions of reformers and idealists, he was less successful than he thought in eliminating metaphysics and dogma from his own philosophy. For "the heavenly city of the eighteenth century philosophers" he substituted the crude analogies of a Darwinized *laissez faire*, which, while equally blinding, were also sterile. If he dispelled the sentimentality of old-fashioned reformers, he also strengthened the most facile illusions of an acquisitive society.

Notes

1. See the discussion at the first meeting of the American Sociological Society, reported in "Social Darwinism," *American Journal of Sociology*, XII (March, 1907), 695-716.

2. *Essays of William Graham Sumner*, edited by A. G. Keller and Maurice R. Davie (New Haven, 1934), II, 22.

3. *Earth Hunger and Other Essays* (New Haven, 1913), 3.

4. *Illustrations of Political Economy* (London, 1834), III Part 1, 134-135, and Part 2, 130-131; VI, Part 1, 140, and Part 2, 143-144.

5. *The Challenge of Facts and Other Essays* (New Haven, 1914), 5.

6. Harris E. Starr, *William Graham Sumner* (New York, 1925), 47-48.

7. *Cf.* Albert Galloway Keller's discussion of Sumner's influence in "The Discoverer of the Forgotten Man," *American Mercury*, XXVII (November, 1932), 257-270.

8. William Lyon Phelps, "When Yale Was Given to Sumnerology," *The Literary Digest International Book Review*, III (September, 1925), 661-663.

9. "When Yale Was Given to Sumnerology," 661.

10. Starr, *William Graham Sumner*, 336-337.

11. *Cf. What Social Classes Owe to Each Other* (New York, 1883), 155-156.

12. For Sumner's early skepticism about the merits of democracy, see the college composition quoted in Starr, 44.

13. *Cf.* the preface to *The Science of Society*, I, xxxiii. Sumner died before the completion of this work, and it was finished by Albert Galloway Keller and published in four volumes in 1927 by the

Yale University Press. The fidelity of the work to Sumner's major conceptions is such that I have not hesitated to use it as a source.

14. See the autobiographical sketch in *The Challenge of Facts*, 9.

15. *Science of Society*, Chapter 1; *cf.* also the essay "Earth Hunger." The main elements of this idea are in the wages fund doctrine and can be traced to Sumner's early acquaintance with Harriet Martineau.

16. *What Social Classes Owe to Each Other*, 17; *cf.* also 70. "Nature is entirely neutral; she submits to him who most energetically and resolutely assails her. She grants her rewards to the fittest . . . without regard to other considerations of any kind. If, then, there be liberty, men get from her just in proportion to their works, and their having and enjoying are just in proportion to their being and their doing." *The Challenge of Facts*, 25.

17. *What Social Classes Owe to Each Other*, 76.

18. At times Sumner distinguished the struggle for existence, which he looked upon as man's impersonal struggle against nature, from what he called "the competition of life," a strictly social form of conflict, in which groups of men united in the conquest-of-nature struggle among themselves. *Cf. Folkways*, 16-17, and *Essays*, I, 142 ff. But the competition of life was elsewhere described as "the rivalry, antagonism, and mutual displacement in which the *individual* is involved with other organisms by his efforts to carry on the struggle for existence for himself." *Folkways*, 16-17 [my emphasis, R. H.]. Thus the distinction was often obscured, so that Sumner's closest student, editing *The Science of Society*, could pardonably identify "the familiar struggle for existence" with "the competition of life" (I, 4). The terms of the analogy between human existence and the struggle of animals seemed to require that men be regarded as struggling against each other, as members of the same species. While Sumner was trying to utilize the analogy, he resisted this conclusion.

19. Bagehot, *Physics and Politics, Thoughts on the Application of the Principles of Natural Selection and Inheritance to Political Society*, 1874; Ludwig Gumplowicz, *Grundriss der Soziologie*, 1885, translated in 1899 by Frederick W. Moore as *The Outlines of Sociology*; and Gustav Ratzenhofer, *Soziologie*, 1907.

Keller, estimating the major influences on Sumner's sociology, has placed Spencer first, Julius Lippert second, and Ratzenhofer third. ("William Graham Sumner," *American Journal of Sociology*, XV (May, 1910), 832-835.) Lippert was a German cultural historian whose method was much like that employed in *Folkways*. See his *Kulturgeschichte der Menschenheit*, 1886, translated in 1931 by George Murdock as *The Evolution of Culture*.

While the influence of Spencer is primary, the differences between Sumner and Spencer should not be neglected. Sumner does not seem to have followed Spencer's identification of evolution with progress. He was not so severe in his conceptions of the proper limits of government. (*Cf.* Starr, 392-393). Less libertarian, he understood the limitations imposed by industrial society upon individual freedom (see *Essays*, I, 310ff.). Finally, his approach to ethics contrasted sharply with Spencer's intuitionism.

For his part, Spencer cordially approved Sumner's way of defending *laissez faire* and property rights. He tried to persuade the Liberty and Property Defense League in England to reprint *What Social Classes Owe to Each Other* (Starr, 503-505).

20. It was this tendency which led to Mr. Justice Holmes's reminder as late as 1905, in the dissenting opinion in Lochner *vs.* New York (198 U.S. 45), that "The Fourteenth Amendment does not enact Mr. Herbert Spencer's Social Statics."

21. *Essays*, II, 56. Charles Page, *Class and American Sociology* (New York, 1940), 74 and 103, has stressed the importance of the economic ethics of the Protestant tradition as a formative element in Sumner's thinking. See also the treatment of these ideas in *Essays*, II, 223, and *The Challenge of Facts*, 52 and 67.

22. *The Challenge of Facts*, 68.

23. *The Challenge of Facts*, 40 and 145-150; *Essays*, 1, 231.

24. *The Challenge of Facts*, 43-44.

25. *What Social Classes Owe to Each Other*, 73.

26. *Essays*, I, 289.

27. *What Social Classes Owe to Each Other*, 54-56.

28. *The Challenge of Facts*, 90.

29. *The Science of Society*, I., 615; *cf.* also 328, where Sumner opposes a communal economy on the ground that it makes variation impossible—"and variation is the starting-point of new adjustment." Sumner considered the masses to be immobile and unproductive of social improvement. Variation is chiefly characteristic of the upper classes, *Folkways*, 45-47.

30. *The Challenge of Facts*, 67.

31. *What Social Classes Owe to Each Other*, 135.

32. *Folkways*, 48.

33. *Essays*, I, 358-362.

34. *Essays* I, 86-87.

35. *Earth Hunger*, 283-317.

36. *Essays*, I, 185.

37. *Essays*, I, 104.

38. *Essays*, II, 165.

39. See "Advancing Organization in America," in *Essays*, II, 340 ff., especially 349-350. In his references to the effects of the frontier upon the unique historical development of the United States, Sumner seems to have anticipated also the theories of Frederick Jackson Turner. Sumner's views on democracy have been discussed in Ralph H. Gabriel, *The Course of American Democratic Thought* (New York, 1940), Chapter 19; and in Harry Elmer Barnes, "Two Representative Contributions of Sociology to Political Theory: The Doctrines of William Graham Sumner and Lester Frank Ward." *American Journal of Sociology*, xxv (July and September, 1919), 1-23 and 150-170.

40. "The Absurd Attempt to Make the World Over," in *Essays*, I, 105.

41. *The Study of Sociology* (1883 edition, New York), 1-24 and 270.

42. *Essays*, II, 215.

43. See "Reply to a Socialist," in *The Challenge of Facts*, 58 and 219: on the ineffectiveness of reform legislation, see *War and Other Essays* (New Haven, 1911), 208-310; *Earth Hunger*, 283 ff.; and *What Social Classes Owe to Each Other*, 160-161.

44. *The Challenge of Facts*, 57.

45. *Essays*, I, 109.

46. *What Social Classes Owe to Each Other*, 101.

47. *Essays*, II, 249-253 and 255.

48. *Essays*, II, 67-76.

49. *The Challenge of Facts*, 27-28.

50. *The Challenge of Facts*, 99; *What Social Classes Owe to Each Other*, 90-95.

51. *Essays*, II, 366.

52. *Essays*, II, 435.

53. Starr, 285-288; *cf. What Social Classes Owe to Each Other*, 146.

54. Page 123.

55. Starr, 258 and 297.

56. See the essays on democracy and plutocracy in *Essays*, II, 13 ff.

57. *Essays*, II, 236-237.

58. "The Forgotten Man," in *Essays*, I, 466-496; *cf.* also *What Social Classes Owe to Each Other, passim*.

59. *The Challenge of Facts*, 74.

60. Starr, 275.

61. Phelps, "When Yale Was Given to Sumnerology," 662.

62. Quoted in Starr, 300-301.

63. For evidence that this aspect of Sumner's thought is by no means dead, however, see some of the comments in *Sumner Today*, edited by Maurice R. Davie (New Haven, 1940).

64 . *Folkways*, 4 and 29.

65. *Cf.* the review of *Folkways* by George Vincent in *American Journal of Sociology*, XIII (November, 1907), 414-419; also John Chamberlain, "Sumner's Folkways," *The New Republic*, IC (May 31, 1939), 95.

66. "The Conquest of the United States by Spain," *Essays*, II, 266-303.

67. "War," in *War and Other Essays*.

American Protestantism: From denominationalism to Americanism

Sidney E. Mead

The late nineteenth century was preeminently an economic age, a time that celebrated the acquisitive instinct and the country's material development. This was also a time deeply under the influence of the scientific spirit, especially in the form of Darwinian thinking. Yet this was by no means an age of secularism; on the contrary, religion exerted a profound influence on late nineteenth century America. "It is a commonplace," Sidney Mead observes in the following essay, "that in the period roughly from 1870 to 1900 evangelical Protestant Christianity largely dominated the American culture, setting the prevailing mores and the moral standards by which personal and public, individual and group, conduct was judged." The most striking proof we have of this religious factor is in the recent statistical studies of voting behavior during this period. The decisive factor in determining party identification appears to have been religious affiliation. And the central issues of political life, until the 1890s at any rate, involved social control of personal conduct—Sunday observance, temperance, education—that, as Paul Kleppner notes, "in turn, derived from religious perspectives."

Not only did evangelical Protestantism thus have a central part in American life, but, as Sidney Mead suggests in his essay, its primary effect was to sustain the prevailing values of the Gilded Age. Above all, it lent a moral defense to the business system. "Godliness is in league with riches," asserted Bishop William Lawrence. This conjunction of righteousness and enterprise, given expression in a variety of ways but widely and deeply felt, provided a powerful justification for the evident inequities and profound dislocations that attended industrialization. Similarly, when the United States embarked in the 1890s on its imperialist adventures, evangelical Protestantism lent crucial moral grounds, especially in the notion of America's providential mission to uplift the world. From a twentieth-century perspective, nothing is more notable about the Gilded Age than the sense of moral rectitude that sustained Americans while they went about the ruthless business of building the new industrial order and creating an American empire.

Sidney E. Mead, "American Protestantism Since the Civil War. I. From Denominationalism to Americanism," *The Journal of Religion*, XXVI (January, 1956), pp. 1-16. Reprinted by permission of the publisher.

That religion played this crucial role is, of course, well understood by historians of the Gilded Age: the evidence is entirely clear on that score. What is less clear is why American Protestantism should have been so powerful a cultural factor in this age, and even more why its influence should have been so profoundly conservative. Professor Mead's exploration of these questions forms the more original part of his essay. His central notion is that contemporary Protestantism involved two intermingled faiths—one specifically religious associated with pietistic revivalism, the other directed at the American democratic society. The conservative character of the second, Mead argues, derived from the pietism of the first, which, instead of asserting the standards by which society ought to live, acquiesced in the standards by which society did live. In the introduction to the preceding essay on William Graham Sumner, the question was raised about how the intellectual historian can explain the success of a set of ideas in meeting the needs of an age. In this essay, Sidney Mead offers one approach: namely, to focus on the ideas themselves and to try to discover the characteristics within them that make them responsive to social conditions.

For further reading: A. I. Abell, *The Urban Impact on American Protestantism: 1865-1900* (1943);——, *American Catholicism and Social Action* (1960);* C. D. Hopkins, *The Rise of the Social Gospel in American Protestantism* (1940); H. F. May, *Protestant Churches and Industrial America* (1949);* Robert D. Cross, ed., *The Church and the City: 1865-1910* (1967); Gail Kennedy, ed., *Democracy and the Gospel of Wealth* (1949).*

By the decade 1850-60 denominationalism was generally accepted in the United States and was assumed to be the proper organizational embodiment of the Christianity of the self-consciously evangelical Protestant churches. Such general acceptance of this form suggests the general prevalence of a state of mind or outlook which I attempted to define in an article on "Denominationalism" published in *Church History* in December, 1954. The argument of the present article is that during the second half of the nineteenth century there occurred a virtual identification of the outlook of this denominational Protestantism with "Americanism" or "the American way of life" and that we are still living with some of the results of this ideological amalgamation of evangelical Protestantism with Americanism.

It is a commonplace that in the period roughly from 1870 to 1900 evangelical Protestant Christianity largely dominated the American culture, setting the prevailing mores and the moral standards by which personal and public, individual and group, conduct was judged. As H. Paul Douglass put it, "despite multiplying sectarian differences, Protestantism's prevalence tended to create a Protestant cultural type. . . . It was a triumph of religion still on a communal level."[1] Indeed, down to the present, a "rebel" in America has to rebel against *these* standards in order to acquire the name.

To the free churches, inasmuch as Christian humility permitted, such dominance was a sound source of pride and a basis for self-approbation, for it demonstrated their success in meeting the terms implied in their original acceptance of the fact of separation of church and state. With religious freedom, these churches had given up coercive power and had assumed the responsibility collectively to define and inculcate in the population the basic beliefs necessary for the being and the well-being of the democratic society,[2] while armed only with persuasive power. Their dominance seemed to demonstrate that they could do this effectively. Then with the Civil War the North became dominant, and "to Protestants of the Northern States, the years of the Civil War furnished the supreme vindication" of their way.[3] The free churches seemed to have been tried and found adequate, and it is little wonder that, in spite of theological differences and multiplying sectarian divisions, "in its most characteristic pronouncements American Protestantism substantially approved the church-state status quo."[4]

What was not so obvious at the time was that the United States, in effect, had two religions, or at least two different forms of the same religion, and that the prevailing Protestant ideology represented a syncretistic mingling of the two. The first was the religion of the denominations, which was commonly articulated in the terms of scholastic Protestant orthodoxy and almost universally practiced in terms of the experimental religion of pietistic revivalism. This defines for our purposes Protestant "evangelicalism."

The second was the religion of the democratic society and nation. This was rooted in the rationalism of the Enlightenment (to go no farther back) and was articulated in terms of the destiny of America, under God, to be fulfilled by perfecting the democratic way of life for the example and betterment of all mankind. This was a calling taken as seriously as every Christian saint or administrator took his peculiar vocation. Said one of its high priests in 1826: "We stand the latest, and, if we fail, probably the last experiment of self-government by the people."[5]

This religion was almost universally practiced in terms of the burgeoning middle-class society and its "free-enterprise" system, the most persuasive argument for which was the plain fact that it worked to the economic and general material betterment of men, until Andrew Carnegie, in summarizing his version of its beneficent effects, could say that such "is the true Gospel concerning Wealth, obedience to which is destined some day to solve the problem of the Rich and the Poor, and to bring 'Peace on earth, among men Good-Will.' "[6]

The primary concern in this article is to deal with the high degree of amalgamation of the two faiths during the decades following the Civil War, giving some attention to the ideological content of the resulting syncretistic view. It is necessary, first, to give some explanation of the situation which enabled the ideological amalgamation of such diverse and even logically inconsistent elements at the time. I suggest three roots of this situation.

The first root was the widespread triumph of pietistic revivalism in the denominations during and following the Revolutionary epoch, at the time when essentially rationalistic assumptions and thinking were largely determining the legal and political structures of the new nation. This meant, aside from a genial lack of concern for logical consistency, a widespread tendency to equate "spreading scriptural holiness over the land" through revivals with "reforming the nation."[7] Assuming, perhaps, that "spreading scriptural holiness" in their fashion was seeking first the Kingdom of God, it was not difficult also to assume that all things else, such as social and political reformation, would be added thereto.[8]

The second root was the almost universal reaction in the free churches against the whole ethos of the Enlightenment that took place at the same time. This threw the emerging denominations back upon scholastic Protestant orthodoxy for their intellectual structure and professed theology and created in them a mood to articulate and defend it stubbornly and uncompromisingly. This, in turn, created a basic and continuing dichotomy, for the emerging civilization continued to be informed by the spirit and ideas of the Enlightenment moving toward the whole world-view of modern science.

The third root was the often noted lack of intellectual interests and structure of the pietistic Protestantism which came to dominance. Pietistic sentiment, with its emphasis on personal religious experience, elaborated its own version of Pascal's "The heart has its reasons, which reason does not know" into a more or less systematic excuse for giving up the intellectual wrestle with the modern age. Nor was pietism in this respect confined to the uneducated revivalists on the geographical frontier and the ignoramuses on the social and intellectual fringes of all places. Horace Bushnell's distinguished theological career began when, during a revival in Yale College in 1831, he finally burst out:

O men! what shall I do with these arrant doubts I have been nursing for years? When the preacher touches the Trinity and when logic shatters it all to pieces, I am all at the four winds. But I am glad I have a heart as well as a head. My heart wants the Father; my heart wants the Son; my heart wants the Holy Ghost—and one just as much as the other. My heart says the Bible has a Trinity for me, and I mean to hold by my heart. I am glad a man can do it when there is no other mooring. [9]

Thereafter, aided and instructed somewhat by Samuel Taylor Coleridge, he spun out over a long period of years his own reflections on the Christianity of the heart that was secure from the "speculations of philosophers and literati"—indeed, even from "the manner of the theologians" [10] —all of whom were thought to have an exaggerated regard for intellectual structure and logical consistency. A fitting end-result of this view was Lyman Abbott's glorying in the fact that, at Plymouth Church, "we do not ask what man believe" [11] as a condition of membership.

It is unnecessary to dwell upon the point that such a view made religion almost impervious to the "acids of modernity" which were already eating away the faith of many; gave systematic theology a security largely untroubled by the problem of its relationship to the emerging scientific world view; and placed the question of the Christian's role as a businessman and citizen in the democratic society beyond the ken of practical theology. Meanwhile, what C. H. Hopkins called "a smug preoccupation with the salvation and perfection of the individual" [12] largely pervaded the revivalistic denominations, tending to focus their attention on the personal vices and morals of individuals, until such personal habits as smoking, drinking, dancing, and Sunday observance became the outstanding indexes to Christian character. From the midst of this period came Daniel Dorchester's exultation that "under Protestantism, religion became purely a personal thing, passing out from under the exclusive control of the sacraments, the arbitrary sway of assumed prerogatives, into irrepressible conflicts with individual lusts and worldly influences." [13]

Francis Wayland had foreseen something like this outcome as early as 1842 and was very unhappy about it. Looking around, he noted that

one man asserts that his religion has nothing to do with the regulation of his passions, another that it has nothing to do with his business, and another that it has nothing to do with his politics. Thus while the man professes a religion which obliges him to serve God in everything, he declares that whenever obedience would interfere with his cherished vices, he will not serve God at all.

He was grieved to observe that "the pulpit has failed to meet such sentiments at the very threshold, with its stern and uncompromising rebuke." The root of the difficulty in the churches, he thought—sensing the meaning of pietistic revivalism—is that "men are told how they must feel, but they are not told how they must act, and the result, in many cases ensues, that a man's belief has but a transient and uncertain effect upon his practice."[14]

But since men, if not given instruction and guidance in such matters as citizenship and conduct in business by ministers and theologians in their churches, will nevertheless be instructed and guided by some prevailing code, the effectual abdication of the Protestant churches left the way open for the sway of the ideas and ideals of the emerging acquisitive society.

Hence the dichotomy noted and stated so well by the two Randalls, between the professed beliefs of the denominations and the "moral and social ideals and attitudes, . . . the whole way of living" which they "approved and consecrated." On the side of the latter, they came "to terms with the forces of the modern age," but "on the side of beliefs" not only did they "not come to terms with the intellectual currents of Western society" but they were "involved in a profound intellectual reaction against just such an attempt at modernism" as was implied therein.[15] A not unexpected result was that when, in 1897, George A. Gordon surveyed the scene with critical eye, he concluded that "the theological problem for to-day" is the almost complete "absence of a theology giving intellectual form and justification to the better sentiment of the time." For example, he added, "among almost all our effective preachers the sympathies are modern; but in the greater number the theology is either ancient or nonexistent. In either case, the mass of prevailing emotion and practical activity has no corresponding body of ideas in league with it." Hence "the scheme entertained is usually some decrepit modification of the Calvinistic kind . . . while the purposes, sentiments, and practical outlooks are all of this new and greater day."[16]

However, as the nineteenth century had moved into the balmy days of the Victorian age, the democratic society with its "free-enterprise" system proved obviously beneficial in terms that could be made tangible and measured in incomes and material goods. As this happened, activistic American Protestants lost their sense of estrangement from the society, began to see that it was profoundly Christian and to bless and defend it in a jargon strangely compounded out of the language of traditional Christian theology, the prevalent common-sense philosophy, and *laissez faire* economics. This compounding was made easier by the teaching of such men as Bushnell and his disciples that the form of expression in words was relatively unimportant, thus sanctifying a studied ambiguity.

In the context of this general interpretation of developments, it is not too difficult to understand why an aura of religious consecration came to surround the acceptance and promulgation of the syncretistic point of view. Especially important in this regard was the matter of religious freedom—how it was originally conceived and by whom. In the first place, it was the rationalists who made sense out of it theoretically and, on the basis of their theory, worked out the legal and political forms for the separation of church and state. In the second place, the churches accepted religious freedom and separation in practice, although there was little obvious theoretical justification for it in the classical Protestant theology which they professed. In effect, then, they accepted it in practice as a good thing, but on the rationalists' theoretical terms. The prevalence of pietistic sentiment at the time enabled this theoretical ambiguity to go largely unquestioned. Nevertheless, the rationalists' theory had far-reaching and devastating implications so far as the free churches were concerned. Most important was the implication that only what the religious "sects" held and taught in common (the rationalists' "essentials of every religion") was relevant to the public welfare of the new commonwealth. For the obverse side of this was that what each group held peculiar to itself, and hence what gave it its only reason for separate existence, was irrelevant to the general welfare of the whole commonwealth. No wonder that a sense of irrelevance has always haunted the most sectarian religious leaders in America. Further, the basic competition between the religious groups inherent in the system of religious freedom has always augmented the sectarian emphases, while at the same time such emphases on peculiarities undercut the sense of relevance to the life of the whole commonwealth.

This dilemma has troubled some religious leaders in America from the beginning. It is revealed, for example, in the typical insistence of Professor Bela Bates Edwards in 1848 that "perfect religious liberty does not imply that the government of the country is not a Christian government." But the most he could assert positively was that there is a "real, though indirect, connection between the State and Christianity."[17] What, then, is the nature of this indirect connection? Tocqueville thought that he saw it. While supposing that there was some "direct influence of religion upon politics in the United States," he concluded that "its indirect influence" was "still more considerable," and added:

The sects which exist in the United States are innumerable. They all differ in respect to the worship which is due from man to his Creator; but they all agree in respect to the duties which are due from man to man. Each sect adores the Deity in its own peculiar manner; but all the sects preach the same moral law in the name of God.[18]

To be sure, he sensed that the situation involved a kind of compartmentalization, and what he said of Roman Catholics might equally be applied to the Protestant groups. Their priests in America, he thought,

have divided the intellectual world into two parts: in the one they place the doctrines of revealed religion, which command their assent; in the other they leave those truths, which they believe to have been freely left open to the researches of political inquiry. Thus the Catholics of the United States are at the same time the most faithful believers and the most zealous citizens.[19]

The same kind of compartmentalization was exhibited by John Leland, the Baptist elder and perennial democrat, who on the matter of religious freedom spoke, on the one hand, "as a religionist" and, on the other hand, "as a statesman," coming to separate conclusions in each that would be hard to reconcile theoretically.[20]

It is suggested that Christianity was made relevant to the public welfare at the expense of cherishing unresolved theoretical difficulties in its mind. And so long as these remain unresolved, discussions of the sects' relation to the general welfare are likely to generate more heat than light. Hence, for example, the common fervency of the insistence upon the dogma of "real, but indirect connection," which, I take it, has usually meant what Tocqueville noted, that the religious denominations in common inculcate the same basic moral standards which are the foundation of the Republic. This it is that makes their work relevant to the general welfare of the democracy. And this comes close at least to tacit acceptance of the rationalists' view of the matter.

Meanwhile, the whole grand dream of American destiny, under God, instrumented through the democratic way, while its tangled roots drew nourishment from many different soils in past centuries, was nevertheless profoundly Protestant Christian in origins and conception. [21] Hence the "democratic faith" had always a positive and apparently independently legitimate place in the religious affections of the people. And this the free churches, in order to make themselves relevant, have always been under pressures to accept on faith and to sanctify.

Grant all this, plus the prevalence of a fuzzy and amorphous intellectual structure in the religious groups, and the way is left open for the uncritical adoption of whatever standards do actually prevail in the society. Hence, as noted, the American denominations have successively loaned themselves to the sanctification of current existing expressions of the American way of life.

John Herman Randall, Jr., by taking a more theoretical route as befits a philosopher, arrives at the similar conclusion that "Protestantism left the way open for the assimilation of any pattern of values that might seem good in the light of men's actual social experience . . . and has thus tended to become largely an emotional force in support of the reigning secular social ideals." However, it is not quite fair to conclude further, as he does, that Protestantism has offered "*no* opposition to any ideal deeply felt" and "no independent guidance and wisdom," [22] although the denominations have always exhibited a surprising lack of ability to launch a cogent criticism of their culture, and during the period we are discussing such criticism was almost non-existent. "The most significant feature of the New Theology" of the period, as W. S. Hudson makes clear, "was its lack of normative content," which made it "compatible with every conceivable social attitude." [23] It is not to be wondered at that, when during a later period of trouble, businessmen looked to their churches for guidance, they complained that they received back only the echoes of their own voices.

But whatever historical explanations are accepted as most plausible, there remains the general agreement that, at the time Protestantism in America achieved its greatest dominance of the culture, it had also achieved an almost complete ideological and emotional identification with the burgeoning bourgeois society and its free-enterprise system, so that "in 1876 Protestantism presented a massive, almost unbroken front in its defense of the social status quo." [24]

Furthermore, Protestants, in effect, looked at the new world they had created, were proud of its creator, and, like Jehovah before them, pronounced it very good. A widespread complacency, a smug self-satisfaction with things as they were (or as they were supposed to be), settled upon them as soot settles on Chicago. This complacency, while a bit incredible to the mid-twentieth century, is not too difficult to understand historically. To do so, it is necessary to keep in mind the almost universal prevalence of a providential view of history—which itself is no mean evidence for the cultural dominance of the denominations. Late in 1864 Horace Bushnell proclaimed:

We associate God and religion with all that we are fighting for. . . . Our cause, we love to think, is especially God's and so we are connecting all most sacred impressions with our government itself, weaving in a woof of holy feeling among all the fibres of our constitutional polity and government. . . . The whole shaping of the fabric is Providential. God, God is in it, every where . . . every drum-beat is a hymn, the cannon thunder God, the electric silence, darting victory along the wires, is the inaudible greeting of God's favoring work and purpose. [25]

Granted this sentiment, it was natural that the outcome of the Civil War should suggest to those of the North that "the sword of victory had been wielded by the arm of Providence," while many in the South tended humbly to submit "to the inscrutable ways of the same Power," [26] as the young South Carolinian interviewed by John Trowbridge, who had concluded, "I think it was in the decrees of God Almighty that slavery was to be abolished in this way, and I don't murmur."[27]

However, the ways of Providence were not to all as inscrutable as to Abraham Lincoln, who, after plumbing the awful depths of the war's events, spoke of the altogether righteous judgments on both North and South of the "Almighty" who "has His own purposes" in history—purposes which might not fully coincide with the desires of either side. On this basis, Lincoln concluded in humility that it behooved finite men to proceed "with malice toward none, with charity for all."

There was little of such humility in the heart and hardly a hint of such somber mystery tinging the thought of the Rev. Henry Ward Beecher—that magnificent weathervane of respectable opinion and on some issues an aboriginal Brooklyn Dodger—when in May, 1863, he addressed the anniversary meeting of the American Home Missionary Society in Chicago. "See," he exulted, "how wonderfully God, in his good providence, is preparing us for the work." For "while the South is draining itself dry of its resources . . . the Northern States are growing rich by war." And "what does this mean but this—that God is storing us with that wealth by which we are to be prepared to meet the exigencies which war shall bring upon us."

And what "exigencies" are to be brought upon us? Beecher expressed no doubts:

We are to have the charge of this continent. The South has been proved, and has been found wanting. She is not worthy to bear rule. She has lost the scepter in our national government; she is to lose the scepter in the States themselves; and this continent is to be from this time forth governed by Northern men, with Northern ideas, and with a Northern gospel.

And the reasons are clear: "this continent is to be cared for by the North simply because the North has been true to the cause of Christ in . . . a sufficient measure to secure her own safety; and the nation is to be given to us because we have the bosom by which to nourish it."[28]

Instructed by such worthy religious leaders, it is not to be wondered at if the final victory was widely interpreted as a vindication of the righteousness of the cause of the victors. And this in turn easily merged with a vindication of what the victorious North was rapidly becoming—an industrialized civilization under "business" control. For, to quote a well-known textbook, "the Northern victory meant that certain forces and interests, long held in check by the combination of the agricultural South and West, could now have free and full play. . . . Finance and industrialism could move forward to completion without effective opposition."[29]

From here it was but another short step to enshrinement of the political instrument which, in the hands of Providence, had guided the Union to victory over slavery and disunion. By 1865 a writer in the Methodist *New York Christian Advocate* had already proclaimed that "we find the political parties of the day so made out, that it may . . . be determined on which side an orderly and intelligent Protestant will be found, and on which the profane, the dissolute and the Romanist."[30] The Republican party, said Henry Wilson, contained "more of moral and intellectual worth than was ever embodied in any political organization in any land. . . . [It was] created by no man . . . [but] brought into being by Almighty God himself." This, of course, meant enshrinement of what the party became soon after Lincoln's death, when "it allied itself with the forces of corporate industry, which represented a greater investment of capital and, consequently, a greater concentration of power in politics and economic life than the slaveholders had ever dreamed of possessing."[31]

But if Americans were religious and idealistic, they were also pragmatic. If it appears that they too simply saw the smiles of beneficent Providence in the trinity of Northernism, business, and the Republican party, it must also be remembered that the system appeared to work—to produce tangible fruits in the great and obvious material prosperity that o'erspread the land like a flood and promised, eventually at least, to saturate all levels of society. Thousands of inventions, garnered up and universally applied by free and daring enterprises, revolutionized transportation, communication, agriculture, and industry, while the prevailing system seemingly distributed the benefits more widely and equitably than any had before it.[32] It was these practical, tangible results that provided the most persuasive argument for "the American way of life" and tended to dampen all critical, as well as carping, voices in whatever realm as "un-American." Further, as time passed, a rather definite and complete ideological structure—constituting an explanation and defense—was compounded out of conservative *laissez faire* economic theory, the "common-sense" philosophy of the schools, and the pietistic orthodoxy of the churches.

The foundation of the whole structure was the idea of "progress." It was belief in progress that made tolerable the very rapid changes to which people were being subjected, as well as some of the less desirable aspects of what was happening. The idea of progress was compounded of the Christian doctrine of Providence and the scientific idea of evolution and was summed up in the slick phrase popularized by John Fiske and Lyman Abbott: "Evolution is God's way of doing things." So, for example, it could be proclaimed as late as 1928 that "the fact of human progress is seen to be part of the inevitable evolutionary process; and religious faith seeks in the cosmos which produced us and which carries us along the evidence of the activities of God."[33]

To those standing on such a theological escalator, change held no terrors. And undesirable features of the passing scene might be endured with patience bred of the knowledge that they would inevitably be transcended, since, as Henry Ward Beecher assured a Yale audience, "Man is made to start and not to stop; to go on, and on, and up, and onward . . . and ending in the glorious liberty of the sons of God."[34] Meanwhile, as John Bascom had said, "death is of little moment, if it plays into a higher life. The insects that feed the bird meet their destination. The savages that are trodden out of a stronger race are in the line of progress." And "We—we as interpreters—are not to bring higher and impossible motives and feelings into a lower field."[35]

That such sentiments were not restricted to the eggheads and/or the well-to-do is suggested by the popularity of some of the so-called "sentimental" gospel songs that the so-called "common people" sang in the churches:

> *He leadeth me; O blessed thought!*
> *O words with heavenly comfort fraught!*
> *Whate'er I do, where'er I be,*
> *Still 'tis God's hand that leadeth me.*

And when bleak failure seemed to encompass them and cankerous despair threatened to eat away the soul, they still sang,

> *We wonder why the test*
> *When we try to do our best.*
> *But we'll understand it better by and by.*

The understanding at the time was aided by the enunciation of a constellation of basic principles or doctrines which together gave content and structure to the idea of progress by explaining its practical workings in human society. One of the most complete statements of these doctrines was achieved by Andrew Carnegie in his article called "Wealth," which appeared in the June, 1889, issue of the *North American Review* and was described by the editor as one of the finest articles he had ever published.[36]

Carnegie eschewed airy speculation and proposed to speak of "the foundations upon which society is based" and of the laws upon which "civilization itself depends"—the laws which "are the highest results of human experience" and "the soil in which society so far has produced the best fruit." And, he added as an anathema, "Objections to the foundations upon which society is based are not in order."

First was the familiar law of "the sacredness of property"—or the right of every individual to have and to hold and be protected by the government of the society in the possession of whatever property he could get.

Second were the twin laws of competition and the accumulation of wealth. The competition is for property, and these laws explain the way in which property gets distributed in a society. All men enter into the competition. But it is recognized that men differ in inherent aptitudes or talents in relationship to it. For example, some men are gifted with a "talent of organization and management" which "invariably secures" for them "enormous rewards, no matter where or under what laws or conditions." Ergo, "it is a law, as certain as any of the other named, that men possessed of this peculiar talent for affairs, under the free play of economic forces, must, of necessity, soon be in receipt of more revenue than can be judiciously expended upon themselves." In brief, "it is inevitable that their income must exceed their expenditures, and that they must accumulate wealth." The wealthy man may be regarded as the victim of circumstances over which he has no control.

Carnegie was realist enough to recognize that "society pays" a great price "for the law of competition," which, indeed, "may be sometimes hard for the individual." Nevertheless, "the advantages of this law are also greater still," for not only has it produced "our wonderful material development, which brings improved conditions in its train," but "it is best for the race, because it insures the survival of the fittest in every department." This suggests a rather clear and universal, not to say comforting, criterion for judging who are the "fittest" in the society.

The Right Reverend William Lawrence of Massachusetts propounded his ecclesiastical version of the agnostic's sentiments in an article published in January, 1901.[37] Sniffing "a certain distrust on the part of our people as to the effect of material prosperity on their morality," he suggested that it would be well to "revise our inferences from history, experience, and the Bible" and shed that "subtle hypocrisy which has beset the Christian through the ages, bemoaning the deceitfulness of riches and, at the same time working with all his might to earn a competence, and a fortune if he can." Having rid himself of such false inferences and hypocrisy, man may now recognize the two great guiding principles for his life. The first is that it is "his divine mission" to "conquer Nature, open up her resources, and harness them to his service." The second is that, "in the long run, it is only to the man of morality that wealth comes" for "Godliness [in God's Universe] is in league with riches." This being the case, the good Bishop added, "we return with an easier mind and clearer conscience to the problem of our twenty-five billion dollars in a decade," confident that "material prosperity is in the long run favorable to morality."

Third was the law or rule of stewardship, which followed upon the views of the sacredness of property and the laws of competition and accumulation. In brief, the use and disposition of the property, as well as its mere possession, are sacred to the man who accumulates it. God gave it to him by endowing him with certain talents, and he is responsible for it *to God* alone, and certainly not to the unfit or the lesser fit in the community.

"We start," said Carnegie, "with a condition of affairs under which the best interests of the race are promoted, but which inevitably gives wealth to the few." And "thus far . . . the situation can be surveyed and pronounced good." Therefore, the "only question with which we have to deal," he continued, is "What is the proper mode of administering wealth after the laws upon which civilization is founded have thrown it into the hands of the few?" There were, he thought, but three possibilities. "The few" might leave it to their families, they might bequeath it "for public purposes," or they might administer it during their lives. He ruled out the first two as irresponsible, even coming to the radical conclusion that the state might well confiscate through inheritance taxes at least half of fortunes so left.

The true duty of "the man of Wealth" is to live modestly and unostentatiously, "provide moderately for the legitimate wants of those dependent upon him," and, beyond that,

to consider all surplus revenues which come to him simply as trust funds, which he is . . . strictly bound as a matter of duty to administer in the manner which, in his judgment, is best calculated to produce the most beneficial results for the community . . . thus becoming the mere agent and trustee for his poorer brethren, bringing to their service his superior wisdom, experience, and ability to administer, doing for them better than they would or could do for themselves.

The main rule to be followed is "to help those who will help themselves" and to eschew the "indiscriminate charity" which presents "one of the most serious obstacles to the improvement of our race," by encouraging "the slothful, the drunken, the unworthy." To this we shall return in the next article.

Here it is necessary only to note that such stewardship was taken seriously by many wealthy men of the day and produced in them an honest and consecrated devotion to their sacred duties which only the sneering souls of the mean in mind could belittle. In 1856 John P. Crozer was somewhat awed to note that "wealth flows in from all sources." And this, he added, made him feel "as often before, in making up my yearly accounts, oppressed with the responsibility of my stewardship. I am, indeed, perplexed how I shall use, as I ought to, the great and increasing wealth which God has bestowed upon me." "I love to make money almost as well as a miser," he wrote but added, "I love to give it away for charitable purposes." But he realized, as he searched his soul, "I . . . must set a guard over myself, lest the good designed be lost in the luxury of giving." For

excuses are so easily framed, and the heart of man is so deceitful, that one can easily reason himself into the belief that, all things considered, he has done pretty well. I find such a process of reasoning in my own mind; but calm reflection tells me that I have not done well. I am a very unprofitable servant to so good a Master; and as he has made me the steward of a large estate, it becomes me "to lend to the Lord" freely of my substance.

And, still troubled, he prayed with real humility, "O my Lord, if it is thy righteous pleasure, direct me clearly and decisively to some path of duty and of usefulness, apart from the absorbing influence of wealth and worldly mindedness."[38]

Later, of course, when such devoted men were harassed by the rise of the unfit and strikes rocked their companies this paternalistic conception of stewardship would show another face, as when George F. Baer, president of the Philadelphia and Reading Railway, wrote in 1902 to an inquirer:

I beg of you not to be discouraged. The rights and interests of the laboring man will be protected and cared for—not by the labor agitators, but by the Christian men to whom God in His infinite wisdom has given control of the property interests of the country, and upon the successful Management of which so much depends.[39]

Meanwhile, as intimated previously, Protestantism—at least in the "respectable" churches—effused a benign sanctity over all. The older "people's" churches were rapidly becoming "middle class," at least in mentality and leadership. As A. M. Schlesinger, Sr., says, even the Baptists "abandoned their contempt for wealth," as God gave gold in abundance to some of their more worthy members.[40] And even in 1866 a writer in the Methodist *Christian Advocate* was pleased to note that "by virtue of the habits which religion inculcates and cherishes, our Church members have as a body risen in the social scale, and thus become socially removed from the great body out of which most of them originally gathered." And he added with a hint of smugness, "this tendency of things is natural and universal, and in its results unavoidable; perhaps we might add, also, not undesirable."[41]

At the same time, American scholars, many of them ministers turned professors, worked out, as Henry May says, "a school of political economy which might well be labeled clerical laissez faire." And in this area, perhaps, the ideological amalgamation of which we have spoken is best and most clearly illustrated. Said the Rev. John McVicker of Columbia: "That science and religion eventually teach the same lesson, is a necessary consequence of the unity of truth, but it is seldom that this view is so satisfactorily displayed as in their searches of Political Economy."[42]

But Americans, in spite of the long century of relative peace and stability in the world following 1814 and their almost complete freedom from embroilment in European affairs, which permitted them to work out their own problems with a minimum of outside interference, were never complete isolationists ideologically. From this they were saved by the strong sense of destiny under God, which pervaded their thinking from the beginning. By 1825 Francis Wayland, Jr., a Baptist minister, had already proclaimed sentiments that should have raised eyebrows in Europe: "What nation will be second in the new order of things, is yet to be decided; but the providence of God has already announced, that, if true to ourselves, we shall be inevitably first."[43]

The keynote of the American idea of destiny was struck by John Winthrop in his address "Written on Boarde the Arrabella" in 1630. He said:

The worke wee haue in hand is by a mutall consent through a speciall overruleing providence, and a more than an ordinary approbation of the Churches of Christ to seeke out a place of Cohabitation and Consorteshipp vnder a due forme of Government both ciull and ecclesiasticall.

If we are faithful to our covenant with him, Winthrop continued,

wee shall finde that the god of Israell is among vs . . . when hee shall make vs a prayse and glory, that men shall say of succeeding plantacions: the Lord make it like that of New England: for wee must Consider that wee shall be as a Citty vpon a Hill, the eies of all people are vpon vs.[44]

Thenceforth throughout American history this strong sense of particular calling, of destiny under God, has remained a constant part of the ideological structure of the nation. Clothed in various languages in various times and places, the theme has remained the same, although God, like Alice's Cheshire cat, has sometimes threatened gradually to disappear completely or, at most, to remain only as a disembodied and sentimental smile.

Perhaps the version of destiny intimated by Winthrop in his reference to the "Citty vpon a Hill" with "the eies of all people . . . vpon vs" has been most commonly dominant—namely, that American destiny is to be fulfilled merely by setting an example for all to follow. Thus in the *Discourse* quoted earlier, Francis Wayland, Jr., held that "our power resides in the force of our example. It is by exhibiting to other nations the practical excellence of a government of law, that they will learn its nature and advantages, and will in due time achieve their own emancipation."[45] Already, he thought, "our country has given to the world the first ocular demonstration, not only of the practicability, but also of the unrivalled superiority of a popular form of government."[46]

William R. Williams in 1846 more obviously wove the strands of evangelical Christianity into those of American destiny: "Our Heavenly Father has made us a national epistle to other lands," he wrote.

See that you read a full and impressive comment to all lands, of the power of Christian principle, and of the expansive and self-sustaining energies of the gospel, when left

*unfettered by national endowments, and secular alliances. The evangelical character of
our land is to tell upon the plans and destinies of other nations.*[47]

It is small wonder that Americans down to the present commonly find it hard to understand why the nations of the world do not automatically adopt the fine way of life which
their country so completely and beautifully exemplifies.

It was the idea of destiny which in the period we are discussing, as in all periods before
and since, added "the inducements of philanthropy to those of patriotism" in the American mind and broadened the idea of progress and its laws to include all of humanity.
America's destiny came to be seen as her call to spread the amazing benefits of the
American democratic faith and its free-enterprise system throughout the world, gradually
transforming the world into its own image. The idea of destiny lay back of and tempered
Bishop Lawrence's belief that "Godliness is in league with riches." So, he concluded, "we
have learned how to win wealth: we are learning how to use and spend it." But wealth
and character go together. "Without wealth, character is liable to narrow and harden.
Without character, wealth will destroy." Therefore,

*the call of to-day is . . . for the uplift of character,—the support of industry, education,
art, and every means of culture; the encouragement of the higher life; and, above all, the
deepening of the religious faith of the people; the rekindling of the spirit that, clothed
with her material forces, the great personality of this Nation may fulfill her divine
destiny.*[48]

But, by the time he wrote in 1901, the United States fresh from its first venture in
imperialistic war, was already beginning to be impressed by the meaning and possibilities
of the physical power which destiny had placed in its hands and the idea had been
hatched that the power as well as the wealth was given by divine appointment to be used.

Josiah Strong, erstwhile Congregational pastor in Cheyenne and at the time secretary
of that denomination's Home Missionary Society, sounded the Christian version of this
view in his very popular book, *Our Country*, first published in 1885.[49]

The Anglo-Saxon race—and in America all immigrants soon became Anglo-Saxon—is
the representative of two closely related ideas, "Civil Liberty" and "pure spiritual Christianity." Hence, he concluded, "it is chiefly to the English and American peoples that we
must look for the evangelization of the world," for there is no doubt that these two ideas
are necessary if "all men" are to "be lifted up into the light of the highest Christian
civilization." Hence it is obvious that "the Anglo-Saxon . . . is divinely commissioned to
be, in a peculiar sense, his brother's keeper."

And when we of this generation add to this fact the equally obvious fact of the
Anglo-Saxon's "rapidly increasing strength in modern times . . . we have well-nigh a
demonstration of his destiny." For "does it not look as if God were not only preparing in
our Anglo-Saxon civilization the die with which to stamp the peoples of the earth, but as
if he were also massing behind that die the mighty power with which to press it?"

The English, however, may be discounted, and the Americans "may reasonably expect
to develop the highest type of Anglo-Saxon civilization." For it follows from the fact that
"human progress follows a law of development" that "our civilization should be the
noblest; for we are 'The heirs of all the ages in the foremost files of time.'"

Thus, he explained, "God, with infinite wisdom and skill, is training the Anglo-Saxon race for an hour sure to come"—the hour of "*the final competition of races.*" And, he modestly concluded, "can anyone doubt that the result of this competition of races will be the 'survival of the fittest?' " Planting his feet firmly on the escalator, he proclaimed the present knowledge that the "inferior tribes were only precursors of a superior race, voices in the wilderness crying: 'Prepare ye the way of the Lord!' "

So this eminent Congregational leader, having to his own satisfaction plumbed at last the depths of inscrutable Providence, knew that "God has two hands. Not only is he preparing in our civilization the die with which to stamp the nations, but, by what Southey called the 'timing of Providence,' he is preparing mankind to receive our impress."

With such well-nigh infallible religious guides abroad in the land, it is small wonder that a mere junior Senator, Albert J. Beveridge, of Indiana, was prepaied to defend annexation of the Philippines on January 9, 1900, with the words:

We will not renounce our part in the mission of the race, trustee, under God, of the civilization of the world. . . . He has made us the master organizers of the world to establish system where chaos reigns. . . . He has made us adept in government that we may administer government among savage and senile peoples. . . . And of all our race, He has marked the American people as His chosen Nation to finally lead in the regeneration of the world. This is the divine mission of America, and it holds for us all the profit, all the glory, all the happiness possible to man. We are trustees of the world's progress, guardians of its righteous peace. The judgment of the Master is upon us: "Ye have been faithful over a few things; I will make you ruler over many things."[50]

But already the worm was beginning to turn—and a Christian note of profounder depth was struck by Senator George F. Hoar, who rose merely to say: "The Devil taketh him up into an extremely high mountain and showeth him all the kingdoms of the world and the glory of them and saith unto him, 'All these things will be thine if thou wilt fall down and worship me.' "[51]

We have noted, then, that the bulk of American Protestantism achieved during this period a working ideological harmony with the modes of the modern industrialized civilization, the free-enterprise system, and the burgeoning imperialism. Professor W. S. Hudson, treating the more purely theological aspects of this development in a most discerning book on *The Great Tradition of the American Churches*, makes good his claim that "the New Theology was essentially a culture religion."[52] The doctrines of the "gospel of wealth" in the context of the idea of destiny under God gave a satisfactory explanation of the facts of human life as experienced in the United States. It should never be forgotten that at this time the observational order coincided in high degree with the conceptual order and that such coincidence defines social stability.

This it was that created an atmosphere in which those actually in control—the only people that really mattered—could live at ease in the vast expanding new Zion. This was Edith Wharton's "age of innocence," Henry S. Canby's "age of confidence"; and its flower was a host of middle-class "fathers" of the type pictured by Clarence Day. Perhaps its outstanding characteristic was complacency, based on the feeling that God was in his heaven and all was right with the world. Surveying the period in retrospect, we may agree with Whitehead that "the prosperous middle classes, who ruled the nineteenth century, placed an excessive value upon placidity of existence" and that this is hardly a sufficient basis for an enduring culture.[53]

Looking backward today from a world which promises to be somewhat different from that Utopia which Edward Bellamy anticipated in 1888, it seems obvious enough to us that the outward harmony was achieved by overlooking certain incongruous elements in the situation that had troubled only such gloomy and lonesome prophets as Nathaniel Hawthorne, Herman Melville, Walt Whitman, and Henry Adams. Hence the world that seemed so fine and stable to Carnegie and Bishop Lawrence, to Crozer and Henry Ward Beecher, to Josiah Strong and Russell Conwell—to all the "fathers" of Day's type—was about to explode. The period of cultural triumph of the denominations merged—not with a whimper, but with a bang—into the period of upheaval and crisis.

But these denominations, however much their normative theology might be eroded, their historical sense blunted, and their Christianity identified with the current forms of the American way of life, still bore latent within them a sense of continuity with the Christian past—with the prophets of the Old Testament God of judgment; with the Nazarene and his Sermon on the Mount; with the Christian church through the ages—and here was a basis for perspective on the immediate scene. Hence the crisis itself carried within it the possibility of religious renewal and theological reconstruction, rooted in the view that, from a Christian standpoint, the whole ideology of the complacent period rested on an idolatry made possible because the dominant churches had largely forgotten to preach and had failed to inculcate belief in the First Commandment.

Notes

1. "The Protestant Faiths," in Harold E. Stearns (ed.), *America Now: An Inquiry into Civilization in the United States* (New York: Literary Guild of America, Inc., 1928), p. 514; see also Mark Sullivan, *Our Times* (New York: Charles Scribner's Sons, 1927), Vol. II, chap. v, "The American Mind: Orthodoxy," pp. 84-93.

2. See, in this connection, Alexis de Tocqueville, *Democracy in America,* trans. Henry Reeve (rev. ed.; New York: Colonial Press, 1899), II, 9, 22.

3. Henry F. May, *Protestant Churches and Industrial America* (New York: Harper & Bros., 1949), p. 39.

4. *Ibid.*, p. 4.

5. Quoted from Justice Story by Ralph H. Gabriel, *The Course of American Democratic Thought* (New York: Ronald Press, 1940), p. 23.

6. This and following quotations are taken from Carnegie's article called "Wealth," which was published in the *North American Review*, Vol. CXLVIII (June, 1889). I have used it as reprinted in Gail Kennedy (ed.), *Democracy and the Gospel of Wealth*, one of the volumes in the Amherst "Problems in American Civilization Series" (Boston: D. C. Heath & Co., 1949), p. 8.

7. See Wade Crawford Barclay, *History of Methodist Missions*, II: *To Reform the Nation* (New York: Board of Missions and Church Extension of the Methodist Church, 1950), 8.

8. It should not be forgotten that from the evangelical revivalists' point of view the salvation of

individuals was primary and constituted the churches' greatest contribution to social and political morality and life.

9. [Mary Bushnell Cheney], *Life and Letters of Horace Bushnell* (New York: Harper & Bros., 1880), p. 56.

10. Horace Bushnell, "Preliminary Dissertation on the Nature of Language as Related to Thought and Spirit." in *God in Christ* (Hartford: Brown & Parsons, 1849), pp. 16, 40.

11. As quoted by Winthrop S. Hudson in *The Great Tradition of the American Churches* (New York: Harper & Bros., 1953), p. 172.

12. C. H. Hopkins, *The Rise of the Social Gospel in American Protestantism, 1865-1915* (New Haven: Yale University Press, 1940), pp. 14-15.

13. Daniel Dorchester, *The Problem of Religious Progress* (New York: Phillips & Hunt, 1881), pp. 31-32.

14. Francis Wayland, *A Discourse Delivered in the First Baptist Church, Providence, R.I., on the Day of Public Thanksgiving, July 21, 1842* (Providence: Published by H. H. Brown, 1842), pp. 22, 23.

15. J. H. Randall and J. H. Randall, Jr., *Religion and the Modern World* (New York: Frederick A. Stokes Co., 1929), pp. 26-27.

16. George A. Gordon, "The Theological Problem for To-Day," in Rossiter W. Raymond (ed.), *The New Puritanism* (New York: Howard & Hulbert, 1898), p. 151.

17. *Writings of Professor B. B. Edwards, with a Memoir by Edwards A. Park* (Boston: John P. Jewett & Co., 1853), I, 490.

18. De Tocqueville, *op. cit.*, I, 331.

19. *Ibid.*, p. 330.

20. *The Writings of the Late Elder John Leland, Including Some Events in His Life, Written by Himself, with Additional Sketches, &c. by Miss L. F. Greene* (New York: Printed by G. W. Wood, 1845), p. 249.

21. See my "Abraham Lincoln's 'Last, Best Hope of Earth': The American Dream of Destiny and Democracy," *Church History*, XXIII (March, 1954), 3-16.

22. J. H. Randall, Jr., "The Churches and the Liberal Tradition," *Annals of the American Academy of Political and Social Science*, CCLVI (March, 1948), 149, 150.

23. Hudson, *op. cit.*, p. 61.

24. May, *op. cit.*, p. 91. Compare Paul Tillich's comment that the churches which "replaced the one Church" after the Reformation "were supported either by the state or by the dominant group in society—the former predominantly in Europe, the latter especially in America. In both situations, the Churches largely surrendered their critical freedom. They tended to become agencies of either the state or the ruling classes" ("The World Situation," in Henry P. Van Dusen [ed.], *The Christian Answer* [New York: Charles Scribner's Sons, 1946], p. 38).

25. Horace Busnell, *Popular Government by Divine Right* (Hartford: L. E. Hunt, 1864), pp. 15, 12, 15.

26. Herman E. Kittredge, *Ingersoll: A Biographical Appreciation* (New York: Dresden Publishing Co., 1911), p. 288.

27. Quoted by Edmund Wilson in a review of Frederick Law Olmsted's *Cotton Kingdom*, in the *New Yorker*, April 3, 1954, p. 115.

28. Henry Ward Beecher, "Home Missions and Our Country's Future," *Home Missionary*, XXXVI (September, 1863), 112.

29. Avery Craven and Walter Johnson, *The United States: Experiment in Democracy* (Boston: Ginn & Co., 1947), p. 418.

30. As quoted in Ralph E. Morrow, "Northern Methodism in the South during Reconstruction," *Mississippi Valley Historical Review*, XLI (September, 1954), 213.

31. As quoted in Craven and Johnson, *op. cit.*, pp. 430, 422.

32. Compare A. M. Schlesinger, *Political and Social Growth of the American Peoples, 1865-1940* (3d ed.; New York: Macmillan Co., 1941), p. vi: "Yet the record as a whole sums up a people who, despite the ills to which mankind is prey, managed to fashion a way of life and a system of government which at every period of American history served as a beacon light for struggling humanity everywhere."
   Robert Baired in *The Christian Retrospect and Register: A Summary of the Scientific, Moral and Religious Progress of the First Half of the XIXth Century* (New York: N. W. Dodd, 1851) held that no one will deny that "in all that relates to their MATERIAL INTERESTS our race has . . . made great progress since the commencement of the XIXth century" and that "the latter half of the century will show still greater progress, we are far from being disposed, either to deny, or to doubt." Further, "that there has also been a great progress in all that has a bearing on the MORAL AND RELIGIOUS INTERESTS of Humanity, during the same era, is a position which none can question." But, he added, the authors "are pained to be compelled to admit" that "the progress in the moral and Religious Interests of our race, during the period . . . has not equalled that of their Material Interests."

33. Gerald Birney Smith, *Current Christian Thinking* (Chicago: University of Chicago Press, 1928), p. 189.

34. As quoted in Hudson, *op. cit.*, p. 175.

35. John Bascom, "The Natural Theology of Social Science. IV, Labor and Capital," *Bibliotheca sacra*, XXV (October, 1869), 660.

36. The following quotations are taken from the article as noted in n. 6.

37. The quotations are taken from the article as reprinted in Kennedy (ed.), *op. cit.*

38. John P. Crozer, *Standard*, XV (May 7, 1868), 4, col. 4.

39. Caro Lloyd, *Henry Demarest Lloyd, 1847-1903, a Biography* (New York: G. P. Putnam's Sons, 1912), II, 190-91.

40. A. M. Schlesinger, Sr., *The Rise of the City, 1878-1898* ("A History of American Life Series," Vol. X [New York: Macmillan Co., 1933]), p. 331.

41. As quoted in May, *op. cit.*, p. 62.

42. *Ibid.*, p. 14.

43. Francis Wayland, *The Duties of an American Citizen: Two Discourses, Delivered in the First Baptist Meeting House in Boston, on Thursday, April 7, 1825* (Boston: James Loring, 1825), p. 29.

44. John Winthrop, "A Modell of Christian Charity," in Perry Miller and Thomas H. Johnson (eds.), *The Puritans* (New York: American Book Co., 1938), pp. 197, 198-99.

45. Wayland, *The Duties of an American Citizen*, pp. 35-36.

46. *Ibid.*, p. 27.

47. As quoted in John R. Bodo, *The Protestant Clergy and Public Issues, 1812-1848*, (Princeton: Princeton University Press, 1954), p. 241. From "Christ, a Home Missionary," in the *Missionary Enterprise* (Boston, 1845), p. 93.

48. Kennedy (ed.), *op. cit.*

49. The following quotations are from chap. xiv, "The Anglo-Saxon and the World's Future," in Josiah Strong, *Our Country, Its Possible Future and Its Present Crisis* (rev. ed. based on the census of 1890 [New York: Baker & Taylor Co., 1891]).

50. As quoted in Sullivan, *op. cit.*, I, 47-48.

51. Winfred E. Garrison, *The March of Faith: The Story of Religion in America since 1865* (New York: Harper & Bros., 1933), p. 174.

52. P. 161.

53. A. N. Whitehead, *Science and the Modern World* (New York: Penguin Books, Ltd., 1938), p. 240.

Sullivan's skyscrapers as the expression of nineteenth-century technology

Carl W. Condit

The term Gilded Age connoted, among other things, an attitude toward culture that prevailed in late nineteenth-century America. In an era of remarkable industrial vitality, the arbiters of taste and art resolutely averted their eyes from the raw mainstream of American life. Architects lined Fifth Avenue with mansions that resembled French chateau or Renaissance palaces, and their millionaire owners filled the rooms with artifacts that bespoke immense wealth but said nothing of the world in which that wealth had been made. The literary magazines championed a poetry and prose that would be appropriately deignated as "the genteel tradition." There was, indeed, a distinctly feminine cast to this phenomenon. Women were the proper bearers of culture, E. L. Godkin remarked, because they alone had the leisure and finer sensibilities for this high calling. Historians have pondered this odd juxtaposition of economic vitality and cultural sterility. Was the latter merely an expression of the insecurity and vulgarity of the new rich? Or was it an aspect of the intellectual design of this era, the "formalism" that diverted thought and expression away from any critical approach to prevailing assumptions? What was, in any case, certain was that Gilded Age culture constituted a holding action at best. Not for long could writers and artists be so diverted, and the turn of the century witnessed a remarkable resurgence of activity that embraced the realities of American life. It was perhaps appropriate that the primary site of this breakthrough should have been in Chicago, the city which seemed to epitomize the vitality of American industrial life, and that the new realism should have received its earliest expression in architecture, the art form most closely allied to the new technology.

The impact of this technology on the pioneering architecture of Louis Sullivan forms the theme of the following essay. In his analysis of the four major buildings that Sullivan designed between the mid-1880s and the opening of the twentieth century, Robert Condit shows not only how Sullivan utilized scientific and technological advances, but how he gave the buildings a form that would express the method of construction and the purpose to which the buildings would be put. They exemplified his famous dictum that

Carl W. Condit, "Sullivan's Skyscrapers as the Expression of Nineteenth Century Technology," *Technology and Culture*, I (Winter, 1959), pp. 78-93. Reprinted by permission of the publisher.

"form follows function." But Condit sees in this principle, as Sullivan understood it, a deeper significance than the mere use of architecture to express function in a technical and utilitarian sense, significant as this was as a departure from the current mode of derivative design. Sullivan was, by his own account, deeply moved by the special genius of his age, by the immense advances man had made in understanding and mastering his environment. This achievement was summed up in the building of the great nineteenth-century bridges. Two of these—the Eads and Dixville bridges—received deep study from Sullivan, and Condit closely analyzes the elements that especially excited the architect. In his own buildings, Sullivan likewise attempted to develop a form that would evoke the innermost spirit of his age, the power and scientific progress of the late nineteenth century. By so doing, Condit implies, Sullivan was developing not only a modern architecture but, in a time that conceived of art essentially as decoration, he was reasserting the role of art as an expression of the spirit of its age, and his architecture therefore constituted a fundamental criticism of conventional notions of culture in the Gilded Age.

For further reading: Carl W. Condit, *The Rise of the Skyscraper* (1952); John Burchard and Albert Bush-Brown, *The Architecture of America: A Social and Cultural History* (1961); Hugh S. Morrison, *Louis Sullivan* (1935); Louis Sullivan, *The Autobiography of an Idea* (1926); ——, *Kindergarten Chats* (1947); Robert H. Walker, "The Poet and the Rise of the City," *Journal of American History*, IL (1962), 85-99; Peter Buitenhuis, "Aesthetics of the Skyscraper: The Views of Sullivan, James and Wright," *American Quarterly*, IX (1957), 316-324; Wayne Andrews, *Architecture, Ambition and Americans: a Social History of American Architecture* (1964).*

It is now a matter of common consent that Louis Sullivan (1856-1924) was the first great modern architect, the first to create a new and powerful vocabulary of forms derived from the major cultural determinants of his age. He was the most imaginative and the most articulate figure among a small group of creative men in Europe and America who, suddenly around 1890, struck out in a new direction with the deliberate intention of breaking once and for all with the traditional architectural forms of the classical and medieval heritage. In Europe the movement called itself *Art Nouveau*, its initiator being the Belgian architect Baron Victor Horta (1861-1947). In the United States it was at first confined largely to Chicago, where the fire of 1871 prepared the way for one of the most exuberant outbursts of creative activity in nineteenth century architecture. The leadership of this movement, now known as the Chicago school, was initially in the hands of William Le Baron Jenney (1832-1906), but by 1890 it had passed to Sullivan and his engineering partner, Dankmar Adler (1844-1900). Within a single decade Adler and Sullivan moved rapidly, if irregularly, from close dependence on past architectural styles to an organic form which derived its character from the industrial and scientific culture which had swept everything before it in the Western world.

By the last decade of the century Sullivan had developed in preliminary terms his organic theory of building art, a system which was later to be presented at length in his major writings, *Kindergarten Chats* (1901-1902) and *The Autobiography of an Idea* (1922). The philosophy of architecture offered in these works contains extensive ethical and social elements as well as formal and aesthetic. Since the doctrine has been discussed, analyzed, and interpreted in detail by historians and critics, we need not here inquire into it at length. Our purpose is to find, if we can, the broad symbolic meaning of Sullivan's major works, for which it may be useful to summarize some of the fundamental ideas in his system of thought.

Sullivan's interest in structural engineering—in part, of course, the product of professional necessity—early developed into a wide-ranging enthusiasm for science as a whole. It centered mainly in biology, from which his organic theory in part stemmed, but it included the new physical theories as well. He read Darwin, Huxley, Spencer, and Tyndall at length and was well acquainted with the writers who were then developing the seminal theories of building art in the past century, chiefly Ruskin, Morris, and Viollet-le-Duc. What distinguishes Sullivan's thought is his profound grasp of the social basis, the responsibility, and the problem of the arts in a technical and industrial society. He felt that he had discovered the rule with no exceptions (to use his own phrase) in the concept "form follows function," but the key to his philosophy lies in the proper understanding of the word *function*. An organic architecture, he believed, is one which grows naturally or organically out of the social and technical factors among which the architect lives and with which he must work. These factors embrace not only the technical and utilitarian problems of building but also the aspirations, ideals, and needs, both material and psychological, of mankind. Thus *functionalism* involved for him something much wider and deeper than utilitarian and structural considerations, as important as these are.

To Sullivan the creation of a genuine architectural style was not a matter of historical styles or of dipping into a vocabulary of contemporary forms and details in order to secure a style which the architect might feel to be consonant with the life of his time. The architect must first recognize the importance of true aesthetic expression for the symbolic recreation, the harmonization, and the emotional enrichment of the many practical and intellectual elements of contemporary civilization. In European and American society at the end of the nineteenth century such an art would begin, by necessity, with the fundamentals: industry, technology, and science. It is the task of the architect, as Sullivan conceived it, to take the products of techniques, on the one hand, and the logic and order of a scientific technology, on the other, and mold them into a form uniting both in a single aesthetic expression. An architecture so developed means the humanization through aesthetic statement of the often cold and non-human facts of industrial techniques.

The early application of this complex philosophy of the organic to a specific building problem appeared in a document which has become a classic of modern theory, "The Tall Office Building Artistically Considered," first published in *Lippincott's Magazine* in 1896. Scattered throughout *The Autobiography of an Idea*, which is Sullivan's final testament, are many sentences of an epigrammatic character that summarize his thought; for example, "As the people are within, so the buildings are without," or again, "It is the task of the architect to build, to express the life of his own people."

The realization of this program in actual commissions reached its mature form in the four largest and most impressive buildings which Adler and Sullivan designed. The first is the Auditorium Building, now Roosevelt University in Chicago, designed in 1886-1887 and opened in 1889. (Fig. 1) The design of this great building, with its huge masonry bearing walls, was much influenced by Richardson (1838-86) and the Romanesque-like forms which he handled so brilliantly. But it marks a transition toward the open and

Figure 1
Auditorium Building,
Chicago, 1887-89. The building
is now owned by and houses the
facilities of Roosevelt University.
(Photo by *Chicago Architectural Photographing Company*.)

Figure 2
Wainwright Building,
St. Louis, Missouri, 1890-91.
(Photo by *Keystone View
Company*.)

Figure 3
Prudential, formerly Guaranty
Building, Buffalo, New York, 1894-95.
(Photo by *Chicago Architectural
Photographing Company*.)

Figure 4
Carson Pirie Scott Store,
Chicago, 1899, 1903-04, 1906.
(Photo by *Chicago Archi-
tectural Photographing Company*.)

dynamic wall forms that were soon to become the distinguishing feature of Sullivan's work. In the year following the completion of the Auditorium he struck out in a new direction to produce one of the most remarkable exhibitions of sheer architectural origin-ality in his own or any age, the steel-framed Wainwright Building in St. Louis (1890-91). (Fig. 2) A few years later the formal character of this structure was refined and enriched in the Guaranty, later Prudential, Building in Buffalo (1894-95). (Fig. 3) In the last of his large commissions, before the poverty and neglect of his later years, he turned in still another direction and produced a radically different kind of expression in the Carson Pirie Scott Store in Chicago, built in three parts over the years from 1899 to 1906, although designed as early as 1896. (Fig. 4)

Behind these steel-framed buildings lay a long preparation in the history of iron construction. The use of iron as a structural material goes back to classical antiquity, but it did not appear wholly emancipated from masonry until the construction of Darby and Pritchard's cast iron arch over the River Severn at Coalbrookdale, England, in 1775-79. The first building with interior columns and beams of iron was William Strutt's Calico Mill at Derby (1793). It was thirty-five years before iron members appeared in American buildings and 1850 before complete iron construction was established, largely through the work of the New York inventors and builders Daniel Badger and James Bogardus. The remainder of the century saw steady progress in the techniques of cast and wrought iron and later steel framing, reaching its culmination in the skyscrapers of New York and Chicago, in which all the essential features of the modern commercial building were given a practical demonstration.

Thus, by 1890, the technical means of a new building art were available to Sullivan. It remained for him to transmute the structural solutions to these unprecedented functional requirements into a symbolic art. His organic philosophy had already come to exist at least in an inchoate form, but so broad an approach to architectural design could not lead directly to a specific kind of formal expression. The key to the process of transmutation may be found, I think, in those passages of Sullivan's writings in which he gives voice to his feelings about particular architectural and structural achievements of his age. We have already mentioned his debt to Richardson. There is a chapter in *Kindergarten Chats*—Number VI, "The Oasis"—in which he acknowledges this debt, and it is the first of various passages that lead us to an understanding of Sullivan's inner purpose. He describes for us, in ironic and impressionist metaphors, his strong emotional reaction to Richard-son's Marshall Field Wholesale Store in Chicago (1885-87) and to what it stands for.

Let us pause, my son, at this oasis in our desert. Let us rest awhile beneath its cool and satisfying calm, and drink a little at this wayside spring. . . .

You mean, I suppose, that here is a good piece of architecture for me to look at—and I quite agree with you.

No; I mean here is a man *for you to look at. A man that walks on two legs instead of four, has active muscles, heart, lungs, and other viscera; a man that lives and breathes, that has red blood; a real man, a manly man; a virile force—broad, vigorous and with a whelm of energy—an entire male.*

I mean that stone and mortar, here, spring into life, and are no more material and sordid things, but, as it were, become the very diapason of a mind rich-stored with harmony. . . .

Four square and brown, it stands, in physical fact, a monument to trade, to the organized commercial spirit, to the power and progress of the age, to the strength and resource of individuality and force of character; spiritually, it stands as the index of a mind, large enough, courageous enough to cope with these things, master them, absorb them and give them forth again, impressed with the stamp of large and forceful personality; artistically, it stands as the creation of one who knows well how to choose his words, who has somewhat to say and says it—and says it as the outpouring of a copious, direct, large and simple mind.[1]

It is clear that Sullivan was profoundly moved by Richardson's building, but even a fine work of architecture did not arouse in him the powerful emotions that were evoked by the great achievements of the bridge engineers in the nineteenth century. There are several illuminating passages in *The Autobiography*, among the most remarkable in the book, in which he tries to analyze his emotional and philosophic response to these monuments of pure structural form. The first records a childhood experience in which he saw a chain suspension bridge over the Merrimack River (possibly Finley's Bridge of 1810, near Newburyport, Massachusetts). The description is loaded with the most extreme expressions of feeling.

Mechanically he ascended a hill . . . musing, as he went, upon the great river Merrimac. . . . Meanwhile something large, something dark was was approaching unperceived; something ominous, something sinister that silently aroused him to a sense of its presence. . . . The dark thing came ever nearer, nearer in the stillness, became broader, looming, and then it changed itself into full view—an enormous terrifying mass that overhung the broad river from bank to bank. . . .

He saw great iron chains hanging in the air. How could iron chains hang in the air? He thought of Julia's fairy tales and what giants did. . . . And then he saw a long flat thing under the chains; and this thing too seemed to float in the air; and then he saw two great stone towers taller than the trees. Could these be giants? . . . [A page follows in which Sullivan records how he ran frightened to his father to tell him that the giants would eat him.]

So [his father] explained that the roadway of the bridge was just like any other road, only it was held up over the river by the big iron chains; that the big iron chains did not float in the air but were held up by the stone towers over the top of which they passed and were anchored firmly into the ground at each end beyond the towers; that the road-bed was hung to the chains so it would not fall into the river. . . . On their way to rejoin Mama, the child turned backward to gaze in awe and love upon the great suspension bridge. There, again, it hung in the air—beautiful in power. The sweep of the chains so lovely, the roadway barely touching the banks. And to think it was made by men! How great must men be, how wonderful; how powerful, that they could make such a bridge; and again he worshipped the worker.[2]

In later years, on his way to becoming an established architect in partnership with one of the great building engineers of his time, Sullivan came to understand how these miracles were accomplished. Then he was prepared to pay his fullest tribute to the bridge engineers and to record it again in his *Autobiography*.

About this time two great engineering works were under way. One, the triple arch

bridge to cross the Mississippi at St. Louis, Capt. Eades [sic], chief engineer; the other,
the great cantilever bridge which was to cross the chasm of the Kentucky River, C. Shaler
Smith, chief engineer, destined for the use of the Cincinnati Southern Railroad. In these
two growing structures Louis's soul became immersed. In them he lived. Were they not
his bridges? Surely they were his bridges. In the pages of the Railway Gazette *he saw*
them born, he watched them grow. Week by week he grew with them. Here was
Romance, here again was man, the great adventurer, daring to think, daring to have faith,
daring to do. Here again was to be set forth to view man in his power to create
beneficently. Here were two ideas differing in kind. Each was emerging from a brain, each
was to find realization. One bridge was to cross to a great river, to form the portal of a
great city, to be sensational and architectonic. The other was to take form in the
wilderness, and abide there; a work of science without concession. Louis followed every
detail of design, every measurement; every operation as the two works progress from the
sinking of the caissons in the bed of the Mississippi, and the start in the wild of the initial
cantilevers from the face of the cliff. He followed each, with the intensity of personal
identification, to the finale of each. Every difficulty he encountered he felt to be his own;
every expedient, every device, he shared in. The chief engineers became his heroes; they
loomed above other men. The positive quality of their minds agreed with the aggressive
quality of his own. In childhood his idols had been the big strong men who did things.
Later on he had begun to feel the greater power of men who could think *things; later the*
expansive power of men who could imagine *things; and at last he began to recognize as*
dominant the will of the Creative Dreamer: he who possessed the power of vision needed
to harness Imagination, to harness the intellect, to make science do his will, to make the
emotions serve him—for without emotion—nothing.[3]

There is a distinct strain of romanticism in this passionate devotion to the builder,
perhaps even a Nietzschean quality in the worship of creative power. For Sullivan came to
see in science and technology the triumphant assertion of man's will expressing itself in a
wholly new way. As he himself put it, "Louis saw power everywhere; and as he grew on
through his boyhood, and through the passage to manhood, and to manhood itself, he
began to see the powers of nature and the powers of man coalesce in his vision into an
IDEA *of power.* Then and only then he became aware that this idea was a *new idea,*—a
complete reversal and inversion of the commonly accepted intellectual and theological
concept of the nature of man."[4]

Thus Sullivan conceived of a bridge as the personal testament of a man, a testament
expressing a unification of the highest energies and skills of the age. What distinguishes
these achievements is not only the technical virtuosity that men like Eads and Smith
commanded, but the integration of many streams of technical and scientific progress in
the nineteenth century. For it was the age that saw the transformation of building from
an empirical and pragmatic technique into an exact science. Since Sullivan chose the St.
Louis and Dixville bridges as his examples, we may use them as representatives of the
transformation that made possible their design and construction. Eads Bridge (1868-74) is
the earlier of the two, and so we may begin with an analysis which reveals how such
structures brought to focus the various scientific and technical currents.

The general staff of Eads Bridge consisted of James B. Eads as chief engineer, Charles
Pfeiffer and Henry Flad as principal assistants, and William Chauvenet, Chancellor of
Washington University, as mathematical consultant. The choice of Eads, who had never

built a bridge before, as head of the St. Louis project rested in large part on his intimate knowledge of the river. For the builder who proposed to found his piers on the rock far below its bed, it was a formidable obstacle indeed. The pilots could read its surface with remarkable skill for the hidden snags and bars that once menaced them, but only Eads knew at first hand its fluid, shifting, treacherous bed. By means of the diving bell which he had invented, he was able to investigate the bottom directly, and he had seen its depth change from 20 to 100 feet at obstacles in the bed as the result of the scouring action of currents. For the first time the topographic and geological surveys of the bridge site could be carried on to a certain extent under water.

With the design of his bridge substantially completed and sufficient capital available, Eads began clearing the site and constructing caissons in the summer of 1867, but difficulties with his iron and steel contractor soon required a suspension of operations. Eads had already decided to substitute steel for the traditional cast iron in the arches and thus became the first to introduce the stronger metal into American building techniques. The Carnegie-Kloman Company at first found it impossible to roll pieces with the physical properties that Eads demanded. The earlier cast steel samples had already failed in the testing machines. At this point Eads insisted on the costly and hitherto unused chrome-steel, an innovation which was to have wide implications for structural and mechanical engineering. Equally important was the application of the methods of experimental science to the investigation of the physical properties of the metal. Eads Bridge is the first major structure in the United States in which testing machines, which had been developed over the previous thirty years in Europe, played a vital role in the successful completion of the bridge.

The initial problem solved, construction was resumed in 1868. Eads began with the east, or Illinois, pier, where the maximum depth of bedrock offered the most serious challenge. The pneumatic caisson was necessity, and thus Eads became the first to introduce its use in the United States, anticipating Roebling by a year. It had been used in Europe since 1849, when Lewis Cubitt and John Wright developed it for the construction of the piers of a span at Rochester, England. Eads built a cylindrical iron-shod caisson of massive timbers heavily reinforced with iron bands. Its diameter was 75 feet, the working chamber 8 feet deep. Within this huge enclosure the masonry pier was built up, the weight of the masonry forcing the cutting edge into the river bed. The Eads caisson extended continuously up to the water surface, successive rings being added as it sank lower. The caisson for the Illinois pier reached bedrock at 123 feet below water level at the time of construction. Five months of excavation and pumping were required to uncover the foundation rock. Since the top stratum of the bedrock rises steadily from the east to the west bank, the caissons for the center and west piers had to be sunk to a progressively smaller depth, reaching a minimum of 86 feet at the St. Louis pier. The river piers and the masonry arches of the west approach were completed in 1873.

The construction of the steel arches and the wrought iron superstructure was a relatively simple matter after the dangerous work on the piers and required only about one-fifth of the time. In this part of the project Eads introduced another of his important innovations. The tubular arches were erected without falsework by the method of cantilevering them out from the piers to the center of the span. All arches were built out simultaneously from their piers so that the weights of the various cantilevers would balance each other and on completion the horizontal thrusts of adjacent arches would cancel each other. With the arches in place, the spandrel posts and the two decks were erected upon them. The bridge was completed and opened to traffic in 1874. The finished structure between abutments is divided into three spans, the one at the center 520 feet long, the two at the sides 502 feet each, the rise for all of them 45 feet. Eight tubular arches, four for each deck, constitute the primary structure of each span. Wrought-iron spandrel posts and transverse bracing transmit the load of the two decks to the arches. The upper one carries a roadway, the lower a double-track railroad line.

The arches of Eads Bridge are the hingeless or fixed-end type and hence are statically indeterminate structures. It is possible that Chauvenet was familiar with the recent work of French theorists in the solution of problems arising from arches of this kind, and certainly he knew of the many carefully designed wrought iron arches which had been built by French engineers before 1865. The successful attack on problems of indeterminacy was the product of an international effort in which a great many mathematicians had a hand, among them the great English physicist James Clerk Maxwell. The chief figure in the development of methods of stress analysis for fixed and two-hinged arches was Jacques Antoine Bresse, the first edition of whose *Applied Mechanics* was published at Paris in 1859. But for all the mathematical computations of Eads and Chauvenet, they relied to a great extent—as the engineers always did until the last decade of the century— on empirical approximations and gross overbuilding. Eads calculated that his bridge would be capable of sustaining a total load of 28,972 tons uniformly distributed—about four times the maximum that can be placed upon it—and of withstanding the force of any flood, ice jam, or tornado that the Mississippi Valley could level against it. Now in its ninth decade of active service, the bridge carries a heavy traffic of trucks, busses, automobiles, and the frieght trains of the Terminal Railroad of St. Louis.

Sullivan could hardly have chosen a better example to represent the new power of his age. As a work of structural art Eads Bridge remains a classic. In its method of construction and its material, in the testing of full-sized samples of all structural members and connections, in the thoroughness and precision of its technical and formal design, and in the close association of manufacturer and builder, it stands as a superb monument on the building art. It is, moreover, an architectural as well as an engineering achievement. Eads was careful to reduce his masonry elements to the simplest possible form, depending on the rich texture of the granite facing to provide the dignity and sense of restrained power that he was consciously striving for. Nowhere does the masonry extend above the line of the parapet to distract attention from the overall profile, the major parts, and their relation to each other. The tight curve of the arches is the primary visual as well as structural element, and Eads knew that the best he could do was to give full expression to the combination of stability and energy implicit in the form.

The Dixville Bridge posed an entirely different and somewhat less formidable problem. The solution, moreover, belongs strictly to the nineteenth century, the particular truss form employed having been abandoned before the beginning of the twentieth century. It was the decision to use the cantilever principle for a large railway bridge, for which there was only the slightest of precedents, that excited Sullivan's interest. The occasion in this case was the necessity of bridging the Kentucky River at Dixville, Kentucky, for the Cincinnati Southern Railway. The engineer in charge of the project was L. F. G. Bouscaren (1840-1904), chief engineer of the railroad company and designer of its Ohio River Bridge at Cincinnati, a structure which was built simultaneously with the Dixville Bridge and which contained the longest simple truss span in the world at the time of its erection. There is no question that Bouscaren deserves as much credit as Charles Shaler

Smith for the Dixville project, but Sullivan and the rest of posterity have always honored Smith and forgotten the other half of the team.

The chief problem at Dixville was that of erecting the trusses. The Kentucky River gorge at this point is 1,200 feet wide and 275 feet deep. The river has always been subject to flash floods of disastrous proportions, a maximum rise of 40 feet in one day having already been recorded when the two engineers made their preliminary survey. The use of falsework under such conditions was out of the question. Smith originally planned to build a continous Whipple-Murphy deck truss, 1,125 feet long, extending over three spans of 375 feet each.[5] At this point Bouscaren made the proposal that hinges be introduced into the truss at two points, one at each end of the bridge between the shore and nearest pier. The use of hinges in a continuous beam or truss was first proposed by the German engineer and theorist Karl Culmann in his *Graphical Statics* (1866). The introduction of hinges and the resulting transformation of the parts of the beam on either side of the support into cantilevers has the consequence that the action of the member more nearly conforms to the theoretical curve of stress distribution, or stress trajectory, as it is sometimes called. The first large cantilever bridge whose design seems clearly to have been influenced by Culmann's theory was Heinrich Gerber's bridge over the Main River at Hassfurt, Germany (1867). The structure excited wide interest and was undoubtedly known to Smith and Bouscaren.

Several other factors, however, led to Bouscaren's decision. In addition to improvement in the efficiency of the truss action, the engineers were concerned to prevent the excessively high stresses which would have occurred in the continuous truss as a consequence of pier settlement. Further, the successful construction of Eads Bridge by the method of cantilevering the arches out from the abutments and piers suggested not only a similar mode of construction for continuous trusses but also the possibility of using the cantilever as a permanent structural form. By adopting Bouscaren's suggestion the designers turned the bridge into a combination of types which were, in succession from shore to shore, a semi-floating span fixed at the abutment and hinged at the free end, a 75-foot cantilever, a simple truss acting as anchor span to the cantilevers, and so on in reverse order to the opposite shore. The material of the structure throughout was wrought iron. There was, as we noted, little precedent for a bridge of this kind, and Smith and Bouscaren staked their reputations on it. They saw it through to successful completion, but the increasing weight of traffic required that it be replaced in 1911 by a steel bridge built on the same masonry.

Sullivan's intuitive grasp of the meaning of these bridges was perfectly sound. The union of science and technology which made them possible was the creation of men who possessed a rare combination of faculties: they were men who could imagine and think things and who, when they translated the products of imagination into physical fact, did so on a heroic scale. It was difficult not to be impressed, however little one understood the methods of their achievement. Sullivan was profoundly moved, and he knew that he would have to create a building art which could give voice to these powerful feelings and thus evoke them in others.

The Auditorium Building marks the initial step, although what is visible both inside and out at first seems to have little to do with the great achievements of the Age of Iron. Perhaps it is the fact of the building itself, rather than what it says in detail, that heralds a new epoch in architectural form. The exterior walls, as magnificent as they are in their architectonic power, are masonry bearing elements disposed in the long-familiar system of stout piers and arcades. Inside this uniform block, however, is the most extraordinary diversity of internal volumes that one can house in a single structure. The huge theatre, seating 4,000 people, is surrounded by a block of offices on the west and south and by a hotel on the east. Offices, hotel rooms, lobbies, small dining rooms, and other utilitarian facilities are carried on a complete system of framing composed of cast-iron columns and wrought-iron beams. The great vault of the theatre is hung from a series of parallel elliptical trusses which are suspended in turn from horizontal trusses immediately under the roof. The same construction, on a smaller scale, supports the vault of the main dining room. Above the theatre at one end still another type of truss is used to support the ceiling of the rehearsal room. The vaulted enclosures are in no way like the traditional barrel vaults of Roman and medieval building. They are great wide-span cylinders of elliptical or segmental section which were derived from the huge trainsheds of the nineteenth century railway station and thus constitute a metamorphosis of a quasi-monumental utilitarian form into one element of an aesthetic complex. The system of truss framing in the Auditorium grew out of the inventions of the bridge engineers. Under the once brilliant colors and intricate interweaving patterns of Sullivan's ornament, none of this construction is visible, yet the light screens with their plastic detail, and the multiplicity of shapes and volumes could not have been created without the structural means that Adler employed. As a matter of fact, the Auditorium embraces every basic structural technique available to the nineteenth century builder.

The three purely commercial buildings—the Wainwright, the Prudential, and the Carson store—rest on the more advanced structural technique of complete steel framing without masonry bearing members of any kind other than the concrete column footings, but because of the uniformity and relative simplicity of their interior spaces they are much less complex in their construction than the Auditorium. Yet it was precisely here that Sullivan saw his opportunity: now he could take full advantage of the steel frame in the treatment of the elevations, the obvious parts of the building that everyone had to see. What he was trying to articulate in the three buildings was not simply structure and utility, which the bridge engineers had done in their wholly empirical forms, but rather his complex psychological response to the structural techniques that the engineers employed so boldly. The idea underlying the Wainwright and Prudential buildings (Figs. 2 and 3) is clearly summed up in the celebrated passage of the *Autobiography* on the skyscraper. "The lofty steel frame makes a powerful appeal to the architectural imagination where there is any. . . . The appeal and the inspiration lie, of course, in the element of loftiness, in the suggestion of slenderness and aspiration, the soaring quality of a thing rising from the earth as a unitary utterance, Dionysian in beauty."[6]

The formal character of the Prudential Building (which is a larger and more refined counterpart of the Wainwright and thus may be taken to represent the essential quality of both buildings) is an organic outgrowth of its utilitarian functionalism, but it is in no way confined by it. (Fig. 3) Above an open base, designed chiefly for purposes of display, rises a uniform succession of office floors, identical in function and hence appearance, topped by an attic floor which carries heating returns and elevator machinery and whose external treatment provides a transition to the flat slab that terminates the upward motion of the whole block. Elevator shafts, plumbing, and mechanical utilities are concentrated in an inner core. Sustaining all roof, floor, wall, and wind loads is an interior steel frame covered with fireproof tile sheathing. All this constitutes the empirical answer to utilitarian necessity.

Beyond the empirical form, however, are the wholly aesthetic elements that transform structure into symbolic art. The great bay-wide windows of the base are carefully designed not only to reveal structure but to separate it clearly from all subsidiary elements and thus to give forceful utterance to its potentially dramatic quality. The columns which stand out so clearly are the forerunners of Le Corbusier's *pilotis,* now so common in contemporary building that they have become a cliché. Above the open base appears the single most striking feature, the pronounced upward vertical movement achieved by the closely ranked pier-like bands of which every other one clothes the true structural column, the alternate piers being purely formal additions without bearing function.

The basic theme of this light screen is movement, the dynamic transcendence of space and gravitational thrust, qualities Sullivan long before felt in the "floating" chains and roadway of the Merrimack suspension bridge. In a broader sense the theme suggests the underlying energy of a world of process, of evolutionary growth in living things, or the dynamic of the electric field in physics. The bridge, like the building, is not seen by Sullivan as a static thing but as something which leaps over its natural obstacle and thus becomes a living assertion of man's skill operating through his simultaneous dependence upon and command over nature. Again Sullivan's intuition led him into the right path, for this is exactly how the bridge behaves. We can sense this directly in the suspension bridge with its wire cables and suspenders: it seems alive, constantly quivering under its changing load. Although we can neither see it nor feel it, exactly the same thing is occurring in the dense and massive members of the big railroad truss as the internal stress continuously adjusts itself to the moving weight that it sustains. It look a century and a half of painstaking scientific inquiry to discover this hidden and vital activity.

The rich and intricate ornament that covers the two office buildings, an ornament created by Sullivan which died with him, offers a much more difficult problem of interpretation. It is so subjective that it is scarcely possible to find objective experiences that might have led to the feelings out of which it grew. In its complex, somewhat abstract naturalism, it appears to symbolize the biologically organic. While Sullivan sometimes allowed his ornament to flow in uncontrolled and undifferentiated profusion over much of the surface, he was generally careful to observe the limits of architectural ornamentation. By spreading it in low relief over whole elevations, and by confining a particular pattern to the surface of a certain kind of structural member—column, or spandrel beam— he was able to distinguish in a striking way the separate structural surfaces. Thus his ornament enhances the major elements of the structure and further heightens the vivid sense of movement. It also seems to suggest the diversity underlying the unitary organic statement.

In the Carson Pirie Scott Store Sullivan turned to an entirely different kind of expression, one derived from the dominant mode of the work of the Chicago school. (Fig. 4) Where he used the close vertical pattern in the older buildings, in the department store he opened the main elevations into great cellular screens which exactly express the neutral steel cage behind them. The form was dictated initially by the requirement for maximum natural light in the store, but again, in many subtle ways, he translated the practical functionalism into art. If the theme of the Wainwright and the Prudential is movement, that of the Carson store is power. Here the elaborate interplay of tension and compression, of thrust and counterthrust in the bridge truss is given a heightened and dramatic statement by means so delicate as almost to escape notice—the careful calculation of the depth of the window reveals and the breadth of the terra-cotta envelope on the columns and spandrels, the narrow band of ornament that enframes the window, the even narrower band that extends continuously along each sill and lintel line to give the whole façade a tense, subdued horizontality. The base in its sheath of ornament is an exact reversal of that of the office buildings. In the Carson store it is a weightless screen, glass and opaque covering (cast iron forming one unbroken plane, making the cellular wall above literally seem to float free of the earth below it.

In the last analysis Sullivan's civic architecture is a celebration of technique, as is most of the contemporary architecture of which he was the foremost pioneer. But Sullivan had carried the expression far beyond the rather sterile geometry that characterizes most building today. If his work seems limited beside the vastly richer symbolism of medieval and baroque architecture, we may at least say that he was responding to the one coherent order that was discernible in the contradictory currents of nineteenth and twentieth century culture. In the absence of a cosmos in which man was conceived to be the central figure, the scientific technology on which building increasingly depended became the one sure basis of architectural and civic art. It is Sullivan's achievement to have understood how this basis could be transmuted into an effective and valid artistic statement.

Notes

1. Louis Sullivan, *Kindergarten Chats* (New York, 1947), pp. 28-30. By permission of Wittenborn, Schultz, Inc.

2. *The Autobiography of an Idea* (New York, 1926), pp. 82-85. By permission of the American Institute of Architects.

3. *Ibid*. pp. 246-48.

4. *Ibid*. p. 248.

5. The Whipple-Murphy truss was a variation on the form patented by Squire Whipple in 1847. Its distinguishing characteristic is the fact that the diagonal members of the web slope in one direction in any one half of the truss and cross two panels formed by the posts, instead of the usual one. A continuous truss is one that is carried on intermediate supports as well as those at the ends, that is, it extends continuously over more than two supports. In a deck-truss bridge the deck, or track level, is located at the level of the top chord of the truss.

6. *The Autobiography of an Idea*, pp. 313-314.